THE OSKALOOSA COMPANY

Last Wagon Train To Skinner's In 1847

A HISTORY OF THE SOUTHERN ROAD TO OREGON

Untold Story Of The Scott-Applegate Trail
Overland Journey Guided By The 1847 Pilot of Record
Life And Death In A Frontier Settlement
Maps Of The Southern Road To Oregon

By Charles George Davis

To Pat
Charles G Davis
Oct 3, 1999

Davis, Charles George
The Oskaloosa company: last wagon train to Skinner's in 1847 / by Charles George Davis.
p. cm.
Includes bibliographical references and index.
LCCN: 96-83881
ISBN 0-939116-42-1

1. Oregon Trail. 2. California Trail. 3. Overland journeys to the Pacific. 4. West (U.S.)--Description and travel. I. Title.

F592.D38 1996 917.804'2
QBI96-40095

Published by Frontier Publishing
Portland, Oregon 97233

For order fulfillments contact your distributors and wholesalers or:
Charles G. Davis
P.O. Box 924
North Plains, OR 97133
503-647-5893

Cover painting: Independence Rock, by William H. Jackson; Scott's Bluff National Monument

Printed in the United States of America

Dedication

In loving memory of my beloved wife
Ione Vienna Poe Davis
1926 - 1994
A loving mother of five children
She put up with my roaming for almost fifty years.

PREFACE AND ACKNOWLEDGMENTS

Background and Thanks

The Oskaloosa Company: The Last Wagon Train To Skinner's is a history of the overland journey of several emigrant families and single men from the Missouri River to Oregon over the Southern Route To Oregon in 1847. The history carries on with the trials and tribulations of one of those families and the rise and fall of a frontier settlement.

The research for this book started with a copy of Edwin Erwin and David Ronald Davis' book, *Our Davis Family Ancestors.* That book contained a copy of James N. Harty's letter home telling friends and relatives that D. D. Davis was elected Captain of the wagon company. I always knew that my grandfather's family came into the southern Willamette Valley in the early days, and I learned of "The Applegate Trail" in grade school. I liked the idea that my great, great grandfather settled on "The Applegate Trail" and my interest was off to a slow start.

I would like to think that I wrote *The Oskaloosa Company: The Last Wagon Train To Skinner's* to the casual observer that likes to increase general knowledge in storage to be brought up when it is needed. That is about where I was in 1985. I also had slight remembrances of Oregon history studies about the Applegate Trail in grade school over fifty year before, and of my grandmothers references, from the early thirties to the mid sixties, to my great grandfather "Tom" Davis. — not much going at that point but more was called to memory as the need came up.

In order to understand our emigrant forefathers, we must beam ourselves back in time to 1846 or 1847. Just as there are more than the three trading posts of yesteryear between the Big Blue River and the Coast Fork of the Willamette River today — so have economics, societies, politics, and everything else changed. Revisionism has no place in history or in this book. I have tried to present history as only citizens of the United States could understand it in 1846 and 1847 — considering all circumstances that existed then including their faith in themselves, their strengths, and their frailties.

James Willis Nesmith, a 1843 emigrant and later one of Oregon's first United States Senators, told the Oregon Pioneer Association in a prepared address in 1880 that: *"Great Britain was the only country with which we had ever had any conflict of arms, and the generation to which we belonged, particularly in the west, had been taught to look upon the 'Britishers' as natural enemies."* (JWN Page 32.)

Earlier, in 1875, James Nesmith told the same association: *"The path * * * * was made by the hardy frontiersman * * * * to the Pacific, and who stood by their rifles here and held the country against hostile Indians and British threats, without Government aid or recognition until 1849, when the first Government troops came to our relief. * * * * (T)he deserving men who made the path, unaided by Government, will be forgotten. 'And such is history.'"* (JWN Page 24.)

It was several years later, after 1985, that I started gaining interest. Merrill Mattes, in the form of *Platte River Road Narratives*, steered me onto Lester Hulin's journal. I obtained a copy from the Lane County Historical Society and my interest began to grow.

If there is a hero in the "Oskaloosa Company," it is Lester Hulin – he kept the only record of its overland journey to Oregon. Lester Hulin guided the Oskaloosa Company wagon train over rivers, plains, mountains, deserts and around lakes in 1847. He bears sole responsibility for piloting these memories over the Southern Route To Oregon and the Scott-Applegate Trail in this book celebrating the event one hundred fifty years later. Without him this history would not have been written.

Lane County Historical Society had made a typescript-copy of Lester Hulin's *1847 Diary of Applegate Trail To Oregon.* Lester Hulin is not the center of attraction in his own journal, and except for the underlying knowledge that Lester Hulin was the writer, the journal could have been written by anyone making that journey with the Oskaloosa Company. His story is the story of each person making the overland journey.

Lester Hulin names Belknap and Ann Davis in his journal. Family genealogical histories identify the families and enlarge Belknap to include two Belknap men and two Belknap women and their four families.

The people at the Oregon Historical Society Research Library started me out with Merrill J. Mattes' book, *Platte River Road Narratives*. In reviewing Peter W. Crawford's *Narrative of the Overland Journey to Oregon* in the Bancroft Library, Mr. Mattes was thoughtful enough to mention that Davis was Captain of the Oskaloosa Company.

Peter W. Crawford was with the Oskaloosa Company for only a short time. However, his remembrances extended the length of the Oregon Trail. His tall tales of his adventures add to the lighter side of the overland journey. He mentions great, great grandfather Davis twice in his three hundred forty-two page handwritten narrative.

David D. Davis established a settlement at Tampico in Soap Creek Valley in northern Benton County a few years after his arrival. He died in 1860. Although some business survived for several years, the settlement soon disappeared.

The Tampico settlement tells the history of the rise and fall of one frontier settlement which may be typical of many lost settlements throughout the Willamette Valley.

Robert Zybach, Forest Historian for Oregon State University Research Forest, has worked in and around Soap Creek and Tampico for quite a few years. He gave unselfishly of his time and service feeding me valuable information.

Arlie Holt, a historian in Polk County, supplied most of the information on James O'Neil and the two younger Davis children.

Devere and Helen Helfrich were probably the first to make the Southern Route to Oregon an understandable series of events. General Land Office Surveyors, through the Bureau of Land Management, provided maps and notes that formed the basis for locating the Scott-Applegate Trail. Arlie Holt kept me on track in Polk County and Larry McLane in Josephine County. Richard Ackerman, the dean of the Scott-Applegate Trail buffs, suggested making changes over the length of the Scott-Applegate Trail.

Pat Pickens with the Bureau of Land Management office was particularly helpful in providing copies of several hundred GLO Township maps. She never got perturbed even when I insisted I knew what I wanted, even when I didn't know. BLM offices in Reno and Sacramento also provided GLO Township maps. The Elco office provided several maps of the Thousand Springs area. T. H. Jefferson and mother nature did a fine job in defining the route down the Humboldt River.

The Oskaloosa Company followed about the same route Gregory M. Franzwa shows in *Maps of the Oregon Trail* from the Kansas-Nebraska state line to Raft River. It's too bad Lester Hulin (1847) and Virgil Pringle (1846) didn't have the Franzwa maps.

Joe Mardis in Benton County Surveyor's Office led me through GLO maps and surveyor's field notes. He taught me enough to make it possible for me to find spots called homes and lines called roads.

Bill Lewis and Judy Juntenen, Benton County Historical Society provided lots of valuable information from their files and opinions of past things.

Fred Renstjerna, Douglas County Historical Museum Research Library, let me spend many hours pouring over the manuscript of Levi Scott's autobiography.

Hallie Hills Huntington, the granddaughter of Emigrant Cornclius IIills of thc Oskaloosa Company, provided more information before her passing in 1994.

In *Jedediah Smith and the Opening of the West,* Dale L. Morgan documented the British plan, originating in London, for obtaining Oregon territory. After the Oregon boundary negotiations ended in failure in 1827, the British implemented a plan looking to the north side of the Columbia River as their share of a division.. The British planned to occupy and establish trade on the south side of the Columbia River so they would have something to give up in settlement. The British would harass American Traders by underselling them to dampen their expectations and diminish their value in a settlement. They placed priority on harvesting all of the animals in the country south of the Columbia and west of the Rocky Mountains.

William A. Slacum investigated the Oregon situation for the President and Congress of the United States ten years later. Among other things, probably not knowing of the plan, he essentially reported its implantation except that discharged former employees remaining in the area were required to settle north of the Columbia in the Cowlitz area in 1837.

Bettie Angeli, Charlotte and Donald Jr. Alcatraz, and Steve Davis tried to correct my mistakes and offered other suggestions. Donald made calculations needed to place marks on maps to show the location of buildings. Many other people and organizations provided information and assistance. They are too numerous to mention.

Tampico residents Roderick Brennerman and Michael Dunnigan gave freely of their time and knowledge showing the details of Soap Creek Valley.

Jerry and Doris Russell, owners of Frontier Publishing, showed extraordinary restraint and professionalism in guiding this book through last minute changes to include new information and corrections of wording and other mistakes. To Doris and Jerry, a well deserved — "Thanks."

About the Author

Charles George Davis is the great-grandson of Thomas W. and Missouri Hall Davis. Thomas W. Davis was eight years old when he made the overland journey with the Oskaloosa Company on the Southern Route to Oregon in 1847. Missouri Hall was born in 1849 near Oregon City a few months after Oregon became a territory. They met and were married at Tampico (Adair) in Benton County.

The author received his early education in a one-room school that was located west of Banks. He also attended Banks High School.

After five years in the U.S. Army, including combat at Guadalcanal and Central Solomon Islands, he joined the Internal Revenue Service, investigating and researching foreign tax shelters. He retired in 1977.

The historical research, started ten years ago, kicked into high gear about 1989 and has been his full-time project since 1991.

Currently the author is researching Thomas A. Hall's activities in Oregon Territory. He is also immersed in information about the first territorial roads from St. Helens to Ashland.

The author does not consider himself a "trail buff." His actual interest is in citizen efforts to repossess pre-territorial Oregon for the United States — who the citizens were, what they did, what they thought, and where they were at what moment in time.

TABLE OF CONTENTS

ILLUSTRATIONS

Credits

Paintings by William Henry Jackson, Credit Scott's Bluff National Monument:
Night Corral At Independence Rock front cover; Returning Astorians; Whitman Mission; Blue Mountains; Barlow Trail; Approaching Platte River Crossing; Approaching Chimney Rock; Fort Laramie; Devil's Gate; South Pass; Rendezvous At Green River

Paintings by William Henry Jackson, Credit Harold Warp Pioneer Village Foundation:
Old Fort Bridger; Fort Hall

Photos by Shann Rupp, Credit Shann Rupp:
Trail Traces Approaching Ash Hollow; Court House Rock; Chimney Rock; Traces Approaching Black Rock Desert; Rabbit Hole Springs; Devil's Gate To High Rock Canyon; Painted Point; Trail Traces Approaching Forty-Nine Lake; Double Traces Across Devil's Garden

Other Photos and Credits
Photo, Tonquin Crossing The Columbia River Bar, March 25, 1811, Clatsop County Historical Society; Photo, Astoria As It Was in 1813, Oregon Historical Society # 71840; Photo, Rev. Jason Lee, Oregon Historical Society # 4342; Photo, Lee's Methodist Mission, Wheatland, Oregon Historical Society # 46192,8; Photo, Dr. John McLoughlin, Oregon Historical Society # unknown; Photo, Fort Vancouver, Oregon Historical Society # 803; Photo, Birth OF Oregon, Mural at Champoeg Oregon State Park; Photo, James Anderson O'Neil, Champoeg Oregon State Park; Photo, Levi Scott, Douglas Co. Museum; Photo, Jesse Applegate, Douglas County Museum; Photo, Canyon Creek Canyon - Circa 1930, Douglas County Museum; Photo, Peter. W. Crawford, University of California, Berkeley , Bancroft Library; Photo, Lester Hulin, Lane County Historical Society; Photo, Hannah Ann Davis, Family Photo; Photo, Grave Creek Covered Bridge, Larry McLane; Photo, Canyon Creek Canyon, Douglas County Historical Society; Photo, North Umpqua River Ford; Photo, Long Tom River; Photo, Davis Family Home Site On Soap Creek From Scott Applegate Trail; Photo, Scott-Applegate Trail Soap Creek Crossing; Photo, Scott-Applegate Trail Through Trees Near Soap Creek; Photo, Scott-Applegate Trail Through Field; Photo, Scott-Applegate Trail Traces On DLC Boundary In Edge of Wood; Aerial Photo, David D. Davis Donation Land Claim - Soap Creek and Tampico; Platt Map, Donation Land Claim Plat, Benton County; Photo, Donation Land Claim Bearing Tree and Marker; Photo, Town Of Tampico Memorial Marker; Drawing, Tampico Town, Oregon State University, Horner Museum; Photo, Tampico Town Site; Photo, Streets of Old Tampico; Photo, Davis Compound: Entrance To Compound, Fir Trees Planted 1858; Photos, Several Scenes Where Compound Once Stood - Circa 1994; Photo; Compound Exit, Same Fir Trees In Reverse Order; Photo, Beatty Fir Trees Planted 1858; Photo, Roberts' Boarding House; Photo, A Survivor, Bill Bower's Arcade Saloon Circa 1900; Photo, Survivor Of A Later Era - Circa 1923; Photo, Tampico Race Track; Photo, Principle Buildings OF Tampico; Plat, Tampico Town Plot, Oregon State University Research Forrest; Photo, Green Berry Smith, Oregon State University Research Forrest; Photo. Headstones in New English Cemetery, Monmouth, Oregon; Aerial Photograph, Distribution of David D. Davis Donation Land Claim Overlay.

MAPS

Index

The Overland Journey

On The Southern Route To Oregon

<>

THE OSKALOOSA COMPANY

May 22 to November 4, 1847

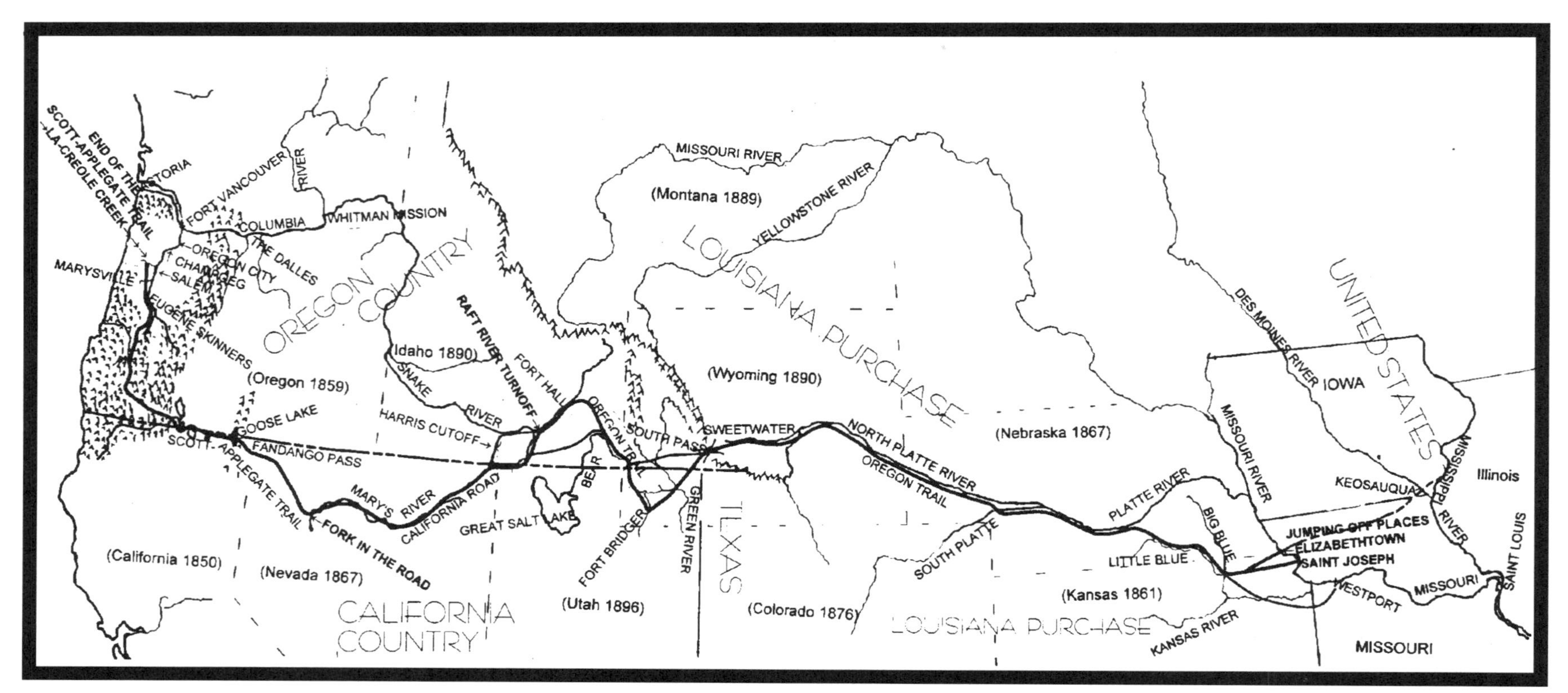

THE OSKALOOSA COMPANY

Last Wagon Train To Skinner's In 1847

A HISTORY OF THE SOUTHERN ROAD TO OREGON

Untold Story Of The Scott-Applegate Trail
Overland Journey Guided By The 1847 Pilot of Record
Life And Death In A Frontier Settlement
Maps Of The Southern Road To Oregon

By Charles George Davis

Frontier Publishing

Portland, Oregon

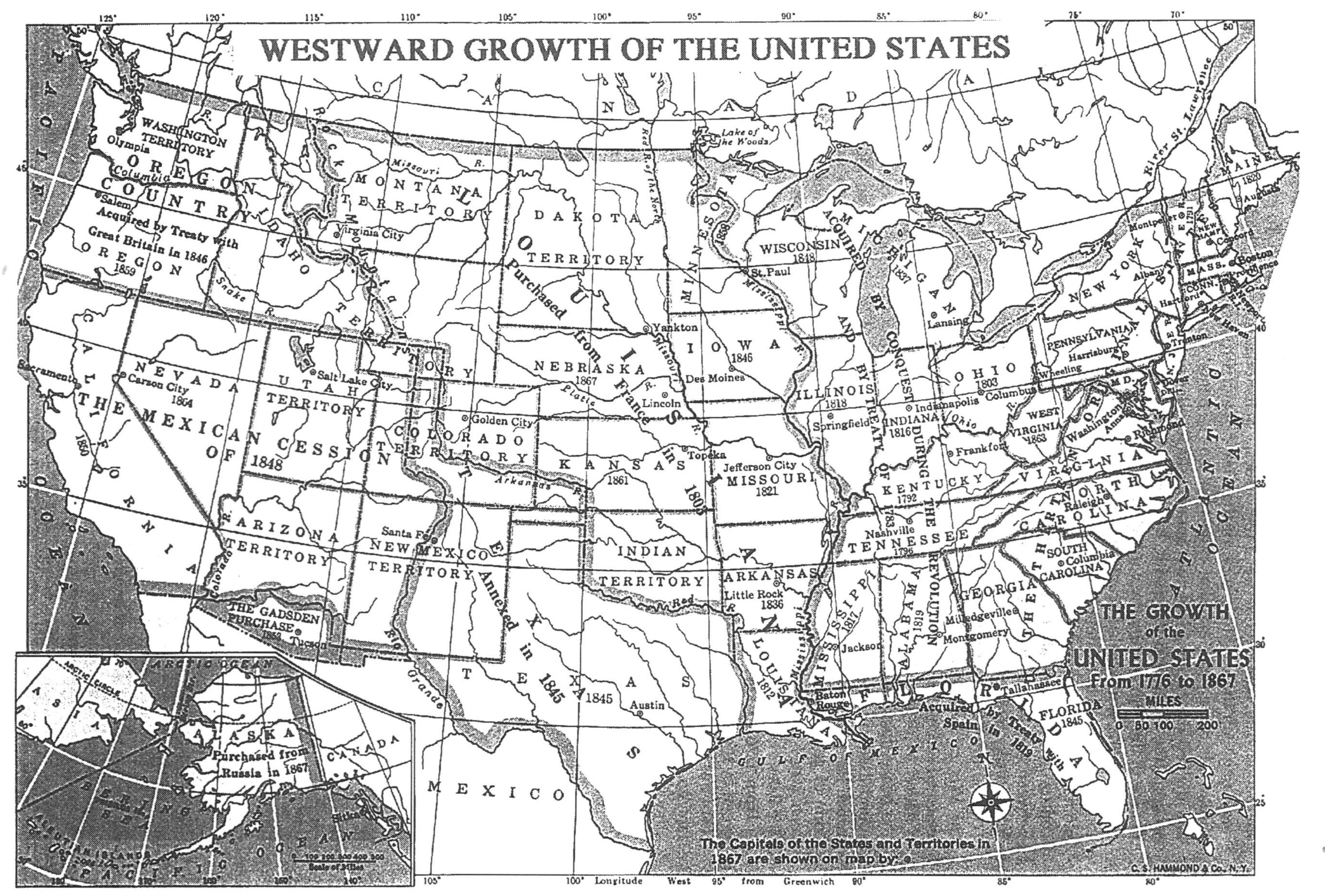

Western growth of the United States

Hammond

CHAPTER 1

Pre-Territorial Oregon History

Spanish navigator Bartolome Ferrelo sailed from Mexico to a point near southern Oregon in 1542-43. His exploit was duplicated by another Spanish mariner, Sebastian Vizcaino in 1602-03. In the meantime, English navigator Sir Francis Drake sailed along the Pacific Coast in 1579, possibly as far north as Oregon. Other Spanish explorers made voyages to Oregon coastal waters during the seventeenth and eighteenth centuries.

Spanish navigator Bruno Heceta sailed to the mouth of the Columbia River in 1775. British Sea Captain James Cook saw the Oregon coast near the mouth of the Alsea River in 1778. Captain Meir, in an English merchant ship out of London, saw Cape Disappointment and entered the mouth of the Columbia between 1780 and 1782. He left the bay under the impression it extended only to Tongue Point. Various British and American vessels frequented the northern Pacific coast within the next decade.

John Meares (1756-1809), a retired British naval officer, founded a commercial house in Macao, China, to trade with the west coast of North America. He made his first voyage in 1786. Meares built at Nootka Sound on the west side of Vancouver Island in 1788. He explored the coast to the south but did not recognize the mouth of the Columbia River as the mouth of a great river. The Spaniards demolished the Nootka Sound establishment in 1789. Meares returned to the British navy becoming a Commander in 1795. (AR note 17.)

Tonquin *crossing the Columbia River Bar, March 25, 1811*
Clatsop County Historical Society

First Americans In Oregon

The first known landing of Americans on the Oregon Coast was in 1788 only five years after Britain recognized the sovereignty of the United States in 1783. Seamen of the American merchant vessel *Lady Washington* commanded by Captain Robert Gray landed near Hobsonville Point on Tillamook Bay.

The *Lady Washington* left Boston in 1787 on an exploration and fur trading expedition with a crew of about fifteen men. *Lady Washington* entered Tillamook Bay in August 1788 in search of "the great river of the west." They were met with violence when one of the men was killed while gathering firewood by an Indian who wanted his sword. This was the first known American robbed in Oregon Country. He was also the first American murdered in Oregon Country. (William A. Slacum, Navy Purser with orders from President Jackson reported that Gray entered the Columbia River in 1783-1884.)

Hobsonville Point is on US Route 101 on Tillamook Bay between Garibaldi and Bay City. US Highway 101 passes a few feet behind Hobsonville Point.

Captain Robert Gray soon discovered that Tillamook Bay was not the great river of the west he was looking for and left the bay. He marked the place on his charts as "Murderer's Harbor."

Captain Gray discovered the great river of the west on his second voyage in 1791. He named the river "Columbia," the name of his ship on the second voyage. The United States later claimed the entire region drained by the Columbia, basing its claim on Gray's voyages.

George Vancouver, a British captain, explored Puget Sound. Fur traders entered the headwaters of the Columbia region in 1793. The immense wilderness was inhabited only by Indian tribes.

Americans Meriwether Lewis and William Clark explored the Columbia region in 1804-05. (FW)

Ouragon, Oregon, or Oregn, Its a Big Wind, A Landing Place For Flights of Fancy

"Ouragon" has had a strange and sometimes exotic linguistic history. At the end of the nineteenth century local historians speculated on the name's possible Indian or Spanish origins. Such conjectures eventually prompted the distinguished regional historian T. C. Elliott to undertake the first comprehensive study of the name. The results of his research appeared in the December 1920 and June 1921 issues of the *Oregon Historical Quarterly*. Elliott traced the word back to 1765 and a petition drafted by Robert Rogers asking royal support for his northwest exploration scheme. Elliott believed that the name Ouragon came from the French word *ouragon*, meaning windstorm or hurricane. The River of the West, another phrase used to describe the Ouragon, came from the land of Chinook winds. Rogers might have picked up that word and its associations from either French or Indian sources. Whatever the accuracy of such an interpretation, Rogers clearly linked Ouragon to the Straits of Anian and other fanciful places. The word *Ouragon* was now rooted in regions remote and fabulous. Jonathan Carver's travels through the interior parts of North America gave the name wide currency.

However it was spelled, Ouragon, Ourigan, or Ourgan (Oregon, Oregun or Oregn) — the invented place captured the imagination. It was the westernmost place, the Eden at the end of the rainbow. Ouragon was the landing place for so many flights of fancy. (OHQ Vol. 94, Summer-Fall 1993, page 137 & 138.).

War With Britain — 1812

The United States was embroiled in war with the British from June 18, 1812, to February 16, 1815. The United States fought the war over maritime rights of neutrals including the United States. The United States population was about 7,700,000 at the time.

286,730 men were in United States military service during the war.

Even though Britain recognized United States independence in 1783, the two countries continued to clash. The United States was fighting Indians who were being encouraged by the British in the Northwest Territories.

During the French revolutionary and Napoleonic wars between France and Britain, both countries were fighting for survival and overrode the maritime rights of neutral powers.

The United States was trying to sell its foodstuffs to both countries and was particularly harmed. Through impressment, Britain seized deserters and other British citizens, including naturalized Americans of British origin, from American ships. These efforts involved blockading all ports being used for trade. Demands were made that American ships dock at a British port for inspection and payment of fees before proceeding to France. From 1802 to 1812 about 10,000 Americans were impressed, causing an outrage in the United States

Demands for war with Britain were growing in 1810. There were problems on the northwestern and southern frontiers where the Indians were being egged on by the British.

Many legislators who supported war against Britain were elected to office in 1810. The faction favoring war came into power during the legislative debates in 1811-1812. They made points that the United States had endured the arrogant British restriction. United States products were rotting in American ports because of the British blockade. The United States economy was suffering because of the lack of export sales. Indians egged on by the British were attacking the frontiers. The United States could achieve an easy victory by an invasion and conquest of Canada.

The United States declared war on Great Britain on June 18, 1812. The President signed the declaration.

First Settlers On The Columbia River 1810 – 1813

The Pacific Fur Company was created in 1809 to establish a string of trading posts along the upper areas of the United States with western headquarters at the mouth of the Columbia River. John Jacob Astor had fifty of its one hundred shares. Astor was to bear all expenses during the start-up period. Wilson Price Hunt, as representative and business manager, received five shares. Alexander McKay, Donald McKenzie, Duncan McDougall, and David Stuart each received four shares each. They were disgruntled former partners in the North-West Company. Ramsey Crooks, Miller, McLellan, and Clarke each received four shares. Alexander Ross and Robert Stuart were to become partners after three years. Other investors, possibly including Robert McLean and Joseph Miller, made up the balance. (AR)

John Jacob Astor was a German by Birth, but a citizen of the United States. He arrived in the United States about the year 1784 and commenced a career trafficking in furs as the American Fur Company in 1809. He purchased Mackina Company and combined the operations as the South-West Company in contradistinction to the North-West Company in 1811. (AR)

The North-West Company was organized as a British company in 1787. It soon became one of the two great rival companies of the north. The other was the Hudson's Bay Company. The North-West Company had recently crossed the Rocky Mountains and had a small operation in New Caledonia. (AR)

The Russians alone had regular trading ports opposite to Kamtschatka. Their capital was limited and their hunting grounds were almost entirely confined to the seacoast around their establishments. Casual American ships frequented the area and seized the opportunity to carry Russian furs to China. Astor saw that such limited and desultory fur traffic produced immense profits.

He perceived that a well-regulated trade supported by capital would confine Russian traders. Coasting vessels would soon disappear. (AR)

Astor intended to employ British subjects in order to prevent arousing the British causing them to speed up their claims of prior discovery to the Oregon country. (AR)

Astoria

John Jacob Astor's Pacific Fur Company established a trading post in the Columbia River region at Astoria in 1811. The Pacific Fur Company extended its activity inland into the present states of Oregon, Washington, Idaho, Montana and on into Canada.

Donald McKenzie and William W. Matthews moved up the Willamette River in April 1812. They were joined by J. C. Halsey and William Wallace and established a hunting camp and trading post near Champoeg. (AR)

Donald McKenzie also established another post near the mouth of the river that bears his name. (HMC P. 78)

Traders under the leadership of Donald McKenzie reached at least as far south as the Umpqua River Valley. Alexander Ross, a company scribe, wrote:

> *"The river (Willamette), towards its head-waters, branches out into numerous little streams, which rise in the mountains. There is also another fine river near the source of the Wallamitte; but lying rather in the direction of east and west, called the Imp-qua; this river empties itself into the ocean. The finest hunting ground on the Wallamitte is towards the Imp-qua. The beaver is abundant, and the party that went there to trade this year made handsome * * * *."* (AR, p231)

Astoria got off to a rough start. Men began clearing brush and cutting trees at the post's site on April 12, 1811. The post was named "Astoria" on May 18th. Hard labor, the rain, poor food and medical care, and Duncan McDougal's leadership wore on the men.

Threats of war with Britain and the aggressive North-West Fur Company threat-

Astoria, as it was in 1813.

Oregon Historical Society Photo 71840

ened the success of Pacific Fur Company from the beginning. The British blockade kept John Jacob Astor from getting ships, reinforcements and supplies to the colony.

John Jacob Astor's appeals to the United States government to protect Astoria went unanswered. He did not get an armed ship to protect Astoria. He got one supply ship, the *Beaver*, through the British blockade. However, Captain Sowle, in command of the *Beaver* and under Astor's instructions, directed the activities of his ship toward Astor's other fur trading activities. (AR, p233)

War Of 1812 Reaches Astoria

Soon after partner Donald McKenzie set up a trading post at She-Whaps in the Nez Perce nation in the winter of 1812-1813 he went over to Spokane to visit Clarke. John George McTavish, a partner in the North-West Company, passed Spokane with strong reinforcements of men and goods. He brought word of a war between Britain and the United States. McKenzie became alarmed and he and all of his men returned to Astoria where they arrived on January 15, 1813. (AR, P216)

The two partners then at Astoria, McKenzie & McDougal, decided to abandon the enterprise. Stuart and Clarke expressed different views when informed of the decision.

On his way back to his post on the Shahaptain River, McKenzie met McTavish and a crew of twenty-two men on their way to the mouth of the Columbia to meet the war ship *Isaac Todd*.

Partners McKenzie, McDougal, Stuart, and Clarke met at Astoria that summer. Preliminary agreement was signed on July 1, 1813, fixing the point of departure as June 1, 1814. Stuart and Clarke were opposed to abandoning the enterprise at first but finally agreed when abandonment was delayed to the next year. (AR. p239)

The Astorians went back into their outposts in the wilderness for another season (year) buying and collecting furs. Stuart went back to his post at She Whaps, Mr. Clark to Spokane, McKenzie on the Willamette, and McDougal remained at Astoria. Stuart seems to have had a post at Okanogan. McKenzie was probably in charge at either Champoeg or She Waps; and there seems to have been another post at Clearwater. (AR. p239)

British Attack By Land Capture Spokane, Advance On Astoria

North-West Company had houses at Rocky Mountain House, Thompson River, Kootenae House, Kootenay, Flathead, Kullyspell House, Spokane House, and Coville in 1813. The small Spokane House was the deepest penetration of the British into Oregon Country before the advance on Astoria. Their provisions were packed over the Rocky Mountains. Furs had to be packed to operations east of the mountains. (MBP P.28)

War came to Astoria when North-West Company forced the Astorians' hand. Seventy-five men under McTavish, a Britain and partner in the North West Company, captured the American out post at Spokane and advanced on Astoria. They arrived at Astoria on October 7, 1813. The British war ship *Isaac Todd* was expected to come into the mouth of the Columbia River to take possession of Astoria by force. (AR. p239)

Alexander Ross witnessed the events from his station at Astoria. He wrote:

> *"Mr. Clarke also accompanied the North-West brigade, on its way to Astoria. With the craft peculiar to Indian traders, they had crammed down Mr. Clark's throat that nothing could be done at Astoria without him, although his accompanying them was like the third wheel to a cart; but it answered their purpose: for his leaving Spokane threw at once all the trade of the district into their hands, and Mr. Clarke found out, when it was too late, that he had been duped."* (AR. p239)

Mr. Clarke had cause to regret his culpability. In quitting his post at Spokane to go with the enemy in time of war, he surrendered the northern part of the Columbia Basin to the enemy. Much of that territory was never recovered and remained in British hands.

The Pacific Fur Company partners knew that the United States was at war with Britain and that the North-West Company represented Britain. Negotiations were quickly completed on October 16, 1813. McDougal agreed to sell out to the North-Westers for $80,500.00 (10% of cost) to salvage what he could. (AR-p244)

McTavish, the British subject in charge of the North-West Company, agreed but wanted more. He delayed closing, expecting the armed ship *Isaac Todd* and a British war ship to come into the Columbia momentarily. If the war ships arrived, Astoria and all American property would be seized as a prize of war. Astoria would become the property of the North-West Company without purchase and McTavish would save the $80,500. (AR. p239)

McDougal and McKenzie, of the Pacific Fur Company assembled a squadron of boats in readiness to transport furs and goods to the Willamette out of reach of warships. McKenzie devised a plan and he and McDougal ordered the seventy-two men at Astoria to man the bastions with guns loaded and aimed at the North-Westers. The Astorians sent the British a message threatening to cut off all supplies from the British camped around Astoria. They would remove them from the vicinity unless McTavish signed the documents delivering Astoria to the North-West Company by 11:00 a.m. on November 12, 1813. McTavish signed.

McTavish's was intent on capturing Astoria and the entire region west of the Rocky Mountains for the British. The logistics for coordinated attack by both land and by sea were great. McTavish may have shown a facade if he was bringing Clarke to Astoria for a peaceful settlement. However, the facade fell when he would not complete the settlement on time, hoping the warship would arrive for an armed takeover of the entire Columbia region.

British Attack By Sea

Captain Black in command of the *Racoon*, a British sloop of war with twenty-six guns, entered the mouth of the Columbia River on November 29, 1813. Two days later Captain Black and his officers landed intent on capturing Astoria. However, he found Astoria already in the possession of the North-West Company.

On December 12, 1813, Captain Black went through the usual ceremony of capturing Astoria and the "whole country." He took possession as a prize of war. The name Astoria was changed to Fort George. Thus done, the *Racoon* and Captain Black prepared and left the Columbia. (AR. p247-248)

Several employees of the Pacific Fur Company stayed on with the British North-West Company. History records the names of several former Pacific Fur Company men as Hudson Bay Company expedition leaders.

Returning Astorians

Pacific Fur Company partners made one more trip into the interior to witness the property delivered to North-West Company.

Pacific Fur Company's partners and employees that were not changing allegiance to the North-West returned to The Sandwich Islands (Hawaii), Canada, and the United States. Some returned by land and some by sea.

The Pacific Fur Company's operations, having been sold to the North-West Company, ended at this point. However, sovereignty over Astoria and the "whole country" was not settled with Captain Black's ceremony capturing Astoria and taking possession as a war prize. (AR)

Warfare Ends

Negotiations to end the War of 1812 started in August 1814. The treaty was signed December 24, 1814, after negotiations were completed at Ghent, Belgium. The news did not reach New York City until February 11,

1815. The treaty was ratified by the United States Senate on February 17, 1815. The treaty provided essentially nothing but a cessation of warfare. The British continued to occupy the "whole country" seized as a prize of war.

The treaty did not secure United States maritime rights, but the end of the wars between Britain and France meant that they were no longer threatened. Britain never impressed American seamen again. The United States emerged from the war with a new sense of national purpose.

Two incidents of the War of 1812 remain in the hearts of every American. (1) During the British bombardment of Fort McHenry near Baltimore, Francis Scott Key wrote "The Star-Spangled Banner." It became the national anthem. (2) The Nation's Capital fell into enemy hands. The British captured and sacked Washington, D. C. They sacked and burned the President's mansion. The stone exterior of the mansion was so blemished by smoke that it was necessary to paint it during restoration. It was painted white and the Presidents mansion became known as "The White House."

Peace Negotiations Continue

Negotiations in 1818 led to establishing the forty-ninth parallel as the boundary between the United States and British possessions as far west as the Rocky Mountains. The convention settled the border problem between the United States and Britain east of the Rocky Mountains. However, some citizens on both sides of the line were dissatisfied. The United States passed a neutrality act in March 1838 and sent federal troops to join local militias in suppressing the planned uprising in what became known as the Patriot War.

"The Oregon Question" Continues

An agreement could not be reached regarding the boundary west of the Rocky Mountains and north of the forty-second parallel. The disagreement became known as "The Oregon Question." The two countries agreed to a ten-year period of joint occupancy of the Oregon Country, from Russian Alaska to Spanish Territory. The convention was extended in 1827. (FW)

British Continue In Oregon

Hudson's Bay Company was made up of a "Company of Adventurers of England trading into Hudson's Bay." Charles II gave his cousin, Prince Rupert, and seventeen other men a charter in 1670. The charter gave Hudson's Bay Company a monopoly in trade and commerce and complete legislative, judicial, and executive control over all seas, bays and straits, and all lands, countries, and territories upon the coasts of such seas, bays, and straits possessed by any English subject, or subjects of any other Christian state. The extensive charter had no parliamentary confirmation or sanction. (Slacum Pg.24)

North-West Company controlled the rich Oregon fur trade. Difficulties and quarrels between the North-West Company and the Hudson's Bay Company caused the British government to step in and compel the two to merge their stock into one company called Hudson's Bay Company. The merger took place in 1821.

The merger transferred the claim of all of the territory between forty two degrees and fifty-four degrees forty minutes north latitude west of the Rocky Mountains to Hudson's Bay Company and its dictatorial powers.

Hudson's Bay Company laid claim to all of the Oregon Country between Spanish California and Russian Alaska.

Governor Sir George Simpson moved the headquarters to Fort Vancouver in 1825. They kept at least one man at Fort George from 1829 to 1846. He was to keep an eye on the Americans who were moving into the region.

Dr. John McLoughlin was Chief Factor of the Columbia department of Hudson's

Bay Company and ruled the whole of the Oregon Country for the British with a heavy iron hand.

Politics In The Oregon Settlement

It was bona-fide settlers, not fur-traders or trappers, that retook Oregon for the United States. The Oregon Question brought fervent religious zeal and had a massive impact on colonization of the Oregon Country.

Hall Jackson Kelley became interested in the Oregon Question soon after the end of the War of 1812, in about 1815. He began writing about The Oregon Question for publication in 1818 and began a campaign for colonization in 1824. Kelley traveled to the Columbia River in 1833. Kelley became sick and was doctored by Dr. John McLoughlin, the primary target of his hatred of the British. Dr. McLoughlin healed Kelley and kicked him out of the country. Kelley did not return to Oregon.

Few American trappers remained in Oregon. Jedediah Smith's party of American trappers was on the Oregon coast in 1826. Fifteen men were killed by Indians, four escaped. Although the Americans were not welcome, Hudson's Bay Company came to Smith's assistance and recovered part of his goods.

Reverend Jason Lee
Oregon Historical Society Photo 4342

Rev. Jason Lee's Methodist Mission, Wheatland, Oregon
Oregon Historical Society Photo 46192

Jason Lee was the first of the missionaries to come to Oregon. He came in 1834 with Nathaniel Wyeth and moved into the Willamette Valley at Wheatland. He moved his mission to Salem in 1841.

The Oregon Question brought people bent on the colonization of the Oregon Country. James Anderson O'Neil arrived in Oregon with the second expedition of Nathaniel Wyeth in 1834 and became one of the first bonafide settlers.

Nathaniel Wyeth built Fort Hall on the upper Snake River and established a trading post there on his 1834 outward journey. James Anderson O'Neil was with Wyeth during the construction of Fort Hall. Goods arrived at Sauvie's Island on board the brig *May Dacre* in August 1834 for Nathaniel Wyeth's Columbia River Fishing and Trading and for Jason Lee's Methodist Mission to be established near Wheatland.

Although there were many Indians on Sauvie's Island earlier, Nathaniel Wyeth wrote;

> *"Mortality has carried off to a man its inhabitants and there is nothing to attest that they existed except their decaying houses, their graves and their unburied bones of which there are heaps."*

That is bleak evidence that the Indian population had been greatly decreased before the arrival of settlers from the United States; a direct affront to the claim by many that Indian deaths due to "white man's diseases" be placed on the backs of our pioneer forefathers from the United States.

Ewing Young Controversy

Ewing Young and Hall J. Kelley arrived in the Willamette Valley with one hundred fifty or more horses from California. Ewing Young settled in the Chehalem Valley in 1834 and was quickly branded a horse thief by Dr. John McLoughlin on information supplied by General Figeroa. McLaughlin, as chief factor of Hudson's Bay Company, prohibited the monopoly from selling anything to Ewing Young.

Bent on survival, Ewing Young and Mr. Carmichael started constructing a distillery for the manufacture of spirits. These factors were causing a three way dissension between Young, Lee, and McLaughlin.

Federal Agent Investigates Oregon Question

The Oregon Question had been rather dormant in Congress since the joint occupancy agreement with Great Britain of 1818 had been renewed in 1827. Everything was quiet in 1836. This bothered President Andrew Jackson, who tried to keep abreast of the happenings in the far-off land.

President Jackson proposed sending a resourceful, courageous, discreet and diplomatic fellow out to the Oregon Country. After some inquiries, the man selected was William A. Slacum, a United States Navy purser. Slacum knew a great deal about the Southwest. He was expected to learn about the Pacific Northwest because he was said to be a fast learner.

Slacum was directed to "go to and up the river Oregon," find out what was going on, and how the settlers felt about the United States. He was to gather such information "political, physical, statistical, and geographical, as may prove useful or interesting to the Government." Slacum was the first American secret agent sent to this part of the continent. He operated covertly as well as overtly.

Slacum arrived at the Columbia River in late December 1836, aboard the brig *Loriot*, which he had chartered in Honolulu. After paying his respects to Dr. John McLoughlin at Fort Vancouver, Slacum set about to pull the talons from the great "White-Headed Eagle."

Slacum considered the matter and the benefit to the country if Ewing Young's distillery was not completed and took action. For Mr. Young's abandoning the distillery project, Slacum arranged for Ewing Young to buy from the monopoly and loaned him the money. He also arranged transportation for Mr. Young to return to California to clear up the matter that had gotten him into the trouble in the first place.

British Monopolize The Beef Industry

It took Slacum only a few days to find that the American settlers needed cattle of their own for their survival and growth. Later, in his report on the Oregon Country to Congress, Slacum put the situation quite bluntly.

> *"Nothing was wanting to insure comfort, wealth, and every happiness to the people of this beautiful country but the possession of meat cattle, all those in the country being owned by Hudson's Bay Company, who refused to sell under any circumstances whatever."*

Slacum organized the Willamette Cattle Company to procure cattle in the San Francisco-Bodega area. He also helped finance it. All of the settlers who had money due them from Hudson's Bay Company contributed to the enterprise.

When Slacum returned to the United States in Mid-January 1837, he took eleven members of the Willamette Cattle Company as far as the San Francisco Bay area. James A. O'Neil was one of eleven members of the Willamette Cattle Company that accepted passage on the *Lariot* as the guest of Slacum. Slacum had concluded his whirlwind tour of the Oregon settlements in less than a month.

The leader of the eleven-member group was Ewing Young. Philip Leget Edwards, was named treasurer. John Turner, James Anderson O'Neil, Webley J. Hauxhurst, Calvin Tibbetts, Lawrence Carmichael, George Gay, William J. Bailey, Pierre DePuis, and Amable Arcouette were the other members. Hauxhurst lost courage at Astoria and left the crew but his investment remained. American Missionaries, American trappers, and French Canadians were represented. John McLoughlin, James Douglas, and Duncan Finlayson, employees of the Hudson's Bay Company invested in the project. (KLH)

In Mid-January 1837, the brig sailed for the San Francisco Bay area where long-horned cattle would be purchased for the long drive north. John Edmunds, William Peter, Benjamin Williams, Samuel Campbell, Henry Wood, C. Mace and Moore joined the Willamette Cattle Company party in California. (KLH)

Ewing Young sought and received permission to drive out seven hundred head of Spanish cattle from Civil Governor, Juan Bautista Alvarado. The cattle had to be purchased from the Mexican Government. The government had recently taken over all cattle when it secularized all Franciscan missions. Seven hundred twenty-nine head of cattle were purchased from military commanders at Sonoma and San Jose.

Six hundred thirty head, mostly heifers, reached Oregon in early October, nine months after the ship's departure. The cattle were distributed from Ewing Young's corral in the Chehalem Valley to those who had invested either money or time in the Willamette Cattle Company. Work was credited at one dollar a day. The cost of the cattle including time and money F.O.B. Young's Corral was $8.30 per head. (KLH)

The long drive was not without incident. Hostile encounters were commonplace between trappers and Indians. Not all encounters were instigated by Indians. Philip Leget Edwards, Treasurer, recorded an incident in southern Oregon. Gay shot and killed an Indian during the cattle drive. Ewing Young and Edwards were disturbed by the killing. However, most of the men supported Gay. Turner, Gay, Bailey and Turner's wife were the only survivors of an earlier Indian attack on eight men on the next river. Bailey became particularly vehement against Indians because he had been disfigured for life with a terrible scar across his face.

James Anderson O'Neil, the former Wyeth man is listed as O'Neal in the articles of agreement for the formation of the cattle company. However, the estate records of Ewing

Young show the name to be James O'Neil. He was credited with $326.725 for products or services that were not shown on the records. He probably received 39 head of cattle in the distribution.

Both names, O'Neal and O'Neil, appear in contemporary records for the man named James Anderson O'Ne?l. O'Neil is the preferred name throughout this book, although for no particular reason other than it appeared on the first documents examined and that name is inscribed on his tombstone. The name should not be confused with "James A. O'Neill" (with two ls), the name of an early mayor of Portland who was later an Indian Agent.

Unfair Business Practices

Americans could not compete with the unfair business practices of the Hudson's Bay Company west of South Pass. American fur companies held rendezvous high up on the Pacific slope of the Rocky Mountains in territory claimed by the United States. Some five hundred American trappers and hunters and Indians would meet to bring the results of their years labors to sell to the American fur traders. They would also purchase their supplies. The traders buy their supplies (chiefly of British manufacture with duty paid) at St. Louis and transport them fourteen hundred miles by land to the rendezvous to sell to citizens of the United States within the acknowledged lines of territory.

The agent of Hudson's Bay Company, a foreign monopoly, began showing up and could afford to undersell American fur traders on their own ground: First by having the advantage of cheaper water transportation on the Columbia and Lewis rivers for seven or eight hundred miles. Secondly, by selling the goods duty free equal to at least a twenty-five to thirty percent advantage.

The British company brought the goods directly from London to the Columbia River duty free. Any American enterprise would bring goods of British manufacture on which duty had been paid, from New York or Boston to the Columbia River. (Slacum Pg. 8)

Orders Straight From The Top In London

William Slacum observations were correct although he probably did not have access to Hudson's Bay Company records nor did he indicate that the problems were parts of a contrived plan. The British battle plan for acquisitions in Oregon Country had been formulated in London ten years earlier. The Governor and Committee in London gave Governor Simpson the battle plan in 1827 soon after the failure of 1826-1827 negotiations:

> "** *The Country on the West of the Mountains remaining common to the Americans and us for an indefinite period, terminable by a years (sic) notice from either Government, it becomes an important object to acquire as ample an occupation of the Country and Trade as possible, on the South as well as on the North side of the Columbia River, looking always to the Northern Side falling to our share on a division and to secure this, it may be as well to have something to give up on the South, when the final arrangement comes to be made.*
>
> *If the American Traders settle near our Establishments, they must be opposed, not by violence, which will only be the means of enabling the Traders to obtain the Interference of their Government, but by underselling them, which will damp their sanguine expectations of profit, and diminish the value which they at present put upon that Trade. It will be useful to give the Americans full occupation by active and well regulated opposition on the South of the river to prevent them advancing towards the North, and the general regulation of the Trapping parties call you best attention and we think merit your devoting a year of your time to it.*" *(DLM Page 273-4)*

In the northern areas in Canada, if Hudson's Bay Company found that districts began harvesting fewer furs, the trappers were immediately ordered to stop trapping. The number of animals would increase in a few years and the trappers would return to trapping. The laws were so strictly enforced among many of the northern Indian tribes that to kill a beaver out of season was a crime punished by death.

However, the British Company encouraged Walla Walla, Lewis, and Snake River Indians to trap the streams relentlessly at all seasons in the territory claimed by the United States. The Umpqua River alone produced ten thousand beaver skins, and double that amount came from the country around the river — all within the lines of the United States. (Slacum Pg. 9.)

As to the territory south of the Columbia River, ten years earlier in March 1827, the Governor and Committee in London instructed Simpson: "***it is extremely desirable to hunt as bare as possible all the Country South of the Columbia and West of the Mountans."* (*DLM page 272*)

Slacum continued in his report to President Jackson through John Forsyth, Secretary of State:

> *"but a greater evil than this exists in the influence of Hudson Bay Company exercises over the Indians, by supplying them with arms and ammunition, which may prove, at some future period, highly dangerous to our frontier settlements. Besides this, the policy of this company is calculated to perpetuate the institution of slavery, which now exists, and is encouraged, among all the Indian tribes west of the Rocky Mountains."* (Slacum pg. 8.)

Indian Slavery

"The price of a slave varies from eight to fifteen blankets. Women are valued higher than men. If a slave dies within six months of the time of purchase, the seller returns one-half the purchase money. As long as the Hudson Bay Company permit their servants to hold slaves, the institution of slavery will be perpetuated, as the price, eight to fifteen blankets, is too tempting for an Indian to resist. Many instances have occurred where a man has sold his own child. The chief factor at Vancouver says the slaves are the property of the women with whom their workmen live, and do not belong to men in their employ, although I have known cases to the contrary. We shall see how this reasoning applies. These whom, who are said to be the owners of the slaves, are frequently bought themselves by the men with whom they live, when they are mere children; of course they have no means to purchase, until their husbands or their men make the purchase from the proceeds of their labor; and then these women are considered the ostensible owners, which neither lessens the traffic, nor ameliorates of the condition of the slave, whilst the Hudson Bay Company find it to their interest to encourage their servants to intermarry or live with the native women, as it attaches the men to the soil, and their offspring (half breeds) become in turn useful hunters and workmen at the different depots of the company. The slaves are generally employed to cut wood, hunt, and fish, for the families of the men employed by the Hudson Bay Company, and are ready for any extra work. Each man of the trapping parties has from two to three slaves, who assist to hunt, and take care of the horses and camp; they thereby save the company the expense of employing at least double the number of men that would otherwise be required on these excursions." (*Slacum Pg.10.*)

"A large cargo of wheat, five thousand five hundred bushels, could at

this time be procured from the settlers on the Willhamett. It would find a good market at the Sandwich islands, the Russian settlements at Norfolk sound, (Sitka,) or in Peru; but some steps must be taken by our Government to protect the settlers and the trader, not from the hostility of the Indians, but from a much more formidable enemy, than any American trading house establishing itself on the Willhamet or Columbia would have to encounter, in the Hudson Bay Company. All the Canadian settlers have been in the service of the company; and from being for a long time subject to the most servile submission to the chiefs of the monopoly, are now, although discharged from the service of the company, still blindly obedient to the will of those in authority at Vancouver, who, on their part, urge the plea that, by the legislative enactment's of Canada, they are prohibited from discharging their servants in the Indian country. Therefore they consider the people of the Willhamett, although freemen in every sense of the word still subject to the protection and authority, otherwise thraldom of the Hudson Bay Company — it being only necessary for the authorities at Vancouver to say, 'if you disobey my orders, your supplies will be cut off;' and the settler knows at once that his few comforts, nay, necessaries of life, are stopped, rendering him more miserable than the savage that lurks around his dwelling." (Slacum Pg. 13.)

Pugitt's Sound Boundary Recommendations

William A. Slacum reported to John Forsyth, Secretary Of State:

" * * * * *Dr. McLaughlin now compels the Canadians, whose term of service expires, and who are anxious to become farmers, to settle on this (Cowlitz) river, as it lies to the north of the Columbia. The reason he assigns is, that the north side of the Columbia River will belong to the Hudson Bay Company. If one side of the river is claimed, with the same propriety they might claim both sides. The navigation of the Columbia is absolutely necessary to the Hudson Bay Company; without this, they have no passage into the heart of their fine possessions in the interior, New Caledonia, &c. I know not what political influence they command; but this monopoly is very wealthy; and, when the question of our western lines of territory is settled, they (the Hudson bay Company) will make the most strenuous efforts to retain free navigation of the Columbia - more important to them than the free navigation of the St. Lawrence is to the people of the United States.*

"I beg leave to call your attention to the topography of 'Pugitt's sound,' and urge, in the most earnest manner, that this point should never be abandoned. If the United States claim, as I hope they ever will, at least as far as 49 degrees north latitude, running due west from the "Lake of the Woods," on the above parallel we shall take in 'Pugitt's sound." In a military point of view, it is of the highest importance to the United States. If it were in the hands of any foreign power, especially Great Britain, with the influence she could command through the Hudson bay Company over the Indians at the north, on those magnificent straits of 'Juan de Fuca,' a force of 20,00 men could be brought by water in large canoes to the sound, 'pugitt's' in a few days, from thence to the Columbia; the distance is but two day's march, via the cowility. I am now more convinced than ever of the importance of the Columbia river, even as a place where, for eight months in the year, our whalers from the coast

Fort Vancouver

Oregon Historical Society Photo 803

Dr. John McLoughlin

Oregon Historical Society Photo 12

of Japan might resort for supplies, which, in the course of a few years, would be abundant, if the citizens of the United States could receive from the Government the protection due to them. A custom-house, established at the mouth of the Columbia would effectualy protect the American trader from the monopoly which the Hudson Bay Company enjoy at this time, and a single military post would be sufficient to give effect to the laws of the United States, and protect our citizens in their lawful avocations." (Slacum Pg. 17)

Dr. McLoughlin, as Chief Factor for Hudson's Bay Company, compelled discharged Canadian employees to settle on the Cowlitz River north of the Columbia River if they wished to stay in the country. McLoughlin believed that possession of the territory north of the Columbia River would ultimately be resolved in favor of the British and the Hudson's Bay Company. He also believed that if they had one side of the Columbia River, they could claim both sides.

The navigation of the Columbia River was absolutely necessary to the Hudson's Bay Company; without this, they would have no passage into the heart of their fine possessions in the interior.

Slacum hoped the United States would

claim to fifty-four degrees forty minutes north latitude.

He urged that the United States should never abandon its claim on Puget Sound. He pointed out that a claim as far as forty-nine degrees north latitude running due west of the "Lake of the Woods" would include Puget Sound. If Puget Sound was in the hands of any foreign power, especially Britain with the influence she had over the Indians through the Hudson's Bay Company, she could raise a force of twenty thousand men. The twenty-thousand men could be brought to Puget Sound in a few days by water. They could reach the Columbia River in two more days.

Slacum reported that Oregon Country was vital to the interests of the United States and should be protected at least to forty-nine degrees north latitude.

Slakum was convinced of the importance of the Columbia River. In addition to being a road of commerce, it was a place where whalers from the coast of Japan might obtain supplies, provided the citizens of the United States could receive the protection due them from their government.

Slacum's presentation appears to be mirrored in the prevailing attitude in the United States in the mid 1840s slogan "fifty-forty or fight." Slacum's report also presented to more conservative alternative boundary at forty-nine degrees north latitude. He may not have liked relinquishing the United States claim to exclusive rights in the Strait of Juan de Fuca by giving the entire Vancouver Island to Britain.

Settlers Request Protection

Slacum enlisted the services of the ever-willing Jason Lee to compile a complete list of white settlers in the Willamette Valley.

There were about fifty-one adult white male settlers in the Willamette Valley when Slacum arrived in January 1837. About half were Americans, including the Methodist missionaries. French Canadians made up the rest.

Jason Lee drew up a petition urging the United States *"to take formal and speedy possession"* of the territory. *"The country must populate,"* the petition stated:

> *"The natural resources of the country, with a well judged civil code, will invite a good community. But a good community will hardly emigrate to a country which promises no protection to life or property."*

The implication was clear. At that, the language was modest, compared to the few who threatened openly to burn Fort Vancouver. Many irate United States citizens had considered the British their adversaries since Britain tightened up its colonial administration after the end of the French and Indian War in 1763. Feelings were still running high in The United States and the Oregon Country wars seventy-three years later.

Patriot Wars were fermenting against the British on the eastern half of the United States border with Canada. A few tried to organize a party to drive out all non-white land-holding settlers in Oregon Country. This was aimed at driving Canadians who had Indian wives and part-Indian children out of the Willamette Valley.

It took some persuading by Lee and Slacum to talk the old voyageurs of the Hudson Bay Company into scrawling their names on the document. Slacum promised that the United States would see to it that the farms remained in their possession. They were partially aligned with the Americans.

Jason Lee was a persuasive businessman. Alexis de Tocqueville defined the frontier missionary:

> *"If you converse with these Missionaries of Christian civilization you will be surprised to hear them speak so often of the goods of this world, and to meet a politician where you expected to find a priest."*

Thirty-six of the fifty-one eligible signed. One was James A. O'Neil. The quicker the

British could be gotten rid of, the better he liked it. He signed everything that might speed that day. The one that he particularly liked was written 23 March 1843 "to the Hon. Senate and House of Representatives of the U. S. of America." In that petition the settlers made a bill of particulars against Dr. John McLoughlin. It accused him of being a despot, a swindler, and a crooked landlord.

Farms Prosper

Bountiful crops made James A. O'Neil well-to-do, and he could hire people to work for him. Sidney Smith, of the Peoria Party, worked for O'Neil upon his arrival in the autumn of 1839. A cow and a calf were paid him for forty-eight days work. Robert Shortess, another member of the Peoria Party, came in the spring of 1840. He said "I then went to work for A. O'Neil, for whom, I continued to labor till the latter end of June, when, having finished his work, I went to work at the mission. The wage for farm work then was $1 per day and board." Almost a hundred years later during the Great Depression, wages on many farms were about the same.

As well established as he was, something was still missing in O'Neil's life. In December 1840 he began attending revival meetings held at the Methodist Mission. The earnest preaching of Reverend David Leslie deeply moved him. One day he stepped forward to become a convert. His zeal thereafter was so dedicated that he became a missionary's aide.

Need For Government

The Oregon Question was the most important part of James Anderson O'Neil's life. It was also the most important thing in the lives of many of his contemporaries including Shortess, Smith and Leslie.

The need for a government came to the attention of the settlers when Ewing Young died in February 1841 without leaving any known heirs. The settlers came together to probate his estate. There they told each other that they needed some kind of organization to handle similar situations that might arise in the future. Dr. Ira Babcock of Lee's Mission was selected to be Supreme Judge.

Eight days before Young's death, Jason Lee had called for the appointment of a committee to draft a constitution and code of laws for the settlers south of the Columbia. Nothing ever came of it.

Other attempts at political organization were aborted. The settlers had little ground upon which even to meet. Finally, two years after Young's death, the strategists devised a reason for bringing settlers of diverse view points together. They did not have far to reach. The farmers who had cattle were losing their stock to wolves.

Wolfe Meetings

Settlers who wanted a government began to look into the matter. William. H. Gray who had left Dr. Whitman and settled in the Willamette Valley was the prime mover behind the movement. He gathered a few trusted settlers at his house to devise a plan for gathering the people together before opposition could develop. A simple but affective plan was devised. It worked like a charm.

Many domestic animals were being destroyed by wolves, bears, lynx, and panthers. How to prevent the small herds from being ravaged by wild beasts was a serious question with the settlers. The small group decided to call a meeting for the purpose of devising some means for protecting cattle from the wild animals. They sent word out for every settler to attend a meeting at the Oregon Institute on the second day of February, 1843.

First Wolfe Meeting
(February 2, 1843)

Dr. Ira Babcock presided over the first wolf meeting. Attendance was very large.

Dr. Babcock was not made aware of its real purpose because he was in opposition to organizing a government.

Judiciously, there was little talk of politics. The real purpose of the gathering was to bring a larger number together at the second "Wolfe Meeting," on March 6, 1843. The meeting was to be held at the French Prairie home of the shrewd trapper and trader, Joe Gervais. A committee to deal with the problem of cattle losses was appointed.

George LeBreton and a Mr. Smith quietly canvassed the sentiment of the people on the subject of a more complete government before the second meeting. They found that there was quite a diversity of opinions.

Dr. John McLoughlin advocated a government that would be entirely independent of the United States and Great Britain. George Abernathy and other Americans advocated that the United States extend its jurisdiction over the Oregon Country within the next four years and that it would not be expedient to form an independent government. Dr. Elijah White, the Indian Agent, advocated a government only if he was placed at its head.

Second Wolfe Meeting (March 6, 1843)

James Anderson O'Neil was presiding officer at the second "Wolf Meeting." Everyone liked and respected him. He was no tenderfoot and had been in these parts when there were very few whites around. Later he became the first settler in what is now Polk County. He owned a copy of the statutes of Iowa and several other law books, so he was considered as having a legal mind.

James Anderson O'Neil was prepared to guide the proceedings as rapidly as possible. The famous "Divide" gathering at Champoeg was on May 2, 1843. The public mind was somewhat prepared for a step of some kind to be taken beyond that of mere protection from wild animals. As a consequence, the second wolf meeting attendance was larger than it would have been.

The first question at the March 6, 1843 meeting was about the wolves, bears, panthers, and other wild animals that were killing cattle and other livestock. The report by the committee appointed at the first meeting recommended the payment of bounties. Fifty cents would be paid for a small wolf, a dollar and a half for a lynx, two dollars for a bear, three dollars for a large wolf, and five dollars for a panther. Indians were to receive half as much as whites.

Each member was levied $5.00 to pay the bounties. A commission of 5 percent was given for each member enrolled to boost payments.

A Quick Turn

As soon as the predatory animals question was out of the way, the political brains turned quickly to what was really on their minds. The diverse elements at the home of Joe Gervais were still fused in unity. Quickly a resolution was introduced and unanimously adopted.

William H. Gray arose and made a little speech to the assembled settlers:

> *"How is it, fellow citizens, with you and me, and our wives and children? Have we any organization on which we can rely for mutual protection? Is there any power or influence in the country sufficient to protect us and all we hold dear from the worse than wild beasts that threaten and occasionally destroy our cattle? Who in our midst is authorized to call us together to protect our own and the lives of our families? True, the alarm may be given, as in a recent case, and we may run who feel alarmed, and shoot off our guns, while our enemy may be robbing our property, ravishing our wives, and burning our houses over our defenseless families. Common sense, prudence and justice to ourselves demand that we act consistent with the principles that we have commenced. We have mutu-*

ally and unitedly agreed to defend our cattle and domestic animals; now, fellow citizens, I submit and move the adoption of the two following resolutions, that we may have protection for our persons and lives, as well as our cattle and herds: Resolved, That a committee be appointed to take into consideration the propriety of taking measures for the civil and military protection of this colony. Resolved, that said committee consist of twelve persons."

A committee of twelve was appointed to consider the propriety of taking measures for "civil and military protection of this colony." James A. O'Neil, Dr. Ira L. Babcock, Dr. Elijah White, Robert Shortess, Dr. Robert Newell, Etienne Lucier, Joseph Gervais, William H. Gray, Sidney Smith, Thomas Hubbard, M'Roy, and George Gay were in the roster of eminent pioneers.

The committee of twelve met a few days later at Willamette Falls, now Oregon City, to take the next step. Many of the most respected men in the area were with them in their deliberations.

Jason Lee, previously a trumpet for Americanization, reversed himself from a position expressed two years before. Now he was alarmed. He felt the movement for independent government was premature. It could provoke the British into moving military power into the area. George Abernathy, a merchant and mill owner who had more to lose than the others, shared Lee's dissent.

Third Wolfe Meeting
The Famous Divide Meeting
(May 2, 1843)

James O'Neil and others would not be deterred. They voted to call a formal meeting on May 2, 1843 to consider the propriety of taking measures for the civil and military protection of the colony. In essence, the committee of twelve had resolved to form a committee of the whole.

The site chosen for the meeting was the former Indian village of Cham-poo-ick, later renamed Champoeg. Hudson's Bay Company had warehouses there that could be used as a gathering place.

Champoeg 1812 -1848

Donald McKenzie and William W. Matthews of John Jacob Astors' Pacific Fur Company moved up the Willamette River in April, 1812. They were joined by J. C. Halsey and William Wallace and established a hunting camp and trading post near Champoeg. The post fell into enemy hands during the war of 1812 and was not recovered by the United States until the treaty with Great Britain was ratified August 14, 1848. (HMC P. 78)

Birth Of Oregon

There is some confusion about the turnout and voting. There was considerable skirmishing going on. The French Canadians invariably voted "NO" on all questions without reference to the bearing they had upon the interests they represented. They became very demoralized as a consequence.

George LeBreton, who had made a careful study of those in attendance, finally exclaimed, *"We can risk it, let us divide and count."* William Gray shouted, *"I second the motion!"* Joseph Meek then quickly moved out, and raising his voice to a high pitch, shouted, *"Who's for divide? All for the report of the committee and organization, follow me."*

Those for the forming a government lined themselves on his side, and a count was taken. Joseph Meek had fifty-two persons lined on his side with only fifty in opposition. Joseph Meek shouted again, *"Three cheers for our side!"* The responsive cheers rose. The defeated Canadians withdrew and gradually left.

Tradition says the vote to endorse the proposal of the twelve-man organization committee was 52 to 50 in favor. Ironically, as legend has it, the vote was tied until Etienne Lucier, a member of the committee, joined

Settlers vote to form a government

Painting by William H. Jackson, Scott's Bluff National Monument

the American side. At that, he was persuaded, not by any arguments advanced by other members of the committee, but by a fellow French-Canadian, Francois Xavier Matthieu, with whom he shared a cabin.

If the legend is correct, it was a French-Canadian that cast the deciding vote setting up a civil and military government.

However, there is evidence that indicates that there may have been a stronger favorable vote. The Champoeg State Park has prepared a different list it claims to be much closer to what really happened. It includes some French Canadians that were some of the most respected men of the time that are not on the list of fifty-two. There was stronger sentiment in favor of forming a provisional government for the civil and military protection of the Oregon colony than is indicated by the traditional 52-50 vote.

Jason Lee and George Abernathy did not vote on the proposal. Lee was not opposed to taking measures for civil and military protection of this colony. He was opposed to the proposal as presented at that time. He was fearful of military retaliation by the British. The British had never been real friends of the United States. Sovereignty over Oregon was a continuous issue with Rev. Lee.

George Abernathy was afraid of British military retaliation. He was a merchant and mill owner who had more to lose than the others. His fear of the British was shown again in 1845. As Provisional Governor he supported a committee to find a Southern Route out of the Willamette Valley. He was "top man" carrying out the provisions of the proposal he did not endorse.

Some declined to attend the July 5, 1843 meeting and said that they would not submit to the authority of any government being organized. The Catholic Missionaries and representatives of the Hudson's Bay Company also assumed the same position.

First Oregon Legislature

The meeting of May 2, 1843, laid the formal groundwork for provisional government, and nine member legislative committee was selected. James A. O'Neil was included in the nine. He owned copies of the statutes of Iowa that formed the working model for the organic laws of Oregon. Oregon was here to stay.

James A. O'Neil was placed on a subcommittee on ways and means and on the judiciary committee when the legislative committee of nine convened. He had a firm hand in writing the report the committee submitted to those who convened on July 5, 1843 at Champoeg.

The people assembled at Champoeg on July 5, 1843. The Committees report was presented by Chairman Robert Moore and read by Secretary George LeBreton. A strong debate followed. The Chair, Gustavus Hines, vigorously opposed the three members of the Executive Committee's proposal. Ira Babcock also opposed on the grounds that it looked like a permanent form of government, instead of the temporary one that he thought was the purpose of the meeting. James Anderson O'Neil and Robert Shortess presented their views arguing in favor of the report. William Gray made a forceful and convincing argument in favor of the report. The report was unanimously adopted.

The preamble to the adopted laws' states:

James Anderson O'Neil

Champoeg Oregon State Park

> *"We, the people of Oregon Territory, for the purpose of protection, and to secure peace and prosperity among ourselves, agree to adopt the following laws and regulations, until such time as the United States of America extend their jurisdiction over us."*

The meeting also voted to purchase James A. O'Neil's books: *Laws of Iowa, A Guide to Judges*, and *Jefferson's Manual* for $10.50. He was paid in full for the books on September 28, 1843. The new government had purchased its first books and started its first library. (RF)

James Anderson O'Neil was elected Justice of Yamhill District in 1843 and Judge of Polk County in 1845 when Districts were divided into Counties. Justices and Judges governed their respective Districts or Counties.

A census in 1845 reported 2,109 people in the Oregon Country, 1,900 were Oregon Trail emigrants, adding considerably to the United States representation. (JT)

National Politics Leading To Statehood

Meanwhile anti-British sentiment was growing back in the United States. War plans were fermenting against the British on the eastern half of the border between the United States and Canada. During the Patriot War in 1838, groups of American citizens and Canadian rebels planned to attack the British armies along the United States-Canadian border and eventually establish an independent republic.

During the 1840s, organized American immigration to the Oregon region began. The "Oregon Question" became a matter of grave concern in the United States. The memory of the War of 1812 was still fresh in their minds. The British had invaded the United States and burned the Nation's Capital only thirty years before. Britain still retained control over the Oregon Country that it had seized during that war.

Britain had been badgering her fledgling offspring from its beginning. James Nesmith remembered:

> *"Great Britain was the only country with which we had ever had any conflict of arms, and the generation to which we belonged, particularly in the west, had been taught to look upon the 'Britishers' as natural enemies." (HQB JWN 32.)*

Americans were demanding that Great Britain relinquish all jurisdiction south of fifty-four degrees forty minutes north latitude in 1843. The Democratic Party slogan, on which James Knox Polk was elected President of the United States in 1844 was "fifty-four forty, or fight." (FW) (GMF)

Missouri's Senators began trumpeting the western movement in December 1821 when Thomas Hart Benton, one of Missouri's first senators was seated. Lewis F. Linn collaborated constantly on the Oregon question. It was Linn who introduced the territorial bill to congress on February 7, 1838. He kept the bill alive for the rest of his life.

Benton pushed congress to appoint Lt. John Charles Fremont to head a federal exploring expedition to the Columbia and report back. Fremont reported that Oregon was indeed as rich as it was said to be and it was easily reached by wagon. Senator Benton reasoned that Oregon should be given territorial status and protection by the government of the United States.

The people became polarized, not between "for or against" but "how much." Henry Clay thought the United States should do everything she could, within reason, to win Oregon. Others wanted Oregon to go all the way to fifty-four degrees, forty minutes — right now. They were aligned behind James K. Polk. The people spoke 1,337,243 to 1,299,068 to go all the way by electing Polk to be President of the United States.

President Polk told the British he would settle for the forty-ninth parallel. They held out for more in the finest tradition of international negotiations. Polk went back to "fifty-four-forty — or fight." (GMF)

The British people, however were relaxed. Fur trade was nearly defunct. There was not much reason to fight over Oregon. There was only token British occupation directed at fur trade. There were no British women in Oregon and no all-British families. The Americans with their families were there in great numbers.

The two countries agreed in 1846, in the Oregon Treaty, on the forty-ninth parallel as the boundary from the Rocky Mountains to the coast, and a line along mid-channel between Vancouver Island and the mainland to the Pacific Ocean. The United States had previously established the forty-second parallel as the southern boundary in a treaty with Spain. (FW)

Congress screamed and true Westerners looked upon their President's action as treasonous. Senator Benton was happy with the compromise and provided the grease on the skids to get the treaty through Congress. (GMF)

Congress ratified the treaty establishing Oregon as a Territory August 14, 1848. It included all of the present States of Oregon and Washington and parts of Idaho, Montana and Wyoming.

Western Migration

The Oregon Question brought fervent religious zeal and had a massive impact on the colonization of the Oregon Country. Jason Lee, the first of the missionaries to go to Oregon Country traveled overland to the Willamette Valley with Nathaniel Wyeth in 1834.

Marcus Whitman was first a man, second a physician, and third a missionary. The West should never forget Marcus Whitman, first a man. Marcus Whitman and Samuel Parker explored the Northwest in 1835 and returned to the United States. Whitman returned to Missouri the following spring. He returned, this time with the first real sign that the West was about to be opened for colonization. He was accompanied by his new bride, Narcissa Prentiss Whitman. They

Whitman Mission

Painting by William H. Jackson, Scott's Bluff National Monument

honeymooned on the Oregon Trail.

Narcissa Whitman wrote many letters to her parents back east. Somehow they got there. Somehow they got published. Somehow she got the point across that the Oregon Trail was receptive to wagon travel though the Whitman's had to abandon the last vestige of the wagon train at Fort Boise when the last of the wagon axles gave out. (GMF)

The Whitmans established and operated the mission on the Walla Walla River until November 29, 1847, when Marcus and Narcissa Whitman and eleven others were chopped up by Cayuse Indians. Most of the rest of the mission population was taken hostages. The Whitman Massacre increased fear within the Oregon population. The people thought there was a general uprising of the Indians against the settlers.

The American press went into in high gear promoting westward migration. Stories appeared constantly. It really got to rural America when the guy from their own area sold out his farm, threw everything he had into a wagon and moved over the trail to Oregon. Neighbors were fascinated and envious. If he made it, why couldn't they?

Letters began coming back from strange places; Saint Joseph, Fort Laramie, Fort Bridger, Ash Hollow, Salem, Fort Vancouver, Whitman Mission. Letters full of stories about the prairies, the Indians, the buffalo herds, the deserts, and even the other emigrants. Stories far different from things they were familiar with. It was like they were leaving to colonize mars, or the moon. (GMF)

David and Hannah Davis, like other Iowa and Missouri farmers, were comfortable and secure with their farms paid for and their ground was all broken and fertile. But they read some of these letters, and heard about many more. They listened to men like Albert Davidson, an 1845 emigrant to Oregon, who came back for their families. They made speeches about the Oregon Country. Men like Mr. Davidson were zealots for the promised land.

Old thoughts welled up in David and Hannah Davis, the same thoughts that made them emigrate from Pennsylvania to Indiana, and again from Indiana to Iowa. The challenge of the new frontier was no longer in the United States, it was in Oregon Country. It was beginning to get crowded back in the United States. Neighbors were coming in and working farms only a few miles away. The paradise of the 1830s had improved, but in the minds of farmers, there was no improvement.

"Manifest Destiny"

John L. O'Sullivan, an editorial writer for the *Democratic Review*, was disenchanted with President Polk's pullback from his warlike slogans like "fifty-four forty or fight." O'Sullivan picked "Manifest Destiny" as his outcry against such disenchantment in the *United States Magazine* and *Democratic Review*. It was picked up by other editors and has been used as a sub-title about the 1840s. Oregon was the United States' "Manifest Destiny."

In the early to mid nineteenth century, people felt a deep personal sense of belonging to the United States and its federal government. David and Hannah Davis thought their duty was to their country, almost as much so as their duty to their family. (GMF)

There was a threat of a "shooting" war with Great Britain over the "Oregon Country." Although a treaty had been negotiated only a few months before the 1847 emigration, there was strong opposition to the treaty in Congress. Almost all of the territory along the Columbia River and the Oregon Trail west of "South Pass" was under British control.

Britain was not the friendly power she is as we approach the twenty-first century. Britain had been aggressively attacking the United States for all of its short life. The United States had been attacked and partially occupied only thirty-five years earlier. The British occupied many points in The United States including the Nation's Capital and New Orleans during the War Of 1812. They had burned much of Washington D. C., including the President's Mansion. Britain still occupied Oregon Country claimed by the United States.

The emigrants knew they could get through. Hadn't a hundred and twelve or more moved west by 1842, a thousand in 1843, three thousand in 1845? About twenty-five hundred went over the Oregon Trail to Oregon in 1846. That was because talk about war over the Oregon Country was hot in 1846. War was less likely in 1847 than it was in 1846. They were ready for whatever they met.

The Oskaloosa Company was a well-organized wagon train of almost fifty wagons when it crossed the Missouri River in the middle of May 1847. During the previous winter the men had been getting together with other men they scarcely knew. They had listened to everybody they thought knew anything about the Oregon Trail or the Oregon Country. They pored over guidebooks and talked about their crops and farm prices. Somehow they had to compress everything they had into the space available in the wagons they could afford to equip.

Many Oregon emigrants left Oregon for California after the discovery of gold in 1849. Congress passed the Donation Land Act in 1850, giving large tracts of land free to settlers in Oregon. A large increase in population and prosperity prompted the settlers to hold a convention in 1857 and request statehood. That portion of the Oregon Territory now known as Oregon obtained statehood on February 14, 1859.

CHAPTER 2

Exploring the Southern Route,
Building the Scott-Applegate Trail in 1846

The Oregon Trail

There is no greater monument to the development of the United States as we know it than the OREGON TRAIL. The Oregon Trail started at Saint Joseph and Independence, Missouri. The two trails soon meet at the Big Blue River in northeastern Kansas. It then stretched two thousand miles across arid plains and forbidding mountains to Oregon's lush Willamette Valley.

The overland route was used earlier by trappers and later by prospectors. Parts of it were pioneered by Lewis and Clark in 1805. Part was pioneered by Overland Astorians in 1811 and Returning Astorians in 1814. William Price Hunt led a group of Astorians

Above, Levi Scott; right, Jesse Applegate
Douglas County Museum

overland to Astoria at the mouth of the Columbia River in 1811. Robert Stuart, another Astorian, led a party of men overland to deliver messages to John Jacob Astor in New York in 1812. Stuart's party has been credited with discovering what was later known as the Oregon Trail. Stuart's expedition was one of the first to locate South Pass. Edward Robinson, John Hoback and Jacob Rizner are credited for telling Stuart of the location of the pass.

Astorians returning to the United States from their defeat at Astoria used parts of the Oregon Trail in 1814 as did Jedediah Smith in 1823 and Nathaniel Wyeth in 1832 and 1834.

Glen Adams, in his Colophon to a reprinting of "*The Earliest Travelers on the Oregon Trail*," an address by T. C. Elliott, gave the best short description of the long trip by the Overland Astorians in 1811:

> *"A possible 300,000 persons traveled over the Oregon and California Trails, with the first of these many weary travelers being the Overland Astorians, under Wilson Price Hunt. Nearly all of the later parties followed the Platte River but the Overland Astorians went some distance north of the Platte. They left on March 12, 1811 and reached the mouth of the Columbia after much hardship, about February, 1812."* (TCE)

William Sublette was the first to take wagons part way over it. Occasionally settlers traveled the trail in the 1830's. The Bidwell party attacked the Oregon Trail in 1841, but the Bidwell party split, the larger group turning south to California. They were the first sizable pioneer party to reach the Pacific. The Oregon section struggled through finally without wagons. Elijah White's party resorted to pack horses beyond Fort Hall in 1842.

Missionary Marcus Whitman guided wagons through the mountains in 1843. About one thousand emigrants got through that year. During the following decade, thousands of covered wagons drove their ruts so deeply into the prairie that traces can still be seen today. Traffic climaxed in 1852, when about ten thousand persons emigrated to Oregon over the Oregon Trail.

The Oregon Trail followed the natural highways of rivers whenever possible. From Independence or St. Joseph, Missouri, it went three hundred sixteen miles north to the Platte River. It followed the South bank of the Platte River to the fork with the North Platte River. It then followed the North Platte to Fort Laramie. The trail crossed North Platte River and went up Sweetwater River past Independence Rock to the summit of the Rocky Mountains.

The Oregon Trail crossed the Rocky Mountains at South Pass and advanced gently to Soda Springs and on to Fort Hall. In 1843 some pioneers detoured south via Fort Bridger, then northwest to Soda Springs and Ft. Hall. David and Hannah Davis chose the route through Fort Bridger in 1847.

The trail divided on the Snake River southwest of Fort Hall. The California Trail went South. The Oregon Trail continued down the Snake River to Fort Boise, winding through steep canyons. The Grande Ronde Valley provided respite before the pioneers attacked the Blue Mountains. Then on to Whitman Mission and The Dalles.

Emigrants were well informed of certain known perils they were apt to encounter along their way while crossing the Great Plains, the Rocky Mountains, and deserts. They traveled with certain expectations over this part of their journey and took some good defensive measures to protect themselves. They were least prepared for their ultimate, last, and greatest hurdle through the Cascade Mountains of Oregon to reach the Willamette Valley.

Another Route Was Needed

Little had been done to improve the trail since the Lewis and Clark expedition in 1803-1804. Some detours and cutoffs had been used, but there was some question of whether they actually improved the journey.

The western end of the trail was causing a lot of trouble. During the years 1843, 1844, and 1845 the travelers over the Oregon Trail had suffered greatly and had losses in both property and lives. Water and grass were in scarce supply and the emigrants met hardships that were nearly unbearable.

In the Blue Mountains there were great forest fires that added to other hardships. Many of the travelers became deathly ill in the area. Calls for medical aid and assistance went out from The Dalles to save the dying. They were becoming so numerous as to create a problem of major significance. It was a major disaster by today's standards.

Trouble was heaped on trouble at The Dalles, for that was literally an end of the wagon trail. Beyond that point were only the crude Indian trails through the Cascade Mountains over which the wagons could not travel. Emigrants bound for the Willamette Valley were forced to leave their needed wagons at that point. However, they could take them apart and float down the Columbia River on hastily made crude rafts.

There was reportedly one other way of getting down the river and on to the Willamette Valley. For one hundred dollars, a boat could be hired to take a wagon and its occupants on down the river. That was beyond the means of all but a few of the travelers.

The trail-weary travelers had met one more disappointment on their way to the promised land. Settlement of Oregon Country seemed important enough to warrant the construction of some roads so the early settlers could reach their destination.

Attempts were made toward finding other routes through the Cascade Mountains into the Willamette Valley. The Barlow Trail south of Mount Hood had been stopped short of the Cascade Summit and it wasn't certain that it could be extended on into the valley before the 1846 emigrants arrived. Other attempts to make a route had also ended in failure. The situation was becoming more desperate each day.

Boundary War - A Possibility

Britain's conquest over the Astorians in the War of 1812 remained to haunt emigrants as they began to settle in their new homes in the Willamette Valley. The Oregon Question was not resolved in the treaty that ended the war.

Negotiations toward sovereignty over Oregon Country had dragged out since Captain Black claimed "the whole country" for Britain in 1813. War with Britain over the location of the boundary between Canada and the United States remained a real possibility. Britain, through Hudson's Bay Company, controlled the only road into or out of Oregon Country. A string of forts from Fort Vancouver to Fort Hall controlled the only overland route from the United States to the Willamette Valley. The United States needed a route to move troops and supplies in, and for the settlers to retreat out of the Country south of the Columbia River in the event of open conflict.

The people of the United States were of a mind to go to war over the Oregon Question if a negotiated settlement could not be reached.

California In Transition

The situation in California was unsettled. Contrary to popular belief, Mexico had no long-standing interest in settling California. The Mexican era in California was a transition from Spanish to U. S. rule that started in 1822. The British extended their activities into Upper California. American trappers and traders included both Upper California and Oregon Country in their expeditions into the West.

The Mexican government neglected California. Governmental institutions were democratized, and Franciscans were expelled between 1835 and 1840. There was no serious resistance to the United States taking over in California in 1846. The U. S. Navy occupied Monterey, San Francisco, and Sonoma. Mexico's forces were defeated in southern California by forces under Major John C. Fremont, General Stephen Kearney, and Jonathan D. Stevenson. (E)

The United States and California settlers were at war with Mexico in 1846. John Craig, a 1846 emigrant to California, and the rest of his little party, volunteered for six months service under Commodore Stockton and Col. Fremont. Another emigrant, William H. Russell, wrote for the *Missouri Republican* on January 26, 1847 about his foray with John C. Fremont:

> *"* * * * an insurrection broke out in this portion of the country, and in this city, which has been the capital of Upper California; to suppress which Col. Fremont, whom I have attached myself to as a member of his staff, forthwith set out by sea, and after a calm of two weeks on the justly named Pacific, we mounted our men, and after a long and tedious march of near two months, met the enemy near this place, who without a regular fight, came in, capitulated, and the country is again at peace, and Col. Fremont is Governor, and, strange as it may seem, I am Secretary of State, and am now writing to you in the Government House of California, in a room of which I have my office."* (WHR pg. 699)

The *Oregon Spectator*, March 18, 1847, issue, reported an anonymous source: *"Nearly the whole of the immigration have been off with Col. Fremont, who has command of all the land forces."*

Although persons were killed, losses were said to be slight on both sides.

A Southern Route To Oregon

Provisional Governor, George Abernathy, ordered that the Southern Route to Oregon be opened in 1845. An unorganized attempt ended in failure in that year.

An article in the *Missouri Reporter* in St. Louis on Tuesday, October 28, 1845, among other things the article said:

> *"Maj. Harris and several others will soon start to view out a road from the headwaters of the Willamette to the Soda Springs beyond Fort Hall, the design of bringing the next emigration through that way into the Willamette valley."*

Moses Harris guided Nathaniel Ford's wagon train over the northern route of the Oregon Trail in 1844. He remained in the Willamette Valley during the winter of 1844 and spring of 1845.

First Attempt in 1845 failed

Settlers subscribed two thousand dollar for the exploration of a new and better way through the Cascade Mountains. Elijah White, Moses Harris, Joseph Gale, Batteus DuGuerre, Joseph Saxton, Orus Brown, John Edmunds and two others set out July 12, 1845, to find an easier pass through the Cascades. They searched the entire length of the west side of the Cascade Mountains parallel to the Willamette Valley but their search was unsuccessful.

Moses Harris
180? - 1849

Moses Harris was a well established mountain man, trapper, trader, and Oregon Trail Guide with twenty-four years experience in 1845. He built an enviable reputation not only for his tall tales around the campfire, but also for his trustworthiness under the pressures of an unfriendly environment. Some of his contemporaries argued that he was a survivor.

Moses Harris had two sobriquets: "Black" because of his appearance. Jerome Peltier in Harris' biography wrote that Alfred Jacob Miller, well-known artist, described him;

> *He was of wiry frame made up of bone and muscle with a face apparently composed of tan leather and whip-cord, finished off with a*

peculiar blue-black tint, as if gunpowder had been burnt into his face."

"Major" was a self-imposed sobriquet. When Moses Harris decided to enter the fur trade, still a neophyte, he observed that everyone of any importance had a title. He selected "Major" to be his title.

Soon after the unsuccessful 1845 attempt to find an alternate route through the Cascades east of the Willamette Valley, Moses Harris met Stephen H. L. Meek near The Dalles. Meek told Harris that he had led a large group of emigrants into central Oregon where they were then in dire straits. Harris secured supplies from the Indians and, together with a few others, whites and Indians, set out to rescue the lost emigrants. A Mr. Goulder said *"They were led by a brave old mountaineer, one of the noblest of his class, who was known to everybody as 'Black Harris.'"*

Moses Harris capped off his historic adventures in Oregon Country as a member of both groups searching for the Southern Route To Oregon in 1846. He was one of the first to carry relief supplies to the beleaguered emigrants along the Southern Route. His first relief trip was closely followed by a second a month later. (TH)

Moses Harris was the only person who was a member of three citizen's groups charged with responsibilities to find the Southern Route and may have been more involved in organizing the road company than history records. When the south road expedition's ranks were depleted and returned for reinforcements, Moses Harris probably enlisted Jesse Applegate, Lindsay Applegate, John Owen, and Henry Boygus, to join the pathfinders.

Harris returned to the United States in 1847. Moses "Black" Harris died of Cholera in 1849. One account relates that he died of Cholera near Chimney Rock. Probably the most reliable account was in the *Daily Union*. It reports that Harris died of Cholera on May 13, 1849, at Independence. Harris was scheduled to guide another wagon train on their overland journey to Oregon.

Efforts to Find a New Southern Route Continued

The *Oregon Spectator* printed the following article on March 19, 1846:

"To the Editor of the Oregon Spectator:

Sir — I am requested to forward to you for publication the proceedings of a public meeting, which was held at Salem mills on Saturday the 14th inst. — said meeting being convened for the purpose of devising means to explore and open a wagon road from the waters of the upper Willamette to Snake river. The meeting was organized by the appointment of Hon. J. M. Garrison to the chair, and Juno. B. McClane secretary, when the following items of business were transacted: A subscription that had previously been circulated, was presented to the meeting, It was resolved, that a committee of six be chosen to still farther circulate said subscription. The following persons were selected as said committee, viz.: Juno. B. McClane, Thos. Holt, Jas. P Martin, J. W. Boyle, A. R. Shaw, and Moses Harris. The aforesaid committee were instructed to circulate the subscription as extensively as possible, and to call a meeting of the subscribers whenever they shall judge proper; also, to inquire who are willing to go on the expedition, and are competent to go as pilots, and to report the result of their inquiries to the aforesaid meeting, which is to convene at the call of said committee.

J. M. Garrison, Ch'mn.
JNO. B. McClane, Sec'y"

Two weeks later, on April 2, 1846, the following article (advertisement) appeared in the *Oregon Spectator*:

"Over the Mountains.
The company to examine for a prac-

ticable wagon route from the Willamette valley to Snake river, will rendezvous at the residence of Nat. Ford, on the Rickreal, so as to be ready to start on the trip on the first day of next May. The contemplated route will be up the Willamette valley, crossing the Cascade mountains south of the three snowy buttes. A portion of the company will return after crossing the cascade mountains. It is hoped that several young men will be prepared to go on to meet the emigration. Those agreed to start at the time above mentioned, are Solomon Tutherrow, Nathan Ford, Gen. C. Gilliam, Stephen H. L. Meek, and Moses Harris, and many others, it is expected will be ready by the time above specified.

Nath. Ford."

The exploring party set out in 1846 to find a way of escape through the southern end of Willamette Valley in event the United States went to war with Britain. The Southern route would also be used to bring in reinforcements and supplies.

First Attack To Find The Southern Route To Oregon

William G. Parker, Bennett Osborn, Levi Scott, John M. Scott, Moses "Black" Harris, Jack Jones, Robert Smith, William Sportsman, B F. Burch, S. H. Goodhue, David Goff, and Solomon Tetherow set out on May 15, 1846, to find a new route into the southern Willamette Valley. Cornelius Gilliam, Nathan Ford, Stephen Meek and a Mr. Wilson listed in the announcement were probably with this party. (LS)

Levi Scott remembered that each man furnished his own horses, arms, ammunition, blankets and provisions. He was at his own risk and on his own time. Considerations were pure patriotism and the gratification of the adventure.

They traveled up the west banks of the Willamette River and Long Tom River to the foothills of the Calapooya Mountains near Coyote Creek. Then east to the junction of the Willamette River where the Middle Fork and the Coast fork met southeast of Eugene.

They explored along the Middle Fork. They traveled up the Coast Fork as far as there was prairie or open ground. They were unable to find a way across the mountains and returned about ten miles and camped on Martin Creek southwest of present day Cottage Grove. Here they found a well-beaten Indian Trail. Some Indians told the pathfinders that the trail led across the Calapooya Mountains into Umpqua Valley. (LS)

Return For Reinforcements

Four or five of the fifteen man expedition returned home when the expedition ran into swollen steams on Elk Creek. The rest continued on to Calapooya Creek before they too returned for reinforcements. (LS)

Hudson's Bay Company traders had used the route from time to time. All traces of their passages had been obliterated before the explorers passed through.

The returning pathfinders discussed the likelihood of raising a new company to push on through. Levi Scott told them that he would join the expedition and would be ready and would go at a moment's notice. (LS)

Scott stopped along the trail eight miles north of Mary's River (Corvallis) on his return trip to take up and work a claim near Peavy Arboretum. (LS)

Levi Scott - Farmer, Traveler, Frontiersman, Trail-Blazer

Levi Scott was born on February 8, 1797, in the part of Northwest Territories later called Monroe County, Illinois. James Scott, the father Levi never knew, died when Levi was very young. When his mother, Rebecca, married a Mr. McCann, Levi and his brothers George and Frank, and sisters, Sarah and Cynthia were placed with relatives and neighbors. There is no known record of them ever seeing their mother again.

Levi gained his frontier experience working for several families in Illinois. He experienced his first pride of land ownership when he and his brothers inherited a right to claim land. They claimed land in St. Clair County, Illinois northwest of Waterloo in 1815.

Levi soon lost interest in that land and returned to his uncle Jehu Scott's place near Alton. Levi found the woman of his dreams near Edwardsville. He courted and married Edy Ennis March 18, 1817, and settled on a rented farm in Madison County.

Levi Scott never stayed in one place very long. He became an entrepreneur buying farm land, developing it, then selling it off and buying another to start the cycle all over again much as carpenters and handymen buy and fix houses up today.

Levi started his own flour mill in 1826. He also spent some time in the militia during skirmishes with Indian Chief Black Hawk.

He claimed land two miles down river from Flint Bluffs in 1834. Levi was chosen to the arbitration board for land claims for Township 70, which included the settlement of Burlington, Iowa. He was also the auctioneer in the land sale.

Levi Scott's wife, Edy, died in September 1842 in a typhoid epidemic. Lust for wandering returned to Levi's mind after Edy's death. His friends were picking up and heading for Oregon County. His son John decided that he would go with his father to Oregon Country.

Levi started his overland journey to Oregon in the spring of 1844. Levi said his last goodbyes at St. Louis and headed west across Missouri toward Independence.

Levi Scott joined a wagon train, Nathaniel Ford was Captain, for his overland journey to Oregon. Moses "Black" Harris, a man Levi Scott was soon to be associated with on the South Road to the Willamette Valley, was scout for the wagon train.

Controversy broke out in the wagon train. Levi Scott remained with the wagon train hoping it would stay united. However, Levi Scott and a party of German emigrants left the wagon train near Laramie. (LS)

The Company disbanded at The Dalles, the end of the Oregon Trail. Most of the emigrants sold their stock to the mission at The Dalles and floated down the Columbia River. Levi Scott chose to leave his wagon and drive his animals over the Cascade Mountains to Oregon City.

Levi Scott served in the upper house of the Territorial Legislature during 1852-1854 and was a member of the Constitutional Convention for statehood of Oregon. He also founded Scottsburg on the lower Umpqua River. Mount Scott in Crater Lake National Park was named for him.

South Road Company

Rumors of war continued and rumors started about the pathfinders' return without finding the Southern Route into the Willamette Valley. The settlers became quite concerned. Nathaniel Ford was more concerned about the rumors and wrote another article that appeared in the *Oregon Spectator* on July 4, 1846:

> *"Mr. Lee - In your last paper, I see that you have noticed the return of the road company party that left Polk county a few weeks ago, and stated that they have returned "unsuccessful and discouraged." It is true they returned, but not discouraged. One of the party turned back, before reaching the Callapooiah mountain, and three others soon after crossing it; but Maj. Harris, Capt. Scott and son, Benjamin Burch, William Parker, and Mr. Boggs continued some seventy miles further - found nothing in the way of a practicable wagon road, and they were prevented from going on only by the hardships of having to stand guard every night; they therefore returned to increase the number of the party, and were successful in procuring the following named energetic, and persevering men, viz; Capt. Applegate, Robert Smith, Lindsey Applegate, David Goff, Ben. Burch, John Owens, J. Jones,*

W. Sportsman, B. Ausburn, and Mr. Goodhue. By the addition of these men, the party is sufficiently strong to insure safety against the attacks of Indians, and to greatly lessen the hardships of the trip. The party left the Rickreal on the 22d inst. In fine spirits and high hopes of bringing the next emigration in at the head of the Willamette valley. They left with a firm determination never to retrace their steps — never to abandon the noble and philanthropic enterprise, until they shall have found a good wagon road, if such a thing be possible.

Yours, respectfully,
NAT. FORD"

Pathfinders Reinforced And Try Again

Moses Harris, Benjamin Burch, William Parker and Boggs returned from the Umpqua River Valley and found several men: Jesse Applegate, Lindsay Applegate, John Owen, and Henry Boygus who joined the pathfinders to insure safety against attacks and lessen the hardships of the trip. William G. Parker, Bennett Osborn, Levi Scott, John M. Scott, Moses "Black" Harris, Jack Jones, Robert Smith, William Sportsman, B F. Burch, S. H. Goodhue, David Goff of the earlier party stayed on with the South Road Company. "The South Road Company," assembled on La Creole Creek (Rickreal Creek) southwest of the present day city of Dallas.

Levi and John Scott were working on Levi's claim about eight miles north of Mary's River in Benton County when Jesse Applegate asked them to join The South Road Company. (LS)

The South Road Company set out on June 20, 1846, traveling the same route through the Willamette Valley, through the Calapooya Mountains, and into the Umpqua Valley to Calapooya Creek, pioneered by the first pathfinders.

They struck an old fur trader's trail at Calapooya Creek. The old trader's trail was the route most generally traveled by the few persons traveling between the Columbia River Valley and the Sacramento River Valley. They crossed the North Umpqua River one mile above its mouth. (LS)(VP)

They traveled an old trader's trail between the Cascade Mountains and the Coast Range from the Umpqua Valley to Emigrant Creek near present Ashland. It had been used from time to time by trappers, emigrants, drovers and The Willamette Cattle Company. It was used by Hudson's Bay Company traders on their yearly forays into the territory, once going out and again on their return. It was suitable only for foot traffic and the detail of where to locate the road had to be worked out when the South Road Company returned with 1846 Emigrants.

The trail was so bad in Canyon Creek Canyon that the South Road Company pathfinders;

> "* * * * *entered the canyon, followed up the little stream that runs through the defile for four or five miles, crossing the creek a great many times, but the canyon becoming more obstructed with brush and fallen timber, the little trail we were following turned up the side of the ridge where the woods were more open, and wound its way to the top of the mountain."* (LA)

Levi Scott remembered that the trail by which The South Road Company crossed the Umpqua Mountains passed up a deep gorge for about two miles, then turned up a ridge to the right which they followed to the summit. They camped on Cow Creek, probably at the base of the ridge between Fortune Branch and Galesville.

The next day Jesse Applegate, W. G. Parker, B. F. Burch and Levi Scott went up Cow Creek to its source on Clear Creek. They went across the pass and down Canyon Creek to examine the canyon. They returned to camp that night and discussed the matter with the entire company and decided a road could be made through the canyon.

Indian Attack

The pathfinders overtook a group of about eighty French Canadians, Indians, and half-breeds. The French Canadians directed the South Road Company to where they should leave the trappers trail and cross the Cascade Mountains near the Green Springs Summit. The Hudson's Bay fur traders left the settlement in the Willamette Valley three or four weeks before the South Road Company. The voyagers probably brought their families as was their custom. The wives were to make camp, prepare meals and pack pelts. The boys to wrangle horses, run errands and otherwise learn the trade of their fathers. The girls followed in their mother's footsteps. Lindsay Applegate probably counted all of the people in the party, Hudson's Bay Company would have counted only its employees. (LA) (JAW)

The Rogue River Indians probably knew the difference between the British fur traders and the Americans. Indians disliked fur traders. The South Road Company got through without being attacked by Indians in the Rogue River Valley. The Indians spent their energy attacking the of the Hudson's Bay Company employees on their yearly quest for pelts.

East Across Southern Oregon

The South Road Company knew the general location of Mary's River and that the California Trailled down it and across the Truckee Route into central California valleys. Their plan was to hit the Mary's River as near the forty-second Parallel as possible and follow up the California Trail eastward if practicable.

Although several explorers had been in different parts of the area, there were no tracks to follow between Emigrant Creek and Mary's River. There was only three hundred forty miles of untamed wilderness.

The pathfinders met their match with this virgin wilderness. Problems that they encountered took their toll in time, much needed food supplies, and the morale of the pathfinders.

Levi Scott remembered that Lindsay Applegate and John Jones became dissatisfied when Jesse Applegate approved one of Levi Scott's suggestions. They threatened to abandon the Company in the Cascade Mountains and return home.

Although Jesse Applegate appeared to lead the Company, somewhere a few miles east of Clear Lake he wanted to quit and go home. He heard grumbling among the men about his leading them in a wild-goose-chase northeast of Tule Lake. They blamed him for the hardships they had to endure. He threatened to resign and could only be persuaded to stay when Levi Scott and David Goff were appointed to take on serious responsibilities. (LS)

The South Road Company was behind schedule due to their wanderings while in search of the Mary's River. Food was getting very low. A bacon rind was their last meat, so they boiled it three times and thickened the soup with flour to make gravy. They finally ate the rind and were completely out of meat. Fortunately, they came upon others with good supplies and completed the outward portion of their mission by reaching their destination.

Their route was somewhat different from that originally planned. They had to make some detours to go around mountains and other physical features that stood in their way.

An alternate route was found to the Oregon Country and Willamette Valley, one that would allow the wagons to travel all the way.

Levi Scott remembered that the pathfinders mistook the Humboldt River for Sprague River which Ogden had labeled "Mary's River". He also remembered that the river labeled Mary's River on Ogden's map ran similar to Humboldt River but ran into Klamath Lake. (LS)

Stone Bridge

A ledge of volcanic rock crossed the stream at right angles. The stream poured over the top of the ledge in a beautiful waterfall straight down to another steppe of the ledge. The second steppe formed a smooth flat roadway across the river over which the water rippled, swift and clear, about six inches deep forming a roadway one hundred feet wide. At the lower edge of the roadway, the current seemed to cease, and the river suddenly assumed an unfathomable depth with scarcely any perceptible current to the lake below. (LS)

Plan Ahead

Levi Scott remembered that the trailblazers were short of provisions when they reached Mary's River. They made an estimate of how much would be required to open a road through the newly found route to the Willamette Valley.

They concluded that it would take thirty able, well-appointed hands to open the road the wagons would travel. If the emigrants were unable to provide thirty well-equipped men with provisions to prepare the way, the trailblazers were not to aid, nor advise any of them to travel to the Willamette Valley by the Southern Route. (LS)

Levi Scott was elected by a vote to guide the emigrants and to lead them through - but only if the emigrants furnished the required workforce and equipment. Scott accepted the position and appointed William G. Parker to assist him. (LS)

Jesse Applegate took the written estimate and started for Fort Hall to get supplies for the trailblazers' return trip. He would also talk to the emigrants about the required workforce. (LS)

Levi Scott, together with William Parker, backtracked to find the route from Mary's River to Rabbit Hole Spring. Then they returned to help improve the California Trail on their way to meet the emigrants.

On The California Trail

Jesse Applegate, Moses Harris, David Goff, John Owen, Joseph Burke, John Scott, and Henry Boygus found their way to the point of interception of the emigrants on the Oregon Trail. Henry Boygus traveled alone. He was never heard from again.

Definitions

Trail is defined as: "A path across a wild or unsettled region, a mountain trail, the Oregon Trail."

Path is: "A walk or way used by man or animals on foot." In the next few chapters it can be seen that early explorers and trappers in the Oregon Country developed a trail (a "walk or way used by man and animals on foot" for traveling from Oregon to California.) It probably could be said that the South Road Company's outgoing expedition established a new "trail" (path) from the fur trapper's trail near the Oregon-California border to the California Trail on Mary's River.

Road is defined as: "an open way for public passage, esp. from one city, town, or village to another; a highway."

Scott-Applegate Trail. The next chapters will show that the 1846 emigrants to the Willamette Valley "opened a way for public passage," from the road known as the California Trail to the Willamette Valley. Although the emigrants followed the South Road Company's outgoing path and the Oregon-California Trail in places, they were "opening a way for public passage" of wheeled vehicles where wheels had never gone before. The 1846 emigrants built the "Scott-Applegate Trail" from Mary's River to the Willamette Valley.

Route is defined as: "A course, road, or way taken in traveling from one point to another." It is a broader term that can include a series of roads or trails, either successive or paralleling each other.

Southern Route is a series of trails and roads used in passing from the Oregon Trail on the Snake River to the Willamette Valley. It includes the California Trail, the new Emigrant Road across northern California and southern Oregon, and old trails and new roads west of the Cascades. The Southern Route To Oregon could also be said to include the Oregon Trail west of the Missouri River to the turn off on the Snake River.

SOUTHERN ROUTE

The California Trail

The junction where the California Trail intersected the Oregon Trail was on Raft River about forty miles west of Fort Hall. Some wagon trains divided at that point.

Most of the Oregon Trail migration continued down the Snake River to destinations in eastern Oregon, eastern Washington, Fort Vancouver, or the northern Willamette Valley.

Some emigrants chose destinations in California and traveled down The California Trail. They went through southern Idaho into northwestern Utah, Nevada, across the Sierra Nevada mountains, and into central California.

The first three hundred eighty-two miles of the California Trail became part of the alternate Southern Route into the Willamette Valley in 1846. The new Scott-Applegate Trail left the California Trail near the sink on Mary's River (formerly known as Ogden's River, and later known as Humboldt River). It crossed northwestern Nevada, northeastern California, through southern Oregon, and up through the mountains to the southern Willamette Valley.

First Wagons Over The Southern Route

Amos "Black" Harris, Jesse Applegate, David Goff, John Owen and Henry Boygus found their way to the point of interception of the 1846 emigrants on the Oregon Trail. Joseph Burke and William Scott, son of Levi Scott, were probably with them.

William E. Taylor, one of the first 1846 emigrants to meet the South Road Company, recorded that he met Black Harris and Applegate on the California Trail on August 3, 1846.

Harris Cutoff

"Meddlers" Vanderpool, former mountain man, was leading a wagon train of fourteen wagons down Snake River.

David Goff, in the *Oregon Spectator*, April 3, 1847, issue, wrote:

> *"Maj. Harris and myself met Mr. Vanderpool's company at Goose creek, where they had encamped on the 5th day of August. * * * * Goose creek is two days' travel for wagons on this side of the forks of the road (at Raft River) * * * *."*

Levi Scott remembered that Harris had known Vanderpool when he was in the mountains a few years before. When Harris heard that Vanderpool was leading the company, he went down Goose Creek and met Vanderpool's Company at its mouth on the Snake River below Raft River. (LS).

Harris told the Vanderpool people that they could drive right along into Oregon on this new route without any trouble at all. Having induced them to take the new route, he led them up Goose Creek till they struck the California Trail and met the South Road Company. (LS)

Moses Harris led Vanderpool's company up Goose Creek so they would not have to retrace their tracks back up the Snake River to the entrance to the California Trail at Raft River. Moses Harris was the leader that pioneered the cutoff up Goose Creek. No wagons are known to have used that cutoff before or after.

Goose Creek originates in the extreme northwestern corner of Utah and extreme northeastern corner of Nevada near the Idaho line. The headwaters of Goose Creek are on up the California Trail in the high country between Raft River and Thousands Springs Creek in the tri-state area.

First Emigrants On The New Route

Emigrants of Vanderpool's company were the first and only emigrants to use the Harris cutoff. They were also the first Oregon-bound emigrants to use the California Trail and the Scott-Applegate Trail on the Southern Route to Oregon.

Since Levi Scott had been elected by The South Road Company to guide the emigrants, he checked to see if they understood the rules. They said they did not, so Scott explained the terms agreed to. They made light of the terms until Scott told them that it was impossible for them to get through without more help and if more help did not come, they must take the old road or they would perish in the mountains. That stopped them for one day.

Jesse Applegate On the Oregon Trail

Jesse Applegate met the Harrison Linville Company of fifteen wagons at the mouth of Raft River on August 6, 1846. The Linville Company brought Levi Scott a note from Applegate stating that he could get the required workforce to open the road and that Scott should move out with the wagons he had. Applegate would overtake them with the required workforce in two days. The Linville company joined up with the Vanderpool company.

Jesse Applegate met another wagon train on the Snake River on August 8, 1846, and turned twenty-one wagons onto the Southern Route. Virgil Pringle was a member and diarist of the wagon train. Mr. Pringle's diary is heavily relied upon in the Scott-Applegate Trail story, second only to Lester Hulin's 1847 journal. Pringle's party overtook Vanderpool-Linville at Stone Bridge on Sacramento River (Lost River) on September 29th. They united, making fifty wagons in the lead wagon train. (DH)

Later on August 8, 1846, Jesse Applegate met J. Quinn Thornton eight miles south of Fort Hall. Thornton was with another party and recorded many of his adventures. (DH)

Levi Scott remembered that Jesse Applegate caught up with them about the time he said he would, but that he only had six men with him instead of the thirty needed. Several trailblazers fell in with the emigrant roadbuilders. The roadbuilders were poorly equipped and poorly supplied. (LS)

California Trail

Levi Scott shuddered at the possible result of such rashness, but started into the wilderness. With wagons pressing from the rear, it was better to go forward and get through as best they could. (LS)

Nicholas Carriger recorded passing part of Vanderpool's company on Mary's River on August 26, 1846. Three in the Vanderpool company were sick and were not expected to live. Carriger was bound for California. (DM)

There were probably more small parties, including Samuel Whitely (Whitley or Whitelsy), using the route in 1846.

Levi Scott was ready to guide the wagons across the desert and beyond as the first wagons moved onto the Scott-Applegate Trail on September 5, 1846.

Scott-Applegate Trail

T. H. Jefferson provided the most accurate and detailed map showing the exact location of where the Scott-Applegate Trail left the California Trail. Jefferson was bound for California in 1846. He arrived at the Scott-Applegate Trail turnoff on September 19, 1846 two weeks after the trail was opened and several days after the last 1846 wagons turned onto it.

In 1846 the California Trail passed through present Winnemucca and followed down the left bank of Mary's River to a point near the railroad siding of Cosgrove. There it forded the river to the right bank. It followed the river to section 28, T33N, R33E M.D.M. three miles west of the Callahan Bridge, northwest of present Imlay, Nevada. The California Trail turned south and recrossed Mary's River to the left side. It passed across a large bend in the river where the Pitt-Taylor Reservoir is now.

The Scott-Applegate Trail continued in the westerly direction on the right side of the river. The "fork" or junction was on the upper end of Lassen Meadows, now covered by Rye Patch Reservoir southwest of Eugene Mountains.

Jesse Applegate wrote:

"The Oregon and California roads fork at a large bend of the river where the river turns directly south - the Oregon road here leaves it and runs on in a west course towards a gap in the mountains."

Mary's River provided a watering point at the forks of the road. Lester Hulin wrote:

"When we came to the forks of the road we watered."

In 1849, the California Trail continued westward along the low land another mile before the trail forked and began climbing the sand ridges.

Emigrants in the last 1846 wagon trains were surprised to find David Goff waiting for them at the fork in the road on Mary's River to turn the wagon trains onto the new road. He stayed with the wagons and was with the first emigrants to reach Soap Creek in northern Benton County.

Later Travel Over The Scott-Applegate Trail

Levi Scott believed that most of the 1846 emigrants reaching Raft River after Jesse Applegate reached there turned onto the Southern Route. A few hundred emigrants chose to travel to Oregon by the Southern Route in 1846 and 1847. Emigrants choosing Southern Route in 1847 may have separated from larger Companies at the junction in southern Idaho.

The portion of the Scott-Applegate Trail from the "fork in the road" on Mary's River to Goose Lake became heavily traveled during the gold rush to California. The Lassen Trail to the Sacramento Valley in California branched from the Scott-Applegate Trail south of Goose Lake. That portion of the trail was used by 48ers and 49ers rushing to the gold fields in central California. The Scott-Applegate Trail also took part in the gold rush days and settlement of Yreka Valley.

Emigrants from the United States later traveled the road to settle in Oregon's Umpqua River and Rogue River Valleys, and in the Klamath Basin.

Emigrants reaching the Willamette Valley over the Southern Road To Oregon after 1847 were few and far between. Few were recorded. Single wagons and small wagon trains may not have been recorded.

The Oskaloosa Company, including David D. Davis, Lester Hulin and Cornelius Hills with about twenty wagons, was the last substantive wagon train to reach the Willamette Valley over the Scott-Applegate Trail in 1847.

Cornelius Hills returned to the United States in 1850 and returned to the Willamette Valley over the Scott-Applegate Trail with his bride in 1851.

Road Building Party

Jesse Applegate assembled a road crew made up of all of the South Road Company except Scott and Goff. Emigrant wagon trains were able to raise only eight men, instead of thirty, for the road building crew. Thomas Powers, Burgess, Shaw, Carnhan, Alfred Stewart, Charles Putnam, William Kirquendall and J. M. Ware joined the road opening crew. There were twenty-one men in the crew as it went on ahead of the combined wagon trains. (DH)(WAM)(VC)(OS)

Levi Scott remembered that the first three hundred miles of the way was on comparatively level open country. Most of it was rock and rather barren desert covered with sage growing from to two to ten feet high. Most of it was from one and a half feet to three feet high and very tough and stiff. The roadbuilders made no attempt to clear the sage away and the emigrant wagons frequently were required to drive over it to break it down in open country. (LS)

The trailblazers had not marked out a road on their way out. They had only carefully viewed the country sufficiently to conclude that a road could be made. (LS)

Jesse Applegate promised to mark the trail they traveled with stone cairns and blaze trees to lead the emigrants to the cleared roadway through the desert, the Cascade Mountains and the Umpqua Mountains.

Jesse Applegate and Road Builders Return Home

Levi Scott remembered that Jesse Applegate blazed one tree, at Goff's Spring, where he left a note buried among the roots of the tree. The note informed Levi Scott that Jesse Applegate had changed the plan breaking the promise made only a few days earlier. Applegate informed Scott that he was taking John Scott and Lindsay Applegate ahead to the Willamette Valley in the hope of getting settlers to return opening the trail from the north. He left the rest of the road-building crew to work from the south. (LS)

Levi Scott felt let down by Jesse Applegate's departure. He had the unexpected and laborious task forced upon him of searching out in advance of the wagons the particular track to be followed. Many times the advancing wagons were delayed while he searched out the way ahead. (LS)

Levi Scott remembered natural landmarks that guided him in keeping the course most of the time. However, there were a lot of obstacles placed in the way that escaped his attention on the way out that had to be avoided or overcome the best way he could find. (LS)

The emigrants became angry at the thought of being deserted three hundred miles out in the wilderness. They became hostile. There was talk of hanging him but since he was the only person that knew where they were and the way to get to somewhere else, they needed his services. (LS)

Emigrants Elect Levi Scott To Lead Them

Levi remembered that he never lied to them and that he had the confidence and respect of most of the emigrants so he got along without too much complaining. He noticed that confidence and respect increased as the difficulties and dangers increased.

The emigrants insisted on electing Levi Scott to be their Captain when the wagons came together at Stone Bridge on the Sacramento River (Lost River) between present day Tule Lake, California, and Merrill, Oregon. He refused the position unless they would agree to obey his orders. He told them that the title of Captain would put burdens on him and would not do them any good unless he had real authority. The emigrants insisted and pledged Scott that his orders would be obeyed. He accepted the responsibility relieving the Captains of the various companies. He was elected unanimously at a mass meeting. (LS)

When the 1846 emigrants reached the foothills of the Cascade Mountains a few days later, no road had been built, or even blazed. Jesse Applegate had departed a few days earlier. Now the whole crew had followed their leader.

The emigrants, both men and women, expressed their anger at the thought of being deserted and there were threats of hanging the Applegates when they arrived in the Willamette Valley.

"They pulled out and left us to either make our own road, or root hog or die." "They led us into this wilderness, then abandoned us to our fate."

Even Levi Scott and David Goff feared for their lives but stayed with the emigrants to find a way through and build a road for the wagons.

Cooler heads prevailed. Rev. Cornwall said: *"It is better that we expend our energy in a more profitable manner. We had better press forward as fast as possible to our destination."*

It is ironic that it was the Cornwall family that was stranded on Cabin Creek for the winter of 1846-1847 and required rescue in the spring of 1847.

First Wagon Train Massacre By Indians Bloody Point On Shores of Tule Lake (A look into the future — 1852.)

The butte now known as Bloody Point

gets its name from a massacre by Indians along the shores of Rette Lake. The exact location of the killings is not known except that it was between the butte and a ravine in the bluffs opposite present day Newell.

From the bluff overlooking Rette Lake later known as Tule Lake, the Scott-Applegate Trail followed down a ravine to the level of the lake. This ravine and the lake shore below were later, in 1852, the scene of a bloody massacre. A party of Indians lay in ambush, until an emigrant wagon train was emerging from the ravine. It then attacked and killed nearly everyone in three parties. Tule Lake afforded a secure retreat where the Indians could escape among the tules. Their light canoes could defy a superior force.

Settlers were moving into the Yreka and Rogue River Valleys in 1852. The settlers were eager to have more settlers move in to help them defend themselves. Indians were becoming hostile and attacking settlers.

As the first wagon train arrived in Yreka Valley in 1852, a company of thirty armed men was organized under the command of Charles McDermitt. They headed eastward to meet the emigrants with provisions.

The McDermitt party met another party of men at Tule Lake. They sent two men back with the emigrants to act as guides. They soon had a skirmish with the Indians. The two guides were wounded. (This was not the massacre.)

McDermitt continued on and met eight packers between Tule Lake and Clear Lake. The eight men continued on and were ambushed as they descended the bluffs toward the shore of Tule Lake. Indians were lying in the brush and attacked when the packers were about half way down the hill. Seven of the men were killed by the attacking Indians at Bloody Point.

A man by the name of Coffin escaped and wandered around in the tules for several days. He joined the next wagon train on August 23rd. Coffin reported the incident upon his arrival in the Rogue River Valley. Twenty-seven men were organized under the command of Ben Wright to go back over the trail and protect following trains.

As McDermitt had continued eastward, he met two small wagon trains near the west shore of Goose Lake. He advised them to join together and sent Thomas H. Coats, John Onsby and James Long to act as guides.

These two small wagon trains were next to leave Clear Lake. They became separated leaving Clear Lake. The three guides were a mile ahead of the lead train of seven wagons looking for a nooning place. The guides were surrounded and killed as they rounded a point in the bluffs.

Captain Morrison of the lead wagon train heard a skirmish in the distance and sent Felix Martin ahead to find out what was going on. Morrison heard a shot from Martin's pistol but he did not return.

The wagons moved in close and every man prepared for the fight as they moved ahead cautiously. They discovered blood on the road as the wagon train moved passed Bloody Point but they did not see the Indians until a shower of arrows fell among the wagons. The Captain corralled the stock and wagons. The Indians advanced and surrounded them.

This wagon train included thirty men, one woman, and one boy. They fought off attacking Indians that day and night. The second train did not arrive until the next day to join them.

The emigrants would undoubtedly have suffered much more — even complete annihilation except for the company of volunteers led by Ben Wright. Ben Wright's group arrived at the scene and without stopping at the corralled wagons, charged forward and drove off the Indians.

The Modocs admitted the loss of twenty in the hand-to-hand battle that extended a mile up and down the shore of the lake. That is said to be about half of the actual number killed. Many more were wounded.

Sheriff Ben Wright's company searched among the tules for remains of the Modocs' victims. They found the mangled bodies of emigrants, whose deaths were not known before. Twenty-two bodies were found and buried, including two women and one child. Wright's company also found portions of wagons, firearms, clothing, camp utensils, money and many domestic articles, showing that an entire emigrant train had fallen prey to the Modocs. No one could tell how many emigrants had been murdered. Fourteen more victims, including horribly mutilated and disfigured bodies of several women and children, were found a few days later by a company of men from Jacksonville under Col. John E. Ross. (HLW, page 130-131.)

Oregon-California Border Is In Wrong Place.

California is part of the territory acquired from Mexico by the treaty of Guadalupe-Hidalgo between the United States and Mexico proclaimed July 4, 1848. It established the northern boundary at forty-two degrees north Latitude. The act of the United States Congress dated September 9, 1850 admitting California into the Union provides in part that the northern boundary of the State of California be at forty-two degrees north latitude. (FKVZ)

The Territory of Oregon was organized August 14, 1848 with its southern boundary at forty-two degrees north latitude. The act of February 14, 1859, admitting Oregon to the Union provides that the southern boundary of the State of Oregon also be at forty-two degrees north latitude. (FKVZ)

All of this establishes the boundary line between Oregon and California on the line of the forty-two degrees north latitude. Right? **Wrong!!!**

An astronomic station was established at Camp Bidwell to determine the proper position of the northeast corner of the State Of California. More than three thousand measurements of lunar distances were said to have been made for longitude in 1868-69. The corner was computed to be nine miles, fifty-six chains north and four miles seventy-eight chains east from the observatory. (FKVZ)

The California-Oregon state line was created by a survey. Deputy Surveyor and astronomer D. G. Major surveyed the boundary line two hundred twelve miles, twenty-eight chains west, from the northeast corner of California to a terminal twelve chains from the shore of the Pacific Ocean. The mile marks along the line consisted of wooden posts or small stones having "O" cut on the north side, "C" on the south, and the mile number and date on the other two sides. (FKVZ)

The N.A.D. position of the post near the Pacific Ocean was 41°59'54.65" north latitude and 124°12'28.31" west longitude in 1927. At that point the border is five hundred thirty-five feet south of forty-two degrees north latitude. The line of the surveyed border resembles the teeth on a carpenter's saw more than a straight line.

The present State line between Oregon and California varies considerably, to as much as five hundred forty feet south of forty-two degrees north latitude.

Two interesting points arise because of this: (1) that portion of the State of Oregon lying south of forty-two degrees north latitude was obtained under the treaty with Mexico; and (2) 1846 and 1847 emigrants crossed from California into Oregon Country at forty-two degrees north latitude. However maps drawn now place the crossing point from California into Oregon about three miles farther south and east.

A Hero Along The Trail

Forty years later Levi Scott remembered the heroic act of one mother in saving her children and emigrants from serious injury or death in the mountains west of Lower Klamath Lake.

As the first wagons were traveling around the lake, Levi Scott knew that there was a treacherous hill ahead. He advised the wagons to travel slowly while he went ahead to find an easier way around. He located a better way but when he reached the wagons he found that they had moved ahead too rapidly and were well past the turn off for the new way. He caught the wagons and wanted them turn back and travel the easier way.

The emigrants told Scott that they could get up the steep treacherous hill.

Levi Scott was impressed by an incident when a wagon broke loose and moved backward down the hill. The mother of some children in the wagon picked up a large rock and jammed it behind a wheel causing the wagon to stop. She saved the wagon, her precious children, and other emigrants following her wagon up the hill.

Levi Scott wondered at the mother's ability to think so quickly and the superhuman strength she mustered to pick up the large rock and jam behind the wheel of the wagon. He remembered that the emigrants knew that the mother had saved them from disaster and expressed their feelings.

His one regret was that although the mother received her five minutes of recognition for her heroic efforts, she would be the only one to remember. The emigrants had to return to their task and the incident was soon forgotten. Levi Scott thought she deserved more recognition for her heroic efforts for saving her children and the emigrants from harm.

It seems that Levi Scott's concerns were correct. Although there are many steep and treacherous places along the route of trail, there is no recorded alternative to show that Levi Scott led the 1847 emigration by the better way he found that day.

Flawed Report

The *Oregon Spectator*, October 1, 1846, issue reported that Jesse Applegate, and at least one road building volunteer from the 1846 emigration had already arrived in the settlements in the northern Willamette Valley.

> *"Mr. J. M. Ware from the States, has arrived and informed us that he came in company with Captain Applegate — that the wagons, numbering some two hundred and fifty, will probably arrive in about two weeks."* (DM)

The first wagons were still crooking round the inlets of Lower Klamath Lake, over three hundred miles back up the trail from Oregon City, on October 1st. They were still making tracks down Rogue River in good weather two weeks later.

Virgil Pringle, one of the first two wagons through the Calapooya Mountains on November 22nd, did not reach Salem until Christmas.

The 1846 emigrants were left with about two hundred miles of wagon road to build through some of the most treacherous mountainous wilderness in the United States. There were only foot paths, from near present day Keno on the eastern slopes of the Cascade Mountains to near Cottage Grove on the Coast Fork of the Willamette River.

Levi Scott Leads Emigrants Works Road

The first emigrants approached the Cascade Mountains at Klamath River on October 7, 1846. They could not find the road opening party, or any sign of them, or road, or even a blazed trail. A recent forest fire had littered the trail with limbs and fallen trees that had to be removed before the wagons could pass through.

Levi Scott and David Goff had expected to find that some of the road work had been done. Levi Scott told the emigrants that they were almost four hundred miles from the nearest settlement at Salem and that the worst road was ahead of them. Levi Scott wrote *"But there had not yet been a stick cut, nor a blaze made."* The emigrants were nearly out of provisions.

Emigration progress bogged down when the first emigrant's had to build their own road through the mountains to the southern Willamette Valley.

A plan of action was decided upon and Harrison Linville, one of the emigrants, went ahead of the wagon trains with a party of road building emigrants to do what they could. Levi Scott went with them. David Goff remained with the wagons.

Levi Scott wrote:

*"I would go forward, view and blaze the way for a considerable distance, and then return to the working party and help them to come up as far as I had blazed. * * * * Then I would blaze ahead again. In this manner we finally got a rude way opened, and by doubling the teams at the steep places, we managed to get nearly all of the wagons over that had now reached the mountains."* (LS)

Progress Slowed

Virgil Pringle reported that they rested their oxen and improved roads on October 8, 1846. They reached the summit at Green Spring Mountain where they got their first view of beautiful Rogue River Valley with majestic mountains on both sides.

A few days later they connected with the old trapper's trail at Emigrant Creek. The old trapper's trail was not suitable for wagon travel - they would have to make their own road through a hundred seventy-five miles of majestic mountains covered with giant fir, spruce and hemlock trees, downed logs, rotten stumps, underbrush, and large boulders.

Levi Scott Resigns — Gets Better Results

One time Levi Scott believed that they were in danger of Indian attack and ordered sufficient guard be maintained for the stock while they were grazing. The emigrants saw no danger and they and their animals were exhausted. A herd of sheep and several other animals were lost to the Indians when they were not guarded.

Levi Scott reminded the emigrants of their promise to obey his orders. He resigned but continued as pilot or guide. After that any suggestion by Scott was followed more closely than any of his orders had been. (LS)

On October 13, 1846, Virgil Pringle wrote in his diary that they rested their oxen and looked for the road in the Rogue River Valley about sixteen miles west of present day Ashland.

Rogue River Crossing

The first 1846 emigrants crossed Rogue River at a point in the hills near Jones Creek and proceeded in a northwesterly direction.

Levi Scott led the 1847 emigrants to cross Rogue River a mile or so below the town of Rogue River. He then followed the north side of the river down to a point known as Pierce Point. The wagons turned northwesterly through the bluffs on the first road built by the 1846 emigrants.

The first 1846 wagon train had to stop near present day Interstate 5 interchange 58, several miles after crossing Rogue River. The old trappers trail Levi Scott planned to follow was rough with rocks and could not be made passable for wagons. Scott searched a long time for a way through and found a place where the wagons could pass after cutting over a mile of road through thick brush near Butcher-Knife Creek. Indians called the creek Tetalum meaning Sunflower. It is now known unpoeticaly as Louse Creek. (LS)

The Scott-Applegate Trail crossed I-5 a few yards west of the interchange and went up a draw through a pass to parallel Butcher-Knife Creek. The trail crossed the creek a mile or so south of northbound Manzanita Wayside. Then it went past the wayside between the parking area and I-5.

The first 1846 emigrant wagons reached Jump Off Joe Creek where it took them several hours work to cut the road through.

Virgil Pringle was back in a following wagon train. He was able to travel right along through the area without road work interruption. The entire country had been burned over until they reached Jump Off Joe Creek. (VP)

General Land Office Survey maps show that the "Road from Willamette Valley To Jacksonville" in 1855 generally followed the way found by Levi Scott and opened by the first 1846 emigrants in 1846 from the river to the summit at Sexton Mountain.

Alternative Road Through Grants Pass

Some of the last emigrants in 1846, those not committed to the first way, may have continued downstream after they heard the first way was blocked. Richard Ackerman, Scott-Applegate Trail historian, points to a crossing near the southwest corner of Grants Pass. That trail would have continued northwestward across Lathrop Creek, and through the hills to emerge at the west end of the railroad pass a mile and a half south of Louse Creek.

From Jump Off Joe Creek

Most emigrants camped at Jump Off Joe Creek. Ahead of them Sexton Mountain raised its majestic back to challenge the weary men and animals. The hill was so steep that it presented an almost insurmountable obstacle to wagons. The men would look up toward the great mass of earth and rocks, then gaze anxiously at their weary animals, and wonder if it was possible to get the wagons over the top. There is no way of getting around it, even today Interstate 5 winds its way up the face of the mountain to Sexton Pass. (WAM)

Several teams of oxen were hitched to one wagon, then with the help of three or four men, the wagon was slowly pulled and pushed to the top of the hill, and over on the north side where it was left while the teams and men returned for another wagon. (WAM)

First Relief Party

Jack Jones and Tom Smith arrived at the camp of the first emigrants the morning after the wagons reached Cow Creek. The relief party had some beef cattle. This was the first relief party to meet the emigrants with supplies from the Willamette Valley. The emigrants were anxious to receive information from the Willamette Valley brought in by the party, so moved only a short distance that day. (LS)

Emigrants Build Road Through Canyon Creek Canyon

The emigrants camped on Cow Creek at Azalea near the south approach to Canyon Creek Canyon. They stayed there four days while every available man built road through the Canyon.

Virgil Pringle wrote:

> *"We started through on Monday morning and reached the opposite plain on Friday night after a series of breakdowns, hardships, and being constantly wet. Laboring hard and very little to eat. The provisions being exhausted in the whole company. We ate our last the evening we got through. Rain started to fall on October 26th, and continued for five days."*

He said that there was a great loss of property and much suffering, no bread, they lived altogether on beef brought in by Enoch Garrison. Pringle lost a wagon in the canyon.

Tolbert Carter wrote:

> *"The Umpqua canyon was a terror to the company. The sides seemed almost perpendicular. It didn't seem possible for a wagon and team to get down it, but somehow they did."*

However, Enoch Garrison from Yamhill County met the emigrants at the canyon. Levi Scott said that he and Enoch Garrison were the only men besides emigrants to work on the road through the canyon and north to the Willamette Valley. Abraham Henry Garrison mentioned that his cousin, Jeptha Garrison, was also there. (LS)(AHG,p28)

A Day To Remember November 22, 1846

Canyon Creek Canyon

Douglas County Museum

Virgil Pringle's party was the first to reach the southern Willamette Valley over the Southern Route. He wrote that his wagon and one other were first to reach the Willamette Valley. The date, November 22, 1846, deserves recognition — but few even know, much less remember.

Skinner's Cabin

Virgil Pringle reached Skinner's Cabin on November 29, 1846. Many emigrants from the same wagon train did not reach the Willamette Valley until the end of January, 1847 and three families had to be rescued in late April, 1847.

Mr. Eugene F. Skinner was the southernmost settler in the Willamette Valley in 1846. 1846 and 1847 emigrants considered that they had arrived in Oregon when they came to his cabin although they had many more miles to travel to before reaching their destinations.

Eugene Skinner's cabin was the first sign of civilization the emigrants had seen in traveling 2,000 miles.

"Skinner's" first cabin was in section 30, T17S, R3W 3,121.9' south 57° 25' east of the northwest corner and 2,801.04' north 42° 44' east of the southwest corner. Translated into plain language, Skinner's cabin was at the foot of the west edge of Skinner's Butte in downtown Eugene.

It was a small pole cabin Skinner built in 1846 without door or window, and was said to be quite homelike. The Skinners left for the winter before the 1846 emigrants got there. One family whose teams were exhausted stayed in his home for the winter. Others spent the winter in the area.

1846 Emigrants Disperse

Rev. Cornwall and about twenty-five or thirty people were stranded on Cabin Creek for the 1846-1847 winter when they ran out of provisions and their oxen died of exhaustion and exposure. They were rescued in the spring of 1847.

The Collins family wintered in Skinner's cabin. James Layton Collins was a thirteen year old boy who was man enough to drive a team of oxen pulling a wagon on the Scott-Applegate Trail. James Layton Collins was a close friend of Scott's until Scott's death.

James Layton Collins collaborated with Levi Scott in writing his autobiography, by placing Scott's notes in final handwritten form. Scott approved the material in final form before his death. Items designated "(LS)" herein are from this source. Both collaborator and collaboratee were reliable eyewitness in their own right, to the building of the Scott-Applegate Trail

Tolbert Carter stopped eight miles north of Mary's River and settled in the area a short distance from the present Polk/Benton County line. Over thirty percent of the families settled in Polk County. Most of the rest settled in Yamhill and Washington Counties as far north as Roy.

1846-1847 Comparison

In a comparison, the last wagon train in the 1847 emigration using the southern route entered the Canyon Creek Canyon on the same date as the first of the 1846 migration, exactly one year later. The last wagon through in 1847 reached Skinner's cabin on November 4, 1847. The 1846 took five days to get through the canyon, the 1847 took only two. The fastest of the 1846 migrants took twenty-five more days than the last of the 1847 emigrants to traverse the little more than a hundred miles from Azalea to Eugene. The toll on the energy of the emigrants and animals was much greater than is reflected in the three extra days it took the 1846 Emigrants to get through the canyon.

A study of a comparative progress graph of the Virgil Pringle Party in 1846 with Lester Hulin's Journal in 1847 shows that Lester Hulin was making better time than Virgil Pringle before they reached the canyon. However, there was a decided increase in the time difference starting at the entrance to the canyon. The best of 1846 lost time with progressively increasing rapidity in to Skinner's cabin — even after they reached the Willamette River. Evidently both emigrants and animals were "spent" long before they reached Skinner's cabin in 1846.

It is almost a sacrilege that a controversy developed over the plight of the 1846 emigrants and that their great sacrifices and accomplishments were thereby greatly diminished. Many of the 1846 emigrants gave their lives, and all gave their all (strength and health) to build the Southern Route through the Cascade, Umpqua, and Calapooya Mountains. The comparatively little difficulty experienced by the 1847 emigrants shows that the road built by the 1846 emigrants was the best way for a road that could be found.

Although the road has been improved to become the great Interstate 5, the route followed by the 1846 emigrants west of the Cascade Mountains has remained unchanged for a hundred and fifty years. The emigrant road across the Cascade Mountains, Oregon Highway 66, remains the primary east - west route in the southern part of Oregon and extreme northern California. The long section through the desert from the Humboldt River to Tule Lake fell into disuse but remains in the hearts of historians and tourists.

Scott-Applegate Trail

"Scott-Applegate Trail" is being used as the name of the Emigrant Road from Mary's

River to the southern Willamette Valley at LaCreole Creek of southwest Dallas, Oregon.

"Scott-Applegate Trail" is more realistic of the immediate exploration and development of the emigrant road in 1846. Levi Scott was a valued advisor and explorer for the South Road Company on its way out and of the earlier finders of the route to Calapooya Creek. He was selected to be one of the triumvirate leaders of the outgoing explorers for the eastern two hundred miles from Goff's Spring to Mary's River.

The South Road Company elected Levi Scott to lead the 1846 emigrants to the Willamette Valley. He alone led the 1846 emigrants from Goose Creek in the tri-state area (Idaho, Utah, Nevada) on the California Trail to the Willamette. The 1846 emigrants elected him to be their leader to the exclusion of all others at a mass meeting at the Stone Bridge on the Sacramento River. Although he soon resigned the position when orders were not obeyed, the emigrants continued to follow his "suggestions" even better than his orders.

The South Road Company had not blazed out a road on their way out. They had only carefully viewed the country sufficiently to conclude that a road could be made. Levi Scott alone picked the way the road would go through three hundred miles of the worst and most treacherous wilderness encountered. It ran through some of the roughest mountains in the country from near Keno to the Coast Fork of the Willamette River southwest of Cottage Grove. The old trappers' trail, a foot path, served only as a guide, it kept him pointed in the right direction. It was followed only when convenient.

When he was not leading, or searching out the way, he got down into the dirt and worked making road.

Jesse Applegate led the South Road Company on their outward journey through previously explored territory of western Oregon as well as into the unexplored wilderness of southern Oregon and northern California. He co-led the explorations after David Goff and Levi Scott were selected to join him as co-leaders.

Moses Harris has not gained recognition as one of the leaders of the expedition even though he was the only one of the South Road Company elected or appointed as a representative of the settlements. He had over twenty years experience as a mountain man and had been involved rescuing other trail parties that were in trouble.

Moses Harris was the only member of the committee assigned to search out a means of locating a Southern Route from the Willamette Valley that went with the South Road Company. He was also with every exploration party searching for the Southern Route from Oregon.

Moses Harris, one of the South Road Company, was with two successive relief parties bringing supplies back to the emigrants. He also led a relief effort to rescue the Meek wagon train stranded in central Oregon in 1845.

Moses Harris probably failed to gain the recognition earned because he lost contact in Oregon when he went east with Levi Scott in 1847 and continued east to the United States. The May 13, 1849, issue of the *Missouri Republican* carried the following: "An old mountain guide, by the name of Harris, died of the same disease (Cholera) on the same day."

"Southern Route" to Oregon is being used to show the way traveled by the 1846 and 1847 wagon trains from Snake River to LaCreole Creek over the California Trail and the Scott-Applegate Trail in 1846 and 1847. The Oregon Trail from the jumping off point to Raft River is also included in the Southern Route to Oregon

The War of The West Was Won by some 400,000 pioneers, fighting for a cause against very high odds. There were 30,000 or more deaths in fighting the battles "Going West"—many more than in most of the more formal wars fought by the

United States of America to this day. Many more pioneer lives were lost fighting to win control of the land after they arrived in the West. David D. Davis, his wife Hannah and three of their children were among those who lost their lives settling in Oregon. (MJM)

CHAPTER 3

Outfitting

Many guide books were written for and were available to emi grants that wanted to do their homework. They offered worthwhile suggestions guiding the emigrant in outfitting for the trip West. Each emigrant had to plan his own outfit according to his own living standard, his own wishes, and his planned way of life in the Oregon Country.

Joel Palmer made the trip west in 1845. He returned to the United States in 1846 to write one of the best guide books of all. His book was distributed widely to the emigrants.

Rolling Stock

Light four-horse or heavy two-horse wagons were the size commonly used. The best wagons were made of the best well-seasoned material, and had falling tongues. The best tires were three inches wide but tires only one and three-fourths inches wide were also used. Tires on good wagons were bolted on with bolts five-eighths or three-fourths of an inch in diameter. Tires on cheaper wagons were fastened with nails.

The Mormon-style wagon bed was the best. They were usually made with straight

Blue Mountains

Painting by William H. Jackson, Scott's Bluff National Monument

side boards about sixteen inches wide with a four inch outward offset at the top on each side. Another sideboard ten or twelve inches wide was at the top. The top side board held the wagon bows in place. Covers were double-thickness. It was advisable to make wagon beds water tight for crossing streams.

Draft Animals and Loading

Ox teams were more extensively used than others. Oxen stood the trip much better than horses or mules and were not as apt to be stolen by the Indians. They were much less trouble. Cattle were allowed to graze at large when not hitched to the wagons. Horses and mules had to be staked up at night. Oxen could graze in many places that horses could not.

Cattle that were raised in Illinois or Missouri stood the trip better than those that were raised in Indiana or Ohio. Illinois and Missouri cattle were accustomed to eating the prairie grass like the grass found along the Oregon Trail. The best cattle were heavy built and four to six years old.

It was not safe to set out with less than four yokes of oxen (eight oxen) for each wagon. Cattle were apt to go lame, get sore necks from chafing against the yoke, or stray away. One six-ox team properly outfitted could start with a twenty-five hundred pound load. Rations were used from the load each day making the load lighter. The load would be reduced before they reached rough country. Everything they took was needed along the way or in settling in after reaching Oregon country.

Loads consisted of provisions and apparel, a supply of cooking utensils, a few tools, etc. The prices of oxen and cows was much higher in Oregon than in the United States.

Barnyard Animals

Each family needed a few cows for milk along the trail. Cows could also be put into teams to relieve the oxen. Cows should be scheduled so some of them would come in fresh on the road. Sheep were well suited for the trail. American horses and mares always commanded high prices and could be taken through. If horses were used to pull wagons, hacks, or carriages, their load was light.

Housewares

Each family needed a sheet iron stove with a water boiler. A platform could easily be constructed on the back end of the wagon, for carrying a stove. A stove was very conveniant along the trail. It was much more conveniant than a camp fire when it was windy and and fuel was scarce. Every family needed a good quality tent with tie downs.

A Dutch oven and skillet of cast metal were essential. Plates, cups, etc. were of made of tin because conventional dinnerware was much heavier and apt to break. It also requires a lot of time to pack it properly. Families needed two churns, one for carrying sweet milk and one for sour milk. They needed one eight or ten gallon keg for carrying water, one ax, one shovel, two or three augers, one hand saw.

Supplies

Farmers needed a crosscut saw and a few plow molds because it was difficult to get them in Oregon. Plows cost from twenty-five to forty dollars each in Oregon. A good supply of rope for tying up horses and catching cattle was carried along. Every person needed a supply of boots and shoes. Many emigrants walked the entire length of the Southern Route from the Missouri River to LaCreole Creek. Every person needed a supply of every kind of clothing.

It was good for each family to carry at least one feather bed and a good assortment of bedding. There were no tame geese in the Oregon Country, but an abundance of wild ones. It was difficult to get enough feathers for a bed.

Firearms

Every man and boy needed at least one rifle. A shotgun was also useful for wild fowl and small game that were in Oregon in abundance. The best size caliber for the mountains was from fifty-two to fifty-six balls to the pound. One from sixty to eighty balls to the pound, or even smaller, was best when in the lower settlements. The larger game animals were elk, deer, antelope, mountain sheep or bighorn, and bear. The small game were hare, rabbit, grouse, sage hen, pheasant, quail, etc. A good supply of ammunition was essential.

Provisions

In laying in a supply of provisions for the journey, emigrants were governed in some degree by their means. However, there were several things that everyone needed.

Each adult needed two hundred pounds of flour for the journey, three hundred pounds of pilot bread, seventy five pounds of bacon, ten pounds of rice, five pounds of coffee, two pounds of tea, twenty-five pounds of sugar, half a bushel of dried beans, one bushel of dried fruit, two pounds of baking soda, ten pounds of salt, and half a bushel of corn meal. It was also good to have half a bushel of parched and ground corn for each adult and a small keg of vinegar should be taken for the family.

These things were needed by each of the adult emigrants. Other good things could be added as long as the emigrant families could afford them and there was room for them. Whatever was good in the United States was nonetheless good on the road. However, most emigrants overestimated the things they could carry exceeding the weight that the cattle could pull. If additional quantities were taken, it could readily be disposed of in the mountains and at good prices. Not for cash, but for robes, dressed skins, buckskin pants, moccasins, etc. It was also good for families to be provided with medicines.

Estimating Time On The Trail

It usually took about five months to travel from Missouri to Oregon City. However, the time could be reduced to four months with the help of someone who had traveled the route before.

Travel Was Their Business

Racing was hazardous to the teams. Emigrants made traveling an everyday business. Camping in one place for two nights was not good policy. The animals became accustomed to the area and were likely to ramble. Indians had more time to observe the operation during the multiplied daylight hours and plan night attacks to steal the livestock.

Large companies were to be avoided because large companies moved slower. Twenty to twenty-five wagon companies were large enough to travel safely.

Indians

The Indians were very annoying because they liked to steal, not because they liked to kill emigrants. They would seldom steal if a good guard was maintained. Most losses due to Indians were to sneak-thieves that avoided confrontation. Indians would sometimes look for opportunities to rob a man for the few personal belongs he had on him, and shoot him if he tried to get away.

Jump Off Places

There are several points along the Missouri where emigrants could get outfitted. Of these, Independence, St. Joseph, and Council Bluffs on the Missouri River were the usual places to outfit and enter the Oregon

Trail. Emigrants from Ohio, Indiana, Illinois, Iowa, Michigan, and northern Missouri usually outfitted at St. Joseph. By taking the St. Joseph route the crossing of several streams was avoided. Outfits could be obtained at St. Joseph as easily as at other places along the river. Work cattle could be bought in the vicinity for between twenty-five and thirty dollars per yoke; cows, horses, etc. were just as cheap.

Most emigrants tried to arrive at St. Joseph early in April to be in readiness to march up the Oregon Trail by the middle of April. Companies often started as late as the tenth of May but they usually arrived in Oregon after the rainy season began in the Cascade range of mountains. (The Last wagon train to Skinners left on May 22, 1847. It was caught by the rains in the Umpqua Mountains a hundred miles short of Skinners cabin.)

Emigrants leaving northern Ohio, Indiana, Illinois, Michigan, etc., needed to start in time to give their teams at least ten days rest near the jump-off place. Ox teams, after traveling four or five hundred miles were unfit for the journey across the mountains.

Tools Of The Trades

Farmers needed to take along a good supply of horse gear. Mechanics needed those tools they could safely carry. Tools stocked in the few stores in Oregon had high price tags when compared to prices in the United States. School books were needed for emigrant children.

Providing Along The Trail

Flour could be bought at Ft. Hall and at Ft. Boise for twenty dollars per hundred pounds. Spalding's Mission on the Kooskooskee would take flour to Ft. Boise for ten dollars a hundred pounds. The price at Grand Round was eight dollars. Spalding's Mission and Grand Round would exchange dry goods, groceries, etc. Ft. Hall and Ft. Boise would take only cash and cattle. At Dr. Whitman's station, flour could be bought at five dollars per hundred pounds, corn meal for four. Beef was six and seven cents per pound. Potatoes were fifty cents a bushel. Emigrants however, were cautioned to stock in a sufficient supply to last them for the entire journey.

CHAPTER 4

Westward Ho – Rendezvous

Westward Growth

Sixty some years earlier the settlers along the Atlantic coast had thrown off their ties with Britain, forced their independence, and set up a nation known as the United States of America. They forgot about the rest of the world and turned toward affairs at home. These noble people, citizens of the United States, turned their thoughts toward the west beyond Cumberland Gap and Alleghenies. Men, such as Daniel Boone (1734-1820), were intrigued by tales of the west and the untold and virtually unknown riches in the interior of the continent. Having an entrepreneurial spirit, thought turned into action and they departed by whatever means they had through the mountain passes leading to the headwaters of the Ohio and Tennessee Rivers.

Since so much has happened in the intervening years to obscure our view, we have all but forgotten this first migration. These first emigrants did not fan out across plains and through forests when they reached the Northwest Territories. There were no roads or railroads. These pioneers came from the seacoast and coastal rivers where they were used to water as a source of transportation. The first emigrants came from all walks of life, uninhibited with the knowledge that they could not populate the west themselves. Thoughts of failure never entered their mind.

The first emigrants followed down the reaches of the Ohio River and the Tennessee River, and up the tributaries of these and other rivers. They settled as near rivers as possible and used the network rivers and streams to move from place to place. This way of life was so striking that the men become known as the "Men of the Western Rivers."

First there were flatboats, or scows, and the many varieties of rowboats and canoes. Sail power was sometimes used, then steam power. The rivers flourished into greater and greater importance. It is not by accident that all large population centers of that time were on the banks of navigable rivers. Even today one can observe that all large industrial centers east of the influence of the Missouri and Mississippi Rivers are on such bodies of water. Even the western railroads that came later, started west from ports established by these first emigrant-pioneers.

David D. Davis
Oskaloosa Company Captain
Farmer, Miller, Family Man

David D. Davis was born in 1807 to a Welsh family in Pennsylvania. His mother was the former Ann Rees.

Pennsylvania declared its independence from Great Britain thirty years earlier on July 4, 1776. However, The United States Of America had to prove itself again when Britain blockaded American ports and impressed American seamen. The United States exerted its rights and declared war on Britain in 1812. Little is known of David D. Davis' father except that he was probably killed in action. The War of 1812 was fought on the Atlantic Coast, in the interior of the continent, and on the Pacific Coast by the infant Pacific Fur Company working to establish a foothold in the Pacific Northwest.

David D. Davis' father was a Welsh farmer. David was born on or near the family farm. David learned farming from his stepfather who was a good farmer and blacksmith. David D. Davis apparently was fond of his stepfather and half brothers and sisters, as well as his mother, Ann Rees Davis Roberts. It was said that he named his own children after his half brothers and sisters.

Cumberland Road

The Cumberland Road, National Road or Great National Pike, extended the 800 miles from Cumberland, Maryland to Vandalia, Illinois. It played an important part in opening up the west to settlement from the east. Construction commenced about 1815. It was completed to Wheeling in 1821. Construction ended in 1840. The road is the National Old Trails Road. It is surfaced from Washington, DC to St. Louis, Missouri. Interstate 70 appears to approximate this route.

David Davis was twenty-three and living in Indiana in 1830 when he married Hanna Donahoe, daughter of John and Elizabeth (Morgan) Donahoe.

The Donahoes probably emigrated from Germany to the United States several years earlier. There were eight Donahoe children; Hannah, Elias, Eliza, John, Morgan, Polly, Rebecca, and Rachel. The exact spelling of the family name is unknown, however Donahawer appears to be the spelling used by John's father. (EE/DRD)

David D. Davis and Hannah Donahoe obtained a marriage license on February 22, 1831, at the courthouse for Dearborn County, Indiana. They married in Lawrenceburg, Indiana, her home town.

David and Hannah remained in Indiana and began raising a family. Jane, the first girl was born in 1832. Hannah Ann was born the following year, 1833. She was named for her mother and grandmother. They nicknamed her Ann to distinguish between mother and daughter. Rebecca was born two years later in 1835. By that time David and Hannah had three little girls. David wondered if he was ever going to have any boys to help him with the work on the farm. David and Hannah had their first son in 1837, Meshach. Meshach is a variation of a name from the Bible. He received the nicknames, Meck or Mack. Later in life many people called him McDavis.

On To Iowa

David D. Davis, Hannah, and family left Indiana and moved on to Iowa Territory in 1838. Family tradition says that they traveled down the Ohio River and up the Mississippi River to Burlington, Iowa on a flat boat or scow. David D. Davis purchased a farm in Green Bay Township, Lee County, Iowa. It was a few miles southwest of Burrington near the Mississippi River.

Thomas was born in Iowa in 1839 soon after they arrived in Green Bay. Elizabeth was born in 1842. She was named after her Grandmother Donahoe. Rachel was born in 1844. She was the baby of the family until William arrived in 1846. Jane was about 14 years of age when William was born. David and Hannah had eight children, a total of ten people in the family, when they made their overland journey to Oregon in 1847. (EE&DRD)

The Davises Prepare To Leave Iowa

Albert Davidson's father was one of the first settlers in the Burlington, Iowa area in 1836. Albert and James Davidson first came to Oregon in 1845. Albert Davidson returned to Iowa and gave a splendid account of Oregon Country and made a number of speeches in Illinois, Missouri and Iowa. Albert Davidson's speeches and discussions convinced many that Oregon Country was their land of milk and honey. Albert Davidson came west again in 1847 leading a small wagon train over Scott-Applegate Trail. He reached the Willamette Valley about a month ahead of the Davises. (TLD)

David D. Davis probably heard and talked to Albert Davidson during the winter of 1846-1847 since they both were from the Burlington area.

Lester Hulin lived in Henry County, Iowa, a short distance northwest of Burlington and adjacent to Lee County. Hulin had experience exploring in Kansas, Colorado, New Mexico, Texas and Indian Territory with John C. Fremont and Colonel Albert. David D. Davis probably met Lester Hulin during the 1846-1847 winter. It is also conceivable that Hulin was hired to pilot the Oskaloosa Company including Davis' seven wagons on the overland journey while they were still in Iowa. (LH)

David D. Davis sold his Iowa farm before he said good-by to all of his friends. David Davis, Oren Belknap, Ransom Belknap, L. D. Gilbert, Samuel F. Starr, Mr. McKee, and others from Burlington, Oskaloosa, and Keosauqua in southeastern Iowa, listened to people such as Albert Davidson and planned their trip during the previous winter.

David D. Davis started getting everything together so he could make the overland journey to Oregon as uneventful as possible. That took a lot of planning and a lot of time.

Many years later Alice Delcina Sims Davis, daughter in law of Thomas W. Davis told the story that David D. Davis started west from the United States with seven wagons loaded with supplies for the trip and goods to start a business in the new country. David was leading a forty seven wagon train. She said that the Davises were very well off before they started on their overland journey to Oregon. They arrived in the southern Willamette Valley with only themselves, their worldly goods tied to the front end of a wagon pulled by two horses, and some loose stock.

It seems a family tradition was true. Seven wagons was a large family group headed by David D. Davis when they left Green Bay Township. Six full time drivers, in addition to David, were needed to drive seven six-ox teams pulling seven wagons. More men were needed to drive the loose stock. There were twenty or more people in the Davis entourage during the journey westward.

Forty-two oxen were needed to pull the wagons. More oxen were needed to spell tired oxen, and as spares. Thirty to fifty milk cows and young stock would have been along, together with a band of sheep to supply wool for clothing for the family. Most of the men, and Mrs. Davis had saddle horses.

In all seven wagons loaded heavy with supplies for the trip west and setting up business in Oregon Country, over twenty people, over fifty oxen, and well over a hundred head of other livestock left the Davis farm in Iowa to make the overland journey to Oregon that spring morning in 1847.

Bullwhackers

Driving teams of oxen was an art. Oxen were not horses and they were not driven with bit and bridle. In theory they were told which way to go by gently whispering in their ears-"gee" to have them turn right or "haw" to have them go left. The theory worked, with some changes when used by gentle farmers working their farm. However, with the longer teams involved pulling big freight wagons, whispering could not work. The drivers had to raise their voices to make them heard over the noise of the ox team. They raised their voice to yell the instructions on where to go, "gee" to turn right, or "haw" to turn left. The oxen were stubborn and did not always follow the instruction of the driver. The drivers developed a special vocabulary to add to the "gee" and "haw" instructions. Drivers became teamsters.

The oxen did not understand the flowery instructions given by the teamsters and would often take off in their own direction. The bull whip was invented. Teamsters became adept at snapping the whip, "whack," close to the ears of the lead oxen. That got their attention. The ox, bull, would shy away from

Peter W. Crawford
Bancroft Library, University of California at Berkeley

the "whack" causing him to move in the opposite direction. The drivers, teamsters, soon became known as "bullwhackers."

Peter W. Crawford Bullwhacker, Adventurer, Bachelor, Diarist

Peter W. Crawford was hired to drive a covered wagon from Valparaiso, Indiana, to the Oregon Country for Mr. Cline. Covered wagons were usually pulled by at least three yoke of oxen. Two oxen yoked together made up one yoke. Three yokes of oxen would be six animals. Oxen were usually steers. Bulls and cows were also used. Extra oxen were taken along so the oxen in the teams could be rotated and given a rest. When the emigrants came up short draft animals such as after an Indian raid, even milk cows were pressed into service.

Peter W. Crawford left Valparaiso, Indiana on April 12, 1847. He was driving for George and Mrs. Cline and their family; Joseph Cline, Lewis Cline, Eunice Brishinel, Oliver Brishinel, Daniel Brishinel, Jane Emily Cline and Peter Cline. The Clines had four wagons, twenty cows and young stock, four mares and sixteen yokes of oxen. The four wagons were driven by Lewis Cline, Wheeler, Simpsons, and P. W. Crawford.

Lewis Savage, Judson, Reason Reace (Cline's Brother-in-law), Mary Margaret, Adeline, Joseph, and Samson joined the Crawford party very early in the trip. The Reads had two wagons driven by Mr. Read and his brother David Read.

The Crawford party crossed the Mississippi River into Iowa at Burlington near Green Bay where David D. and Hannah Davis lived with their family. They traveled through Iowa to Keosauqua on Des Moines River. Mr. Crawford reported that they crossed from Iowa into Missouri in Sheridan County. (No record was found of a Sheridan County in either Iowa or Missouri.) They traveled through Missouri. They crossed the Missouri River at Elizabethtown thirteen miles above St. Joseph on May 27 and 28, 1847. The water was muddy and the current was fast. All were over safe on the afternoon of May 28. They camped near the river. They saw some tombstones. The country looked wild.

"Leaving all civilized life ale, all, behind. Launch into the wild, plains among wild savages, with which were not acquainted. Neither their ways nor language. Farewell to all society back beyond the eastern ocean or that just left in the region of the fast growing center of the west, Chicago on the Lakes.

"Now leaving all settlements, all civilization and emerging into the Indian Country. The sensation to a man or woman of a family must have been one of distrust-commingled with a hope and trust of reaching that para disal home in the far west six or eight months roaming through savage plains and artimis'a dust - But the young blossom little knows the many scorching sunbeams the many frosty nights, the many severe blasts it is going to be exposed to. But taking its place side and side with the many neighboring flowers - it stands the storms and is fed and nourished by those providential elements, the gentle dew, the muted rain. The moistening showers and warmed by the glowing sun shine until bursting forth into life and vigor and as then final as the fragrant blooming bulky hardy rose. So with the early pioneers who cross the plains in 1847.

"Camping day-by -day a little nearer, a little nearer their western homes. But alas, many never saw it. As sickness came the Indians came, and many things came to snatch, even some of the fair ones. To leave thus fair remains in a rude ruthless savage county

and relieve the spirit of its load of earthy clay to wing its way on high to fairer climes.

"After crossing the Missouri River 13 miles above St. Joe the Immigrant road leads about northwest over very rolling country until it gains a point far enough from the breaks of the Missouri River — Through some small skirts of timber until the old Missouri is past about 70 miles out on the plains.

"Then comes the Country of the Minahawes, two streams of that name running southward with some belts of timber on their borders as it is the custom for the immigrants to concentrate and rendezvous for the purpose of defense against Indians.

We have overtaken our friends from Lakeport Indiana; Mr. Stanton & Family, Mr. Kimble & Family. Mr. Hill & Family, one Batchedlor wagon, Gustaves Cane, Bill Molten and another Jerry Manbeing, All Hoosiers in journey together." (PWC)

Crawford also wrote "*After crossing the Nimahaws we overtake other trains of wagons who are anxious to double up so we form a Company with Ascalousa (Oskaloosa) Company, Davis Captain, sixty wagons strong*". (PWC)

Lester Hulin
Pilot, Explorer, Bachelor, Diarist

Lester Hulin let it be known throughout southeastern Iowa that he was available to pilot a company of wagons to the Oregon Country. The Oskaloosa Company needed a pilot and Lester Hulin had the experience necessary to be a pilot so the organizers of a Company leaving for Oregon Country hired him to be the pilot. Lester Hulin was waiting up the trail to pilot the Oskaloosa Company on the overland journey to Oregon.

Lester Hulin was born to Peter Hulin and Elizabeth Smith (Hulin) on March 22, 1823. In 1844 at the age of twenty-one, he moved to Henry County, Iowa. A year later he went to St. Louis where he met Captain Fremont and Colonel Albert. He was hired to go on an exploring expedition with them through Kansas, Colorado, New Mexico, Texas and the Indian Territory. He returned to Iowa for a short time but the new country to the west was calling. In April 1847 he went to St. Joseph, this time to act as pilot for a Company traveling west.

Lester Hulin kept a daily record of his travels in a "Day Book or Journal." That portion recorded for the "Oregon Trail and Scott-Applegate Route" in "1847" was reproduced by the Lane County Pioneer Historical Society in 1959. It is from the original Day Book that is owned by Wilbur S. Hulin, Eugene, Oregon. The book is six by eight inches with a marbleized paper cover

Lester Hulin
Lane County Historical Society

and a leather hinge. It is said to be excellently preserved. It begins with accounts in Missouri, 1843. The day-by-day diary follows the 1843 Missouri accounts. The book continues with more business accounts and notes in Oregon Territory.

This writer has studied all entries that Lester Hulin made on the overland journey to Oregon. Lester Hulin's entries have been compared with other 1846 and 1847 trail writers. Lester Hulin's entries were professional as well as reliable. There is one place where they may be off by one day or date - identified at Monday and Tuesday, October 11th, 1847. That is 99.37% accuracy in days and dates accounted for. Although there are indications of "catching up," the book is reliable.

Lester Hulin's "Day Book or Journal" has been accepted by the Lane County Historical Society and the Klamath County Historical Society. Devere Helfrich, Applegate Trail historian, made extensive use of Lester Hulin's own words in rewriting the history of the Scott-Applegate Trail. Lester Hulin's works have never been questioned.

Lester Hulin Leaves Iowa

Lester Hulin was twenty-four years old when he left his friends in Iowa on April 23, 1847. He started a journey that would take him more than two thousand miles over the Rocky Mountains to the Oregon Country. He traveled the first two hundred fifty miles to St. Joseph, Missouri in nine days.

Saint Joseph was a "jumping off" place for the far west and presented a very rough appearance. This frontier town was just beginning to get set for the rush of business that was to be pressed upon it. It still had unready, mud-lined streets lined with crudely thrown up shops and supply stations. (HHH)

Prices were high and commodities limited. Some of the most sought-after services were found in the blacksmith shops where it was possible to have horses shod and wagon tires reset. Wagons were built to near specifications with water-tight bodies for crossing streams. These large water-tight wagon beds were later to prove a sound investment, for the rivers were many and varied in the problems they created. (HHH)

Oxen sold at prices ranging from a small amount for green "broke" up to one hundred fifty dollars and often more for one span of well-wintered and properly broken work stock. (HHH)

On Monday, May 4th, 1846, Virgil Pringle wrote *"got my bacon this day for which I paid $3.75 per hundred"* in Jackson County. The next day he wrote we *"went ahead with my wagons and commenced loading in my flour for which I pay $2.00 (per barrel) for S(uper) fine and $1.75 (per barrel) for fine."* (VP)

Talk was rough and even then guns were fast and often deadly. The law was not too much concerned. It wanted to stay away from conflict with these hardy characters that burned with a desire to head westward. (HHH)

Some families waited in St. Joseph so they could join together forming wagon trains with leadership so they could push into the beckoning sunset with some measure of safety. Others waited about seventy miles down the trail.

Lester Hulin Starts The Story His Overland Journey To Oregon

1847 April 23rd. On this day I took my last leave of the friends in Iowa and commenced a journey of more than 200 Ms. over the Rocky Mts. or to the territory of Oregon. After a travel of nine days I Arrived at St. Joseph a distance of 250 Ms. Here I waited one week for the man I expected to accompany. Spent the next week in making our preparations to leave the land of civilization. Accordingly on the 20th day of May we emerged from the land of society so long dear to us and night found us on the opposite bank of the Missouri River. Camped here in the bushes.

May 21st. With some difficulty we traveled through the muddy bottom and camped in the edge of the prairie. Distance 5 miles. Wood, water and grass.

May 22nd. Traveled over a ridges and in 5 miles camped at a fine spring.

Sun. 23rd. In camp to day.

M 24th. Made about 6 miles through rain and camped on Musquito Creek.

James Harty, an emigrant wrote home saying that he camped on Mosquito Creek a day or so later after Hulin camped there. Harty's small party waited for more wagons so the wagon train would be large enough to pass safely over the road ahead. They soon joined the Oskaloosa Company and the David D. Davis family, also on their way to Oregon.

T. 25th. To day we passed over fine ridges (for this road runs altogether over ridges) and 15 miles brought us to the agency of the Saux & Fox. Passed it a mile or two and camped.

W. 26th To day we made 20 miles and camped at the usual camping ground of the emigrants. Grass nearly eat up, water good.

T. 27th. Passed on over the ridges and sought out a new and very good camping grounds 1/2 mile from the usual place. Weather fine.

F. 28th. In camp all day.

S. 29th. To day McKean and Ross went back to meet company and ascertain how long we must wait. In the after noon we had a very heavy shower with wind.

Lester Hulin mentions only a few persons in his overland journey to Oregon. No person is mentioned a second time. McKean and Ross are two emigrant men that are important in Oregon history. They are remembered only in this brief note in Lester Hulin's journal but are worthy of your attention.

S. 30th. In camp today. Morning rainy, evening fair.

M. 31st. To day a large caravan of emigrants came in sight. Some camped with us, others passed on 2 miles and camped.

It is not clear whether the break up of the Oskaloosa Company was prearranged on May 30th and completed on May 31st by division into two camps. It seems probable that the breakup council mentioned by Peter W. Crawford was on the evening of May 31st with McKee being elected Captain of the forty-one wagons in the second section camped with Lester Hulin.

June 1st. This morning we left those with whom we have been camped and overtook those who passed last night. Today we made a good drive and camped on Big Burr Oak Creek.

The Davises Start Their Overland Journey To Oregon

David D. Davis was thirty-nine or forty years old when he, his wife, Hannah, and their eight children: Jane (15), Hannah Ann (14), Rebecca (12),Meshach (10), Thomas (8), Elizabeth (5), Rachel (3) and William (1), left Iowa in April 1847 on an overland journey to Oregon. It would take them five months and more than two thousand miles over the great plains of Missouri, Kansas, and Nebraska; over the Rocky Mountains through Wyoming, and Idaho, the deserts of Utah, Nevada, and northeastern California; then through the mountains of southwestern Oregon and into Oregon Country's Willamette Valley and their new home.

David D. Davis, his wife, Hannah, and their eight children headed in the general direction of Keosauqua the last week in April 1847. Seven covered wagons carried their possessions. The seven wagons were pulled by twenty-one yoke (forty-two oxen) accompanied by more work oxen in reserve. There were loose stock, cattle, milk cows, horses, and a herd of sheep, enough to supply their needs during the trek to Oregon Country.

The Davis family probably met the Belknap, Watts, Starr and Gilbert families near Keosauqua in Van Buren County, Iowa. (BCM) They joined up other families along the road to Keosauqua where they crossed the Des Moines River into Missouri.

The Oskaloosa Company traveled west through northern Missouri and crossed the Missouri River into Kansas at Elizabethtown the last week in May 1847. Elizabethtown is thirteen miles above St. Joseph.

They overtook other companies, and were overtaken by others. Some companies joined the Oskaloosa Company for defense against Indian attacks. The Oskaloosa Company grew in numbers to about eighty-one wagons.

They soon found that it took too much time for all of those wagons to get in camp at night and out in the morning, and too long to coral the wagons if Indians attacked.

The Oskaloosa Company camped in two camp grounds some seventy miles west of St. Joseph. They picked up the pilot, Lester Hulin, the evening of May 31, 1847.

About forty-one wagons formed a separate Company, with Mr. McKee captain. He was with Davis in the Oskaloosa Company. (PWC)

Those leaving the Oskaloosa Company included Cooper, Fullison, Read (Reak), Cline, McKee, and the Abe Peak families. (PWC)

The Oskaloosa Company and the McKee Company totaled about eighty-one wagons. Forty wagons remained with the Oskaloosa Company, forty-one left with the McKee Company. (Seven wagons of the McKee Company returned to the Oskaloosa Company on June 17, 1847.)

David D. Davis was camped at the forward camp ground and led the Oskaloosa Company. Lester Hulin would pilot the Oskaloosa Company.

The Oskaloosa was organized for the overland journey to Oregon. David D. Davis, Hanna Davis and their family were ready to go.

David D. Davis, Captain

Peter W. Crawford's brief association with the Oskaloosa Company supplies two important historic facts in the life of David D. Davis. First, the name of the wagon train David D. Davis made their overland journey to Oregon with was "The Oskaloosa Company." Second, "Davis" was the name of the Captain.

Later events identify D. D. Davis and show that David D. Davis was elected, or reelected, Captain of the wagon train. James N. Harty reported that D. D. Davis of Green Bay (Township), Lee County, Iowa was (re)elected Captain. Lester Hulin recorded the election of officers and on September 29, 1847 noted that Ann Davis, David D. Davis' daughter, was badly injured and fell into a fire during an Indian attack in Fandango Valley.

This evidence indicates that the Davis, Captain of the Oskaloosa Company, and the D. D. Davis that was elected Captain of the company was David D. Davis.

CHAPTER 5

The Oregon Trail

St. Joseph, Missouri, to Raft River

Company Business

Emigrant wagon trains entered an untamed wilderness when they crossed the Missouri River in 1847. They had to rely on each other for protection as they traveled the Oregon Trail. Explorers such as John C. Fremont had been through the area. American and British fur trading companies had established trading posts, commonly known as forts, along the way but they were manned by civilian fur traders. Although there were a few soldiers passing through traveling between the United States and California, there were no military installations. There was no military protection of any kind. Emigrants on each wagon train were entirely on their own.

All of the companies that traveled the Oregon Trail faced the same problems. Some problems were known and were planned for well in advance. Many of the problems were

Approaching Platte River Crossing
Painting by William H. Jackson, Scott's Bluff National Monument

unknown until they exploded into their lives. Each of the companies had its own way of doing business and organizing the travel of the wagon train. The well-being of the wagon train depended on people's cooperation within the wagon train and how well the company handled its business.

The day would start between four and five in the morning. The last shift of guards would wake up the people on the wagon train. The drovers would check the cattle to make sure none had wandered away and move them back toward camp. Teamsters would check and lay out gear. Others would prepare breakfast.

Breakfast was enjoyed from six to seven, or earlier if a long day's drive was expected. The emigrants ate inside the circle formed by their forty-seven wagons. As the departure time neared, the tents would start coming down.

The hired pilot then moved out with the hunters behind him, ready to search out the buffalo or antelope. Chains that linked the wagons together, wheel to wheel, were removed. Teamsters hitched their oxen to the wagons. The lead wagon for the day would move out. The rest of the wagons fell into line behind the lead wagon, one by one.

Along the Platte River where the nature of the terrain was flat, the wagons fanned out into horizontal lines. Usually the terrain did not permit a wide road. The wagons would form in single file.

The guide usually was at the nooning place (where they stopped for lunch) about an hour before the wagon train would arrive. The teams were brought in, unhitched from the wagons but not unyoked. The wagons stopped where they were comfortable, in shade if there was any, and there usually was not. They did not form a corral at noon.

There was always bickering along the line of march. The council frequently was charged with favoritism. Certain cliques would form in loosely organized wagon trains. Some would reserve the best campsites by arriving early. Some would change the line of march. Urgent disputes were settled at the noon rest by the elected council that held both legislative and judicial powers. When the problem got too severe, it was sometimes solved by changing leaders. The line of march would resume by one o'clock.

The pilot would arrive at his chosen campsite and stake out a one hundred yard circle near sunset. He would guide the lead wagon around the complete circle directing it to stop after the wagon had almost gone around the complete circle. He directed the next wagon to head in slightly so its left front wheel was opposite the right rear wheel of the lead wagon. This procedure was followed by following wagons until the circle was complete – except for one wagon that was left out. The teams were then unhitched and driven out through the opening. The last wagon was moved into the opening to close the corral.

Each of the families prepared their own campsite and raised their own tents. Within forty-five minutes to one hour they were eating their evening meal.

Sources of Information

There are no known family records of the overland journey of the David D. Davis family. However, the details of its journey can be shown by following Lester Hulin's daily journal. Hulin's journal provides a bare bones no nonsense narrative of the overland journey. There are few personal incidents in his writing that did not happen to every other member of the wagon train. It is assumed that David D. Davis is walking in Lester Hulin's shoes from their meeting on May 31, 1847 to November 4, 1847 when they reached Skinner's Cabin.

Passages in this book that are printed in *Script* are the words written by Lester Hulin in his "Day Book or Journal."

Memories of Peter W. Crawford, and James N. Harty's letter home provide more information and elaborate on Hulin's narrative.

Oskaloosa Company Gets Together

M. 31. To day a large caravan of emigrants came in sight. Some camped with us. Others passed on 2 Ms and camped.

June 1st. This morning we left those with whom we have been camped and overtook those who passed last night. To day made a good drive and camped on Big Burr Oak Creek.

Eighty-one wagons in the enlarged Oskaloosa Company moved to the rendezvous on the evening of May 31, 1847. The wagon train divided by camping in two locations along the St. Joseph branch of the Oregon Trail. About forty-one wagons set up at the Lester Hulin's camp. Forty wagons, including those of David D. Davis, went another two miles down the road before they camped for the night.

David D. Davis was Captain of the Oskaloosa Company, and Lester Hulin was its Pilot. They got together and discussed the organization of the Company well into the night. Lester Hulin would take up his position as Pilot of the Company as they moved out on June 1, 1847. Everything was organized and they were ready to go.

Lester Hulin moved through the front camp early on the morning of June 1, 1847, and out onto the trail that would take the emigrants on their overland journey to Oregon. A few hunters moved out behind him. Then the lead wagon moved out, followed by the rest of the wagons in the train. The Davis family, the Oren Belknap family, the Ransom Belknap family, the Gilbert family, the Starr family, the Watts family, Lester Hulin, James N. Harty, McKean, John Ross, Cornelius Hills, and the rest of the Oskaloosa Company were on the trail to Oregon. They made good time that first day and camped on Big Burr Oak Creek.

Peter Crawford remembered that the company divided into two Companies. McKee was Captain of the second wagon train of forty-one wagons.

W. 2nd. This morning being fine and feed good we yoked early but missing a few of our oxen we were detained an hour or two before we could start. Followed the ridges 12 or 14 miles and camped on a fine neck of prairie with groves of hickory, oak, &c. on 3 sides of us.

T. 3rd. Passed over the ridges, crossing (Burr Oak), Little Burr Oak, headed one branch and crossed another. Passed over a large level prairie, turned off to the right and camped with but little wood, good grass.

The Company camped on the prairie northwest of present day Marysville, Kansas after crossing the Big Blue River,

Crossing the Big Blue River was uneventful for our travelers although some other companies had problems with high, turbulent water. Earlier in the season many companies had to wait several days for the stream to subside before they could cross. They raised the wagon beds by placing blocks between the beds and bolsters so the contents of the wagons would remain dry during the crossing. The caravan was in hurricane country during hurricane season.

Virgil Pringle was on the main trail when he recorded a violent hurricane in 1846 on the Little Blue River:

"About 3 o'clock the most violent hurricane I ever experienced overtook us. The wind blew from every point of the compass with utmost violence

but principally from the southwest, and the rain fell in torrents. Its severity was as to blind a man and take his breath to face the storm. It continued about 45 (minutes). When it abated every prairie branch was a river. We went 12 miles and camped. Everything in our wagon appeared wet. Went to bed tonight with wet beds." (VP)

The next day they *"examined our wagons and put our clothing to dry. We found most of our provisions dry and in good order. There was little damaged by the storm."* (VP)

On to The Big Trail To Oregon

F. 4th. Passing on, we soon came to Republican Creek and nooned. Republican is a large fine stream, plenty of timber and wide bottom. Again over ridges. In about 3 miles came to the Independence trail or the junction. This now in the big road to Oregon. 2 miles more to Wyeth's Run. Two graves here on the right + over one. In two miles more we camped.

The Oskaloosa Company crossed Republican Creek and nooned there on June 4th. They came to the junction where the trail from St. Joseph meets the trail from Independence, Missouri about three miles east-southeast of Hanover. They saw two graves on Wyeth's Run southeast of Hollenberg Ranch Historic Site.

Out of Kansas - Into Nebraska

S. 5th. Moved over a high ridge, crossed some branches and camped on the bottom of a branch. Distance to day about 14 miles.

Sun. 6th. Passing finely along, we crossed Cannon Ball Creek, well timbered. stopped about noon during a shower, dined. Continued farther on and at night turned off left and camped with grass, wood & water.

The emigrants traveled fourteen miles on the Oregon Trail on June 5th. They crossed a high ridge and several small branches. They camped near one of the branches near present day Rock Creek Station northeast of Endicott.

The Oregon Trail crossed the present day Kansas-Nebraska State Line about ten miles from the junction of the Independence and St. Joseph trails. That is three or four miles south southeast of present day Fremont Springs.

They stopped for noon during a shower and camped near Powell on a branch with grass, wood, and water at evening on June 6th.

This part of Kansas and Nebraska was beautiful and very fertile, but there was little timber. Trees were plentiful after they crossed Cannon Ball Creek. There were plenty of antelope along this part of the Oregon Trail.

The Oskaloosa Moved Up Little Blue River

M. 7th. Left the branch and passed on to Otto Creek (probably so called from its being the residence of the Otto Indians). Passed Dry Sandy, Big Sandy and camped on a sandy branch. Game consists of antelope, wolves &c.

T. 8th. Passed Middle Sandy and Little Sandy. We, in about 6 miles came to Little Blue. Went up about 6 miles and camped. Good Grass, wood and water.

W. 9th. No traveling done today. Hunting, fishing, &c.

The emigrants camped on a branch of Big Sandy River west of present day Alexandria, Nebraska.

The next day, in about six miles, they camped on a beautiful spring branch on the right bank of the Little Blue River near Kiowa Station south of Davenport. There was plenty of grass and wood, and was the most beautiful and convenient spot for a farm they had seen.

They stayed there on June 9, 1847. This was relaxation. However, David and Hannah Davis and the other travelers had to get food where they could. Fish and antelopes were plentiful here. Emigrants had to rely on the country for all of their fresh food. The lay over also gave their animals a chance to relax and recuperate.

T. 10th. Left camp this morning with a good sun and fine roads. Followed up Little Blue until near noon. We then left the (river?) for about 3 miles and thereby went about 2 miles out of the way. We should kept the bottom. About the time we came in the bottom again our cattle were scared by two horses galloping by, and commenced running. We did not succeed in stopping them until 3 of the oxen had fallen and each one lost a horn in the scrape.

About the time that they came to the river again, several ox teams were scared by two horses galloping past. The cattle were startled and ran. It was almost impossible to stop them. The drivers could not stop them before three of the oxen had fallen. Each of the three lost a horn in the scrape. The runaway happened near present day Liberty Farm Station at Deweese, Nebraska. (LH)(HHH)(JNH)

F. 11th. This morning some of our cattle being among the missing, we were detained until near noon and of course made a short drive, perhaps not more than 12 miles. The day warm and dry.

Some of the cattle had wandered off during the night. It took most of the morning to find them and move out. They started late and camped near Pawnee Creek near present day Ayr, Nebraska.

Both the Little and Big Blue Rivers were enjoyed for their cool, but strangely murky waters. The day was warm and dry. (LH)(HHH)(JNH)

Cross Country
Little Blue River to Platte River

S. 12th. Having left our place of our camping which is the last on Little Blue, we marched up it until near noon. Here we dined and left Blue. Passed up the ridge. Soon crossed a branch and in about 6 miles came to the last camping place between Blue and Platt. There we camped, wood, water, & grass.

Sunday 13th. To day we had to make a long drive, 23 or 25 miles. We could not do better but we crossed and was in camp before sunset. Good grass but no wood. Here it might be well to mention that there is no wood along Platt except on the islands.

The Oskaloosa Company camped two miles southwest of Juniata on June 12 and made one of the longest drives of the overland journey to Oregon on June 13th. They had one of the most romantic views of the scenery just before they stopped at sunset as the reached the Platte River near Lowell. There was good grass but no wood. There would be no wood along the Platte River.

Marching Along

Drovers usually rode horseback to keep the loose stock in line. Scout's duties required them to ride out front or to the side of the wagon train. They chart its progress and warn the emigrants of possible attack. Some also went back along the trail to help stragglers and to pick up stray stock. Hunters went wherever they thought they could find food. They usually rode on horseback. Of course, there were others who just wanted to ride all of the way and refused to walk.

There were many sick and dying people on the trail to Oregon. Their only consolation was in the covered wagon. Many Oskaloosa Company women and children walked almost all of the way from their home in the United States to their new home in Oregon.

Up Platte River

M. 14th. Moved about 15 miles up Platt. Good roads and good grass. To day we passed the grave of J. H. Fisher who died June 6th, 1847. The miserable Paunees had dug him up or rather dug down to him. We covered him again and some mourned with his bereaved wife and children.

The river looked majestic when there was nothing but a broad vale of sand with banks about three feet high. The banks were full at high water and the sand was dry in a dry period. There was enough water to barely cover the sand bars, leaving them in sight at times. However, flat boats loaded with furs are able to travel this river. They draw about a foot of water and were continually scraping bottom as they floated down the river.

They passed the grave of J. H. Fisher on June 14th. Mr. Fisher died eight days earlier on June 6, 1847. The Pawnees had dug him up, or rather dug down to him. Our travelers covered him again and some mourned with his bereaved wife and children. (LH)(HHH)(JNH)

John H. Fisher died on the Platte of camp fever caused by bad drinking water. He was survived by his wife, Rachel Fisher (Mills). She kept going because *"I had no one to take me back."* She lost a daughter, Angeline, on August 11, 1847. Her driver drowned in the Snake River soon after that. She arrived in Portland on November 15, 1847. The Fishers were from Henry County, Iowa and traveling with the Thomas Hockett company. (JMT)

The Oskaloosa Company camped near Platte Station across the river from present day Kearney, Nebraska.

T. 15th. Continued coasting along up Platt. Always camping on the river. Generally good grass.

The Davis' wagon train continued coasting along up the Platte. The morning was cool but the day pleasant for traveling and the roads were among the best - level bottom and firm. There was good grass and plenty of antelope where they camped near Phelps County Canal.

W. 16th. This morning Mr. Hill and myself went back after a cow that had left during the night. In about 6 miles we met McKee's Co. They had been visited by Pawnees and seemed much scared. We again overtook our Co. by camping time but did not find cow.

The McKee Company, the company that had pulled out of the Oskaloosa Company back on the St. Joseph Trail, had been visited by Pawnees.

Peter W. Crawford was traveling with the McKee wagon train. Mr. Crawford wrote later that upon leaving camp the previous Sunday morning a band of Indians were discovered. They were coming six abreast over the Indian trails in Pawnee Country. They came from the north as thick as buffalo riding at a good lope. They were well armed and riding side by side. They were well mounted, some on mules and some on good-looking horses. Some had branded guns showing they had been taken from a wagon train on the Santa Fe Trail.

The Indians told them to stop and not go through their country without paying them. Captain McKee ordered the wagon train to turn back. Many of the young men would rather fight than turn back. They turned back until they found a place to form a "closed A" corral so they could defend themselves.

They got out their "*shootin irons*." Mr. Crawford got out his long whip and shouldered his "*good Old Yuager that carries a half ounce ball and is seen every shot.*" He went outside the circle to drive some young impudent Indians from those wagons having women and children.

When Mr. Crawford returned he found an Indian in his own wagon. The Indian was in the sugar bowl eating sugar. Another Indian got into a barrel of soft soap, hauled out his bare arm, looked at the soap, smelled it and said something in Indian talk. Other Indians jeered him and laughed. He laughed. Mr. Crawford laughed.

Mr. McKee had captured an Indian Chief by the time Mr. Crawford got back inside the circle. Mr. McKee was treating him as royalty and giving him presents to keep his men back and to let the wagon train pass through their country unmolested. The women gave up nearly all their bread that they had baked to carry them through to the Platte.

The wagon train moved out with the Indians going with them. The Indian Chief whipped some of his young men to keep them quiet and keep them from stealing. The Indians were seen as strong, stout of build with muscles like a highland soldier. The Indians that did not have guns had strong bows and their quivers filled with arrows.

The travelers supposed that the Indians thought that it would be sporting to kill the people and take the whole wagon train. But the wagon train was armed to the teeth. There were forty good men and desolate boys eager to fight. The Indians must have thought they outnumbered the wagon train with five hundred well-mounted Indians.

Mr. Crawford said;

> *"But, we would have had breast-works of wagons and oxen-and two oxen abreast would have been hard to have shot through. The Indians would have needed stamina and hardihood to have charged them through the mouth of the corral. So many skeletons would have been left to bleach on that plain. We were lucky to get off so well. "* (PWC)

The Oskaloosa Company camped near Johnson Lake across from Lexington.

A Child Is Born

T. 17th. To day we are obliged to lie by to attend to the case of a Mrs. Balch who upon this day gave birth to an infant son. So our company has not only increased one by birth but has also increased 7 wagons and about 10 men who being dissatisfied with McKees Co. joined ours and so our Co. now consists of 47 waggons and about 75 men. To day we saw buffalo at a distance.

The Oskaloosa Company not only increased one by birth but also increased by seven wagons and about ten men. They joined the train after becoming dissatisfied with McKee's Company. The wagon train then consisted of forty-seven wagons and about seventy-five men. The McKee Company moved through as the Davis Company did not travel on June 17th. (LH)(JNH)

The scenery of the country looked almost the same since they came to the river. There was enough of change to make it agreeable. The breadth of the river, the many islands, and the variety of shape in the sand hills all kept the mind relieved from sameness.

There were plenty of buffalo signs along the road. They occasionally saw dead buffalo in the bottom land. The live ones were all on the highland plains beyond the sand hills at that season. In the fall they come in the bottom for water. The appearance of their range was like an old pasture closely grazed. (VP)

F. 18th. Continued coasting up Platte. Made about 15 miles and camped without wood but with plenty of Buffalo chips.

The day was a good cool day. The sand hills were more romantic than any David and Hannah Davis had seen before. They rose into high, irregular peaks, resembling majestic snow drifts in form. They made about fifteen miles coasting up the Platte. They camped without wood but with plenty of buffalo chips across the Platte River from present day Willow Island near Gothenburg.

Recycling Grass-Buffalo Chips

David and Hannah Davis learned to substitute buffalo chips for wood as fuel for their fires. Cooking food over an open fire was an art that they acquired when they were emigrating from Indiana to Iowa. Cooking food over a buffalo chip fire was something new to them.

Buffalo chips are sun-dried buffalo pies left on the open prairie as the buffalo pass through. They were plentiful, and a person could pick up a bushel of them in less than three minutes. They could be used as they were gathered. The buffalo chips did not have to be chopped down to size as wood did.

A Child Is Lost

S. 19th. Last night a child of Mr. Kimballs met the king of terror and we had to remain in camp to bury her.

James N. Harty wrote that they dug her grave deep and sunk a vault and lay her in it with the winding sheet around her. They did not have anything they could use to make a coffin but covered the body with pieces of short board. They thought of her as cemented in. They placed her inscription a little way from the grave to deceive the prowling Pawnees. They drove the entire wagon train across the grave to remove all traces of the grave. Nobody wanted the body to be dug up by the Indians like Mr. Fisher's body had been. (LH)(JNH)(HHH)

Prowling Pawnees

Sun. 20th. Last night the prowling Pawnees succeeded in leaving one of our men minus a horse. Myself and 50 others ran them close but caught them not. Made about 15 miles and camped near the lower end of Bradys.

The guard was not alert enough to detect the Indians. About fifty men from the wagon train chased and almost caught up with the Indians but they got away.

The Indians had a clever way of inching through the grass with the silence and smoothness of a snake. They would leap onto the back of the startled horse. Their moccasined feet would dig in behind the shoulders of the horse. They were away like the wind into the darkness. Knowing the country as they did made pursuit impossible. (HHH)

The emigrants camped across the river from present day Brady, Nebraska.

M. 21st. This morning we soon crossed several hollows upon which was considerable timber. Road passed over high prairie and ran nearer the bluff than usual. Turned off to the right and camped on a stream of running water. Good Grass.

T. 22nd. Today we moved on with good progress. Buffalo plenty. The road running along and over the bluff having traveled about 18 miles we camped on the S. fork of Plat about 4 miles above the mount. No wood, poor grass, and muddy water.

They camped near the present day city of North Platte, Nebraska where Platte River divides into the South Platte and the North Platte. The Oskaloosa Company and the Oregon Trail followed near the south bank of the South Platt River before crossing it and crossing overland to the south bank of the North Platte at Ash Hollow. They camped about four miles up the South Fork of the Platte River after following it for ten days.

They continued up the South Platte River, down O'Fallons Bluff, and camped near Sutherland Reservoir on June 22, 1847.

Meat To Eat And Lost Horses

W. 23rd. Made an early start and a good drive but bad luck. One of our men lost 2 horses by one going after buffalo, the other followed and both got away and ran off with the buffalo with which the plains abound. I killed a good cow to day and the camp got their first meal of good buffalo meat. 2 men were in pursuit of them but returned about 12 at night without them. Camped about 12 miles below ford.

T. 24th. Did not leave camp today on account being out after those horses but had no luck. Conclude the Indians got them.

The Oskaloosa Company camped southeast of Ogallala on June 23, 1847 and stayed there on the 24th looking for two horses that wandered off into a buffalo herd and could not be rounded up. Two men returned about midnight empty handed.

Lester Hulin killed a cow buffalo and the emigrants had their first taste of the meat.

Crawford's Encounter With Indians

Peter. W. Crawford, a bullwhacker with the McKee Company, recorded an interesting story of his experience with Indians at this location a few days earlier. (PWC)

During a heavy thunderstorm one night, Indians cut the lariats that tied their horses to the outside of the wagons. Then they tried to stampede the horses. Mr. Crawford was on guard duty with two other men. He assumed the other two guards went to sleep but he stayed awake. He took shelter under his wagon so he would not be out in the very heavy rain.

The lightning flashed and he saw the legs of an Indian leading a horse. Instantly there was another flash of lightning — because they were as quick as lightning. He shot his big rifle in the direction of the Indian without taking aim. The sound of the rifle shot in the dead of night instantly awakened the whole camp. All the people with horses tied to the outside their wagons checked. All lariats were cut. Everyone had lost their horses. They began looking for them and calling for them after the storm stopped. To the surprise of everyone, all horses were found. The Indians had lost their prey — but kept trying and were successful the next time. (PWC)

F. 25th. Traveled up the south fork and camped about one mile from the ford.

The emigrants joked about the river being a mile wide and a foot deep as they prepared for the crossing. When they finally got there, they found it was a not joke at all - that it was a mile wide and a foot deep. Actually the river bed is closer to a mile and a quarter wide. A June 8, 1846, report said that the river channel was almost level with the plain and a big sand bed. The channel was only half a mile wide and only a foot and a half deep on June 25, 1847. The Lower California Crossing is four hundred forty miles from Independence.

Ford South Fork Of Platte River Travel Up North Fork

S. 26th. Crossed Platt. Made up it about 6 or 8 miles and camped with good grass.

Emigrants found that the river was a half mile wide and quite shallow. The sand was the main problem in crossing. If a wagon was not kept in motion for even a moment, one wheel might sink into the sand. In some cases the wheel would sink swiftly to a point where the wagon would tip over, spilling its contents into the river.

The emigrants were cautioned to incline their travel downstream when crossing the river at Lower California Crossing. This causes the pressure from the moving water to be directed slightly forward against the back of the oxen's legs. The reverse would be true if they were inclined upstream. The pressure from the water would be directed against the front of the oxen's legs. By traveling slightly downstream, the oxen are not fighting the current in the river quite as much. The animals are not swimming upstream in deeper water, and pressure of the current against the wagon box is not as great.

David and Hannah Davis found the water was never over the front axle of their wagons, seldom that deep. They doubled the teams but pulling was still hard through the sand. However, it was not as bad as it looked. The distance with the angle they took was about a mile and a half across sand and water.

California Hill

The wagon train headed up California Hill after completing the crossing of the Platte. They pulled hard at this one because they knew there was a fine plateau at the top. It went all the way to Ash Creek and the North Platte River. The day was fine and the wind was from the east. They camped for the night with good grass.

Sun. 27th. Five miles found us at the place the road turns off to the north fork of Platt. Passed on over fine roads and camped about 5 miles from the river without water. Cool night.

Ash Hollow

M. 28th. Sun arose pleasant. We passed on and soon came to the bluffs. They are high and ragged. Descended into the sandy bed of Ash Creek. About 1/2 mile brought us to the river. Timber pleanty, ash and cedar. Here we camped for the day.

The sun was pleasant. The wagon train soon came to the high rugged bluffs. As the emigrants approached the bluffs the hills formed a smooth low horizon from left to right. The foreground behind the smooth plain was gone. The distant horizon was still there but there was nothing between the observer and it but thin air. As the wagon train approached the bluffs, the plain below began coming into view, the far end first.

From the top of the bluffs, the full plain below was in full view - with one big hill immediately at their feet. Ash Hollow was three hundred yards below. Ash Hollow was a level plain, six miles long, reaching all the way to the North Platte River. There was a beautiful grove of cedars and the best water on the Oregon Trail is only an hour away.

One emigrant described the descent as breaking the monotony — also the legs of the horses, the legs of mules, the legs of the oxen, and the arms of the teamsters. The ravines were filled with wagon wrecks. Wagon bows were broken and there was no willow to replace them. This was the first of many wagon slides David and Hannah Davis would find along the Trail to Oregon.

The road was steeper than any David and Hannah had ever taken a wagon over before. The scenery was really magnificent. The brown hills for miles around presented

Trail Traces Approaching Ash Hollow

Photo by Shann Rupp

a picture varied in height and shade rarely exceeded in beauty. David and Hannah Davis descended into the sandy bed of Ash Creek.

Many have written about the "windlass" activity of Windlass Hill. The sheer weight and volume of nine hundred feet of one inch (or larger) rope makes it unlikely that any wagons were let down on a windlass.

Sometimes ropes were attached to wagons and people slid on their feet, and other body parts, on the ground to provide as much braking power as possible.

The road down Ash Creek was bad for three or four miles. They found lots of currants and chokecherries. There was a fine spring near the mouth of Ash Creek. A cabin called "Ash Grove Hotel" was there. Inside they found a treat, cards of all the companies that had come through before them. They camped in the ash and cedar trees for the rest of the day.

T. 29th. To day we made coal and repaired our waggons which by this time began to get out of repair.

David and Hannah stayed in Ash Hollow. They had been making good time but the wagons were wearing out. They took time out to make necessary repairs to their wagons.

Constant use over the last couple of months was wearing on the wagons. The wheels dried out in the dry air. Tires rolled off wheels, spokes pulled out of the hubs and brittle wagon tongues snapped.

Regular maintenance of the wagons in hot dry country required that the wooden wheels be taken off wagons and placed in creeks or rivers when water was available. The water made the spokes swell and tighten so they would not fall apart. Even so, the weather was hot and dry and the wheels dried out fast. Also the steel wagon tires had to be repaired quite often.

James Harty was not happy with his wagon. He had been stuck with a bad wagon and he complained to his folks back home that he was repairing a half-made wagon. He cautioned relatives following him that Mr. Nutt made wagons inferior to most. (JNH)

Some History of Ash Hollow

There are two incidents that happened at Ash Hollow that ought to be remembered now. Old Ignace, the persistent Nez Perce who came to St. Louis in search of the "White Man's Book of Heaven," was ambushed here by a band of Brule Sioux. He was returning to Oregon from his second St. Louis trip in 1837 with another Nez Perce and three Flathead companions when he lost his scalp. (GMF)

Earlier, in 1837, a companion of Dr. Marcus Whitman was escorting six "civilized" Indians back east. They came upon the Brule Sioux, maybe the same band. They said through a white companion that they wanted no white blood but they were behind on their quota of Flathead scalps. While the escort and the interpreter were talking it over, the Sioux killed all of the Flathead Indians. Without regard to the escort's self-righteous diary to the contrary, experienced men of the West knew what had happened. The escort had traded Indian lives, the lives of his friends, converts and parishioners, to save his own scalp. (GMF)

Up North Platte

W. 30th. Traveled over a very sandy road. Poor grass and no wood but buffalo sedament.

July 1st. To day we still found the roads still sandy. Distance about 15 miles.

The emigrants camped near McCulligan Butte across the river from Oshkosh on June 30, 1847, and across from Lisco on July 1, 1847.

The country was poor and sandy. It had

the appearance of being formed by the wind blowing out the sand into basins, some of which were left forty feet deep.

Buffalo Country

Hugh Cosgrove, traveling with the one hundred fourteen wagon Lot Whitcomb Company in 1847, said that their wagon train encountered a vast herd of buffalo that bore down on the caravan. It divided before reaching the wagons and passed on both sides of the caravan. It took four hours for the buffalo to pass.

Mr. Cosgrove also reported that wolves were plentiful at the time. He had two greyhounds that could overtake an antelope. They could overtake wolves too, but the dogs soon learned to leave the wolves alone. The dogs were chased back even more ferociously than they attacked the wolves.

A travel associate said that the greyhounds chased the wolves over a hill out of sight. The dogs returned even faster, with the wolves in pursuit.

Beautiful Scenery

F. 2nd. Moved finely along. came in sight of two noted works of nature, Castle Rock and Chimney Rock. Roads yet sandy. About 6 miles back we passed a fine creek and soon a fine spring.

S. 3rd. Continued up Platt. Found the roads good. Crossed another creek the ? ? ? of which is bout 100 ft. wide. Nooned at or opposite Castle Rock. It looks 1-1/2 or 2 Miles from the road and yet it is said to be five miles. This deception is owing to the purity of the air and want of objects by which to judge distances.

The Davises continued up the Platte River. They had good roads. The Davises stopped for their noon meal on a creek three miles southeast of Bridgeport on July 3rd. Court House Rock and Jail House Rock (shown as Roudhouse Rock on USGS maps) were about six miles to the southwest. The famous rock was five miles from the road but looked as if it was only two miles away. This deception was due to the purity of the air and lack of things to compare distances.

Court House Rock, reminded some emigrants of pictures they had seen of the Capitol in Washington, D. C. Others said Court House Rock was named because it resembled the Court House in St. Louis at that time. However, Court House Rock had the name before the Court House in St. Louis was started in 1845. Court House Rock and Jail House Rock are about five miles south of Bridgeport.

The company camped at the Jackson Panorama Site (see W. H. Jackson's panorama herein) almost five miles east of Chimney Rock on July 3, 1847.

A Fourth Of July Picnic

*Sun. 4th. Upon this Columbus natal day we passed the towering and interesting natural object. * * * * This is said by some to be 250 ft. high. I ascended it to the 2nd bench. Nooned here. Distance 10 miles.*

David and Hannah Davis passed Chimney Rock on the Fourth of July. Chimney Rock was said by some to be two hundred fifty feet tall and about a mile and a quarter off the Oregon Trail. It was a great attraction to the early emigrants. Many early diarists reflect that a large percentage of the emigrants, men, women, girls, and boys, visited Chimney Rock. The level to which the young men could climb reflected on their ego and gave them something to brag about.

Courthouse Rock

Photo by Shann Rupp

Chimney Rock

Photo by Shann Rupp

Lester Hulin, some of the older Davises, and others, climbed to the second bench and had a fourth of July Picnic. They earned their bragging rights on July 4, 1847.

Virgil Pringle said Chimney Rock might pass for one of the foundries in St. Louis, were it blackened by burning of stone coal.

They passed other romantic scenery, Castle Rock, a most beautiful place in the meadow of a tributary of the Platte. Castle Rock has a strong resemblance to a real castle of ancient times.

Even though Chimney Rock has lost height, Chimney Rock, Court House Rock, and Castle Rock remain among the best known tourist attractions today as much as they did in the time of our forefathers. Many postcard size pictures of Chimney Rock are sold tourists. It is background for many commercial advertising promotions.

The Oskaloosa Company camped near Melbeta on the river on July 4, 1847.

M. 5th. To day we gradually re-

Approaching Chimney Rock
Painting by William H. Jackson, Scott's Bluff National Monument

ceded from the river in order to pass up behind Scotts Bluffs. Follow up a broad valley and about 16 miles found us at the spring near the gap in the bluffs. Camped here without grass for our animals.

T. 6th. Made an early start. By sun up we were on our road. Passed down another valley. Roads being fine, we soon found ourselves on Horse Creek. 12 miles here by passing down toward the river we found grass and good spring water.

Oskaloosa Company passed behind Scott's Bluff, possibly following the old Oregon Trail camping near Mitchell Pass, west of Gering. However, Lester Hulin's note on July 6th where it says that they "*found ourselves on Horse Creek * * * * by passing (12 miles) down toward the river*" indicates the more southern route to Robidoux Pass was followed. Either way they would have traveled in Gering Valley surrounded by historic Scott's Bluffs. The name of the southern pass was not known. Robidoux Trading Post was not established there until 1849.

They camped near the later site of Robidoux Trading Post just east of Robidoux Pass on July 5, 1847. The next day they camped on Horse Creek near Lyman, Nebraska just east of the Wyoming State Line.

A Look Into The Future

Horse Creek was later, in September 1851, to become the place where more than ten thousand Indians; Arapaho, Cheyenne, Sioux and nine other nations held the largest council ever held.

The council was held on the west side of Horse Creek and the south bank of the Platte River. The Indians agreed to cease their depredations on the trail. The whites agreed to respect the tribal boundaries and pay annual fees for crossing Indian lands. The Indians accepted the gifts from the Great White Father and went on home. (GMF)

From Nebraska Into Wyoming

W. 7th. Left Horse Creek. Crossed points of bluffs, sometimes sandy and sometimes good roads. Passed a very large spring and camped on the river. Grass not good.

The emigrants crossed the present border from Nebraska into Wyoming three or four miles after breaking camp and traveled up North Platte River. They camped across the river from Lingle, Wyoming.

Cholera - The Unseen Destroyer

Cholera took more of a toll along this stretch of the Oregon Trail than anywhere else along the trail. Oscar Hyde, in the edition of the *Frontier Guardian* dated May 2, 1850, said that he had counted as many as five hundred graves along the North Platte east of Fort Laramie. "Sickness" lasted usually but a day. Many beds and blankets were abandoned by the roadside. No person, not even an Indian, dared to touch them for fear of the unknown, unseen destroyer. (GMF)

T. 8th. Having good roads today. We soon found ourselves within 3 miles of Mt. Laramie. Camped here. Grass very poor.

Indians Require Tolls At Laramie

F. 9th. To day we moved on across Laramies Fork (this is a fine stream) taking the right hand road, we passed up Platt about 3 miles and camped.

S. 10th. All day in camp. Somewhat troubled by our Sioux visitors which we met yesterday and gave presents.

An old Indian Chief came into camp with many of his Indians. He boasted that his people had never taken white blood, nor were they thieves in general. However, there were some bad Indians in his tribe that would steal. He said that while we stayed there and anything was stolen by his people to let him know and he would punish them.

He also said that his people expected presents from the emigrants passing through his county. They spread out robes on the ground and the emigrants gave them provisions such as salt, flour and bread. All emigrants resented this because they were giving up provisions that they could ill afford. They resented it even more when they were without provisions near the end of their journey and throughout the following winter. Many emigrants lost their lives when they ran out of provisions.

This should have been resolved at Horse Creek when the Indians agreed to cease their depredations on the trail and the United States government agreed to respect the tribal boundaries and pay annual fees for crossing Indian lands.

The treaty may have worked except when an Indian stole and killed an emigrant's cow, the Indian Chief claimed a higher responsibility to protect the Indian than his responsibility to honor the treaty and refused to produce the thief. A Second Lieutenant overacted in his search for the thief by shooting up suspected hiding places. The Indians also overreacted and overran the fort when they realized they had broken the treaty and that the annual fees would probably not be paid.

Fort Laramie

David and Hannah Davis stayed at Fort

Fort Laramie

Painting by William H. Jackson, Scott's Bluff National Monument

Laramie on July 10th. The Sioux Indians that came into camp July 9th were still hanging around. Chester Ingersol found about three thousand Sioux camped around the Fort on June 23, 1847, waiting to tie into the Crows.

There were only forty white civilians stationed at the fort. Fort John was the trading post operated by the American Fur Company at Fort Laramie. Pierre Chouteau was the owner in 1847.

The emigrants were disturbed when they found out here were no army troops at Fort Laramie. They found no consolation in the Indians being much more interested in fighting other Indians than in fighting the white men. Indian tribes had been at each other's throats for many moons.

United States troops were not stationed anywhere along The Oregon Trail, The California Trail or the Scott-Applegate Trail in 1847. So-called "Forts" were merely civilian trading posts established to trade with trappers and Indians. Most were trading posts established by the British west of the Rocky Mountains. Two exceptions were Ft. Bridger established in California and Ft. John at Laramie established in the Louisiana Territory. Both were established and operated by Americans. Fort Hall was established by an American, Nathaniel Wyeth. It was in British hands in 1847.

The U. S. Army authorized the purchase of Fort Laramie in 1848. Lt. Daniel Woodbury, Corps of Engineers, negotiated the purchase of the fort for four thousand dollars. The deal was completed on June 26, 1849. Two officers and sixty enlisted men occupied the fort. Fifty-five more men moved in on August 12th. (GMF)

There were groups of United States troops passing along the trail during 1847. Those troops that were mentioned in 1847 writings were transitory travelers like the emigrants themselves. Most were traveling from California back to the "United States" after the end of the Mexican War.

Sun. 11th. To day after a late start

we passed up Platt on the bottom. Found some good grass and camped 1/2 mile below good springs.

They camped a few miles southwest of present day Guernsey, Wyoming, near the National Historic Landmark where deep wagon ruts are cut in the sandstone.

Lost Cattle Found

M. 12th. This morning through remissness of guards or carelessness of Company, about 1/2 of our cattle were gone which we did not succeed in finding all until afternoon when it was too late to make another camping ground. So we were obliged to lay in camp. We employed ourselves part of the day in making some new officers and regulating matters so that we might have things go straight another time. Day cool.

One of the worst scares of the entire trip happened southeast of Guernsey, Nebraska. Through negligence of guards or carelessness of the company, about half of the cattle were gone. They did not succeed in finding them until after noon.

This was a bad spot for straying cattle. Virgil Pringle reported that his Company was detained the morning of Friday, June 26, 1846, hunting lost cattle at about this location. Elizabeth Dixon Smith Geer also reported a similar incident, but that was before they reached Ft. Laramie. See the June 24th entry.

David D. Davis Elected Captain - Again

It was too late to travel so the company went to the business of electing some new officers and regulating matters to assure proper security in the future. Lester Hulin does not name the new officers. However "making some new officers and regulating matters" indicates that new positions were created and filled. Peter Crawford mentioned guards sleeping on duty, so the company must have taken a strong stand regulating the conduct of guards. (HHH) (JNH)

James N. Harty is more direct. He identifies "D. D. Davis" as being elected Captain in a letter home.

> *"We passed smoothly along for several days, nothing worthy of notice taking place, except the organization of our Co. which terminated in the election of D. D. Davis Capt. of Green Bay (Township), Lee Co., Iowa."*

The David D. Davis family had seven wagons and was traveling with the same wagon train as Lester Hulin and James N. Harty.

Peter W. Crawford earlier identifies "Davis" as Captain of the Oskaloosa Company early in the journey:

> *"After crossing the Miniahaws we overtake other trains of wagons who are anxious to double up so we form a company with Ascaloousa (Oskaloosa) Company, Davis Captain, sixty wagons strong in all."*

Both J. N. Harty and Peter W. Crawford were contemporary writers writing about different events taking place with the same wagon train. Both say that "Davis" or "D. D. Davis" was, or was elected, Captain.

T. 13th. This morning we left Platt and wound our way among the hills and valleys for about three miles. Past warm springs and soon was on the big road again. For the first two or three miles we had a rough hilly road. It then grew better, running over high ridges and about 8 miles from W Spring brought us to Bitter Cottonwood creek. We passed up this creek about 3 miles and camped. Good Spring water, tolerable grass for this country and wood pleanty. Distance about 14 miles..

In 1847 the Oregon Trail went overland from Guernsey to near Glenrock, Wyoming. The Oskaloosa Company made the overland journey in about five days. They camped on Cottonwood Creek the first night.

W. 14. Marched up B Cotton Wood about 5 miles, then turned off N by W. We followed up dry fork 8 miles to a spring. This spring is nearly dry. Camped here. Distance to day 13 miles.

T. 15th. Left this dry and baren campment early and six miles brought us to Horseshoe Creek. This part of our road was rough, hilly, crooked and dry, and at H Shoe we found a fine spring. Stoped here an hour, then rolling on we crossed two or three branches with wood and some grass and water. Tolerable camping might be found here. We camped at the third. Distance 14 miles.

F. 16th. To day we traveled over a hilly, though, very good road and in 10 miles came to Rock Creek. The after noon being rainy we camped here.

The Oskaloosa probably camped on Crow Creek on August 14, 1847. They crossed Horse Shoe Creek near the Platte-Converse County Line on the 15th and camped on Trail Creek.

At least some of the 1846 emigrants followed this trail through the Black Hills. Virgil Pringle recorded crossing the Black Hills in 1846:

"Wednesday, June 24, (1846)— Traveled about 9 miles and intersected the old road at the spring which is very bold and rather warm (Warm Spring at Gurnsey). We now enter the Black Hills. Rose from a valley onto high rolling prairie. Went 6 miles from the spring and encamped on the banks of a clear mountain stream (Cottonwood Creek).

"Thursday, June 25 – Our course in the fore part of the day was up the aforesaid creek. Passed a large, fine spring about 10 o'clock, and timber plenty on the creek consisting of cottonwood, box, willow, choke-cherry and ash. Passed over the highlands towards another creek. Camped at a small spring 14 miles (from) last encampment.

"Friday, June 26. – Detained this morning hunting cattle till 10 o'clock. Went to a bold running creek (Horseshoe creek) to noon. Passed over the hardest pulling hill we have had on our route to a small branch of spring water and camped. 8 miles.

"Saturday, June 27. – Traveled this day 12 miles over hilly and rock road. 12 miles

"Sunday, June 28. – Traveled 20 miles and camped in sight of the Platte at a spring. (Edited)

Later, the Oregon Trail may have taken a route a few miles to the right of the old 1846 -1847 Oregon Trail.

Buffalo Hunt

The way Indians hunt buffalo was most interesting. First the hunters took pride in their buffalo horses. A buffalo horse had to be exceptionally fast and fearless. Fleetness of foot was necessary to overtake the intended victim. The Indian hunter would run his horse until the toe of his moccasin touched the rear of the fleeing buffalo. Then from the back of his running horse, the Indian would shoot a heavy arrow into the flank. The arrow was directed to range forward, through the vital organs of the buffalo. The horse was trained to put on a burst of speed when the arrow was released. Increased speed was needed to pass the buffalo and get out of its way. If the arrow did not hit a vital spot, the furious buffalo would charge both horse and rider. (HHH)

Peter Crawford, A Fine Brood Mare, And A Wounded Buffalo

(Peter Crawford's words, paraphrased.)

The McKee wagon train was headed for Oregon along The Oregon Trail in the summer of 1847. Peter W. Crawford was bullwhacking for George Cline.

The wagon train was traveling up the North Platte River nearing Independence Rock. Early one morning the night guard awakened the camp with the news that a herd of straggling buffalo was within sight. Abe Peak, Peter Crawford and another young man from another camp moved around the herd so they would not to be seen.

They approached the herd and the three fired simultaneously. They wounded one of the animals. The rest of the herd took off. The wounded animal could only move slowly and went in a different direction than the rest of the herd. Abe Peak and Peter Crawford followed at a distance.

Peter Crawford loaded his yaugar again. His yaugar carried a half ounce ball. He broke his ram rod while loading the gun. Abe Peak was not a young man and was getting tired so he turned back. Only Peter Crawford continued following the wounded animal, following it into a small valley.

Crawford crossed the canyon and moved up on the other side of the buffalo. The buffalo stood still. He took aim at his lights but may have been out of range. The shot was probably low but the animal fell. He tried to load again because he was eager to kill the buffalo. But he had broken his ram rod and could not find a stick to pack the load down with.

Crawford laid his gun on the ground and rushed down to the wounded buffalo. He was lying down groaning. There was no butcher knife to cut the animal's throat but Crawford wanted to finish him off before leaving to go for help. He picked up the largest round boulder he could lift. He threw it on the animal's head with all the force he could muster. The blow brought the animal back to life, or to his senses. He opened his great wide eyes and looked at Crawford. Crawford retreated, went back for his gun and stood looking at the animal. The buffalo lay down again. Crawford wondered what he could do with a dead buffalo way out here away from any help or transportation.

He ran for camp as fast as his legs would carry him. It was getting late for starting. However, he had become so involved with the wounded buffalo that the thought of breakfast had never entered his mind. He ran high up on a rolling hill so he could see the lay of the country. Then he shot off for camp the closest way he could guess.

The wagon train was packed up and ready to start when Peter Crawford arrived back at camp. He told them of his adventure. Mr. Cline, Crawford's boss, thought that the animal would surely die and that the wagons needed grease and the emigrants needed meat. The guide said that this would probably be the last buffalo they would see.

Peter Crawford ate a hurried breakfast while one of Cline's boys hitched up and drove his team. Crawford saddled up with the American saddle. He showed Abe Peak, the guide and Cline's stepson the way back over the rolling high sand hills.

The buffalo was sitting up like a hog on his hind quarters when they first saw him. They talked it over. Crawford offered Abe Peak his trusty old yaugar. Abe Peak preferred his own rifle and told Crawford to ride down the hill to the buffalo trail in the valley. If the buffalo started down the old buffalo trail, Crawford was to scare him back.

They went for the kill. Crawford on the old mare holding on to the old American saddle the best he could. It had no cinch or surcingle. Abe Peak got across the hollow and pricked the animal with a small rifle ball. That made the animal kick a little but only enraged him more. He headed down the hill.

Crawford had stopped the mare on the buffalo trail, turned her head towards the buffalo that had already started the charge towards them. He tried to get the old mare turned up the hill but he had no whip, no stick, no spur — nothing but the reins of an old bridle to steer the horse in the right direction.

The mare eyed the huge black shaggy old ferocious buffalo. The buffalo eyed the mare and Crawford. Crawford was sure the charging buffalo knew he was the same chap he had in his large red eyes a few hours before.

Without ceremonies of any kind the animal came like a rush of a big wind. The buffalo came like a locomotive rather than an animal, running his head under the mare's flank trying to run Crawford's legs through the mare. He sent the mare end over end before you could say Jack Robinson, or anything else. The buffalo never stopped or stayed his pace — on he went.

Crawford went into the air holding on to the saddle, not knowing which came down first. Crawford was thrown on his back over the mare's head. She, in her fright trying to get to her feet, kicked Crawford in the chin with one forefoot, and in the chest with the other forefoot. The first thing he thought of was the buffalo, where he was and what his next intentions were.

Looking down the trail, he saw the animal in the distance, by itself, alone, walking leisurely away. Crawford all the while had fears of his returning and taking revenge on him while he was down, or going after the wounded mare.

Looking up the hill Crawford saw that the mare was headed for camp whickering as she went. Crawford went after the old mare with the saddle upon his back.

The mare had a large piece of hide cut and flesh torn out of her flank about 8 inches by ten inches. Crawford caught the mare and headed for the road and wagon train. He was really mortified when he reached the train that was behind his train. He borrowed a needle. There were plenty of buckskin needles, everyone had one. With the buckskin needle and some silk thread, he stitched up the wound. He poured spirits of turpentine into the wound to disinfect it and led the old mare on to their own train.

He wondered what Cline would say about his fine brood mare. Cline expected to make part of a fortune breeding her in Oregon. The wagon train camped that night near Independence Rock. Cline was very much out of humor about the old mare.

Peter W. Crawford promised himself that would be the last buffalo meat he would go after with any body else's mare.

Over The Hills From Rock Creek

S. 17th. Left Rock Creek. Upon starting, passed over the hills and in about 3 miles came to Cotton Wood Fork. Passed this and one or two branches and camped on the branch near a creek. This creek, we have been informed, is Table Fork, a fine creek affording pleanty of water.

Sun. 18th. In about one mile we crossed Table Fork. In about 3 miles more we crossed a small stream. Nooned on the hill and passing on, we in about 2 miles, came to a fine clear stream and in about 3 miles farther, came to

Mark Head Fork. This is a good sized stream and afording good camping. From here, 6 miles brought us to Platt. Up Platt about 4 miles we camped, turned our animals over the river, found good grazing.

The Oskaloosa Company returned to the Platte River on August 18, 1847. They camped near Glenrock, Wyoming.

M. 19th. Upon leaving camp, in about 1 mile we passed Deer Creek. Passed up the river about 14 miles and camped on a fine stream of water. Good grass but little wood.

T. 20th. Crossed the stream on which we camped and continued to coast along up the river passing one or two small streams and camped about 2 miles above the Mormon Ferry at what I shall call Cotton Wood Grove, a fine place. Distance about 14 miles.

W. 21st. This day we passed up the river about 3 miles, came to the ford, crossed and camped for the day. Grass short.

The Davises marched up North Platte River and camped on Muddy Creek on August 19, 1847, and across from Casper on the 20th. Their camp was two miles above the ferry Brigham Young established during his trek to found Salt Lake City in 1847. The first ferry was his leather boat.

T. 22nd. Left Platt and also left a co. of travelers from Oregon. Some like the country, others did not. Pursued our way along the road. About 5 P.M. came to the Red Butte spring. This would be a fine camping ground if it had wood. Distance 12 miles.

F. 23rd. Left the Red Butt Camp and pursued our way over very good roads. Passed about noon what I should call the Chinese wall. About one mile from this, we came to the soap mine. A place so marshy that it is dangerous for man or beast to go in it. In about 5 miles we came to the Willow Spring. This a good camping ground for a small co. but large Co's had better divide and part camp about 1-1/2 miles from this before we get here. Distance to day 15 miles.

The Company camped at Red Buttes on July 22nd. The Sweetwater was a beautiful and unspoiled country. Cattle caused a lot of trouble by venturing into deceptive banks. The marsh land looked stable. However, it was underlayed with a type of quick sand and many of the cattle became mired down. This made fast and heavy work necessary. Unless they could be gotten out in a short time, they gave up and refused to try to help themselves. They waited for whatever fate might have in store for them. (HHH)

S. 24th. Left the Willow Spring and going over the hills we, in about 4 miles, came to very fine creek. This small creek on our left affords very good camping ground. Passed on about 6 miles farther and camped on Horse Creek.

Sun. 25th. Left this creek. Pursued our way over sandy roads and in 10 miles came to Independence Rock on Sweet Water. This rock bears the names of many travelers. We crossed Sweettwater. Passed up six miles to a pass of the river through the rock called the Devils Gate. The bluffs tower up on each side for 3 to 5 hundred feet. Good grass and water.

Independence Rock, Sweetwater River, and Captain Fremont

The name "Independence Rock" is believed to have been given by Tom Fitzpatrick. He was a new principal of the Rocky Mountain Fur Company. He cached his furs here on July 4, 1824.

John Charles Fremont may have lost his bid for the Presidency of the United States because he left his mark on Independence Rock. Fremont, while returning from one of his many trips exploring the West, committed an act that some say cost him the presidency. Fremont's highly circulated "Report to Congress" contains this quotation: "*Among the thickly engraved names I made on the hard granite the impression of a large cross, which I covered with a black preparation of India rubber, well calculated to resist the influence of wind and rain.*" Many of the electorate considered this a popish act. Dynamite took the cross away some years later, but it was too late. History records that Fremont lost in his bid for the presidency in 1856. (GMF)

David and Hannah Davis met and passed General Stephen Watts Kearney and his escort going down the Sweetwater River to the United States within a few miles of Independence Rock. They were returning to the United States from California at the end of the Mexican War. Captain John Charles Fremont was with General Kearney. He was being returned to Leavenworth under arrest for disobeying orders in California. He went on to become

Night Corral at Independence Rock

Painting by William H. Jackson, Scott's Bluff National Monument

a General and a candidate for President of the United States.

David and Hannah Davis kept going. They crossed the Sweetwater near Independence Rock, then up about six miles to where the river runs through the rock called the Devil's Gate. The bluffs tower up on each side from three hundred feet to five hundred feet.

Emigrants Abandon Effects to Lighten Loads

Many emigrants cut down or lightened their loads along a grade up the Sweetwater River. They left everything they thought unnecessary. It was a long haul up the Sweetwater although they did not perceive the ascent to be steep. Still, they could see when looking back that they were gaining altitude fast. Peter W. Crawford reported that Mr. Davis was compelled to leave and abandon his mill stones. (PWC)

Oskaloosa Company Divides At Devil's Gate

M. 26th. Upon leaving this Devils Gate and having separated in small Co's, we started early and passed rapidly along considering the sandy roads to sepparate enough so we would not be oblige to camp together. Made 20 and some 23 miles and camped on Sweetwater. During the last two days we passed large ponds of saleratus and saltpeter. Both a curiosity and useful to travelers.

The Oskaloosa Company separated into two or three smaller Companies near Devil's Gate the previous evening so they could camp at different places in smaller camp grounds.

Small companies were needed so they could move faster. Also they would fit into the smaller camp grounds that lay ahead. Lester Hulin and the David and Hannah Davis family probably were in the same small company. Lester Hulin's journal entry Friday, September 24th shows that two companies kept in close contact and rejoined forces at that time. They may have been traveling as one company in two or three sections.

The Oren Belknap family, the Ransom Belknap family, the Watts family, the Samuel Fletcher Starr family, the L. D. Gilbert family, and six other wagons were in a second, or "other" company following the Davis company. (BCM)

They passed several ponds of saleratus (baking soda) and salt peter during the previous two days. One lake was said to contain Epsom salts. *"When the sun has evaporated the water and left good tasting Epsom salts."* (PWC)

T. 27th. Following up the river, we passed some grass and the roads sandy running away from the river. about 1 PM came to the river. Nooned. Passed up a gap, crossing and recrossing. Found good grass and camped behind a bluff on the river. Distance about 16 miles.

W. 28th. Left our beautiful camping place this morning. Followed up the river about 2 miles, crossed and saw no more of it for about 16 miles. When we again came to the river again but found the grass nearly eaten up by the thousands that have grazed there. Camped here having traveled 18 miles but called 20.

T. 29th. Crossed Sweet Water. Passed over the hill and down on the

Devil's Gate

Painting by William H. Jackson, Scott's Bluff National Monument

South Pass

Painting by William H. Jackson, Scott's Bluff National Monument

bottom again. Followed up about 6 miles and camped near another gap through the Mts.

F. 30th. To day we left the river and passed up the Mts. for several miles. Our road was much better than one would expect for an ascent of the Stony Mts. In about 14 miles crossed a branch of Sweetwater. In 2 miles crossed another and in about 4 miles, we turned off to the left and camped on Sweetwater. Distance to day 20 miles. A good drive for a Mt road, yet easier than many days in the sand.

The Oskaloosa Company crossed Sweetwater River at Devil's Gate. The company crossed three times on August 27th, once on the 28th, and again on the August 29, 1847. They crossed several branches of the Sweetwater on August 30th and camped on the river.

Continental Divide At South Pass Oskaloosa Company Enters Oregon Country

S. 31st. Upon leaving Sweet Water we gradually arose the Mt. For about 6 or 8 miles and then the descent was just perceptable and 12 miles from Sweet Water brought us to a green marshy place affording plenty of water but so miry cattle could not approach it with safety this is called the Pacific spring. The water runs to the western Ocean. From this spring we traveled 12 ms farther to Dry fork and camped almost without grass after a stride of 24 Ms across the south Pass. Dry Fork has some water in it now but goes dry sometimes. For the last 2 days Snowy Mts has been in sight and one of our Co found a drift in S. W. valley. Surely it seem strange to have snow in July and August.

The wagon train crossed and left the Sweetwater. They gradually went up the mountain for about six to eight miles to the South Pass on the Continental Divide. The place is called "the Continental Divide" because it divides the continent's watersheds, the east from the west. It is the summit of the Rocky Mountains. Looking back, they could see the wagons in the rear like small carts. They come wending their way serpentine winding up the long grade.

The emigrants had reached the South Pass. Gregory M. Franzwa described the pass:

> *"To the North is the end of the Wind River Range of mountains. To the South is Pacific Butte and the Antelope Hills. In between is the great saddle, 950 miles west of Independence and fully 29 miles across. Through this pass the suffering humanity that wrote the most dramatic chapter in American history. Over that slope the threads all came together forming an umbilical cord over the national spine to tie the West forever to the United States. A nation in its undying gratitude has marked it with two little rocks, neither of them so much as three feet high, and both placed by private citizens at their own expense. The USA has ignored it completely on highway maps and left access only to those who don't mind driving their cars over craggy sage and wretched roadways."* (GMF)

The emigrants seldom stopped at the pass. They knew fresh water was only a couple of miles away at Pacific Springs. They wanted to see what water looked like that was to flow to the Pacific Ocean. All of the water that they had seen before flowed east into the Atlantic Ocean. (GMF)

Also, the emigrants were leaving their home back east in the United States and entering into a new adventure that would last them a lifetime, a new life in a new land — Oregon Country.

The treaty of 1818 with Britain established United States possession as far west as the summit of the Rocky Mountains at this continental divide. Sovereignty over the Oregon County ahead was still in dispute with Britain. It was not resolved until congress ratified the treaty with Great Britain in 1846.

One reason for the South Road Company's expedition to find the southern route to the Willamette Valley was to find a way of escape for United States citizens in case of war with Britain. The other reason was to provide another route to move more settlers into the southern Willamette Valley to reinforce those already there in event of war.

Ft. Vancouver, Ft. Hall and other forts west along the Oregon Trail were British. The United States Senate was still undecided whether to ratify the treaty with Britain or to fight for fifty-four degrees forty minutes north latitude. Congress ratified the treaty with Britain and accepted Oregon as a Territory on August 14, 1848.

The descent from the South Pass was barely perceptible. Pacific Spring was twelve miles from the Sweet Water River. There the water runs to the western ocean.

For the last two days snowy mountains have been in sight and one man in the company found a drift in the valley. Surely it seemed strange to have snow in July and August.

Parting Of The Ways

Sun. August 1st. Left Dry Fork. Pursued our way over good roads and crosing Little Sandy, we camped about one mile below the ford. Distance 15 miles, grass & water good, no wood but willow.

Between dry fork and Little Sandy we passed the forks of the road, one leading to Ft. Hall and the other to Ft. Bridger.

Oskaloosa Company left Dry Fork over good roads. They passed the forks of the roads, both branches leading to Fort Hall. The one known as the Oregon Trail went south through Fort Bridger, then turned north and northwest to Fort Hall. The other was Sublette's Cutoff that continued west in a more direct route but over a rugged mountain range to join the Oregon Trail on Bear River. Oskaloosa Company took the fork south to Ft. Bridger.

Sublette's Cutoff led westerly through mountainous country. Part of it was known as the long drive. It then went over the Bear River Mountains. The passage from the top of Bear River Mountain to Bear River was known as the Beaver's Slide.

The Davises crossed the Little Sandy and camped about one mile below the ford. They had traveled fifteen miles to good grass and water. There was no wood there except willow.

M. 2nd. This morning we left Little Sandy and having good roads, by 11 A.M. we were at Big Sandy. A distance of 8 miles. Crossed this, watered and in one hour nooned. Then rolled on about 15 miles and found the road approached the river at a place where we found good feed. Camped here.

Distance 23 or 24 miles.

7. 3rd. Left camp about 8 o'clock. About noon arrived at Green River. This is a clean cool and rapid stream. Had but little trouble in crossing. Passed down it about 4 miles and camped. Distance to day about 12 miles.

The wagon train left camp at eight o'clock and arrived at Green River about noon. The river was clean, cool and fast but they forded the river without trouble. The forty-second parallel between Oregon Country and California is about here. Green River is part of the great Colorado River system.

Rendezvous At Green River: Rocky Mountain Summit Fur Trade Show And Swap Meet

(JKT Pages 189-195)

Thomas Fitzpatrick, Nathan Wyeth and the men of the Rocky Mountain Fur Company were first to arrive at the "Rendezvous At Green River" on June 19, 1834. William Sublette, Captain Serre and other leaders, with their companies were there and the camp was crowded. James Anderson O'Neil, David D. Davis' future friend and (step)-son-in-law, was on his way to Oregon with Nathaniel Wyeth. Jason Lee and his mission were also traveling to Oregon with Nathaniel Wyeth.

Nez Perce, Shoshone Tribes, and Banneck Indians came in with furs and peltries they had collected during the previous winter and spring to trade for ammunition, trinkets, and "fire water." There were mountain men, French-Canadians, half-breeds, etc., as wild as the Indians with whom they constantly associated.

These people, with their obstreperous mirth, their whooping, and howling, and quarreling, added to the mounted Indians, who were constantly dashing into and through camp, yelling like fiends, the barking and baying of savage wolf-dogs, and the incessant cracking of rifles and carbines, rendered the camp a perfect bedlam. A more unpleasant situation could scarcely be conceived.

One had to listen constantly to the hiccoughing jargon of drunken traders, the sacre foutre of Frenchmen running wild, and the swearing and screaming of the Rocky Mountain Fur Company mcn, who were no less savage than the rest.

They were heated by the detestable liquor that circulated freely among them. Liquor was sold to the men at three dollars a pint. An inferior quality of tobacco that could be purchased back east for ten cents a pound was sold for two dollars. Independent mountain-men paid in beaver skins and buffalo robes. Company men had a charge made against their wages.

The pasture was rich with lots of good grass. It did the hearts of the men good to see the satisfaction and comfort of their poor horses. They were camped in a pretty little valley. The plain was surrounded on all sides by low bluffs of yellow clay. The deep clear water of the Siskadee (Green River) flowed nearby. Beyond, on every side, was a wide level prairie with some gigantic mountain peaks and conical buttes in the distance.

The river contained many large trout, some grayling, and a small narrow mouth white fish resembling herring. The fishermen were delighted that the fish could be taken on a hook baited with grasshoppers or minnows. Isaac Walton would have been in his glory there. He would not have needed the precautionary measures that he recommended in approach a trout stream because the fish were not shy. They were quick to take the bait.

Buffalo, antelope and elk were abundant so the people were eating well. They saw a new kind of game bird. It was a beautiful bird, the size of a half grown turkey, called the "cock of the plains." It traveled in flocks of fifteen or twenty. It was so tame that it approached within a few feet, running before horses like chickens. They shot a few of the grouse the first day but the men were disappointed because they were too strong and bitter to be eatable. After that, the cock of the plains was allowed to roam unmolested. The men were content to admire the beauty of its plumage and the grace and spirit of its attitudes.

William Slacum reported to President Jackson that goods of British manufacture were purchased by the American fur companies at various American seaports. Duty was paid when the foreign goods were brought into the United States. The American fur companies moved to goods overland at a high cost.

The Hudson's Bay Company began entering the American market at the rendezvous selling the same goods of British origin to Americans at reduced prices. The British monopoly was bringing the same goods to the rendezvous duty free and cheaper water transportation was used.

The investigator reported that the American companies were victims of the unfair business practice. (Slacum)

David D. Davis' future friend, James A. O'Neil left the "Rendezvous At Green River" on July 2, 1834. The Wyeth party was increased by about thirty Flathead and Nez Perce Indians headed for the Snake River with their families and dogs. The Indians wanted to avoid their enemies, the Blackfeet. (JKT)

The Oregon Trail crossed Green River about six miles northwest of James Town. The Fur Traders Rendezvous 1834 site was a few miles up the river.

W. 4th. In about 2 miles we left Green River. Then gradually arose for about 4 miles to the dividing ridge. Then descended most of the time until we arived at Blacks Fork. Here we camped. Good grass. Distance about 17 miles.

T. 5th. Left camp following up the river 2 or 3 miles. Then crossing the two forks, we traveled until about 5 P.M. before we came to it again. Here we camped on Black's Fork again. Distance about 16 miles.

F. 6th. Followed up Blks Fork. Crossed and recrossed. Then crossed a branch of the river and after a stretch of about 10 miles, came to Ft. Bridger and Camped. The whole distance from Laramie to Bridger is 409 miles.

S. 7th. Remained in camp today visited there &c.

Fort Bridger

Fort Bridger was a trading post founded by James Bridger and Louis Vasquez in 1843. It was built to trade with trappers in the area and emigrants traveling the Oregon Trail near Black's Fork. It consisted of one or two adobe buildings and a lot of wigwam type tents covered with matting, skins or rawhide.

James Bridger was operating the trading post, "holding down the fort," while David and Hannah Davis were there. Louis Vasquez was on a business trip to Fort Laramie and did not return until August 9, 1847.

James Bridger looked the part of a frontiersman, hunter, trapper, and trader. Mr. Bridger talked freely of California and claimed to be a citizen of California when David and Hannah Davis were there. He advised them that his trading post was in California. The Davises had crossed from Oregon Country into California Territory upon leaving camp the day before.

James Bridger was born in 1804 in Richmond, Virginia and moved to St. Louis as

Rendezvous at Green River

Painting by William H. Jackson, Scott's Bluff National Monument

a boy. He came west as a member of the Ashley-Henry Fur Company. He soon established his reputation as a trapper, trader and guide during the height of the beaver trapping era. James Bridger discovered the Great Salt Lake in 1824 or 1825 while seeking to determine the course of the Bear River. Despite his many exploits, James Bridger could neither read nor write.

The political history of the area was in turmoil in 1847. The first American emigrant wagon to enter California arrived there in 1826. Trading operations had been expanding over the next twenty years. Sentiment for annexation of the province by the United States was developing in California. A band of American settlers revolted against the Mexican government and seized the town of Sonoma on June 14, 1846.

The United States declared war on Mexico in May, 1846. On July 7,1846, John Drake Sloat, Commander of the Pacific Squadron of the United States Navy, ordered his crew to occupy Monterey and Yerba Buena. California was declared a Territory of the United States on August 15, 1846. John C. Fremont served in the land forces under Sloat. Many of the 1846 Emigrants to California volunteered to serve with Fremont. One emigrant, William Henry Russell, was a Major. Russell also served as Secretary of State for the new territory while Fremont served as California's first Governor. The terms of both Fremont and Russell were cut short when General Kearney arrested Fremont for disobeying his command in a political power struggle between the Army and Navy. General Kearney was taking Fremont back to the United States for courts martial when they passed the Oskaloosa Company on Sweetwater River two weeks before, about July 25, 1847.

The government of Mexico ceded California to the United States on February 2, 1848, after the Treaty of Guadalupe Hidalgo ended the Mexican War. That was six months after David and Hannah Davis passed through Fort Bridger with their family. (This short narration does not include all things involved in the Mexican War nor in the Guadalupe Hidalgo Treaty.)

Congress established the region made up of most of the present States of Nevada and Utah and the Southwest corner of Wyoming as the Territory of Utah on September 9, 1850. Brigham Young was then appointed the first Governor. This area around Fort Bridger that had been the extreme northeastern corner of Utah Territory became part of Wyoming when Wyoming was admitted to the Union as a State in 1890.

Sun. 8th. Left the fort. Our general course was N.W. over crooked, hilly, and rocky roads. In 8 miles we crossed Little Muddy. No camping ground here. In 9 miles more we came to Big Muddy. Up one mile found very good camping for the night. Distance 18 miles.

M. 9th. Followed up Big Muddy all day. Roads rough and hilly. Found very good camping in about 16 miles.

The Oskaloosa Company crossed Little Muddy Creek about eight miles after leaving Fort Bridger. They moved on another nine miles to Little Muddy Creek (Big Muddy) and moved up it another mile and camped on August 8, 1847.

They followed Little Muddy Creek for sixteen miles and camped near Chicken Creek about 18 miles southwest of Kemmerer, Wyoming on August 9, 1847.

Most of the road traveled over the Bear River divide west of The Hogback on the 8th and 9th retains wonderful pristine wagon ruts. About half are on Bureau of Land Management land, the balance on ranch roads. They should only be traveled by experienced backpackers and never alone. Some of the stream crossings are too deep even for four wheel drive high-slung vehicles.

Back Into Oregon Country

T. 10th. Upon leaving camp this morning we in about 2 miles passed 3 fine springs. Soon left Muddy. Then up a dry branch 4 miles to the divide across the Mt. Down a dry Branch again 4 miles to a spring. Still down to Bear River or to the valley, it being impassable for wagons. We were obliged to camp on a creek after following down the bottom 3 miles. No grass here but our cattle went to the river (where we might have went had it not been dark) and found grass. Roads rough and crooked. Distance 20 miles..

The Oskaloosa Company left camp on August 10, 1847. They passed three fine springs within two miles. They went four miles up a dry creek to the pass across the mountain. Then they marched four miles down a dry creek to a spring. They kept going down to Bear River or Bear River Valley until dark.

They camped on a creek near Beckwith. There was no grass here. The cattle found some on nearby Bear River. The roads were rough and crooked for the twenty miles traveled.

W. 11. Upon leaving camp this morning we passed down the river. In 2 miles found a very large spring. Followed it down over a very smooth bottom to the cut off road and camped. Distance 10 miles

Parting Of The Ways - Back Together

The Oskaloosa Company recrossed the

Old Fort Bridger

Painting by William H. Jackson, Harold Warp Pioneer Village Foundation

line, this time from California Territory into Oregon Country on August 11, 1847, a few miles before they camped at Sublette Creek south of Cokesville, Wyoming. The road from Beaver Slide and Sublette's Cutoff met the road from Fort Bridger here.

Some travelers thought they had traveled twenty-five miles farther by going through Fort Bridger than they would have traveled using Sublette's Cutoff. Others claim Sublette's Cutoff is fifty miles shorter. The cutoff is over very mountainous country and the twenty-five or fifty miles to go through Fort Bridger were considered well spent.

Marcus Whitman Sticks Jim Bridger

Gregory Franzwa cites an interesting aside about Dr. Marcus Whitman and James Bridger that happened just east of the Idaho-Wyoming border. In 1835, as many Nez Perce and Flathead Indians stood around,

> *"Dr. Whitman gave James Bridger a bullet to bite, rolled him over, sliced his back open and removed an iron arrowhead three inches long." It was a souvenir of his little altercation with the Blackfeet Indians in 1832. The gallery had applauded wildly as Dr. Whitman held up the blackened object, now covered with a tough cocoon of cartilage. Old Gabe stood up and tried to make like it did not hurt. Whitman marveled that the man had not died. 'Shucks Doc,' Bridger is reported to have said, 'yknow meat don't spile in the mountains.'"* (GMF)

7. 12th. Continued down this smooth bottom. In 12 miles we passed Miles camp. In 8 more we passed Smith's camp known as Peg Leg Smith. In about 5 miles more we camped on Bear River. Good grass, willow wood &c.

13th. Continued down this bottom about 3 miles to __________Fork. Crossed it. Turned up the Mts. In 4 miles came to Little creek again. Over Mts and in about 6 miles more descended into the Bear River Bottom. Followed down the bottom about 6 miles and camped on a fine stream.

Peg-Leg Smith

Gregory M. Franzwa reports:

> *"The fort consisted of four log cabins and some indian lodges. It was established with the idea of farming the fertile land of the Bear Valley."* (GMF)
>
> *"Smith was one of the legends of the Oregon Trail. He was a bona fide mountain man. He worked quietly and efficiently* * *. In the late 1820s he was forced to amputate his own leg, sealing up the arteries with a red hot bullet mold. In his younger days Smith became skillful at kidnapping Indian babies and younger children to sell as slaves to the Mexican trade."* (GMF)

The emigrants crossed the present Wyoming-Idaho State line at Bolder Junction and continued down Bear River and camped south of Wardboro on August 12, 1847. They camped on a fine stream. There were many huge mosquitoes at this camp. No one had ever seen them that large back in Iowa.

They continued down Bear River on the 13th and camped several miles from Bennington.

> *S. 14th. To day our roads were good and we soon made a distance called by Mountaineers, 18 miles. We crossed several very fine streams tumbling down from the Mts. At length we crossed one larger than the rest and camped at the foot of a hill. Good grass and water.*
>
> *Sun. 15th. Passing up the hill and down again, we were (going) along in sight of the river the rest of the day. In 8 miles passed a branch. In 7 more another fine stream. Just across this stream what are called the Soda Springs commence. There at the creek one hundred yds or less from the crossing below. I call the best though no great similarity to soda. The Steamboat Spring is about 3/4 of mile from the creek on the river bank. This night as well as one other of Bear River has been frosty.*

The Davises camped north of Nounan on the 14th and continued on to Soda Springs on the 15th.

Soda Springs were across the river from the Oregon Trail. Lester Hulin called Soda Springs the best but did not believe it contained soda. Steamboat Spring was about three-quarters of a mile from the creek on the river bank.

Tar Springs water tasted a little like tar. Soda Springs water tasted a little like soda. Steamboat Spring resembled the escaping of steam from a steamboat as it threw up a volume of water. At intervals it gets higher than at other times. The rise and fall seemed to be at regular intervals. It was considered one of the wonders of nature. Hannah Davis could make some bread with the water from a soda spring.

> *M. 16th. To day in about 4 miles we left Bear River. Turning to the right we passed up a broad valley about 14 miles and camped in the bottom of Fourtneth Creek. This is a broad and fertile valley. The grass being like a meadow but no timber. During the day about the middle we passed some very fine springs. One of them being a large and beautiful soda fountain.*

They left Bear River after traveling four miles. They passed Sheep Rock (now Soda Point) three miles west of Steamboat Spring.

Passed Hudspeth's Cutoff

The Bidwell-Bartleson party split earlier at Sheep Rock. Half the emigrants went on to Oregon and the rest took an agonizing trek south through the Idaho and Nevada deserts to California. No other wagon trains had used the Hudspeth Cut Off before David and Hannah Davis passed through.

T. 17th. Followed up Fourtneth about 10 miles. We left the creek and in the course of the after noon we passed several small but fertile valleys with good grass. Camped in one at a fine spring. Distance to day about 16 miles.

W. 18th. This morning is cloudy and about 9 A.M. we had a fine shower. Passed over hills and down valleys. In one long valley we found good grass or wild rye and a good spring. Continued down to a small creek and in about 6 miles came to Snake River. Distance today about 20 miles.

T. 19th. Followed down Snake River a piece, then to Black Foot Fork. Crossed and then crossing the plains in about 9 miles came to a creek within about 5 miles of the Fort Hall. Camped here. Pleanty of grass and water. The route came is 25 miles out of the way.

F. 20th. In 5 miles came to the fort. Drove below on Ross's Fork and camped and repaired waggons and done other business.

The emigrants camped south of Gay, Idaho on August 17, 1847, and on Ross Fork on the 18th. They followed Ross Fork westward. Then they crossed a plain. They camped on Jimmy Creek 5 miles from Fort Hall on August 19th. They moved past Fort Hall and camped on Ross Fork on the 20th.

Fort Hall

Fort Hall was in its dying days when David and Hannah Davis were there in 1847. Apparently Hudson's Bay Company had seen this operation as a dying cause for some time. The Fort had fallen into disrepair. Britain had given up all claim to the area the previous year and Oregon was on its way to becoming a Territory of the United States.

Captain Grant was Master of Fort Hall. Captain Grant had a full grown son. Peter W. Crawford was impressed by him. That was probably because they were both Scotch. Others found him to be overbearing and pompous.

Grant was a long-time employee of the Hudson's Bay Company. Grant and other Fort Hall employees were loyal to Britain. They were concerned with the increased American emigration into the Oregon Country — an area they considered British territory.

The British at Fort Hall had earned the reputation of trying to divert immigration away from the Oregon into California. They used any means they could. They exhorted the virtues of California, amplified the problems on the Oregon Trail, and played down the attributes of the Willamette Valley. They even resorted to outright lying.

The Trading Post was closed in 1849, soon after the Senate of the United States ratified the treaty.

The last bastion of British colonialism in the United States went with the death of Fort Hall. Now if we can only get them to quit referring to the United States as "The Colonies."

Nathaniel J. Wyeth Builds Fort Hall

(JKT Pages 211-231)

Nathan Wyeth and three others located an excellent site for Fort Hall on July 14, 1834. They killed a buffalo in the vicinity. The entire party was pleased when they arrived on the location the following day. The stock of dried meat was almost exhausted and they had been depending almost exclusively upon fish.

The fort was named for Henry Hall, a senior member of the firm furnishing financial backing. Most of the men went to work falling trees, making horse-pens and preparing various materials for the building. Others prepared to back-track to hunt meat for the camp.

The hunting party of twelve men rode out of camp on July 16th, 1834. They rode about sixty-four miles in two days before spotting a herd of buffalo. They killed four buffalo that day and cut one into thin slices and hung it on bushes to dry. The other three were cut and hung out to dry the next day.

The buffalo were plentiful and less suspicious of man than at other places. They frequently passed slowly along within a hundred yards of camp.

One evening John Kirk Townsend was able to shoot one between the eyes from a few feet away. The monster shook his head, pawed the ground, sprang into action with a roar and turned to escape. At that instant, the ball from Tounsend's second barrel penetrated his vital organs and the animal stretched out on the ground - dead. The first ball had penetrated the matted hair and skin on the buffalo's head. It was completely flattened against the skull without making even the smallest crack.

They started baling the meat in buffalo skins dried for that purpose on July 25, 1834. Each bale contained about a hundred pounds. Each of their twelve mules carried two bales. The men at Fort Hall were glad to eat again because they had been on short rations for several days.

There was a party of traders and Indians camped near the fort. Their lodges were of a conical form, composed of ten long poles. The lower ends are pointed and driven into the ground. The upper ends are blunt and drawn together at the top by thongs. Several dressed buffalo skins, sewed together, are stretched around the poles. A hole is left on one side to form the entrance.

Fort Hall looked great, the stockade was

Fort Hall

Painting by William H. Jackson, Harold Warp Pioneer Village Foundation

finished, two bastions had been erected, and the workmanship was good. The house was almost habitable and could be completed at leisure by those that would be left to operate the fort.

Nathan Wyeth's party left Fort Hall across the Snake River Desert on August 6th, 1834. James Anderson O'Neal, later to become David D. Davis' friend and (step)-son-in-law, was with them. (JKT)

Down Snake River

S. 21. Left Ft. Hall. Made 10 miles it being in the afternoon when started and camped on a branch of Snake River. Good Grass

The camp ground is now under the waters of American Falls Reservoir.

Sun. 22nd. Good bottom about one half the day. Then left the river and in about 18 miles camped on Little Fall Creek.

M. 23. Made about 12 miles and camped on Big Fall Creek. For the last 2 nights, grass was poor.

Onto The California Trail At Raft River

T. 24th. Pushed on over dusty roads and in about 12 miles came to Raft River. Passed up (Raft River) about 2 miles and camped.

David and Hannah Davis made the greatest commitment, short of starting the overland journey To Oregon, on August 24, 1847. They turned onto the California Trail at Raft River after traveling twenty miles. They went up Raft River, on the California Trail, two miles and camped.

CHAPTER 6

Oregon Trail's Southern Route

Introduction

The Southern Route To Oregon is the series of roads that emigrants used to emigrate from The United States to the southern Willamette Valley. Emigrants used the Oregon Trail, the California Trail, and the Scott-Applegate Trail to reach the Willamette Valley in 1846 and 1847. One wagon train led by Meadors Vanderpool and guided by Moses Harris also used a little known trail up Goose Creek from the Snake River to Pole Creek and the California Trail called Harris Cutoff.

The California Trail.

The South Road Company was formed from settlers in the Willamette Valley to find a route to leave the Willamette Valley if the border dispute between the United States and Britain erupted into a war. The new route would also be used to bring reinforcements and supplies into the Willamette Valley. The South Road Company settled on a route that included the section of the California Trail from the Snake River to a point on Mary's River. The junction where the California Trail turned south from the Oregon Trail was on Raft River about forty miles west of Fort Hall.

Most of the Oregon Trail migration continued down the Snake River to destinations in eastern Oregon, eastern Washington, Fort Vancouver, or into the northern Willamette Valley.

Some emigrants chose destinations in California and traveled down The California Trail. They went through southern Idaho into northwestern Utah, Nevada, across the Sierra Nevada Mountains, and into central California.

Levi Scott believed that most of Oregon's 1846 emigrants who heard about the new Southern Route turned on to the Southern Route.

Emigrant wagon trains bound for the southern Willamette Valley traveled the California Trail from the Snake River to a the "fork in the road" on Mary's River near present day Imlay, Nevada. The California Trail turned south and crossed Mary's River, the South Road continued westward.

1846 Emigrants Build Scott-Applegate Trail

The emigrants were faced with another six hundred miles of wilderness when they reached the "fork in the road". The first 1846 emigrants to arrive at the fork in the road were faced with another problem. There was no road. Although the South Road Company had carefully looked at the route, they had not made it passable for wagons or even blazed a trail. They did not even know where the road could be built.

The first 1846 emigrants that chose the Southern Route to Oregon built over five hundred miles of new road through the wilderness where no wagon had traveled before. They built road from the fork in the road on Mary's river to the Coast Fork of the Willamette River.

Wagons had penetrated the entire length of the Willamette Valley by the time the emigrants reached the Coast Fork the last part of November 1846. Settlers were moving in a few miles down the road at present day Eugene. One or two relief wagons met the emigrants at the foot of the Calapooya Mountains on the Coast Fork of the Willamette River

The portion of the Scott-Applegate Trail from the "forks in the road" at Humboldt River to Goose Lake became heavily traveled during the gold rush to California. The Lassen Trail to the Sacramento Valley in California turned off the Scott-Applegate Road south of Goose Lake. The Scott-Applegate Trail also took part in the gold rush days and settlement of Yreka Valley. Emigrants from the United States again traveled the road to settle in Oregon's Umpqua River and Rogue River Valleys, and in the Klamath Basin.

Emigrants reaching the Willamette Valley over the Scott-Applegate Trail after 1847 were few and far between. Few were recorded. Single wagons and small wagon trains may not have been recorded. The David D. Davis, Lester Hulin and Cornelius Hills wagon train with about twenty wagons was the last substantive wagon train to reach the Willamette Valley by the Southern Route.

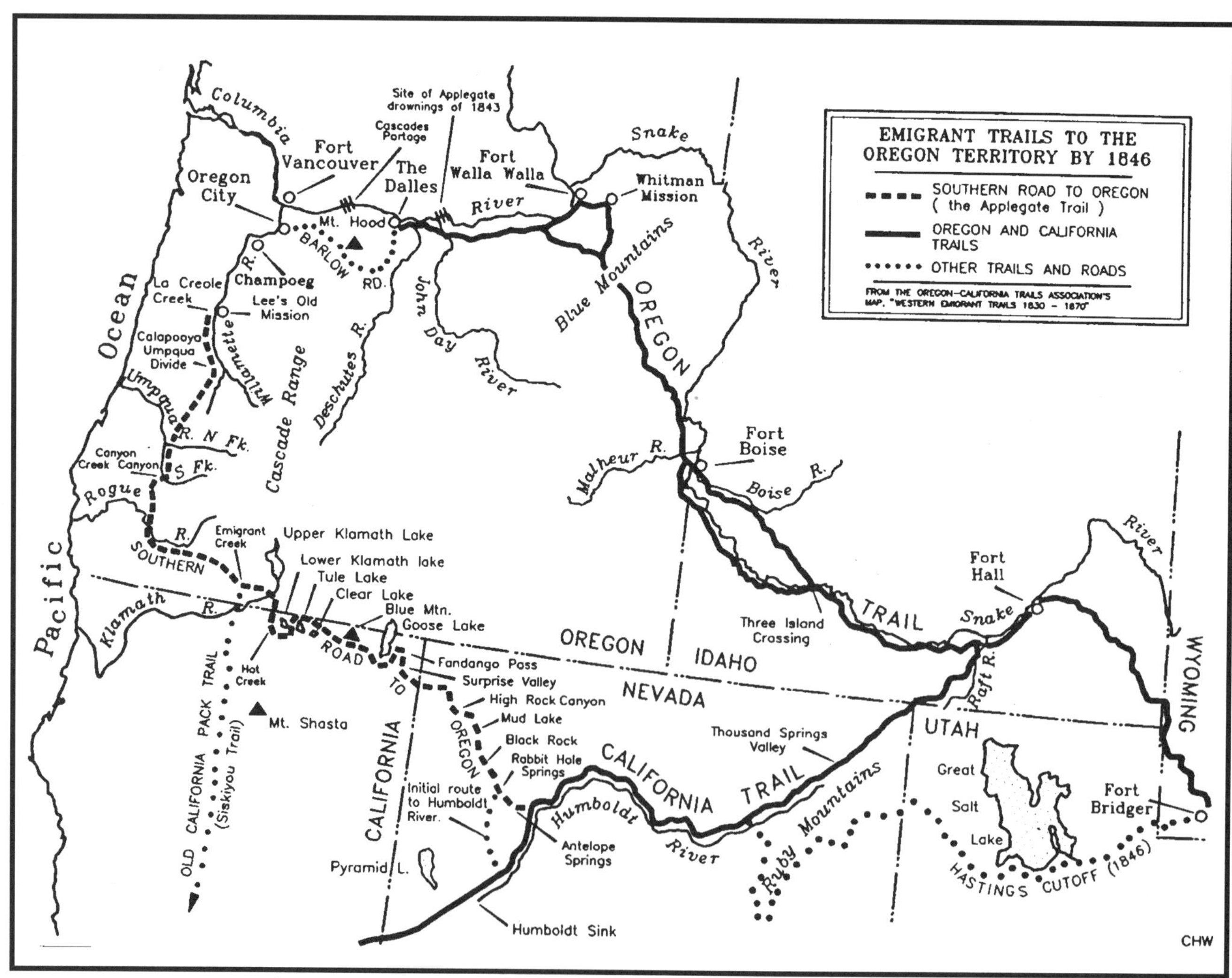

Courtesy of Overland Journal Vol. 11, Number 1, Page 3. Oregon California Trails Association

CHAPTER 7

The California Trail

T. 24th. Pushed on over dust roads and in about 12 miles came to Raft river. Passed up about 2 miles and camped.

David D. Davis turned The Oskaloosa Company, The Last Wagon Train To Skinners, off the Oregon Trail onto the California Trail at Raft River on September 24, 1847. The Oskaloosa Company continued two miles up Raft River on the California Trail before camping.

Lester Hulin was pilot of the Oskaloosa Company. He kept a daily record of the wagon train's progress along its overland journey to Oregon.

The Oregon Trail's new Southern Route to Oregon's Willamette Valley separated from the old trail on the Snake River at Raft River. The Southern Route followed the first four hundred miles of The California Trail to the

Traces Approaching Black Rock Desert

Photo by Shann Rupp

place where the Humboldt River turns from its westerly direction to south.

W. 25th. Continued up Raft River. Found good grass on the river in most places. Made about 12 miles and camped.

T. 26th. Followed up Raft Creek to the head, a distance of 16 miles. The whole distance up Raft Being 30 miles.

The Oskaloosa Company continued up Raft River on The California Trail. The emigrants camped near present day Keogh, Idaho, on August 24, 1847, and near Edward Creek the 25th.

F. 27th. Passed a divide into a valley afording plenty of grass and water. Nooned here. Continued on over a small creek, then up through a gap in the Mts. to a small valley with a spring branch in it. The whole presenting a very rocky appearance. Over another ridge or two, then into a broad dry valley. About the middle of this valley is good grass and about 1-1/2 miles above the road is water. We camped here after a drive of 20 miles.

Out of Oregon Country Into California Country

The wagon train left Raft River and passed through a divide into a valley with plenty of grass and water. Granite Pass is in Idaho but near the present day Idaho-Utah border on the 42nd parallel. They had lunch, then continued over a small creek, up through a gap in the mountains to a small valley with a spring and creek. They went over another ridge or two, into a broad dry valley. There was good grass in the middle of the valley and Birch Creek was about a mile and a half from the road, so they camped.

S. 28th. After crossing the valley we came to a spring. Made a halt here, then passed on over rough hilly roads to a spring branch. Then over to Goose creek. Up the same about 3 miles and camped. Distance to day 15 miles.

Cross Present State Line From Utah Into Nevada

The Davises crossed the valley to a spring and rested. They moved on over rough hilly roads to Pole Creek and a spring. Then they marched over to and up Goose Creek for three miles. They camped on Goose Creek after traveling fifteen miles.

Sun. 29th. Followed up Goose Creek about 14 miles and camped.

M. 30th. After following up Goose Creek about 3 miles we crossed and left it. Then we had very good hilly roads for 12 miles and no water during the 12 miles. Came to a spring branch and camped with tolerable grass and water. Distance to day 15 miles.

The Oskaloosa Company crossed over the divide to Rock Spring Creek on August 30, 1847 and camped near Texas Springs Canyon. The road was quite sideling through the area and the wagons were often in danger of being overturned. (JQT)(LH)

T. 31st. Left camp. Passed down the

branch and in 5 miles came to Horse Spring. Passed down a smooth valley 12 miles to Prairie Spring and camped. Distance to day 17 miles

The emigrants passed down Thousand Springs Valley and camped near Toano Creek on August 31, 1847.

Sept 1st, 1847. After leaving Prairie Spring, we found good water in 5 miles. Then passing some hot springs, we came to another small branch. Nooned here, then on to the bluff and camped at a spring in the bluffs. To day 15 miles. Good grass all day and water or small spring every little way.

The Oskaloosa Company marched down Thousand Springs Creek and up Brush Creek Draw. They camped at a spring in the mountains north of Melandco on September 1, 1847.

Mary's River

T. 2nd. Crossed over the divide. Then down to a creek. Followed down to a pass. Here we nooned. Then passed through this narrow horrible rocky pass about 2 miles long coming out into a level bottom with good grass. We camped on the creek we nooned on but it being enlarged by a warm spring, the water was disagreeable to drink until it cooled by standing in a vessel over night. Distance to day 12 miles.

The Oskaloosa Company crossed over the divide through a narrow horrible pass. They reached a level bottom with good grass at Cricket Creek where they nooned. They moved on to Bishop Creek and down it to Mary's River. Mary's River is now known as Humboldt River. They camped near present day Wells, Nevada on September 2, 1847. A warm spring fed the river. The water was disagreeable to drink until it was cooled by standing in a vessel overnight.

F. 3rd. Followed down this creek or Mary's River as it is called 12 miles & camped.

S. 4th. Continued down the river 20 miles and camped.

The Oskaloosa Company traveled down Mary's River and camped near Rasid on September 3, 1847. They crossed Mary's River to the south side on the 4th and camped near Elburz.

Sun. 5th. Last night these miserable root diggers took the liberty of driving off a couple of our cattle. I with 4 others hunted them up after a hard days drive and scaring one of the M diggers nearly to death. To day we made 15 miles.

Indians Rustle Cattle

Paiute Indians drove off a couple of head of Oskaloosa Company cattle during the early morning. Lester Hulin and four others hunted them down after a hard day's drive. They scared one of the Indians nearly to death in the process.

The company moved on and camped above Elko, Nevada.

M. 6th. We kept a strong guard last night and lost no cattle. But this morning there being but two men to guard, the Indians crept along in the willows and soon put arrows in 7 of our oxen. We killed one of them (oxen), the others are living. Myself and one other got a shot at them but do not know whether we hit or not. Passing on we soon came to the co. ahead of us and found them in the same trouble we had, only worse. We united with them and passed on toward night: Distance to day 8 miles.

The Oskaloosa Company kept a strong guard during the night, however they relaxed too much the morning of September 6th permitting Indians to approach through the brush along the river. They lost seven oxen.

The Company traveled about 8 miles and found another company in trouble on Mary's River near Dixie Creek.

Earlier 1847 Companies Had Their Troubles Too

The first 1847 emigrant company traveling through this area less than a month earlier did not find it so easy. T. L. Davidson was about fourteen years old when he came through this area in 1847. In 1878 he told a pioneer camp rally that five of their cattle were stolen along the Mary's River. The men tracked them for five miles out to the edge of the mountains. When they got there, they found three of the animals spread out to dry upon a drying apparatus. Two other animals were standing nearby. They saw one of the Indians and captured him. They brought the Indian and one of the animals back into camp. (TLD)

They held the Indian prisoner that night. The men of the camp got together the next morning in a council. The younger men wanted to whip the Indian for stealing their cattle, then release him. The older men wanted to turn him loose. "*He got Whipped.*" (TLD)

Levi Scott remembered the incident differently. He was one of the older men as well as their guide. He was not for turning him loose. (LS)

1846 Emigrants Had Their Problems Too

J. Quinn Thornton took The Southern Route To Oregon in 1846. He reported that the Indians, along the whole length of the river, were very troublesome. They would steal the cattle and conceal themselves behind rocks and bushes, from which they attacked the emigrants and their stock. Two men in his Company shot an Indian with a rifle and shotgun during an attack during a layover. It was always necessary to guard the cattle while they were grazing. (JQT)

The cattle, the oxen, pulled the covered wagons. Killing "cattle" took away the emigrant's transportation over six hundred miles from the nearest settlement. It took David and Hannah twenty-seven more days to reach the nearest cabin. The nearest settlement was Salem, over six hundred miles away. Salem could have had as few as four houses in 1847.

One of the first 1846 wagon trains had a skirmish with the Indians as they attacked from the trees along the river. Some Indians were killed. Two men from the wagon train were seriously wounded. One of them died. It was reported that he was shot with a poison arrow. However, he apparently died of blood poisoning. (JQT)

The Oskaloosa Company continued on down Mary's River.

T. 7th. Passed on down the river

about 20 miles we saw no diggers.

W. 8th Today we soon crossed a clear cool stream and passing up a low Mt. was 16 Ms away from the river about half way or 8 miles we passed small spring but did not camp and night overtook us before we reached the river. But finally camped at about 9 o'clock with poor grass. Distance 20 miles.

The Oskaloosa Company crossed Mary's River to the north side and camped near Carlin on September 7, 1847. They crossed a bend in the river through Emigrant Pass on September 8th. They passed a small spring at the pass but did not stop. Darkness caught them before they reached the river again.

The Oskaloosa Company avoided Palisades Canyon by crossing a large bend in the river. The oxen pulled hard for the first eight miles over good road from Carlin to Emigrant Pass. The emigrants found everything they had ever heard about the desert took on new meaning when the desert began in earnest. Temperatures near 100° with nights near freezing were normal. However, the 100° daytime high was misleading because that was in the shade where none existed. Also, with single digit humidity and no breeze, the burn factor is enormous. The animals pulled unusually hard on this one to get the semi loaded wagons up the hill over several steep ridges.

Mr. Thornton reported that the Mary's River Valley varied in width from two to ten miles. The soil was fertile in many places. The grass was usually good and there was lots of it. There were no trees. The road was usually good. Water was usually, but not always, convenient. Sometimes the river would disappear into the ground. It came out of the ground at another place. (JQT)

T. 9th. Did not leave camp until late. Passed about 12 miles down the river and camped.

F. 10th. Continued down the river with good roads for about 18 miles and camped.

S. 11th. Continued down the river about 18 miles and camped. Roads good.

Sun. 12th. Down the river 20 miles and camped. Roads first rate. Good grass.

The Davises crossed Mary's River to the South side soon after leaving camp on September 9, 1847. The went only a few miles before they crossed the river again to the north side.

The emigrants camped near North Battle Mountain on the 10th.

They crossed the river to the south side on September 11, 1847, and camped near Valmy.

They camped near Red Horse the 12th.

Two Shall Continue As One

Joseph Gaston says that Benjamin Davis had just entered Indian country when Catherine Davis, his wife, became seriously ill with fever. The fever continued to grow worse. One morning her condition was so bad her husband decided to stay in camp until she became better. It would surely be fatal to her to proceed. The Captain and the rest of the wagon train decided to go on their way. They were in a hostile Indian country and far from their destination. (JG)

Benjamin Davis stayed with his decision to remain at the camp site, fearing that it would prove fatal to his wife to go farther. The remainder of the wagon train started on their way - except the wife of one prominent member of the train, who was ministering to Mrs. Davis. When her husband called her to join the others, she replied: "Father, you can go on if you want to, but my duty is with Catherine and these little children, and I will stay with them." (JG)

The husband turned his wagons to rejoin his wife. The next wagons, seeing this, also turned, and soon the whole train was in corral again. They stayed there until the fever abated and Catherine Davis was able to resume the journey. (JG) (Note: There is no known relationship between Benjamin Davis and David D. Davis.)

Catherine Davis lived to become a Pioneer Doctor, doctoring people on the frontier whenever an emergency called her. She rode a horse so fast that nobody could catch her. (JG)

M. 13th. Made today about 20 miles down Mary's River.

T. 14th. To day we traveled about 18 miles and camped in good grass with some of the Mormon Battalion from California.

W. 15th. About 28 miles brought camping time. No wood on this river but willow.

T. 16th. In about 3 miles we crossed Mary's River for the last time. Crossed a bend about 12 miles and camped about 4 miles above the forks of the road. Distance 15 miles.

The Company crossed the river to the north side near Peble and immediately recrossed to the south side near Goloconda on September 13, 1847. They camped near Tule, Nevada.

They camped south of Winnemucca on September 14, 1847, and near Rose Creek on the 15th.

They crossed the river for the last time, to the north side near Cosgrave and camped four miles from the fork in the road.

F. 17th. When we came to the forks of the road we watered.

Lester Hulin, David and Hannah Davis and The Oskaloosa Company came to the forks of the road and watered their stock. Then the wagons left the California Trail and moved out on the Scott-Applegate Trail — on the Southern Route to Oregon.

CHAPTER 8

The Scott–Applegate Trail
Northern California and Southern Oregon

1847 Emigration

In 1847, Levi Scott, accompanied by B. F. Burch, "Black" Harris and a party of about thirty young men going back to the states, made their way eastward over the Scott-Applegate Trail. Levi Scott returned to Oregon guiding emigrants over the Scott-Applegate Trail. (D&HH) (LS)

The Davidson party, guided by Levi Scott was the first Oregon-bound company that entered the California and Scott-Applegate Trail in 1847. (TLD)

The Wiggins party, some knew it as The Gordon party, was seventeen wagons bound for California. The route chosen had never been used before. It was probably the second or third party to turn into the Scott-Applegate Trail in 1847. They planned to go to the headwaters of the Pitt River and follow it to the Sacramento Valley. They followed the plan, turning southward at Goose Lake. They were forced to turn back and eventually fell in with the Oregon migration. They arrived in the Willamette Valley on October 25th. (DH)

The Thomas Smith party was eleven wagons with fifteen men and boys. They arrived in the Upper Willamette Valley on October 14th. That was eleven days before the Wiggins

Black Rock

Photo by Shann Rupp

party. The Thomas Smith party may have included the Davidson group. (DH)

The Benjamin Davis party traveled the Scott-Applegate Trail with eighteen able bodied men. They arrived in Oregon on October 28, 1847, seven days ahead of David and Hannah Davis and four days after the Wiggins party. (DH)

Of the wagon trains that traveled the Scott-Applegate Trail in 1847, only the Thomas Smith party was as small as the Benjamin Davis party. It is unlikely that the Benjamin Davis party and the Thomas Smith party were the same company because of the disparity in arrival dates.

The Oskaloosa Company entered the Scott-Applegate Trail on September 17, 1847. It arrived in the Willamette Valley with about twenty wagons on November 2, 1847. The Oskaloosa Company was probably the last company to travel the length of the Scott-Applegate Trail to the Willamette Valley.

Lester Hulin's day by day diary shows there were at least two sections of the wagon train entering the Scott-Applegate Trail. The Oskaloosa Company divided back on the Sweetwater River on July 26th so they could camp at different small campgrounds. The two sections combined forces on September 24th after Indians killed some cattle in the second section. The company had been separated by only a few hours travel time for the two months.

Less than half a dozen wagon trains had used The South Road when The Oskaloosa Company entered it on Friday, September 17, 1847. David and Hannah Davis came to the fork in the road after traveling four miles. They stopped long enough to water their livestock. Then they turned onto the Scott-Applegate Trail-The Southern Route to the Willamette Valley.

Another Company had problems with Indians on The California Trail and had joined the first Company of the Davis-Hulin-Hills wagon train on September 6th. It may have turned onto Scott-Applegate Trail as part of the Oskaloosa Company.

The Fork In The Road

F. 17 When we came to the forks of the road we watered. 12 miles farther brought us to the foot of the Mts. Here is a spring but no grass. Camped here. Distance 16 miles.

T. H. Jefferson, an 1846 emigrant, arrived at the Scott-Applegate Trail turnoff two weeks after the trail was opened and several days after the last 1846 wagons turned onto it. T. H. Jefferson prepared very accurate and detailed maps that are the best source for locating the fork in the road. (D&HH)

In the beginning Scott-Applegate Trail left the California Trail near where the California Trail crossed Mary's River to the south side one or two miles below Callahan Bridge four or five miles northwest of present Imlay, Nevada. The ford was on the upper end of Lassen Meadows, now covered by Rye Patch Reservoir southwest of Eugene Mountains.

Jesse Applegate wrote:

> *"The Oregon and California roads fork at a large bend of the river where the river turns directly south - the Oregon road here leaves it and runs on in a west course towards a gap in the mountains."*

The fork of the road was close to the river because Lester Hulin wrote: *"When we came to the forks of the road we watered."*

In 1849 the California Trail continued westward about two miles before climbing the sand ridges bordering the meadow to the plain. The road entered sand ridges before it forked. (D&HH)

The Oskaloosa Company entered "the dry stretch" of their journey. (JA)

The emigrants let the animals drink all they wanted preparing them for the long journey through the desert. They also filled all of the cans and kegs that could be found.

Only two small springs, Antelope Spring and Rabbit Hole Spring, were ahead.

They reached the foot of the mountains and a place called Antelope Spring after twelve miles on the Scott-Applegate Trail.

Antelope Spring is actually four small springs, the first now known as Willow Spring is nine miles from the river. David and Hannah passed the first spring on their way to three small springs clustered another three miles down the road where they camped.

One of the tragedies of the trail occurred thirteen years later at these springs. Susan Coon, the wife of a wagon master died in childbirth in 1860. The grave was marked with a granite headstone. The son she bore survived and was raised by two pioneer ladies. Seventy-two years later he returned in search of his mother's grave and was led to his birthsite. (PMJ)

Also there is a stone slab set in the ground marking the spot where two prospectors were killed by Indians. (PMJ)

18. Moved off by sunrise in hopes of finding grass but found none but found a small spring at 15 miles. We used up all the water we could get. Took supper and moved on about 15 miles and stopped in a place deserted by everything living. Distance 30 miles.

There was no grass at Antelope Spring so they broke camp at sunrise. They moved up the trail hoping to find grass. The wagon train headed northwest across a broad sage plain and through a ravine at Kamma Mountains south of Rosebud Canyon. They came to Rabbit Hole Spring in fifteen miles. They ate supper and used all the water. The grass they had hoped for was not there.

Lindsay Applegate describes the discovery of Rabbit Hole Spring:

Rabbit Hole Springs

Photo by Shann Rupp

*"After traveling about fifteen miles (east of Black Rock) we began to discover dim rabbit trails running in the same direction in which we were traveling. As we advanced the trails became more plained, and there were others constantly coming in, all point in the general direction toward a ledge of granite boulders which we could see before us. Approaching, * * * * we could see a green mound where all the trails seemed to enter, and on examining the place closely we found a small hole in the top of the mound, in which a little puddle of water stood within a few inches of the surface * * * *. Digging down in this clay we made a basin large enough to hold several gallons and by dark we had quite a supply of good pure water. * * * * Great numbers of rabbits came around us and we killed all we wanted of them. This is the place always since known as Rabbit Hole Springs."*

From Rabbit Hole Spring, the emigrants had a clear view of Black Rock on the northwestern horizon. The Oskaloosa Company continued on another fifteen miles toward Black Rock to the southeastern edge of The Black Rock Desert. The Company was in trouble at this point. Their livestock had no grass or anything else to eat for two days. They had already traveled thirty miles. The dreaded Black Rock Desert was still ahead.

The trail from Rabbit Hole Spring to Black Rock was probably the cruelest segment of the whole trip. There was no water in the twenty-two mile stretch across a rugged sage plain and the unvegitated Black Rock Desert.

Quinn Thornton, an 1846 emigrant, wrote of this place:

"Just as the sun was sinking, we resumed our journey, and after descending a little hill we entered a country more forbidding a spot and repulsive than even that I have described. There were occasional spots where we saw a stray and solitary bush of artemisia. It was a country which had nothing of redeeming character.

"Nothing presented itself to the eye, but a broad expanse of uniform dead level plain, which conveyed to the mind the idea that it had been the muddy and sandy bottom of a former lake; and, that after the water had suddenly sunk through the fissures, leaving the bottom in a state of muddy fusion, streams of gas had broke out in ten thousand places and had thrown up sand and mud, so as to form cones, rising from a common plane, and ranging from three to twenty feet in height. It seemed to be the River of Death dried up, and having its muddy bottom jetted into cones by the force of the fires of perdition. It was enlivened by the murmur of no streams but was a wide waste of desolation, where even the winds had died. It was wearisome, cull, and melancholy scene that had been cheered by the beauty of no verdure since the waters of the flood had subsided, and the dove left the patriarch's window to return no more." (JQT)

An exploring party traveling through the area in 1959 found the preserved remains of oxen that had been there for over one hundred years proving that this was a perfectly sterile environment. (D&HH)

Sun. 19th. In about 3 miles we came to a muddy creek. Watered our animals and pushed on about 5 miles to Black Rock, or a blk Mt. near some redish looking (rocks?). Here is a hot spring and course grass. We of coarse camped here. Distance 8 miles.

The wagon train came to muddy Quinn River after traveling only three miles. They watered their animals and pushed on another five miles to Black Rock. They camped after traveling only eight miles. The people and the animals were exhausted after the long journey through dry country. They needed water and grass for the starving animals.

Lindsay Applegate recorded his impressions of the hot springs at Black Rock as the South Road Company made their way east.

> *"On starting out on the morning of the 12th of July, we observed vast columns of smoke or steam rising at the extremity of the black ridge. Reaching the ridge a few miles north of its extremity, we traveled along its base passing a number of springs, some cold, and others boiling hot.*
>
> *"At the end of the ridge we found an immense boiling spring from whence the steam was rising like smoke from a furnace. A large volume of water issued from the spring which irrigated several hundred acres of meadow.*
>
> *"Although the water was strongly impregnated with alkali, it was fit for use when cooled, and the spot was, on the whole, a very good camping place for the desert. The cliffs at the extremity of the ridge were formed of immense mass of black volcanic rock and all about were vast piles of cinders, resembling those from a blacksmith's forge. This place has ever since been known as 'Black Rock'."*

> ***M. 20th. This morning we yoked and moved on to the hot spring (5 miles) and camped until about 4 o'clock P.M. Then pushed on by moonlight about 15 miles and stopped until morning. Distance 20 miles.***

The wagon train yoked up and moved five miles to Double Hot Springs on September 20, 1847. There were approximately one hundred acres of lush meadow and sink holes fed by the runoff from the hot springs so they camped until about four in the afternoon. Then they pushed on about fifteen miles through deep sand in the moonlight and stopped until the following morning.

Thornton remembered the 1846 migration:

> *"We remained at Black Rock one day and night, for the purpose of resting and recruiting our exhausted cattle; after which we resumed our journey and traveled about eight miles, to the Great Hot Springs, in the vicinity of which we found a limited supply of grass. Our road between these two camps conducted us over a dry, grassy plain, and usually near the foot of a high and naked precipitous bluff. The tops of these bluffs or hills appeared to be covered with volcanic scoria, or a substance resembling the slag formed in iron furnaces. Their side presented a great variety and blend of colors, including almost all those of the rainbow. These have evidently been produced by the action of intense heat, which had left different colors in different places, according to the degree of heat applied, and the temperature of the atmosphere into which the masses had been suddenly projected while thus heated. Indeed, without attempting to account accurately for the phenomenon, the hills appeared to have been in some way scathed and blasted by subterranean fires."* (JQT)

> ***T. 21st. This morning we moved early, about 5 miles, and finding some grass and water we stopped until about 8 P.M. Then on again about 5 miles farther and camped in a valley with grass and water. Distance 10 miles.***

The wagon train moved about five miles

Tuesday morning. There was good grass and water so they stopped until about eight in the afternoon to let their livestock eat, get water and recuperate.

The Oskaloosa Company moved past Paiute Peak, on the left just before reaching Mud Meadows. Peter Lassen was murdered on its slopes in April 1859, either by Indians or by a disenchanted Lassen Trail emigrant. His bones may still rest on its barren slopes. (PMJ)

The company moved on another five miles before camping at Mud Meadows. There were several hundred acres of level, deep grassy plain, watered by Springs Canyon to the northwest, Mud Meadows Creek to the northeast and several warm springs. (PMJ)

Slide Into Fly Canyon

W. 22nd. Did not start very early. Found our road ascending for about 5 miles, then down a steep rocky hill through a kanion. Then on about 4 miles and into another kanion to good grass and water. Camped here. Distance 12 miles.

The wagon train left camp late and began climbing a hill parallel to Fly Canyon for about five miles. After reaching the top, the wagon train was faced with several hundred feet of 45⁰ downhill travel, the wagon slide into Fly Canyon. The younger children had fun running down the hill to wait while the rest of their party caught up with them. The rest made it down locking wagon wheels by tying them with rope to hold the wagons back. They used anything they could to avoid rolling over, sideways or end-over-end, and being smashed to smithereens.

After completing the descent, the emigrants continued along the rock canyon floor for about a half a mile. They climbed out of the canyon and worked their way along a narrow ledge bordering the northern edge of the canyon. They continued on in a westerly direction across the northern shore of High Rock Lake and into High Rock Canyon before they camped. There was grass and water so they made camp for the night.

Rev. A. E. Garrison, an emigrant of 1846 wrote:

> *"* * * * in coming down into the canyon, the hill was so steep that one wagon with all its wheels locked fell over forward on the team. When we got down, we turned around to look up the perpendicular wall four or five hundred feet high. It was truly frightful."*

High Rock Canyon

T. 23rd. Moved on up this branch through a deep cut for 12 miles and camped. Good grass.

The Oskaloosa Company turned north toward the towering red rock walls of Devil's Gate and High Rock Canyon. They traveled twelve miles and camped.

High Rock Canyon is about twenty-one miles long. The best words that can be said about it is that it furnishes an almost perfect trailway for travelers through several ranges of hills. The hills would have made crossing difficult except for the canyon. The perpendicular walls were over one hundred feet high at some points along the trail. At some places the trail in the canyon was only wide enough for the wagons to pass through. (EE&DRD)

Jesse Applegate wrote after passing through High Rock canyon in 1846:

> *"The High Rock Canyon is a great curiosity, a good road, handsome little meadows and excellent water. The canyon is enclosed by betling cliffs,*

rising in places hundreds of feet perpendicular."

Digger, or Paiute Indians inhabited caves in the base of the canyon walls. David and Hannah Davis and their family were watching for an ambush as they passed through the canyon. They made it through without incident. However, the second section of the Oskaloosa Company was not so lucky.

Second Section In Trouble Oskaloosa Company Back Together

F. 24. Last night Towner and Belnap of the other Co. came up and informed us 12 of their cattle had been shot that morning by the Indians. They wished help from us so we sent 2 or 3 yoke of oxen to help them up and we laid in camp waiting for (them to catch up.)

The "other company" was a company created when the larger Oskaloosa Company divided near Independence Rock on Sweetwater River the morning of July 26, 1847. "The other company" included at least the large Belknap family: L. D. and Hannah Belknap Gilbert and their six children; Oren and Nancy Starr Belknap and their four children, Ransom and Mahala Belknap and their two children; Samuel Fletcher and Tolitha Cumi Belknap Starr and their two children. They were from Van Buren County, Iowa, and probably were with the Oskaloosa Company from Keosauqua to the Sweetwater. Cornelius Hills was probably with "the other company". Hills and Towner were probably bullwhackers.

Smaller companies could travel faster and get into, and out of, smaller campgrounds. However, they were more vulnerable to Indian attack. (BCM)

"The other company" created when the Oskaloosa Company divided back on Sweetwater River, had divided again on the Oregon Trail when Marcus Whitman talked Watts, a millwright, into erecting a sawmill at the mission. Watts and six others left

Devil's Gate High Rock Canyon

Photo by Shann Rupp

Painted Point

Photo by Shann Rupp

Trail Traces Approaching Forty-Nine Lake

Photo by Shann Rupp

"the other company". Mrs. Watts insisted on going to Oregon and they left Whitman Mission on November 19, 1847, a week before the missionaries were chopped up or kidnapped and the mission was sacked by Indians. (BCM)

Painted Point

S. 25th. Continued our journey up the creek. In 1-1/2 miles we passed a spring branch. In 1 mile farther we entered a kanion, very rocky, about 2 miles long. Here the branch heads. Passed on over good roads and in 6 miles more we passed a fine piece of grass. A spring near. Then on about 5 miles and camped without water. (Good grass.) Roads fine except in the kanion. Distance about 14 miles.

The other company caught up with the first company and they rejoined forces. Lester Hulin continued as pilot for the reunited wagon train.

The wagon train continued their journey up the creek. They passed a spring branch one and a half miles up the road. In another mile they entered Upper High Rock Canyon. The canyon was two miles long and very rocky. The creek they had been following started there.

The wagon train moved on over good roads. It passed Massacre Creek Meadows and Emigrant Spring in six miles. There was fine grass there. After another five miles, they camped near Painted Point. They were without water but had good grass for the cattle.

Forty-Nine Pass

Sun. 26th. Moved on by day break to the little pass and camped for the day. Good grass & water. Here lay an Indian that had been shot about 4 days. Distance about 8 miles.

M. 27th. Passed on over the divide and in 12 miles came to hot springs and camped. Grass and water not very good.

David and Hannah Davis crossed Forty-Nine Lake and marched on to Forty-Nine Pass where they camped on September 26, 1847.

The Oskaloosa Company crossed the present Nevada-California State Line on the 27th and camped at Leonard Hot Spring after traveling twelve miles.

28th. Pushed ahead. In one mile we passed another hot spring, then on over good roads. Crossed a naked bottom or plain and came to a fine stream in 8 miles. Then down the foot of the Mt. to Plumb creek and camped near the foot of the Mt. Road distance 14 miles.

The wagon train crossed the naked alkali flatland at the southwestern end of an alkali Lake. They came to the fine stream now known as Goose Creek in eight miles. They continued around the foot of the mountain to Plumb Creek at the eastern edge of Fandango Pass. They camped near the foot of the mountain road.

Fandango Pass

W. 29th. To day we only passed over the Mt. and camped in the val-

ley below. Distance only about 4-1/2 miles. (*To be Continued.*)

The wagon train only traveled four and a half miles but they had conquered another mountain pass, the worst they had encountered this far. The road climbed seventeen hundred feet in about two miles. That is over an average of eighteen percent grade. They had to double up the teams to haul the wagons up the hill. That is six yokes of oxen, twelve animals, to pull one wagon. The last quarter mile was the hardest because it was loose sand and very steep. Many other wagon trains lost wagons on this hill. They broke loose and careened back down the steep grade smashing into anything and everything they came in contact with. Sometimes a careening wagon would pull oxen back with it.

Finally when they reached the top they were rewarded with a grand view. Looking west from this 6,155 foot summit, a person could see the beautiful, green, grassy Fandango Valley edged by tall pine-covered mountains. They also could see Goose Lake about ten miles in the distance.

The Oskaloosa Company passed over the summit and descended into Fandango Valley. They camped on the beautiful Fandango Plain surrounded by stately pine and cedar trees. There was excellent water and grass for their stock.

The entire company was jubilant over its success. Everyone thought that they had just crossed the killer Sierra Nevada Mountains where many people in the Donner Party had died less than a year before.

What Is In The Name?

The source of the name "Fandango" remains a mystery to this day. "The Fandango" is a Mexican dance but why was "fandango" used in naming the pass and the valley?

Erbee Menefee Mulkey tells this story in his book "Fandango Valley With Love". The Wolverine Rangers, a company of men traveling west from Michigan had just crossed the summit and camped in the valley. They were breaking up the company to permit each of the members to go his own way.

The Smith company, a company of eight brothers and their families traveling west had also just crossed the pass and were camped in the valley. E. H. Todd headed a relief party that was also camped in the valley.

All were jubilant having thought that they had conquered the dreaded Sierra Nevada Mountains. All wished to celebrate. William Swain of the Wolverine Rangers may have picked the "Fandango" title when he recorded the celebration on October 13, 1849. "This evening our boys, and those of another train lying here, joined with the Smith girls and had a tall time in the way of a fandango which lasted till ten o'clock."

The news of the dance at the campfire by the 'boys and Smith girls' celebrating the crossing of the 'Sierras' spread as any gossip of the time.

The isolated pass and valley have been known as "Fandango Pass" and "Fandango Valley" ever since.

Another story tells of a huge massacre that probably never took place when some wagons met in the valley. The emigrants were so happy at having crossed the dreaded Sierra Nevada Mountains that they danced the "Fandango" around a blazing campfire throwing all caution to the winds. They were a perfect target for the Indians. The Indians rode in and massacred all of the men, women and children except one. One man was able to hide and lived to tell the tale of the tragedy.

Although many believe the story of the big massacre and a marker was placed at a spot, there is no real evidence that the event took place. Historians say that several people were killed around the valley and Ann Davis of the Oskaloosa Company was severely injured in an attack on September 29, 1847.

Devere Helfrich, a noted local trail historian, wrote in *Klamath Echoes* Number 9, 1971, on page 68:

> *"It was the scene of the supposed "Fandango Massacre", yet there is no documented evidence of such an event. Fandango Valley was the location of many companies dividing into smaller ones, and the abandonment of much property when the wagons were cut down to carts, or abandoned entirely when the owners took to pack horses. This came about when the distance yet to travel was realized and that they had yet to arrive at the dreaded Sierra Nevadas. Much of this equipment was burned and the remainder became so scattered that later day travelers, and even the first settlers assumed a massacre had taken place. From this fact the "old wives tales' grew."*

Ann Davis Attacked By Indians In Fandango Valley

September 29th. (Continued) This night we were sadly visited by savages. They approached and finding they could get no cattle, vented their spite at a young lady who had been baking and was then by the fire. They shot 3 arrows at her. Two of them hit her. One passed through the calf of her leg and the other through her arm into here side. We fear she is mortally wounded but hope for the best. Her name is Ann Davis. Four arrows more were found that had been shot at a man on guard. These prowling indians are as hard to find as the deer.

Cumi Belknap Starr had reason to remember an earlier incident. The wagon train captain told her not to have a fire at night. One evening she decided to make some bread over the campfire. Shortly thereafter she had an arrow in the bread pan. That ended her cooking at night. (BCM)

Hanna Ann Davis

Thomas W. Davis

Not everyone in the Davis camp that night was celebrating. Some were busy with necessary chores including baking over the campfire disregarding the advice given earlier.

Fourteen years old (Hannah) Ann Davis was busy baking bread at the campfire. There was darkness all around but the campfire clearly illuminated her outline. At some distance, probably near the wooded edge of the valley, Indians were lurking in the darkness. They were not in good spirits that evening. They were out to give vent to some pent up emotions. They probably approached the camp expecting to steal some of the emigrants' cattle, or a fine horse, but could not. Or maybe they were out for revenge for one of their brothers killed earlier by another party of Emigrants.

The peace and quiet of the night were broken when three arrows were shot at Hannah Ann Davis. One of the arrows went through the calf of her leg. Another arrow went through her arm and into her side. She fell into the fire. Although she was rescued quickly, the fire had burned her, her hair, and her clothing. There was a severe burn covering the right side of her face.

Most of the emigrants thought that Ann Davis was mortally wounded and would not survive the arrow wounds and burns. The Davises, and the rest of the company, were jolted by the attack on their beautiful daughter and sister.

No Instruments, No Doctor, No Anesthetic, One Big Operation

Several of the men set to the dreadful task of removing the two Indian arrows and treat the massive burn to her face. Gangrene, also known as blood poisoning, had to be avoided. Any of these would have been a formidable task. All three without the aid of anesthetic of any kind was almost insurmountable.

The operation took place in the dead of night in the moonlight or the light of a camp fire. They also had candles but the campfire shed the stronger light.

There was nothing to ease the pain as the arrows were removed. It took the strength of several men to hold Hannah Ann down while another cut the arrow out of her flesh with a sharp knife. This was a brutal operation but without it she would have died a more painful and brutal death.

One of the men that assisted with this operation told a younger relative some years later the full details. He concluded by saying: "*As long as I live, her screams will ring in my ears.*" (EE&DRD)

Several contemporary writers report that Hannah Ann Davis' pain was so bad in the days following that she had to be carried on a makeshift stretcher by several men. A person cannot imagine the pain caused by the Indian arrow wounds. Neither can they imagine the pain of the massive facial burn on a hot summer day in alkali country. Then add to all this, she had to be carried in the open sun over boulders so thick that the stretcher bearer's feet could not touch the ground. There was no end in sight. (LH)(HHH)

Ann Davis' injuries were particularly aggravating to Ann's family and the entire wagon train. Lester Hulin was so perturbed that he broke from his no-nonsense approach to recording the history of his overland journey to Oregon to record that *"savages" "* * * * vented their spite on a young lady * * * *."* Although Lester Hulin recorded Indian attacks on animals, this was the only attack by Indians on a person in this company he recorded. Lester Hulin and other members of the company took the attack on a pretty young lady in his charge personally.

Ann Davis survived the ordeal. She married Caswell Hendricks and they had ten children. She was living at Hendricks Ferry on the McKenzie River in Lane County when she died in 1904. She was buried next to Caswell in Mt. Vernon Cemetery at Eugene. Her brother Thomas also lies next to her.

> *T. 30th. To day 5 of us laid in the bushes to watch for indians. We heard them halloo but they kept at a proper distance. We think they saw us go in the willows. Or caravan moved on to the lake, then about 3 miles up it and camped. Distance about 10 miles.*

Lester Hulin places the attack on Ann Davis in California seven miles back on the trail from Goose Lake. The emigrants with the Oskaloosa Company were among those who thought they had crossed the Sierra Nevada Mountains. Ann Davis' obituary, in 1904, says the attack took place on Pitt River. However, there were no emigrant trails down Pitt River in 1847.

The first part of the route down Pitt River was developed the next year by Peter Lassen before he ran out of supplies. A party of Oregonian gold seekers, "48ers," led by Peter H. Burnett caught up with Lassen and finished the trail. Thomas McKay guided the Burnett party on a new route southward from The Scott-Applegate Trail near Bloody Point on the eastern shores of Tule Lake. The party probably planned to connect with the California Trail in the Nevada Desert. They intercepted Lassen's tracks and followed them. The Burnett-Lassen trail from Tule Lake to the Sacramento Valley opened in 1848.

Around Goose Lake

Goose Lake covers one hundred ninety-four square miles in northern California and southern Oregon. Just where the original 1846 and 1847 Scott Applegate Trail came to Goose Lake is unknown. It was near the mouth of Willow Creek. The Scott-Applegate Trail turned southward on the bed of the lake headed for McGinty Point on the west side of Goose Lake.

The 1846 & 1847 emigrants took a more direct line of march from near the mouth of Lassen Creek to McGinty Point than would be possible in normal years. Goose Lake was nearly dry in 1846 & 1847. It was only three or four feet deep in the deepest places. That is five or six feet lower than is shown on the USGS map.

Eighteen forty-six and eighteen forty-seven emigrants traveled on the bed of the lake. Virgil Pringle wrote that he traveled on the beach in 1846. Levi Scott remembered that the waters of Goose Lake were dried up until a large portion of the lake-bed at the south end had dried out and cracked in great fissures. They had to travel near the edge of the water to avoid the large cracks in the ground back from the water as they moved around the lake.

The lake was very shallow so the boys could wade out a mile or more shooting ducks.

Virgil Pringle recorded that one of the first wagon trains *"Travel 14 miles on the beach of the lake, road good."* The waters had receded quite a distance exposing a wide beach and the wagons were able to travel on the beach.

The most recent USGS maps published in 1990 show the elevation of the lake to be 4701, over five feet higher than it was in 1846 and 1847.

A paper received from the Watermaster at Lakeview, Oregon, identified only as "Goose Lake, California-Oregon, Records of water level," says that there are credible reports that the lake overflowed in 1868 or 1869 and for 2 hours during a strong north wind in 1881.

The paper reports that the years 1840 through 1851 were dry years indicated by tree growth rings. Water was at the 4,695 foot level in 1846 and down to 4,694 in 1848 and 1852. A road across the lake bed was in use. The lake was dry in 1926 and each summer 1929-1934. The lake was dry again in 1993 & 1994.

These records indicate that the lowest point in the lake has an elevation of 4,692.

The Scott-Applegate Trail was out of the water in 1926 when Getty Studio of Lakeview, Oregon, photographed its clear traces at the McGinty Point crossing. (D & HH)

The level of the lake returned to normal and later emigration to Yreka and southern Oregon had to detour farther south around Goose Lake. Since the earlier 1846 and 1847 emigrations did not travel on the low land bordering Goose Lake, Peter Lassen probably left the Scott-Applegate Trail much farther north, in the Fandango Valley, in 1848 than is proposed by most trail historians.

F. October 1st. Passed around the lake about 10 miles and camped on a small cool stream.

There was no time to linger with winter coming on. The wagon train continued their journey ten miles around Goose Lake and camped on a small cool stream between McGinty Point and McGinty Reservoir.

Across Devil's Garden

S. 2nd. To day our roads were very rocky, so much so that Miss Davis could not ride. She had to be carried on a stage and a waggon broke so we did not make more than 6 miles. Camped without water.

The road was very rocky over the high plain in Devil's Garden. There were lots of pine and cedar timber. The roads were so rocky that Hannah Ann Davis could not stand the pain of riding and had to be carried on a stretcher. The wagon train could only travel six miles. They camped without water north of South Mountain. (LH)(HHH)

Sun. 3rd. Moved this morning at sun rise down to a branch about 2-1/2 miles and camped until noon. Then pushed on about 6 miles down the branch and camped. Distance 8-1/2 miles

The Oskaloosa Company moved out at sunrise. They went down Fletcher Creek two and a half miles and camped until noon. They pushed six miles down Fletcher Creek branch to near its junction with Willow Creek. There were not as many mountains as there had been.

M. 4th. After traveling down this branch about 4 miles, we turned to the right, passed a ridge and in 6 miles from branch we came to Goffs springs.

Double Traces Across Devil's Gardem
Photo by Shann Rupp

Camped here. Distance to day 10 miles. The roads here are very rocky and have been since leaving the lake.

The wagon train traveled four miles down Fletcher Creek then right, passed a ridge later called Blue Mountain. They camped at Pot Hole Spring, six miles after leaving Fletcher Creek.

This was where Jesse Applegate, in 1846, blazed a tree at Goff's Spring. He left Levi Scott a note giving directions and informing him that he had decided to travel ahead to the Willamette Valley and was taking John Scott and Lindsay Applegate with him. He wrote that he hoped to get settlers in the valley to come back along the trail to assist in opening the South Road. He said he was leaving the rest of the party to mark the trail and clear it from the south. (LS)

> *5th. Upon leaving the springs, In 4 miles we came to another fine spring and followed down the branch about 3 miles. Then crossed a ridge to another good camping place. Down the same to its confluence with the first branch and camped. Distance today 12 miles.*

They arrived at Steel Swamp Springs in four miles. They followed the creek another three miles and crossed a ridge to Mammoth Spring. They traveled down the creek to where it joined Willow Creek. The wagon train crossed a swampy portion of Clear Lake Meadows at a spot that is now under the waters of Clear Lake Reservoir.

The company crossed Sacramento River (Lost River) for the first time in the swampy portion of Clear Lake. Lester Hulin does not mention the river so it is assumed that it was lost to the swampy condition of the trail.

> *W. 6th. Passed around a large swamp filled with ducks, geese and cranes. Then passing a good spring, we came to a lake. Watered our cattle and passed on over stony roads and at last camped without water, good grass, in sight of another lake. Distance about 14 miles.*

The Company passed Clear Lake Meadows. It was filled with ducks, geese, and cranes. They passed Applegate Spring and on to Clear Lake, where they watered their cattle, and moved on over rocky roads. The wagon train finally camped with good grass but without water, in sight of Tule Lake.

> *7th. This morning we moved by 5:30 A.M. Soon came to a broad rich bottom. Good grass and in about 12 miles came to the Sacramento River and camped. This water stretch is about 18 miles. About 3 miles farther brought us to the ford where we camped for the day. Here we saw Indians who appeared more brave than the Diggers. They are probably the Clamet Indians.*

The wagon train broke camp about 5:30 a.m. They came to the bluff overlooking the broad rich bottom of The Tule Lake Basin. The Tule Lake Basin has plenty of water and is rich with good grass.

Burnett Road

Peter H. Burnett led a party of about one hundred fifty gold-hungry Oregonians to California over the Scott-Applegate Trail in 1848. Thomas McKay was guide. They followed the Scott-Applegate Trail as far as the eastern shores of Rette Lake now known as Tule Lake. They followed the shores of Tule Lake past Bloody Point. They continued south to a ravine where the Scott-Applegate Trail turned east ascending the bluffs toward Clear Lake. Thomas McKay guided the party as they opened road from the shores of Tule Lake to the Sacramento Valley. The Oregonians picked up the newly opened trail of Peter Lassen along the way and soon caught up with them. They found the Lassen party in trouble and short of provisions. The Oregonians finished the Lassen-Burnett Trail into California.

Bloody Point

Bloody Point got its name from the first wagon train massacre by Indians in history that took place along the shores of the lake within a few miles of the butte. In 1852 a wagon train on the Scott-Applegate Trail descended the bluffs to the junction with the Burnett Road. The wagon train continued toward Oregon — but that story is in Chapter 2,Page 41, of this book.

Descent To The Shores Disputed

The place where the Scott-Applegate Trail descended to the shores of Tule Lake is one of the more important yet disputed mysteries of the Oregon Trail. Three highly respected trail researchers, Richard Ackerman, and Devere and Helen Helfrich, believe that the Scott-Applegatge trail went west from Clear Lake past Horse Mountain and descended the bluff to the shore of Tule Lake a few miles south of the small butte shown as Bloody Point on USGS maps. Other authorities accept GLO maps that show a wagon road traveling northwest from Clear Lake to descend a bluff to the shore of the lake near Bloody Point

After passing on the north shore side of Clear Lake the road builders moved west through the Sage Lake area. They continued west passing north of Horse Mountain to the bluffs overlooking Tule Lake. The trail descended a ravine to the level shore of the Tule Lake opposite the high ground that leads to present day Newell.

Westward Along The 42° Parallel

The Oskaloosa Company came to the forty-second parallel and the Oregon-California border after passing the point later known as Bloody Point southeast of present day Malin, Oregon. The first documented massacre by Indians happened here in 1852. The Scott-Applegate Trail continues westward along the Oregon side of the border for several miles before returning to the California side.

The Oskaloosa Company reached Sacramento River twelve miles from camp and stopped for a short time. Three miles up Sacramento River brought them to the ford at Stone Bridge where they camped for the night. The Indians they saw here were braver than the Diggers (Paiutes). These may have been Klamath or Modoc Indians.

Stone Bridge was a natural bridge across Sacramento River southeast of present day Merrill, Oregon. It was an underwater ridge of rocks about four rods wide at the top.

F. 8th. Crossed the Sacramento, over the hill or divide to a large swamp. Down this to a lake (Clammet) about 3 miles down the lake and camped. Distance about 12 or 14 miles.

The wagon train crossed Sacramento River over an underwater stone bridge. It crossed the same Sacramento River at Clear Lake on October 5th. Sacramento River, or Lost River, connects Clear Lake with Tule Lake. The two lakes are only six miles apart. The river meanders about one hundred miles through the hills to the north between Clear Lake and Tule Lake. The water level in Clear Lake was about 4,423 feet in 1847 and it was about 4,040 in Tule Lake.

The Oskaloosa Company moved over a low divide to Lower Klamath Lake. They moved another three miles around Lower Klamath Lake and camped.

S. 9th. Continued around the lake and swamp. Then through a small pass and in about 5 miles from our last camp we came to a small creek. I call it crooked creek. On about 2 miles and crossed another stream & camped. Distance 7 miles.

The wagon train continued around the lake and through a small pass southwest of Laird's Landing. They came to Willow Creek five miles from camp. In another two miles they crossed another creek and camped. Gold was discovered in the Yreka Valley a few years later and a new trail branched from the Scott-Applegate Trail near Willow Creek.

Out of California Into Oregon Country

Sun. 10th. We found plenty of water for 5 miles today. We should have come here to camp, but did not so we did not make the next camping but took a ridge in the timber and found a small opening with good grass but no water. Camped here. Distance 16 miles.

The Oskaloosa Company followed Hot Creek and Indian Tom Lake for five miles. There were several camping spots that would have been better than the one they left. Lester Hulin thought they should have come here to camp the night before.

The company took to a ridge through thick timber northwest of Miller Lake and crossed into Bear Valley. The road was littered with fallen logs and big rocks. They camped with good grass without water in Bear Valley southwest of Keno.

The 1847 emigrants traveled a more direct route from Miller Lake to Stewart Creek on the north bank of Klamath River than the 1846 emigrants traveled.

Green Springs Mountain

M. 11th This morning we, in about 6 miles, came to Clamett River. Crossed. Then passing in the timber we did not come to grass or water before dark. We were obliged to camp in heavy timber. Distance 12 miles.

The Oskaloosa Company followed the trail and roads built by earlier 1847 emigrants. About six miles from camp they joined the 1846 emigrant road on the north side of Klamath River.

The company traveled six miles before crossing the Klamath River. They moved into the mountains with heavy timber, fallen logs and big rocks. They could not find grass or water before dark. They camped among the pine trees near the 5,000 foot level short of the summit southeast of Buck Mountain. They were almost a mile above sea level.

It was in this general area that Levi Scott and the first 1846 emigrants realized that they were all alone in the wilderness. They would have to build about three hundred miles of road to get their wagons through to the southern Willamette Valley. The trail blazing roadbuilders had left them to their own fate.

T. (12)th. Passing on over this mountain we, in about 9 miles, came to the beaver dams and camped for the day.

W. (13)th. Followed down this branch over hills &c and about noon came to big hill creek. Nooned there. Then on to Little Prairie and camped. Distance about 11 miles.

(Note: Lester Hulin's journal duplicates October 11th date but retains proper continuity in days of the week. All of the following dates are corrected by adding 1 to the dates shown in the Journal. The 1847 calendar reflects these days and corrected dates.)

The Company crossed over the pass, over hills, valleys, and more hills and on to Sheepy Creek. They camped for the day at Puckett Glade.

They moved down Sheepy Creek, then Johnson Creek on Wednesday. About noon they crossed over a hill and down a slide to Jenny Creek. They rested before moving on to Round Prairie near Pinehurst where they camped for the night.

The Davis family was traveling through some of the finest hunting and fishing country in the world. The streams abound with fish and Klamath River Steelhead are among the best. Deer and bear are plentiful.

7. (14) Th. Continued on over the Mts. through the timber. In about 8 miles we descended a steep hill to a creek up to the top of the Rogue River Mt. Then down for about 2 miles and camped. Distance about 10 miles.

The wagon train continued through the timber over the mountains following much the same route as the present highway from Lincoln to Tub Springs. The company slid into Keene Creek at the Keene Creek Reservoir spillway and climbed in a southwesterly direction to Green Springs Summit a half mile away. It crossed the summit within a few feet of the west end of section 33, T39S, R3E's south line. They went over the top and down School House Creek. The Company camped on Tyler Creek, two miles below the summit.

(15)th. Continued descending the stream on which we camped last night. The valley increased in width and the face of nature became more interesting. During the day several Mt. branches had increased the main stream considerable. At noon we saw some Indians and their lodges or shanties. They ran like wild men from us. Passed on to one of these streams and camped. The grass and water, timber and soil is of good quality. Distance today about 10 miles.

The Davis train continued descending the western slopes of Green Springs Mountain on Tyler Creek, Emigrant Creek and through a pass near Songer Butte to Neil Creek. The valley became wider and the scenery was beautiful.

The emigrants came to the old route between Oregon and California and camped on Neil Creek west of Dunn Butte. That is near Interstate 5 interchange #5. Highway 66 crosses over the Interstate in the vicinity of present day Ashland, Oregon. The grass and the water were good. They found that the timber and soil were also good. They were very happy.

The Davis family had traveled three hundred twenty-eight miles along the new Scott-Applegate Trail toward their new home in the Willamette Vallley. They had traveled through what is now northwestern Nevada, northeastern California, and southern Oregon. They had traveled about seven hundred fourteen miles since leaving the northern route on Raft River.

CHAPTER 9

The Scott-Applegate Trail

Western Oregon

Old Trails

The first white men to travel through western Oregon were employed by John Jacob Astor's Pacific Fur Company. Astorian Alexander Ross had been into the Umpqua Valley during the Astoria's short life as an American trading port. American fur trappers and explorers Jedediah Smith, Bailey, Gay, Turner, Lt. Edmmons, Lansford Hastings, Leese, McLure, Ewing Young, and Hall J. Kelley had used the old route.

North-West Company and Hudson's Bay Company men Peter Skene Ogden, Joseph Gervais, John Work, Alexander McLeod, Michel LaFramboise, and others had been through the area.

The South Road Company was not blazing a new route through western Oregon.

John Work's Impression Of The Old Fur Traders' Trail

The old traders' trail, The Hudson's Bay

Miss Martha Leland Crowley Grave Creek Covered Bridge Memorial

Photo by Larry McLane

Company Trail, the old trappers' trail, and The Trail From Oregon To California appear as names loosely assigned to a route between Thomas McKay's farm near present day Scapoose and northern California. It was closely confined through the Tualatin Mountains.

The trail originated on the Columbia River at the southern edge of Scapoose where it entered the mountains near present day Callahan Road. A mile or so up the creek it began to climb ridges toward the summit. The main trail reached Rocky Point Road a short distance east of Skyline Blvd. The trail followed Skyline Blvd., Johnson Road, Jarrell Road and Mason Hill and Jackson School Roads to Tualatin Plains on McKay Creek at Mason Hill Road in Tualatin Plains.

A local tradition says that travelers passing south through Tualatin Plains "aimed" straight for "Bald Peak" on Chehalem Mountain. Travelers going south would travel in a reasonably straight line from Mason Hill Road on the north side of Tualatin Plains toward Bald Peak on the south side. (JW)

On an expedition in 1834, John Work used a branch of the trail now known as Logie Trail that entered the hills about six miles south of Scapoose. The southern trail approximated Logie Trail before joining the main trail near the junction of Mason Hill Road and Jarrel Road. (JW)

Travelers followed their own whims traveling through Tualatin Plains, Chahalem Valley, Yamhill Valley, and the Willamette Valley west of the Willamette River to Veneta. Their only restriction was water; fording rivers and passage through swampy land. The Tualatin River was the most formidable obstacle in the Tualatin Plains. Most travelers did an end run avoiding the river by fording several branches, Dairy Creek, Gales Creek, Scoggins Creek, and the South Fork of Tualatin River west of Gaston. (JW)

John Work, on his 1834 trip, forded Dairy Creek below its forks. He moved to the foothills of the Coast Range of mountains where he forded the North Fork of the Tualatin River, now known as Gales Creek, west of Forest Grove. Gales Creek had an abundance of smooth rocks. John Work continued to follow the foothills fording Skoggins Creek at Shady Side. He passed through Cherry Grove and forded the Tualatin River near Gaston. (JW)

He moved around the north and the east sides of Wapato Lake. The next constriction to the southbound trail was the ford above Yamhill Falls at present day Lafayette. John Work crossed the Yamhill River at Yamhill Falls. More venturesome travelers probably crossed at other more convenient places. The first Territorial Road crossed the Yamhill River at Yamhill Falls. The common name changed to LaFayette Falls after the town that rose on the north bank. (JW)

John Work continued south past Dayton and on to Amity. He went through Salt Creek Valley and crossed La Creole Creek at the end of River Drive in the western edge of present day Dallas. The Hudson's Bay Company Trail crossed the Luckiamute River near the present day highway 223 bridge near Lewisville. (JW)

John Work traveled southeast through Airlie, Soap Creek Valley, and on to Adair. Present day highway 223 is almost exactly the same — just straightened up a bit. As it approached Adair going south, it went through the Donation Land Claim of David D. Davis in Soap Creek Valley and the Soap Creek - Tampico town site. USGS maps call this stretch of the old California trail, the "Old Portland and Umpqua Valley Wagon Road." (JW)

John Work camped near the mouth of Mary's River in present day Corvallis on June 1, 1834. The river was too high to ford but Indians told him it could be forded farther up the river. On July 2,1834, he said *"The Indians set fire to the dry grass on the neighboring hills, but none of them came near us. The plain is also on fire on the opposite side of the Willamette."* (JW)

John work continued south between Long Tom River and the western foothills through Fern Ridge to Coyote Creek ten miles west of the present day city of Eugene. He crossed the Siuslaw River near the present day town of Lorane. He crossed the headwaters of the Siuslaw River, then over the mountains to the headwaters of the Umpqua River at Pass Creek. He went up the Umpqua River Valley a short distance before returning. (JW)

On his return to Scapoose, John Work changed his route to go over the Calapooya Mountains to the Coast Fork of the Willamette River. He traveled down the Coast Fork and the Willamette River to Long Tom River.

The Ewing Young Trail

Ewing Young traveled the old fur traders' route west of the Cascade Mountains at least twice. First in 1834, when his drovers herded 154 horses and mules north from California. Three years later, he was with the Willamette Cattle Company cattle drive that brought six hundred thirty Spanish cattle north from California in 1837. That was the first ever long distance cattle drive.

He could have used either of the two routes into the Willamette Valley in 1834. He could have followed the old fur traders' trail north from Yoncolla and Safley, over the mountains to the headwaters of the Siuslaw River, down Coyote Creek, past Fern Ridge, and down the west side of Long Tom River.

Ewing Young probably followed the route John Work took returning to Vancouver earlier in the year. Young crossed the Calapooya Mountains to the coast fork and stayed on the west side of the Coast Fork through Cottage Grove, Saginaw, Creswell, and Goshen to the forks of the Willamette River near Skinner's Cabin.

Ewing Young stayed west of the Willamette River, crossing Long Tom River at present day Monroe, past Bellfountain and on to Mary's River.

The Scott-Applegate Trail Over Mountains And Through Rogue, Umpqua and Willamette River Valleys

The Scott-Applegate Trail is an entirely new road built by 1846 emigrants where no road had ever been before. The Scott-Applegate Trail west of the Cascade Mountains is not an improved "old fur traders' trail."

The first pathfinders followed the old traders' route from LaCreole Creek to Long Tom River eighteen miles south of Mary's River.

The route from the Long Tom River crossing to Martin Creek at the foot of the Calapooya Mountains was resolved by the first pathfinders after attempts to get through at least two other ways: (1) through the mountains south from Coyote Creek, and (2) through the Cascade Mountains east from the Middle Fork Of The Willamette River.

The first pathfinders apparently had no knowledge of earlier expeditions through the Calapooya Mountains. All traces of the earlier expeditions had been removed by father time so could not be used as a guide. The first pathfinders found the way through the mountains to the Umpqua River Valley, and followed the old traders' route down to Calapooya Creek.

The South Road Company picked up where the first attack was turned back by high water at Calapooya Creek. The South Road Company continued south to Emigrant Creek following the old fur traders' route before turning east leaving the route to California.

On his return trip, Levi Scott and the 1846 emigrants were unable to use the tracks of the outbound explorers in many places. The old trails were suitable for foot traffic only. No wagons or other wheeled vehicles entered the Willamette Valley from the south before 1846. Levi Scott had to find a way suitable to be improved so the wagons could travel the entire distance to LaCreole Creek. Levi Scott located a suitable way and helped the first 1846 emigrants build the wagon road to the Coast Fork at the foot of the Calapooya Mountains.

Two of the major changes made by Levi Scott were: (1) When the 1846 emigrants reached a point on the old fur traders' trail in northern Grants Pass they found the trail to be impassable for wagons because of obstructions and Levi Scott had to spend considerable time locating a new way, and (2) The old fur traders' trail crossed over the tops of ridges through the Umpqua Mountains. Levi Scott led the 1846 emigrants as they built road and went down Canyon Creek through the Canyon. Henry Garrison mentions another place north of the North Umpqua River crossing where he was attacked by an Indian near the old fur traders' trail on a hill over a mile from the road they were following in 1846.

Settlers were moving into the southern Willamette Valley while the pathfinders were away. Eugene Spencer built a cabin at present day Eugene. One or more relief wagons broke the way to meet the 1846 emigrants when they came out of the mountains on the Coast Fork near present day Cottage Grove.

Summary
Scott-Applegate Trail, Start To Finish

The first 1846 emigrants broke the Scott-Applegate Trail from the fork in the road on Mary's River through to the Cascade Mountains. The first 1846 emigrants built the Scott-Applegate Trail from the Cascade Mountains to the Coast Fork of the Willamette River. The Scott-Applegate Trail continues on to the LaCreole Creek Crossing at Dallas. Thomas Holt reported that five 1846 emigrant wagons led by David Goff, a member of South Road Company, had reached Soap Creek, only a few miles short of the LaCreole Creek Crossing.

The Scott-Applegate Trail was the main route of travel in 1848 and 1849 when the Oregon population emptied out through the southern Willamette Valley with gold seekers going to California. James Neall remembered that he, Joseph Gale and Newbanks entertained a proposition during the summer of 1847 to form a party to go to California to dig for gold. Joseph Gale and Newbanks had found gold nuggets on their trapping expeditions into the California mountains. They did not know that California had been acquired by the United States. The idea fell through. Neall was amused at the idea that gold was first discovered at Sutter's mill because he knew many people that knew of that gold long before Sutter's discovery. (JN)

Not all emigrants over the Scott-Applegate Trail were destined for the Willamette Valley. In 1848 Peter Lassen traveled the Scott-Applegate Trail about one hundred seventy-five miles to Goose Lake. He pioneered a new cutoff from the Scott-Applegate Trail into northern California. Later Yreka Valley emigrants and gold seekers traveled the Scott-Applegate Trail to Lower Klamath Lake and turned off on a new trail. Oregon emigrants soon began settling in the Umpqua River Valley, then in the Rogue River Valley. Gold was discovered in southern Oregon in 1851 near Jackson bringing an onslaught of gold seekers into the Rogue River Valley. The Scott-Applegate Trail soon lost its identity as an emigrant road and became a road of commerce.

Down Rogue River

The Oskaloosa Company, The Last Wagon Train To Skinners, left their camp on Neil Creek east of Ashland early in the morning Saturday, October 16, 1847.

> *S. 16th. The roads today were excellent and the face of nature appeared full as interesting as yesterday. Followed down Rogue River about 12 Ms & camp.* (LH)

The roads were excellent, spirits were high, and the whole country appeared fully as beautiful as the day before. They traveled twelve miles down Neil Creek and Bear Creek to present day Phoenix. They camped a block or so northwest of the center of town.

(Note: Lester Hulin's daily journal, being quoted in *Script*, lost one date by making two entries dated September 11, 1847. The day of the week was correctly shown on both entries. Dates have been edited in the following pages while the days remain as correctly shown in the journal.)

Sun. 17th. Our cattle have good grass but do not appear to eat early while the frost & dew is on. So we concluded to travel while the dew was on and stop about 9 o'clock but not finding a convenient place we were obligee to travel until 11 A.M. Then, we took breakfast and moved on again about 1 P.M. Found very good camping ground about 5 on the river bank with plenty of Indians who brought us fish to trade. Distance to day about 15 Ms. (LH)

Sunday, October 17th, the Company continued down Bear Creek through present-day Medford. Near Central Point, the Scott-Applegate Trail turned northwest toward a notch in the hills. The trail went down Kane Creek to the Rogue River where the emigrants camped. There was a good campground with lots of water and grass for the cattle. Also there were many Indians. The Indians brought fall run Chinook Salmon and resident Cutthroat Trout to trade

Benjamin Davis Avoids An Indian Attack

Benjamin and Catherine Davis had an interesting meeting with the Indians when they reached the Rogue River. They were only a few days ahead of David and Hannah. Two hundred warriors surrounded their camp. There were only eighteen men capable of bearing arms in the Benjamin Davis party. Complete annihilation was almost certain. By a bit of strategy however, Mr. Davis prevented the attack. In the back part of his wagon was a cook stove with a drum. From this the smoke was coming through a pipe that extended through the top of the wagon cover. Mr. Davis made signs that this was a cannon or some sort of explosive machine that at his direction would destroy them. The Indians gradually withdrew and allowed the wagon train to pass.

The Chief recalled this incident at a council of these Indians and whitcs somc timc latcr. He said they had planned to destroy the whole wagon train. They would have done so but for the "big gun" in the Davis wagon. (JG)

Unwanted Company

M. 18th. Followed down the river (with some of our too neighborly indians) about 12 Ms and camped.

The Oskaloosa Company traveled twelve miles down Rogue River past Gold Hill to a point across from the present day city of Rogue River. The wagon train camped one mile upstream from the upper ford at Grants Pass.

Some of their neighborly Indians accompanied the wagon train on its journey down the river. These Indians were probably the same Indians that had planned to massacre the Benjamin Davis party only a few days earlier. David and Hannah Davis did not know that.

Little Billy Davis was only a year old when the last wagon train to Skinner's passed through here in 1847. Many years later he returned to look for gold and was quite successful. A younger stepsister later wrote that her two bachelor brothers (William and Thomas) gave her and her sister one thousand dollars each in gold. William Davis died on his ranch at Beagle in Jackson County in 1925.

Wagon Train Fords Rogue River

T. 19th. In about one M we crossed

the river and left it after following it about 50 MS in all. Passed among the bluffs and camped after a distance of about 12 Ms. Some of the Indians are yet following us. Their room is better than their company.

David and Hannah Davis left their camp near the present day city of Rogue River. They forded Rogue River to the north side about one mile downstream from the bridge over the river. They continued down the river for another five miles before turning northwesterly as they passed the foot of Pierce Point. They left the river near Interstate 5 interchange #55 at Fairview Avenue and Foothill Boulevard in Grants Pass.

The Scott-Applegate Trail continued through Craxton Pioneer Memorial Park and on to Washington Boulevard and Morgan Lane west of Interchange 58 on Interstate 5. Then up Granite Hill Road through a pass and down to Butcher Knife Creek now known as Louse Creek. They camped south of the present day golf course.

During the late 1960's and early 1970's you could travel from Ashland to Grants Pass in 45 minutes without breaking the seventy MPH speed limit. It took David and Hannah Davis four days to travel the same distance.

Some Indians were still following the wagon train. The people liked the country but did not appreciate being followed by Indians. Their wagon train had been attacked less than a month previously in High Rock Canyon by Paiute Indians, and again in Fandango Valley. There was reason to be afraid. Ann Davis was still in serious condition after the attack at Fandango Pass less than three weeks before.

Over Sexton Mountain

W. 20th. Upon leaving camp we soon came to a fine creek. Then bad roads ensued (rough hilly and sideling) but by night we were in a valley with good camping ground at hand. Distance 8 Ms.

The Oskaloosa Company moved along the east edge of Interstate 5 near the sewage disposal ponds passing between the northbound lanes and the parking area at the Manzanita Rest Area. The Scott-Applegate Trail crossed present day Interstate 5 at Sportsman Park on its way to Schoolhouse Creek and Jump Off Joe Creek in Pleasant Valley.

The road went over the summit at Sexton Mountain Pass and down Rat Creek. The Oskaloosa Company camped near Miss Martha Leland Crowley Grave Creek in Sunny Valley.

Sexton Mountain was the first in a series of high, rocky, rugged mountains they had to go over on their way to the Willamette Valley.

These mountains were steep and rocky. They were heavily timbered with large fir trees several feet in diameter at ground level. Levi Scott had to select the way among the trees so the wagons would have room to pass.

Death Names A Creek

Miss Martha Leland Crowley was one of the most beautiful and popular young ladies of the 1846 emigration. She became severely ill with typhoid fever and died as the wagon she was riding in descended from Sexton Mountain. The wagon she died in stopped and those behind could not pass. Those ahead kept traveling because they did not know what had happened. The wagon train broke into two parts.

Indians approached closely to the creeping wagon train. Arrows showered down upon both animals and people. An ox hit by the arrows later died. Arrows whizzed past the beleaguered emigrants but no person was injured. Three dogs from the wagon train were "hissed" on the concealed Indians. There was a fierce struggle that was heard from the wagon train. The Indians were run off. One of the dogs was severely injured but recovered. (TC)

The broken wagon train got itself together a few miles down the road and camped. The next morning they moved on about one mile and crossed Grave Creek. Miss Martha Leland Crowley was buried near the crossing. The first General Land Office Survey Maps of the area show the name of the creek as Martha Leland Crowley Grave Creek. The little stream has been known as Grave Creek since then. One of Oregon's historic covered bridges was built across the creek in 1920 as part of the Pacific Highway.

This was only one of many distressing incidents befalling the Crowleys in their 1846 journey to Oregon. In another incident, Talbert Carter wrote that a mother and newborn son from the Crowley family, died of exposure after crossing Long Tom River south of Avery's Cabin.

Thurs 21. To day we had bad roads and reached a good camping ground at dark. Distance 9 Ms.

The wagon train traveled rough and hilly roads over one mountain pass and down to Wolf Creek, then over Stage Road Pass on bad roads. They reached a good camping ground near Glendale on Cow Creek. They had traveled nine miles.

F. 22. We today made about 8 Ms farther and camped at the entrance of the Umpqua Mts. During the day we followed a creek and passed several fine pieces of grass.

The last wagon train made about eight miles on Friday. It followed Cow Creek passed several fine pastures for the cattle. They camped at the entrance to the Umpqua Mountains. They were near Azalea at the mouth of a canyon leading north from .

1847 Emigrants Enter Top Of Canyon Creek Canyon

S. 23. To day we entered the worst roads we ever traveled and made only 6 Ms by dark.

The Oskaloosa Company entered some of the roughest roads of their overland journey in Canyon Creek Canyon. They were in very rugged country and worse off than they were a few days before. They made only six miles by dark. The diary of Lester Hulin only hints about the problems they met on this day.

Dreaded Canyon Creek Canyon Rivals Donner Pass

The 1846 emigrants experienced extreme hardships moving across the pass and through the canyon on Canyon Creek.

The same storm that caused such hardship to the Oregon emigrants in the Canyon Creek Canyon gave the Donner Party problems on the California Trail in the Sierra Nevada mountains. Reports show that the fall rains started on October 28, 1846 from Sacramento to Oregon City.

The Original Donner Party consisted of ninety persons. Of these, six people died along the way before reaching Truckee River; twenty-two died of starvation at several snowed-in camps near Donner Lake. Another fourteen persons died trying to make their way to the settlements in the Sacramento Valley. Cannibalism was resorted to by some of the forty-eight survivors. (D&HH)

The 1846 emigrants traveling the Scott-Applegate Trail had hardships almost as

Top of Canyon Creek Canyon

bad as the Donner Party. Many gave up their lives. Several emigrants were buried along the trail from the top of Canyon Creek Canyon to Long Tom River. Most survivors got through by the last of the year.

Some survivors had it so bad that they had to stop along the Scott-Applegate Trail for the winter and did not reach the Willamette Valley until spring.

The three miles from Azalea to Canyon Creek Pass are very steep and rugged. But that was only an introduction to the to the road through the canyon itself.

Talbot Carter was a boy driving a wagon carrying a widow lady and two small children. Talbot Carter wrote that they met nothing worth noticing until they reached the entrance of the Umpqua Canyon. Before starting into that impassable barrier, it was decided to lay over a day and give their lean jaded oxen needed rest.

The first day they made the ascent and camped with the oxen chained to trees. The next day they crossed a long plateau and went down the steepest hill that wagons had ever slid down. They were in a jungle of trees and bushes and could only see a short distance in front or behind them. They would stop for hours with no knowledge about the cause of detention.

Talbot Carter's wagon was about the middle of the train of fifty wagons. As each wagon came to the bad spot each wagon had to be prepared, then let down over the bad spot. It took a lot of time for each wagon. The next wagon had to stop and wait its turn while the wagons behind caught up and stopped like compressing an accordion.

As each wagon was let down, those behind would move forward the length of one team and wagon.

Carter remembered that once when he came to where the trail jumped down, the wagon in front of him carried a man who had been sick for twenty days with typhoid fever. There was no medicine to relieve his suffering. He could not raise his hand to his head, and could not speak above a whisper. He was at death's door.

The crew rough-locked all the wagon wheels, and to make sure, a man got on each hind wheel to hold the wagon back. Half way down this precipice a ledge of rock projected that was visible only to the first that passed down. Many wagons and much stock had passed, forcing the dirt below away from the rock. By the time this wagon reached it there was a perpendicular fall of almost two feet. With all precautions arranged and the men on the hind wheels, they started down. They got along all right until they came to the rock. The front wheels rose up and went off the rock. The hind wheels rose up and the wagon went crashing down the bank.

Of course, the men on the wheels let go. The wagon landed bottom side up. The wagon bows were smashed with such a crash that no one thought that anything underneath could be alive. The men rushed down and removed the wagon box and bedding. Strange to say, they found their fellow-traveler was still alive. The man recovered.

Most of the road was in the creek. When night came on they bivouacked in the lonely, dismal canyon. The poor oxen were chained to trees. This was the third night without food of any kind. They went on, pell mell down Canyon Creek. They were shut in on each side with precipitous mountains. The mountain sides were covered with dense timber with a dense growth of underbrush along the creek. The narrow, winding path that had been cut out followed the tortuous meandering of the stream.

Fortunately about 3 o'clock the third day they emerged from the mountain prison. The emigrants that preceded the Talbot Carter wagon train opened the way and made it passable had nothing to eat. They only had the game they killed.

The last day's march out of the canyon was the worst for the destruction of property. In fact, everything that could possibly be dispensed with was thrown away. The route was strewn with articles, all valuable to the owners, if they could have been preserved. Extra wagons, various kinds of tools, and farm implements, were abandoned. The owners were glad to escape with their lives.

Alonzo Wood had brought a hive of bees safely that far. The wagon that was carrying them tipped over into the creek. The wreck broke the hive into pieces and the bees all drowned. The hive of bees cost Wood a great deal of trouble. Wood had to feed and water them during the long journey. He had been offered five hundred dollars for them if he had gotten them through. One of Mr. Wood's sons was among those that died in the Canyon.

Another company that came through the canyon a day later than Talbot Carter fared worse, if possible, than he did. The rain had swollen the stream to almost a swimming stage. Judge J. O. Thornton, remembered that a lady gave birth to a child. The condition of the road was so terrible that in a few hours the infant died. The mother soon followed because of the treatment she had to undergo. Only one out of almost a hundred wagons got through without breaking. (JQT)

After lying over two or three days recuperating, preparations were made to resume their journey. They thought that they were out of all danger of savage Indians, so their large caravan broke into small caravans for the sake of convenience. The little party that Talbot Carter was in consisted of eight wagons. They had only meager provisions and no prospects for getting any more. (D&HH)

Another emigrant, Tabatha Brown, wrote:

> *"We lost nearly all our cattle. We passed through the Umpqua Mountains. At the risk of my life, I rode the twelve*

miles through the Umpqua Mountains on horseback in three days.

"I had lost my wagon and all that I had except the horse I rode. Our families were the first that started through the canyon so we got through the mud and rocks much better than those that followed. Out of hundreds (less than one hundred), only one came through without breaking. The canyon was strewn with dead cattle, broken wagons, beds, clothing and everything but provisions, of which latter we were nearly all destitute. Some people were in the canyon two or three weeks before they could get through. Some died without any warning, from fatigue and starvation. Others ate the flesh of cattle that were lying dead by the wayside."

1846 Emigrants Were Maligned

Some said that the situation the 1846 emigrants found themselves in was of their own making. Self-appointed leaders would not follow advice of the roadbuilders. Some elderly persons had various infirmities and were not inclined to hurry. There were those that lingered seemingly almost languid.

The situation that the 1846 emigrants were in started on the east side of the Cascade Mountains when they discovered that the roadbuilders were nowhere to be found. The old fur trader's trail followed by the outbound pathfinders did not show any signs of improvement. The emigrants had been improving the road all of the way from the forks in the road back on the Humboldt River. Things got real rough when the emigrants had to start carving their own road through the untamed wilderness on the east side of the Cascades. Even worse when they had to look for the trail. Being let down was wearing on the spirits of the emigrants

Virgil Pringle took 9 days to build road and move through the canyon. He wrote:

"Wednesday, October 21—The time from this to Monday, 25th, we were occupied in making 5 miles to the foot of Umpqua Mountain and working the road through the pass, which is nearly impassable. Started through on Monday morning and reached the opposite plain on Friday night after a series of hardships, break-downs and being constantly wet and laboring hard and very little to eat, the provisions being exhausted in the whole company. We ate our last the evening we got through. The wet season commenced the second day after we started through the mountains and continued until the first of November, which was a partially fair day. The distance through: 16 miles. There is great loss of property and suffering, no bread, live altogether on beef. Leave one wagon."

Were the 1846 Emigrants falsely malingering or lackadaisical for taking time out to build road through one of the most treacherous canyons in the country?

Although Levi Scott did not keep a daily journal and his record is from memory forty years later, it provides reasonable figures for comparison. He remembered that he spent a lot of time looking for a way through north of Rogue River.

Levi Scott remembered that the first wagons lost four days at the entrance before the emigrants began building road:

The first day Jack Jones and Tom Smith met the Emigrants with some beef cattle. The emigrants were anxious to get news from the settlements so they moved only a short distance that day and they stayed in the same camp two more days.

Levi Scott was able to get four men to go with him to explore the canyon on the fourth day and it took them four more days to work through the canyon before they could move the wagons.

Levi Scott is strangely silent about Moses Harris' coming to the rescue of the emigrants. Some of the emigrants said that Harris was with one of the early relief parties reaching this area.

Meadors Vanderpool, an old mountain man who knew Moses Harris from his fur trapping days, was the Captain of the first wagon train on the Southern Route. Harris was the person who induced Vanderpool to the Southern Route. Vanderpool may have still been Harris' friend. However, sentiment against the roadbuilders that had left for home was running high.

Vanderpool would have been the one person among the emigrants who knew of Harris' reputation as a survivor among mountain men. (JP pp.66)

The Vanderpool wagons were bearing the bulk of the work building roads. They had been short on food for quite some time and the relief supplies did little to relieve their condition.

Were these 1846 emigrants falsely malingering or lackadaisical for taking time out to gain back some of their strength before they built road through one of the most treacherous canyons in the country?

Conduct Of Malingering(?) Emigrants Analyzed

A hasty review of the situation shows that only the first wagons stopped for a few days to get some much needed rest. Virgil Pringle was near the front of the wagons by this time and he went right into the canyon with no delay. Only the few wagons ahead of Pringle in the 1846 emigration could have lingered. These same wagons had been breaking down the brush for the first four hundred miles after leaving the California Trail on Marys River. (LS) The few emigrants in the first wagons had been clearing and building the wagon road on top of their teamster duties for over a hundred miles since entering the Cascade Mountains.

All 1846 emigrants were short on provisions and were in a starving condition. The lead emigrants were particularly worn out because they used what little energy they had to build road and were at their limits when Jones' relief party reached them.

These badly debilitated men took a few days to gain strength and mounted an attack on the worst wilderness encountered on the journey. The group was strengthened as reinforcements arrived when wagons came up accordion style over the next three days.

The 1846 emigrants were able to punch a crude trail through to the Umpqua Valley but their wretched condition and experiences in Canyon Creek Canyon caused a rout condition. Upon escaping from the canyon, the 1846 emigrants moved ahead in families, each family for itself, or in small groups.

David And Hannah Davis Continue Down Canyon Creek Canyon

Sun. 24. Continued over these horrible roads and dark found some of most of the company in the timber. Only 5 waggons got through. The rest had to keep their animals over another night without feed. Distance to day 5 Ms.

Sunday, October 24, 1847. David and Hannah Davis' wagon train continued down the dreaded canyon. The wagons were compelled to stop continually while bad spots were repaired or fixed. The Canyon was so narrow that if one wagon stopped, all wagons behind it had to stop. Most of the Company did not get through but stayed in the timber near the south edge of Canyonville. Only five wagons got through to the South Umpqua River.

Grass needs sunlight to grow. Grass is unable to grow in thick timber because thick timber keeps the sunlight out. When sunlight cannot reach the ground, the grass is starved and it dies. There was no grass for the animals until they could reach an open space that could be reached by the sunlight.

The last wagon train took two days to travel the few miles from Azalea to Canyonville. It was hard work getting through in good weather, but no lives were lost. It took Virgil Pringle five days to get to the first South Umpqua River ford. His was a lot harder trip in stormy weather and high water pioneering the trail.

M. 25. This morning after 1 1/2 ms of toiling over these horrible roads they all reached the valley after upsets, breakdowns and losses of various kinds. 2 1/2 Mss to day.

The rest of the Oskaloosa Company got through Canyon Creek Canyon. The company moved on to Tri-City Area on Monday, October 25, 1847.

Look at The canyon today as you travel over Interstate 5 designed to handle traffic safely at seventy miles an hour. The four lane highway completely obliterated most of the stream bed. Most of the rugged hills above the level of the road remain. Some have slid down onto the highway leaving large scars on the hillside. At places Canyon Creek sneaks its way from under the roadway around short bends. You can travel the whole length of the canyon in less than ten minutes where our pioneer ancestors took days, or even weeks, and experienced so many hardships.

T. 26th. This morning we moved about 2 Ms down the creek (or one branch of the Umpqua river) and camped for the day to wait for those who were back after lost cattle, broken wagons &c. Last night was rainy but to day is clear.

The Oskaloosa Company moved only a few miles down the South Umpqua River on Tuesday, October 26th and camped on a creek in Myrtle Creek. Some waited while others went back after lost cattle, broken wagons, etc. It rained during the night but was clear during the day.

W. 27. Last night was another showery night, but today is clear. The rainy season appears to have commenced & today we made about 4 Ms down the river.

The emigrants traveled down the South Umpqua River to Round Prairie on Wednesday, October 27, 1847.

Beleaguered 1846 Emigrant Killed In His Tent

John Newton was killed by renegade Indians on Newton Creek on November 16 or 17, 1846. Late in the afternoon Mr. Newton met three Umpqua Indians. One spoke English. The Indians informed him that he should camp there because there was no water and grass ahead that he could reach that day. The Indians asked for food, and it was given them. Then they asked for three loads of powder and ball, and said they would bring in a deer. The ball and powder were given to them. They put it all in one gun as one load. Mr. Newton finally suspected that the Indians were up to no good and asked them to go away. They would not leave. He sat up near the door of the tent to watch them. He was overcome with exhaustion and went to sleep and was shot. He immediately rose, and sprang into his tent for his gun. One of the savages seized Newton and chopped his leg nearly off. They robbed the tent and loaded the articles on his horse and fled. Mr. Newton did not survive his injuries. Mrs. Newton remained with her dead husband while Sutton Caldwell (or Burns), an orphan boy traveling with the Newtons, ran back to get help. (D&HH)

Several weeks later, Widow Newton was one of the first known emigrants of the Southern Route to pass through Soap Creek Valley in northern Benton County. Thomas Holt, traveling south from Rickreall Creek (west of Dallas) on a rescue mission, reported that he met the first wagons of the immigration on December 5, 1846. They camped on Soap Creek nine miles north of Mary's River. Mr. Goff was bringing Mrs. Newton through. (TH)

Last Wagon Train To Skinner's Fords North Umpqua River

T. 28th. Continued down the Umpqua valley to the crossing of the N.W. fork of the river about one M above the forks. Camped here. Distance 18 ms.

The Oskaloosa Company, The Last Wagon Train To Skinner's continued down the South Umpqua River Valley. They Crossed Newton Creek, now in the northwest section of Roseburg near Interchange 123 on Interstate 5. They camped on the North Umpqua River about one mile above the forks several miles below Winchester.

There were at least two, probably more, North Umpqua River crossings prior to the arrival of the 1846 and 1847 emigrants, The lower crossing where David and Hannah Davis crossed was about one mile above the forks. Another crossing was several miles upstream.

F. 29th. Spent the whole day in crossing the river which was done by means of the assistance of Indians and canoes.

The emigrants crossed the North Umpqua River Friday, October 29th. Indians with canoes helped them cross.

S. 30th. Left the river and made the calipooya river in 10 ms, then on about 4 ms and camped. 14 Ms in all.

The Last Wagon Train left the North Umpqua River and crossed the Calipooya Creek in ten miles. They camped on Cabin Creek north of Oakland.

1846 Emigrants Stranded For The Winter In Umpqua Valley

Not all 1846 emigrants reached the Willamette Valley. Some beleaguered 1846 emigrants camped on the Scott-Applegate Trail to wait the winter out. The Josephus Adamson Cornwall family was one such family. The Rice Dunbar and James Campbell families may have wintered near the Cornwall family. There were twenty-five or thirty people at the winter camp on Cabin Creek four miles north of Oakland.

Joseph H. Cornwall wrote a Historical Sketch of the Josephus Adamson Cornwall family in 1900:

> *"After resting a few days, Mr. Campbell's family and ours and some others, as best they could, went on leisurely (slowly) until we reached the vicinity of Oakland in the Umpqua valley. There we met some men (the Thomas Holt party) with a small supply of provisions from the Willamette and some of us decided to winter there.*
>
> *"****Cousin Israel Stoley rejoined us and decided to remain with us for the winter. ****Father was anxious to save his wagons and a fine library which he brought with him. Therefore he considered it absolutely necessary to wait for better weather and better roads before resuming our journey.*
>
> *"* * * * Our only supply of flour was eighty pounds sent by a friend from the Willamette. * * * * The supply of flour and bacon with which we left Missouri was exhausted when we were at the canyon; * * * * Father purchased*

a fine beef driven from the Willamette and slaughtered it at camp. We also milked two or three cows, and the above mentioned flour, beef and milk were our only known supply of provisions for the winter, except the venison, which our hunters might secure and a little camas, a wild tuber, which we could purchase, at times, from the Indians. Fortunately wild deer were then abundant in the Umpqua hills, and our hunters kept us well supplied with venison while we stayed there.

"During the winter Stoley and two others from our camp visited the Hudson Bay fort (near present Elkton), far down the Umpqua River, where each was supplied with a bushel of wheat or peas, according to choice; and a few handfuls of salt, nothing more being obtainable from there.

" * * * Father having brought a crosscut saw and a frow with him and there being excellent cedar timber near our camp, we went to work in early winter to build a cabin. About Christmas it was completed, with excellent cedar shakes for the roof, and excellent cedar puncheons for the floor and a comfortable chimney.*

*Father had sent word by some of our company (in the Thomas Holt party) the previous fall that we would need aid to reach the settlements * * * * and three men (Joseph Hess, Josiah Nelson, and Clark Rogers), * * * * came to us and brought us to the settlements in Chehalem Valley, Yamhill County, * * * *."*

*We left our camp in Umpqua Valley on the tenth of April, 1847; * * * *."* (DH)

Mr. Cornwall sent word ahead by Thomas Holt that they needed help to get out. Josephus Adamson Cornwall's impassioned plea, as printed in the March 18, 1847 Vol. II, No.3 issue of the *Oregon Spectator*, follows.

Cornwall's Letter

"The following letter has been received in this city and handed us for publication. The information which it contains may be considered reliable and we therefore hasten to publish it.

UMPQUA VALLEY, DEC. 27th. 1846

"Dear Sir - At the suggestion of a Mr. Holt, who says he is personally acquainted with you, I am induced to write to you, and through you to arouse the sympathies of the good people of Oregon, in behalf of a small company of emigrants who are unable to cross the Callapoia mountains before sometime next season - myself and a large family among them. We are not, it is true, in a state of actual starvation, as yet, but of great want, and we do not know what the consequence will be, unless we receive some aid from the settlement, as soon as practicable.

"We are in number about 25 or 30 souls, who are the last of the unfortunate ones who took the route to Oregon recommended by Mr. Applegate, and have lost nearly all our property, and almost every means of subsistence. And indeed, about the one half of the company was just at the point of starvation, when Mr. Holt, (whose liberality we shall not easily forget) helped us to three tolerably good beeves. We have scarcely any flour or salt in the camp; and nothing in prospect but a little poor beef, and occasionally a poor venison - which, is quite uncertain, for deer are very scarce, as well as very wild.

"We have made an effort to go to the Fort near the mouth of the Umpqua, to try to procure some provisions, if possible; but it proved ineffectual, as the waters were very high, and none of us know the way. We shall try again, but from information, it is very uncertain whether we shall be able to pro-

cure any assistance from that quarter or not.

"Some say it will be May or June next, before the road will be dry enough for us to reach the settlements, and that we shall be detained here at least some three or four months. And in conclusion, we are sorry to say, that we have been credible informed, that some of our fellow emigrants, who were more fortunate than ourselves, and had crossed the mountain, actually misrepresented our condition, to prevent bringing us supplies and pack-horses, by stating that we had plenty, and might have reached the settlements long ago, had it not been for our indolence, in order to receive fresh aid themselves, though so near the settlement.

"Now, in conclusion, we wish you to use your influence in our behalf, and try to induce some hardy young men to bring us some provisions, such as beef, flour and salt, as soon as the weather will permit. In doing which, you will confer, a lasting favor, which we will, as soon as possible, endeavor to remunerate.

Yours, respectfully,
J. A. CORNWALL"

Joseph Hess, Josiah Nelson, and Clark Rogers reached the stranded families in the spring in response to Mr. Cornwall's plea printed in the *Oregon Spectator*. They left their winter camp on April 10, 1847, slightly over a month after the plea was published. The families were taken to settlements in Chehalem Valley in Yamhill County near Newberg.

Holt's Rescue Mission

Thomas Holt, in company with five half breeds and one Frenchman, started on December 3, 1846, to assist the immigration then coming in on the Southern Route. They had a band of thirty-four horses.

Holt's party crossed LaCreole Creek and traveled fifteen miles on December 4, 1846. They camped on the north fork of Luckiamute River. Holt had two hundred pounds of flour and twenty-seven pounds of salt pork. J. B. Baldrouch sent one hundred pounds of flour and one bacon ham.

The party crossed both forks of Luckiamute River and camped on Soap Creek on December 5th. Mr. Goff was camped on Soap Creek. He was bringing Mrs. Newton out of the wilderness. Mr. Holt wrote that Mrs. Newton's husband was killed in the most barbarous manner.

The party crossed Mary's River on December 6th. There were five families with their wagons on the south bank of the river, and one family with only pack animals.

They reached the Long Tom River on the seventh. The party overtook Captain Campbell, Mr. Goodman, Mr. Jenkins, and Moses Harris headed for Canyon Creek Canyon. They had twenty-five horses and some provisions.

A Persistent Moses Harris

Moses Harris seems to be running back and forth-up and down the Scott-Applegate Trail in 1846. He was with the unsuccessful 1845 attempt to find a way out of the east side of the Willamette Valley. He represented the settlers in organizing the 1846 attempt to find a Southern Route out of the valley. He was with the road hunters from the May 15, 1846, beginning. He turned the first wagon train, the Vanderpool Party, onto the Southern Route on August 5, 1846. His record seems silent until he turns up in the first relief parties to reach the emigrants north of Rogue River Valley in late October. Harris was probably with the roadbuilders through August and most of September. It seems that Harris returned to the settlements after a previous rescue expedition to mount the second. One must admire his stamina and ability in mounting two relief expeditions in a little over two months after leaving the roadbuilders in late August, 1846. That shows a turn-around time of only a little over one month.

Holt's Rescue Mission Continues

Holt's rescue party met eight wagons and eight families out of provisions on December 9, 1846. Mr. Owens, Mr. Patten, Mr. Duskins, Mr. Hutchins, Mr. Howell, and Mr. Burrows overtook the Holt party with 24 horses. They also met several families out of provisions and waiting for assistance near present day Eugene on the 10th.

Four of Holt's party turned back on December 11, 1846, because they were afraid that if they went over the mountain, they will not get back before spring. Holt talked Mr. Baptiste into continuing on. The skeleton relief party moved on and met four or five families about noon. They could not get any farther without assistance. Mr. Goodman, Mr. Hutchins, and Mr. Howell turned back to help them in to the settlements. The remaining relief party moved on to the foot of the Calapooya Mountains where they found three families without teams or provisions. The full effect of his responsibility hit Thomas Holt. He felt for them and it was hard for him to pass, but he knew that there were other helpless families among hostile Indians ahead and he was bound to go and assist them.

As they crossed the mountain, they met one family on the top of the mountain and two families on the south side getting ready to cross on December 13. 1846. As they continued back on the Scott-Applegate Trail on December 14th, they met five families.

Mr. Campbell met his family and two others, Mr. Cornwall, and Mr. Dunbar on December 15th. Mr. Harris and Mr. Jenkins stopped here to help them. The Cornwall and the Dunbar families remained on Cabin Creek and Mr. Campbell left nearly all his property with him.

Thomas Holt, Mr. Owens, Mr. Patten, Mr. Duskin, Mr. Delore, and Mr. Batiste continued back up the Scott-Applegate Trail to a point ten miles south of the North Umpqua River where they met the last of the 1846 of immigrants. The last five families of 1846 Emigrants were: the Crump family, the Butterfield's family, widow Butterfield's family, the James Townsend family, and the Baker Family

Returning with the Baker family, Mr. Holt crossed Calapooga Mountain on January 1, 1847. He broke into a chache of provisions he had left on the way out. (TH)

The Oskaloosa Company

The Oskaloosa Company, The Last Wagon Train To Skinner's, left camp on Cabin Creek and moved to Scott's Valley near Yoncolla on October 31, 1847

S. 31 Passed on about 10 Ms and camped. Good camping anywheres but it has rained for the last 4 days.

Levi Scott believed that Scott's Valley was the most beautiful farm area in Oregon Country. He moved into the valley the next year. His home became the first mail stop in Umpqua County. Levi Scott's two sons, John and William Scott took out Donation Land Claims in the valley.

Levi Scott went farther west to stake his claim at Scottsburg on the tidewaters of the Umpqua River. Scottsburg developed as a seaport. Supplies and equipment moved through the port on their way to the gold fields in southern Oregon and the Yreka Valley in the middle 1800s.

The First Emigrant Wagons Over Calapooya Mountains in 1846

Virgil Pringle recorded the last few miles traveled by the first wagons to reach the Willamette Valley. His was one of the first two wagons ever to reach the Willamette Valley from the south. He was with the Levi Scott's crew building the first wagon road as they moved over Calapooya Mountain. Road building took time so their progress was much slower than the progress made by the 1847 emigrants.

"Wednesday, November 18, (1846.)— Go over one ridge of the mountains and make 2 miles. 2 miles.

"Thursday, November 19, (1846.)— Climb another ridge with double teams and make 3 miles headway and camp with little feed. 3—2308 miles (total miles from his home in Missouri.)

"Friday, November 20, (1846.)— Move forward to the top of the mountain on gently rising ground and camp with the foremost wagons 4 miles from last camp. One steer dies at this camp. 4 miles.

"Saturday, November 21, (1846.)— Make 2 miles headway and camp. Rains yesterday and today. 2 Miles.

Virgil Pringle went up a ridge northeast from the junction of Lee Creek with Thief Creek. The ridge was like a "hog's back" of a skinny hog sitting down with the vertebrae sticking up. Virgil Pringle went over one ridge (vertebrae) in two miles on November 18, 1846. He climbed another ridge (vertebrae) in three miles on the 19th, and another to the top of the mountain in four miles on the 20th. Although he says only on the 19th that the teams were doubled, it seems likely that double teams were required all three days.

Pringle's November 20, 1846, entry gives a major clue showing that he did not go up one side of the mountain, then down the other side near Cedar Creek. Pringle says *"Moved forward to the top of the mountain on gently rising ground * * * *."* He was on top of the mountain traveling its gently rising ridge toward its 1,965' peak.

A DAY IN NEED OF RESPECT

"Sunday, November 22, (1846.) — Help finish the road and complete the pass of the mountains and camp 2 miles from the foot in the Willamette Valley. My wagons and one other the first that entered the valley. All in good health and well pleased with the appearance of the country. Headway, 5 miles—5." (VP)

Virgil Pringle helped finish five miles of road to complete the pass of Calapooya Mountain and camped in the Willamette Valley two miles from the foot of the Calapooya Mountains.

Virgil Pringle's recording shows that Virgil Pringle's wagon and one other wagon were the first wagons to reach the Willamette from the south-on November 22, 1846.

The date that the first Oregon emigrants, through many trials and much hardship, successfully traversed the Scott-Applegate Trail into the southern Willamette Valley has been forgotten by the generations. It is known only in this one obscure reference by Virgil Pringle that never gets off the paper it is written on.

Levi Scott Completes The South Road Company's Road

Levi Scott wrote that several wagons met them at the foot of the mountains. The first emigrant wagons, upon reaching the Willamette Valley after passing through the Calapooya Mountains, were able to follow wagon tracks. Levi Scott felt his work was completed and went forward with a few of the lead wagons.

The Last Emigrant Wagon Train Over Calapooya Mountain

M. Nov. 1st. In about 3 Ms we commenced ascending the Calipooyah Mts. Passed up one or two hills and camped about 2 o'clock P.M. on a large hill with good grass. Distance to day about 7 Ms.

The wagon trail climbed the ridge north of Lee Creek from the five hundred foot elevation at the creek's mouth to the summit of the Calapooya Mountains four miles away and fourteen hundred feet higher. The peak of the large hill is one thousand nine hundred seventy-six feet above sea level and the pass is only fifty or sixty feet lower. The average grade up the ridge from the junction of Lee Creek with Thief Creek was 6.6%. The first part is much steeper.

A Pitiable Story of One Emigrant

Tolbert Carter wrote of a pitiable occurrence at the top of the Calapooya Mountains in 1846. Carter wrote of it as a comedy, however, it was a tragedy if it really happened.

Salal berries grow in an abundance west of the Cascades. It has strong vines that form three feet to as much as six feet of matted carpet that had been slowing the progress of the emigrants for days. The berries have an unusual flavor and are not commercially marketed. The emigrants were in dire straits and the salal berries could have been giving them some nourishment.

> *"On that day they met on the summit of the mountain a man named Durbin, with some provision on pack horses. At the place of meeting there was an abundance of wild (salal) berries * * * * but our hungry companion, not knowing but they might be poisonous, was afraid to eat them, as they made their distress known to Mr. Durbin, **** Tool, of Missouri, a large, portly young man, and a very agreeable gentleman, and, by the way, a Methodist. Dan Tool devoured a quarter of an acre, vines, berries and all."*

The Last Wagon Train Continues On To Skinner's

> *Nov. 2nd. Tues. Continued across the Mts where we camped in the Walammett valley at sunset. Distance 7 ms. Last two days rainy.* (LH)

The Oskaloosa Company continued north on November 2, 1847, descending to nine hundred feet in three or four miles to Martin Creek. They followed down Martin Creek another three or four miles, and camped in the rain near present day Monett southwest of Cottage Grove. The Last Wagon Train to Skinners had passed over the Calapooya Mountains and was in the Willamette Valley only a stone's throw from the Willamette River.

> *3rd. Passed down the valley about 10 ms and camped on the Wallamette river. Cloudy in the morning but little rain for the day.* (LH)

Little Tommy Davis was eight years old when he arrived in the Willamette Valley with the last wagon train to Skinner's. He was thirty-one when he returned to the Cottage Grove-Saginaw area with his wife, Missouri Hall Davis, to start their new family.

Missouri was the daughter of Thomas and Lucinda Robinett Hall, early Cottage Grove pioneers. Thomas and Lucinda emigrated to Oregon by the northern route in 1847. Lucinda was a relative of one of the founders of Cresswell. They lived on Hall Creek now at the southern edge of Saginaw. They provided a watering spot for the trail-weary travelers because they wanted to. Missouri was born in Oregon City in 1849 and claimed to be the first white child born in Oregon City after Oregon became a territory in 1848.

Thomas Davis' second son, Chester A. Davis lived with his grandparents on Hall Creek in Saginaw. Chester founded Davis Hall, an early social hall in Cottage Grove.

> *4th. Continued down the valley crossing the river once or twice and at*

sunset we arrived at Mr. Skinners, the first settler of the valley. Distance 18 MS. No Rain. (LH)

The Last Wagon Train To Skinner's continued down the Willamette Valley. They crossed and recrossed the river. At sunset they arrived at the Eugene Skinner's cabin in present day Eugene, Oregon on November 4, 1847.

Eugene Skinner's Cabin

Mr. Skinner was the southernmost settler in the Willamette Valley in 1846 and 1847. His first cabin was in section 30, T17S, R3W Wm. It was 3,121.9' south 57°25' east of the northwest southwest quarter section corner, and 2,801.4' north 42°44' west of the southwest corner.

He completed another home in late 1854 or early 1855 on his Donation Land Claim on section 31. It was 3,814.81' north 78° 24' east of its southwest corner and 2699.4' north 73° 30' west of its southeast corner.

Eugene Skinner's home was a small pole cabin he built in 1846. It was the first sign of civilization the emigrants had seen in traveling two thousand miles. The little cabin, without door or window, looked quite homelike to arriving emigrants. Several families whose teams had become exhausted stayed in the area for the winter. Some emigrants settled in the area.

Most of the beleaguered 1846 emigrants continued down the Scott-Applegate Trail and on to separate destinations in the Willamette Valley. Others made canoes and completed the rest of their journey down the Willamette River to Lee's Mission at Salem.

Others remained in and near Skinner's Cabin. James Layton Collins, co-author of Levi Scott's autobiography, stayed in Skinner's cabin during the 1846-1847 winter. Eugene Skinner, later in a document supporting a land claim dispute with a Mr. Shaw, wrote:

*"As to the house J. Q. Thornton Esqr. with all the Emigration of 1846 that came the Southern or Applegate route can testify also the breaking and sowing of wheat. One Mr. Collins of that emigration wintered in my house & many of them leaving their things and cattle here all winter * * * *."* (DC)

Lester Hulin continued his journal:

5th. Laid in camp near Skinners all day. Very rainy. (LH)

6th. Moved down (the river) about 4 Ms and camped. Day Rainy. (LH)

The Oskaloosa Company moved down the trail about 4 miles and camped on November 6, 1847. It rained all day.

David and Hannah had traveled The Scott-Applegate Trail five hundred thirty miles from the forks in the road on Mary's River to Skinner's Cabin on the Willamette River in forty-seven days.

Oskaloosa Company Disbands

Lester Hulin's day-by-day journal ends with the November 5th entry. Wagon trains broke up soon after reaching the Willamette Valley. Each family had its own destination in the Willamette Valley. Some families traveled together for a short distance, some as far north as Long Tom River. L. D. and Hannah Belknap Gilbert and their six children; Oren and Nancy Belknap and their four children, Ransom Belknap and Mahala and their two children; Samuel Fletcher and Tolitha Cumi Belknap Starr and their two children moved another twenty miles up the Scott-Applegate Trail and settled west of the present Monroe. They completed their overland journey to Oregon November 13 or 15, 1847.

Gilbert Hulin, great grandson of Lester Hulin, says that Lester Hulin continued on to the Monroe area before returning to settle in Eugene. There was quite a concentration of people from the Oskaloosa Company west of Monroe in southern Benton County during the 1847 - 1848 winter. It would be interesting to know if there were any Davises that stayed there while David and Hannah took Ann to Salem for medical attention.

Similarities in Lester Hulin's Journal And Incidents In The David D. Davis Family Journey

Ann Davis' obituary supplies the next information on the activities of David and Hannah Davis after they arrived in Eugene. But first, Joseph Gaston, in Centennial History of Oregon, lists several similarities in incidents that took place along the route to Oregon to the Lester Hulin day-by-day journal and David and Hannah Davis' trip: (l) They took exactly the same route from Ft. Hall (actually from northeastern Kansas); (2) Trouble with the same Indians at the same place: and (3) Trouble with the Indians at the place Ann Davis had her encounter with the Indians. (JG)

Levi Scott and Lester Hulin reported that Miss Davis was shot with Indian arrows in Fandango Valley and that she was with the same company that lost oxen in High Rock Canyon. Ann was the second daughter of David and Hannah Davis. (Her name was probably "Hannah" or "Hannah Ann" but she was always known as "Ann.") Family records show that she was injured in the Indian attack. Family pictures show her face to be badly scarred. Her 1904 obituary says she received arrow wounds on Pitt River. Levi Scott and Lester Hulin place the attack in Fandango Valley a few miles before reaching the river.

James N. Harty says D. D. Davis from Green Bay (Township), Lee County, Iowa was (re)elected Captain of the Company. Both Harty and Hulin wrote of several incidents happening at the same place, in the same manner, and at the same time: (1) Passing J. H. Fisher's grave that had been disturbed; (2) Blach baby is born; (3) Kimball child dies; (4) Cattle were scared by two horses, three fell and each lost one horn; and (5) officers were elected under the same circumstances.

Peter W. Crawford remembered that D. D. Davis was Captain of the Oskaloosa Company when he joined the Oskaloosa Company for a short time.

Report on Ann Davis' Health

David and Hannah Davis and their family had been in constant turmoil since the attack on Ann on the evening of September 29, 1847. They had been giving her all the medical attention they could along the trail and she was on the road to recovery. However, she needed professional medical attention that was available at Lee's Mission on the Willamette River in Salem, over seventy miles down the river.

The Davises Travel To Salem

The roads ahead were almost impassable because of heavy rains. Travel over the trail during the rainy season was dangerous and slow. It took Virgil Pringle almost three weeks in 1846. It would have taken the Davis family a month more to reach the settlements.

David Davis chose to float down the Willamette River. He went to a point on the Willamette River, probably near Goodpasture Park and cut down a large fir tree. It was much larger than anything he had ever seen in his life before reaching Oregon Country. He chopped out a "dugout" canoe and put it in the waters of the Willamette River. He loaded his family into the canoe and headed for Salem in search of medical help and supplies.

River travel was not new to David D. Davis. He had floated down the Ohio River from Dearborn County, Indiana, to the Mississippi River with four children in 1839. He traveled up the Mississippi to Lee County, Iowa where he farmed for about eight years before moving on to Oregon.

Comparing Travel Times
Virgil Pringle: Lester Hulin

Virgil Pringle was among the first emigrants to travel the length of the Scott-Applegate Trail in 1846. Lester Hulin was pilot of the last of the emigrants to travel the length of the road in 1847.

Virgil Pringle took 85 days to traverse the trail from the fork in the road to Skinner's Cabin in 1846. Pringle was one of the fastest travelers in 1846. He was back in the wagons when he left Rogue River. He moved past most of the wagons and drove the second wagon into the Willamette Valley.

Lester Hulin took 47 days, 38 days less, in 1847. Most of Virgil Pringle's added time was lost west of the Cascade Mountains.

Virgil Pringle traveled slower from the fork in the road to Fandango Pass, two days slower than Lester Hulin. He lost another day getting to the Sacramento River and another day moving through Lower Klamath Lake. At Keno he was 4 days behind Lester Hulin's time.

It took 9 days for Virgil Pringle to get from Keno to Emigrant Creek. It took Lester Hulin only 4 days. Most of the 5 days seems to have been lost "improving roads."

It took Virgil Pringle one day more than Lester Hulin to reach Jump Off Joe Creek, and an extra 2 days to reach the base of Cow Creek Canyon near present day Azalea. Virgil Pringle camped at Azalea on October 21, 1846. Lester Hulin camped there exactly one year later, on October 21, 1847.

Virgil Pringle took 5 days to the top of the mountain, Lester Hulin may have taken one. Virgil Pringle was in Canyon Creek Canyon for eight days, Lester Hulin only two.

CHAPTER 10

The Scott-Applegate Trail

Willamette Valley

Levi Scott remembered that there was no organization after the 1846 emigration entered Canyon Creek Canyon. Scott moved up the trail with the first emigrant wagons to his claim eight miles north of Mary's River. He stopped only a short time, then moved on when he found that his claim had been jumped. Other emigrants moved into the Willamette Valley on their own. Some emigrants stayed in and near Skinner's Cabin until spring before moving on. Most seem to have traveled on up the Scott-Applegate Trail to cross LaCreole Creek before moving on.

David Goff and five wagons were traveling up the Scott-Applegate Trail when Thomas Holt met them at Soap Creek on December 5, 1846.

Long Tom River

1847 Wagon Train Companies Break Up

The Oskaloosa Company, the last wagon train in 1847, broke up a few miles north of Skinner's Cabin. David Davis chopped a canoe out of a fir log and floated his family down the Willamette River to Salem. The Belknap-Gilbert-Starr family moved across Long Tom River in the Monroe area where they took up claims. Gilbert Hulin says that his great grandfather, Lester Hulin moved up the Scott-Applegate Trail to Monroe. He returned to Eugene area before he settled down.

Benjamin Davis arrived at Skinner's cabin a few days before the Oskaloosa Company. He and several other Davises settled about four miles north of Skinner's.

The Scott-Applegate Trail Skinner's Cabin To LaCreole Creek

In 1846 and 1847 the Scott-Applegate Trail ran along the Willamette River from Skinner's Butte past the old Day School to the present location of Junction City in 1846. The trail approximated present highway 99W north from Washburne Wayside. It crossed the Long Tom River near the Hubbard Road bridge at Bellfountain Junction on Highway 99 fourteen miles south of Mary's River.

Richard Ackerman, Scott-Applegate Trail historian, believes that the trail crossed the Long Tom River at present-day Monroe before going through Bellfountain to cross Mary's River west of Marysville.

Since Belknaps and Starrs settled west or west southwest of Monroe on November 13 and 15, 1847, there was an emigrant road there at that time. It is not known whether they were following the Scott-Applegate Trail or opening a new branch as they passed through.

Tolbert Carter says he was a boy driving a team for a widow lady in 1846. She became ill the night before the crossing of Long Tom River and a baby girl was born. Carter constructed a tent for the woman and child on the other side of the river. He returned and stayed with the woman and child while the others made the river crossing. They returned and took the bed on which the mother and baby were lying by the four corners. They took her across the river and placed her in the tent Tolbert Carter had prepared.

Another woman and child from the unfortunate Crowley family had died under similar circumstances the night before.

Tolbert Carter says that a ferry for the crossing was constructed of two small Indian canoes, a little larger than the wagons. The canoes were fastened together with a fir log. The contents of the wagons had to be taken out and placed on, not in, this frail boat. The process was repeated until the job was done and the property and people were on the other side of the river.

The Scott-Applegate Trail joined the old trapper's route on the west bank of the Long Tom River crossing. The Scott-Applegate Trail continued northward on a course near present day Highway 99 to Mary's River.

The Carters still had two wagons when they reached the river. Tolbert Carter drove one of the teams and his cousin drove the other. Tolbert Carter's younger brother drove the loose stock all of the way across. Tolbert Carter's cousin was thirty-five years old and had been a pioneer all of his life. He was manager of the caravan. (TC)

Mary's River was about fifty feet across at the place where Tolbert Carter crossed. J. C. Avery had a cabin near the crossing.

The Scott-Applegate Trail followed the route of Highway 99W north from Mary's River, for the first eight miles. The first night the Carters camped in the foothills near the residence of Harmen C. Lewis three miles north of Corvallis. The next day they reached Thomas Read's place. Read told them of an unoccupied cabin a short distance from his place. (D&HH)

The original Scott-Applegate Trail left the Willamette Valley and present day Highway 99W eight miles north of Mary's River near Peavy Arboretum, one and seven-tenths miles south of the Tampico Road Junction with 99W. The trail passed through a pass between the hills and across Soap Creek Valley to Soap Creek where Thomas Holt met the leading wagons of the emigration in 1846.

The Scott-Applegate Trail continued among the foothills to avoid flooded land as much as possible. The north fork of the Luckiamute River was out of its banks many times during the rainy season. Levi Scott wrote that when he approached it was a mile wide. The high water made it necessary to travel along marginal land above high water until the travelers were south of the present day bridge over the river. Then they took off straight across the valley through the water to high ground on the other side. They continued on to the crossing of LaCreole Creek at present day Dallas.

Holt Party Used An Alternate Trail

Thomas Holt traveled back on the trail to meet the last of the 1846 emigrants ten miles south of the North Umpqua River crossing before returning. Each of the five men remaining with the rescue party brought one family out of the wilderness. Rescuers and rescued followed the Scott-Applegate Trail into Soap Creek Valley. They turned from thc main trail as they entered the valley and continued northward on the east side of Soap Creek. One or both of the two Butterfield families stopped at a second Soap Creek Crossing twelve miles north of Mary's River.

The remainder of the Holt Party stopped with Mr. Williams on the Luckiamute River before traveling westward, stopping at Mr. Harris' place.

Barlow Trail

Painting by William H. Jackson, Scott's Bluff National Monument

Thomas Holt crossed a flooding Luckiamute River below the forks. Both James and David Townsend families stopped at the forks. Holt left the Baker family at Judge James Nesmith's place and turned toward home.

Barlow Trail

Samuel Kimbrough Barlow was an 1845 emigrant Captain of one of the divisions of Presley Welch's company. While in the Blue Mountains of eastern Oregon, he ascertained that there was a low spot in the Cascades just south of Mt. Hood. A small seven wagon company was formed to attempt to reach Oregon City from The Dalles by a new route south of Mt. Hood. Joel Palmer induced another twenty-three wagon to attempt the route. It was late in September and it seemed unnecessarily hazardous to some and they turned back. Reuben Gant drove the first wagon over an old Indian trail. They had a difficult time and finally found it necessary to leave the wagons under the care of William Berry. The others experienced considerable hardship but reached Oregon City.

Barlow was given a charter for a toll road and built a passable road. He donated all right, title and interest to the Territorial Government. The Territorial Government leased the road to other individuals who let the road deteriorate.

CHAPTER 11

Life on Soap Creek

Introduction to Rural Life in Oregon

James Willis Nesmith, among other things, was a 1843 emigrant and one of Oregon's first United States Senators. Nesmith addressed the Oregon Pioneer Association on two occasions; first in 1875, and again in 1880. His first address was a statement about Oregon as he found it in 1843. The second address was on internal and external commerce. He remembered that a rough form of hospitality of settlers was given with a liberal hand. The traveler went out with his own horse, blanket and lassrope. He had his own transportation, bed and security for his horse. Doors to settlers cabins always stood open to furnish him shelter and food without cost to the traveler. A traveler could count on this hospitality — and it was the custom that the guest sleep on the floor with his own blanket. (JWN Page 23.)

"The pioneer home was a log cabin with a puncheon floor and mud chimney, all constructed without sawed lumber, glass or nails, the boards being secured upon the roof by heavy poles." (JWN Page 37.)

"Sugar, coffee, tea and even salt were not every day luxuries, and in many cabins were entirely unknown." (JWN Page 37.)

*"Moccasins made of deer or elk skins and soled with rawhide made a substitute for shoes, and were worn by both sexes. Buckskin was the material from which the greater portion of the male attire was manufactured, while the cheapest kind of course cotton goods furnished the remainder. A white or boiled shirt was rarely seen, and was a sure indication of great wealth and aristocratic pretension. Meat was obtained in some quantities from the wild game of the forest or the wild fowl with which the country abounded at certain seasons, until such time as cattle or swine became sufficiently numerous to be slaughtered for food. The hides of both wild and domestic animals were utilized in many ways. Clothing, moccasins, saddles and their rigging, bridles, ropes, harness and other necessary article were made from them. A pair of buckskin pants, moccasins, a hickory shirt and some sort of cheaply extemporized had rendered a man comfortable as well as presentable in the best society, the whole outfit not costing one-tenth part of the essential gewgaws that some of our exquisite sons now sport at the ends of their watch chains, on their shirt-fronts or dainty fingers. Buckskin clothing answered wonderfully well for rough and tumble wear, particularly in dry weather****"*

*"There was no importation***beyond a few old-fashioned and illy constructed English Scythes, sicles and augers, and the simpler indispensable tools used by very primitive people. The grain was all cut with the cradle, or sickle, bound in bundles and tramped out in pens by horses or oxen, and winnowed by the breeze."* (JWN Page 37.)

Plows, mouldboard and all, except for the cutting portion, known as the share, were constructed of wood, while the harrow teeth

Panorama of David D. Davis Soap Creek Home Site

1848 Davis Home was in the cherry, pear, apple and oak trees near the center of this picture. The Applegate Trail emerged from these trees to cross the field and exits the left foreground. Landscapes below were taken back from among the trees at the place where the Davis' lived for five years.

were made of tough, seasoned white oak. Axes, chains, and other tools of iron or steel consisted of the rough article as they came from the hammer of not very expert blacksmiths." (JWN Page 37.)

David D. Davis, Captain of the last 1847 wagon train, built his first log cabin on a low bluff overlooking Soap Creek in 1848.

The Soap Creek settlement takes its name from the rippling little stream that starts at Sulphur Springs. The stream winds its way between the hills in a northerly direction out of Benton County. After many meandering miles, Soap Creek reaches the Luckiamute near its mouth at the Willamette River. The creek has the look of soapy water.

The first settlers arrived in Soap Creek Valley in 1846. They were the David Carson, Thomas Read, D. D. Stroud, Robert W. Russell, Smilie Carter, Tolbert Carter, Johanon Carter, J. S. Halter, and Green Berry Smith families. The David and Hannah Davis family were the first to settle in the Tampico area at the Southeast corner of Soap Creek Valley.

There were only a few pioneer cabins south of the Soap Creek Settlement in 1847. Eugene Skinner built a cabin in 1846 at the foot of Skinner's Butte where he established the town of Eugene. A. C. Avery lived on Mary's River where he established the town of Marysville, renamed Corvallis. Harman C. Lewis' lived a few miles north of Mary's River. Carters lived in the area. Thomas Read was a mile and a half south of Soap Creek Valley. Several of the 1847 Scott-Applegate Trail emigrants stopped and settled between Eugene and Corvallis. Three families of the 1847 Benjamin Davis party settled a few miles north of Eugene. Four Belknap families settled west of Monroe in November 1847.

David and Hannah Davis were in Salem with their children in the winter of 1847-1848. A doctor at Lee's Mission checked the injuries of Ann Davis and found that she was recovering nicely. Everything was back to normal after several months in the Salem area recuperating from the hardships endured on the Scott-Applegate Trail. The Davises were in high spirits, ready to settle in on their "land of milk and honey."

First, they had to find their own place in this magnificent new country. Then they had to recover their cattle and other property left near the Willamette River north of Skinner's cabin.

Land Of Milk And Honey

The details of the Davis' move from Salem to Soap Creek are unknown. However, the circumstances, and Levi Scott's apparent familiarity with details in their overland journey, suggest that they left Salem in the late winter or early spring in 1848. They found their way west to the 1846 LaCreole Creek Crossing used by the South Road Company, then back up the Scott-Applegate Trail.

David D. Davis Finds His Home

Levi Scott probably told David Davis of his preference for the Soap Creek area. David's destination was near Levi Scott's old claim. David was probably not aware that Levi himself would not settle in the area but would return to the northern end of the Umpqua Valley to establish his claim, also in 1848.

David D. Davis was looking to find a place to farm that also had water with power he could harness to run a mill as he made his way back up the Scott-Applegate Trail. He found it where the trail crossed Soap Creek. He settled his family in a safe place near a bluff overlooking Soap Creek. He returned for the possessions left near Skinner's Cabin.

The main thing on David's mind when he found the location on Soap Creek has been overlooked by Soap Creek Valley historians for many years. He wanted to build a flour mill and needed water he could harness to operate the mill. He had to abandon his millstones on Sweetwater River on his journey to Oregon but they could be replaced. Historians have told that Meshach Davis operated a wagon-making business and that he had a lathe and turned out furniture and wagon parts. Soap Creek rapids were in the yard of the Davises first home. It furnished that power needed to power the lathe.

David D. Davis Takes Inventory

The Davises were well off back in the United States. David D. Davis left his home in Iowa, United States, with seven wagons loaded with provisions and things to establish a new beginning in Oregon. He planned the journey well and had enough help to make their overland journey to Oregon.

The Davises left their property in the southern end of the Willamette Valley while they went for provisions (and apparently medical help for Hannah.)

Thomas W. Davis Memories Retold

Alice Delcina Sims Davis had many fond memories of her father-in-law, many years after his death. He was her knight in shining armor. She was sixteen when she married Elmer Davis, Thomas Davis' son and David D. Davis' grand-son. She was only eighteen when Thomas died in 1890. Thomas must have spun many tales while Alice listened. She is the only source of personal information about the Davises known.

She remembered that "Elmer's family settled in the southern valley". Only when pressed would she say that Corvallis was somewhere near the place. Once she related that the Davis' left back east with forty-seven wagons. David D. Davis had seven wagons of his own. The Davises arrived in the southern valley with the front end of one wagon. All of their possessions were tied to one axle and were pulled by two horses. They also had some loose livestock.

When asked what happened, or where did all that stuff go, she said that some was abandoned along the trail, some was lost to Indians, some was lost to the trail, some to the weather, and the what little was left was left in the valley while they went to the settlements. All of the oxen and some stock wandered off. Some property was pilfered by the Indians and emigrants in the area. Most of the property that was not stolen was permanently damaged by the harsh winter weather.

It seems David D. Davis recovered some live-stock kept by friends and rounded up some wandering animals. He got more back from local settlers. David D. Davis converted one of the wagons to a "cart." He salvaged enough personal possessions to load it.

Mrs. Ann Hendricks' (Ann Davis') obituary supports her story. The obituary says in part:

> *"Reaching the Willamette Valley * * * * they cut a tree just this side of the railroad crossing at McVey point, dug out a canoe and left their cattle and effects and firnished their journey by water to Salem."*

Losses - One Interpretive Argument

Joel Palmer, in a guide book, advised emigrants that a well-equipped wagon with four yokes of oxen could start from Missouri with a load of twenty-five hundred pounds. He also advised that:

> *"(E)ach adult should be provided two hundred pounds of flour, three hundred pounds of pilot bread, seventy-five pounds of bacon, ten pounds of rice, five pounds of coffee, two pounds of tea, twenty five pounds of sugar, half a bushel of dried beans, one bushel of dried fruit, two pounds of baking saleratus, ten pounds of salt, and half a bushel of corn meal. It was good to have half a bushel of corn, parched and ground for each adult."*

There were two adults and eight children in David D. Davis' family. Family tradition says that he had seven covered wagons on the trip. Ten or more single adult men were required to bullwhack and drive loose livestock. Twelve adults and eight children under fourteen were on his overland journey To Oregon. If three of the older children required as much as an adult and the other five children required an average of half as much, and each adult needed seven or eight hundred pounds of food. David had between twelve and fourteen thousand pounds of provisions distributed among his seven wagons.

If David D. Davis loaded his wagons exactly to Joel Palmer's recommendations, the total load of seven wagon loads would have been seventeen thousand pounds. All of provisions were used by the time they reached the Willamette Valley. The Davis family may have lost three thousand pounds of personal property, or as much as five thousand pounds, by abandoning it along the trail and through pilferage. If they had the four yokes (eight oxen) pulling each wagon, they also had fifty-six cattle and six wagons consumed, lost, strayed, or stolen along the trail or in the Willamette Valley.

That does not look like a great loss by 1996 standards but to our ancestors, although not unexpected, it was devastating. They were almost destitute. They had lost all of their personal effects, things they needed to start a new life in Oregon. But more important to them, many things could not be replaced in the Oregon frontier settlements. They also needed the oxen and untold loose stock to start up their farming business in Oregon Country, their Manifest Destiny.

The Davises Move To Soap Creek

The David D. Davises returned down the Scott-Applegate Trail to Soap Creek from Eugene. The trail turned into the hills from the Willamette Valley eight miles north of Mary's River a mile and a half north of Peavy Arboretum. The trail went through the small pass from the Willamette Valley to Soap Creek Valley. They saw the most beautiful sight of Soap Creek Valley as they emerged from the pass that evening. Their future home site was in the setting sun almost due west of the pass. The Scott-Applegate Trail continued straight to their new home on the bluff overlooking Soap Creek.

The Davis family was the first to settle in the Tampico area of Soap Creek Valley. The Davises built their first home on a short bluff overlooking Soap Creek Valley. The western edge of Soap Creek Valley is a hundred feet away and fifteen feet lower than the home. The Davises knew what they wanted and they wanted what they saw.

Soap Creek cut through alluvial deposits and into the basalt rock forming a shelf about ten yards wide on the west side of the creek. David D. Davis built his home on a bluff overlooking the shelf. Soap Creek is quite swift with rapids and white water as it runs over rocks between its steep banks. There is a loud roaring sound as the water bounds over the basalt rocks below the cabin site. Government land Office Surveyor's Field Notes say that Soap Creek was thirteen feet wide near the house. It was twenty feet wide and two feet deep one half mile downstream.

Government Land Office Surveyor's Field Notes show the home was in Section 24, T10S, R5W WM., four hundred forty feet east of the west section line. It was about three thousand thirty feet north of the south section line.

The home was probably typical of first pioneer homes in the year 1848, a log cabin about twelve by eighteen feet. Windows were covered with oiled paper to keep the weather out. Oil paper was opaque and worked almost as well as glass. Glass windows would be installed when glass became available. The one door was probably installed about the time the family moved in depending on their rush to get into their new home.

David D. Davis harnessed the power of the water in Soap Creek and used the power to turn a lathe to turn out wheel spokes and furniture parts. He built a blacksmith and carpenter shop next to the creek on the shelf between the bluff and the creek. The lathe was probably run by an undershot water wheel powered by the pressure built up by the rapids as they flowed between the perpendicular banks of Soap Creek.

However, an overshot water wheel using the pressure built up behind a dam of basalt rocks and alluvial deposits across Soap Creek could have been used. The banks are ten or more feet high in some places.

He left his prized millstones back on Sweetwater River to lighten his load on his way to Oregon. He was unable to build his flour mill, or maybe he looked things over when he arrived and decided upon a wagon factory.

The Scott-Applegate Trail Traces

The Scott Applegate Trail crossed Soap Creek a few yards from the carpenter shop. The blacksmith & carpentry shop was between the home and the trail.

The crossing was a mystery to historians until Bob Zybach found it in 1989. He is a Cultural Resource Specialist and Forest Historian for Oregon State University Research Forest. OSU owns the property where they built the first home. Mr. Zybach says that he had a particular interest in locating a Scott-Applegate Trail crossing. He surveyed Soap Creek with Milt Madden, Professor of History at Lane County Community College, and Kevin Sherer, archaeology student at Oregon State University. They found the Soap Creek wagon crossing and a nearby dump site. Mr. Zybach looked for confirmation of the finding. He interviewed Gene Glender, whose family owned the property in the 1920s. Mr. Glender told Mr. Zybach that he did not know anything about the emigrant crossing. However, when Mr. Zybach asked about the dump site, Mr. Gender replied that the dump site was "down by the old wagon crossing." Mr. Zybach had his needed confirmation.

This writer was going to walk Soap Creek looking for the Scott-Applegate Trail crossing and contacted Mr. Zybach to see if he had any tips he might share. He said that he had found the crossing and showed me where it was. The crossing was about five hundred feet from the southern boundary of David D. Davis' Donation Land Claim. There are a couple of places where old trappers could have crossed Soap Creek within a half mile downstream. However, there are none between the crossing and the claim Boundary.

The banks have traces of a ramp going into the water, and another on the other side coming out of Soap Creek. The water was less than three feet deep but could be deeper following a good rain. Soap Creek has worn itself into volcanic basalt rock. In the valley the basalt rock is covered by several feet of alluvial deposits and top soil.

William and Charles Glender discovered a fifteen pound elephant tooth about fifteen feet below the surface in the early 1920's. The Glenders were making improvements to a spring on David and Letitia Carson's claim next door. Several thousand years ago cataclysmic occurrences filled the entire Willamette Valley with hundreds of feet of water, mud, and gravel. Everything that lived here must have been crushed or drowned and buried among sediments. Glender's elephant was probably among them. (BZ)

Archeological Site

Joseph Hunter was about Thomas Davis' age when there were few boys that age in the community. Joseph Hunter was a longtime friend and was in the Davis house many times. He told Dr. Blake in an interview almost seventy years later the house was on Soap Creek near a spring. The Davis home was only a few feet from a spring on David Carson's Donation Land Claim. Cows belonging to Oregon State University Research Farm have developed quite a quagmire around the spring and it could not be approached.

Fragments of a fruit orchard with several large cherry, pear, and apple trees up to eighteen inches in diameter are on the site. Mr. Zybach has taken an inventory and marked the trees. All have historic significance and trees now bear historic "Davis" apples. The fruit trees are intermingled with native oak and other hardwood trees. Many flowers still grow in the yard and have spread into the field. There are many varieties of native flowers and several rose bushes about three feet high.

The site is in Oregon Geographic Names as the first Postoffice on Soap Creek and David D. Davis is shown as the first and only Postmaster. The store was operated by James O'Neil in the D. D. Davis home. James Anderson O'Neil, one of the founders of Oregon's provisional government, became David Davis' step-son-in-law about that time.

Pre-State Roads

Transportation through Soap Creek Valley developed in four phases. The first phase was before the immigrant began coming from the south into the southern Willamette Valley. The second phase was the immigration into the southern Willamette Valley in 1846 and 1847. The third phase involves movement of pioneers before Territorial Roads developed. The fourth and last phase were County Roads under County and Territorial governments.

The Indians, the Trappers, the drovers, and the first emigrants developed a system of trails through Soap Creek Valley. They were able to cross Soap Creek Valley from northwest to southeast in a more direct way during dry weather because they could ford Soap Creek almost anywhere when the water was low.

They altered their way of travel during rainy weather to go farther up Soap Creek to where they could cross more safely. They did not travel with wheeled vehicles so they did not need roads.

Scott-Applegate Trail

Emigrants who came into the southern Willamette Valley and Soap Creek Valley in 1846 and 1847 made roads suitable for the first wagons where none existed. Before 1851, roads developed in the Willamette Valley where the settler drove his wagon. Other wagons followed in the tracks made by the wagon. When many wagons followed making tracks, the tracks became a road.

The way the road went was controlled by where the wagon was, where the driver wanted it to be, and the obstacles hindering a direct approach to where he wanted to be. The Indians burned the vegetation in the valleys yearly leaving an almost unobstructed way. Accessible fording points were needed to cross streams. Hills, rock, mud, trees, logs, and buildings were avoided. Settlers moved in, putting up more obstacles, fences, plowing fields, and building buildings.

The Scott-Applegate Trail from the forks in the road on the Humboldt River to Skinner's Cabin was usually confined to a narrow corridor.

Travel throughout the Willamette Valley was not as confined. Emigrants could travel almost anywhere they chose. They were limited on the east by the Willamette River, and on the west by the Coast Range of Mountains, and by various water obstacles, streams and swamps in between. Wagons began leaving their tracks all over the Willamette Valley. These tracks soon became a network of roads north from Skinner's Cabin to the settlements in the northern part of the valley.

The Scott-Applegate Trail Defined

The Scott-Applegate Trail is narrowly defined in these pages as "the Emigrant Road used by the westward moving emigrants in 1846 and 1847." The Scotte-Applegate Trail was also used by the first 1848-1849 gold seekers traveling south to California. The eastern end of the trail was also used by people emigrating from the United States to California.

Pioneers began settling in and immediately began to developed a network of roads feeding into Scott-Applegate Trail. Such pioneer roads are excluded in the definition of an Emigrant Road

The commercial road through Soap Creek Valley was known by many names: The old fur trader's trail, Road to Marysville, Scott-Applegate Trail, Portland-Umpqua Valley Road,

The Applegate Trail crossed Soap Creek (lower left), went through an opening in the trees (upper left), and through the open field and turned right (upper right). The line of trees in the lower right picture are growing in the old wagon road.

Benton County Road No. 3, Territorial Highway, The Road To California, and Tampico Road.

The road was straightened up a bit starting in 1854 when the county surveyed the road. The new road was surveyed straight across Soap Creek Valley. The new road that followed the survey was not in the tracks of the Scott-Applegate Trail. Pioneer roads were available by the time 1851 emigrants arrived over the Southern Route.

Most 1846 & 1847 emigrants moved north from Skinner's Cabin through Soap Creek Valley during rainy weather when Soap Creek was high. The Scott-Applegate Trail followed the route of the old fur trader's trail from the southeast to northwest across Soap Creek Valley. The Scott-Applegate Trail passed from the Willamette Valley to the Soap Creek Valley through a pass in the hills east of the valley. The trail crossed into David D. Davis' Donation Land Claim at the pass. It left the pass at a point in the hill and went west across the valley. It crossed Soap Creek and turned north along the west boundary of David D. Davis' Donation Land Claim.

The Portland to Umpqua Valley Road, or Territorial Road, replaced the Scott-Applegate Trail. Except for the tracks on the west boundary and the Soap Creek wagon crossing, only memories of the Scott-Applegate Trail remain.

The rights of land owners should be respected. The land north of Tampico Road through Soap Creek Valley is private property in 1996. The land owners deserve your respect of their rights. The land on the south side of Tampico is owned by Oregon State University as part of the Research Forest and access is restricted.

Thomas Holt's Rescue Mission Through Soap Creek Valley

Thomas Holt, in recording his rescue mission in December 1846 and January 1847, chose two routes through Soap Creek Valley. On his outward journey to the Umpqua Valley, Holt crossed both the north and the south forks of the Luckiamute River on December 5, 1846. He camped on Muddy Creek nine miles north of Mary's River. On his return on January 11, 1847, he traveled twelve miles north from Mary's River and camped on Muddy Creek. He crossed the Luckiamute below the forks on January 17th.

The distances recorded by Thomas Holt show that he recorded Soap Creek as Muddy Creek, maybe because he saw its "soapy" appearance as "muddy".

Thomas Holt, on his outward journey, traveled eleven or twelve miles south from the LaCreole Creek crossing before crossing the South Fork of the Luckiamute. The trail changed to a southeasterly direction at the South Fork of the Luckiamute. It went through Soap Creek Valley, and through the pass at Tampico and into the Willamette Valley north of Thomas Read's cabin. On his return, Thomas Holt retraced his steps through the pass to Soap Creek Valley.

Thomas Holt used another convenient trail from the pass at Tampico north to cross LaCreole Creek east of Dallas. History seems to ignore the trail that branched northward from the northwest end of the pass. It is shown on the General Land Office Surveyor's Field Notes. It crosses Soap Creek about thirteen miles north of Mary's River - downstream from the outbound crossing. The trail continues in a northerly direction, slightly west of north, and crosses the Luckiamute River below the forks. It continues in that direction almost to LaCreole Creek. The extra distance to the crossing on the return trip shows that Thomas Holt stayed on the east side of the creek for three or four more miles. (TH)(GLO)

The Government Land Office Surveyor's Notes record that another road went southwesterly from the Scott-Applegate Trail on the eastern side of Soap Creek Valley near the present day junction of Soap Creek Road with Tampico Road. Settlers in the upper reaches of Soap Creek Valley may have traveled up and down both sides of the valley.

Benton County Road 3, Territorial Road-Now Tampico Road

An Act of road legislation passed by the Oregon House on June 30, 1851. Four days later the council provided that Territorial roads should be viewed, surveyed, and established. The roads were to be clearly marked by stakes or blazed trees. The roads were to be platted sixty feet wide.

John H. Kendall surveyed a "Road leading from the Public Square in the town of Corvallis to the Polk County line near the house of Wm. J. Berry." He filed the plot on December 11,1854, and there was an official road through Tampico. Present day Tampico Road is close to the first Benton County Road #3 surveyed in 1854.

Benton County Road #3 was a portion of the Territorial Highway system although there are no Benton County records that say so. There are no records that say when the bridge across Soap Creek was built.

John Horner said that the 1926 Tampico Road followed the same course as when Edward Marsh carried the mail riding a mule. Later Thomas Morgan drove his stagecoach sounding his bugle as he approached the young town.

Territorial Road

"County Road #3" became Territorial Road and was used as Tampico's main Street in 1854. The Scott-Applegate Trail remained as the lower of the two Tampico Town streets for several years before it faded from use. The new County Road #3 is the Tampico Road you see today.

Benton County Commissioners' notes still referred to this village as Tampico in 1866. David D. Davis had probably named the location "Tampico" when he started his store and hotel in 1853. He was named postmaster of "Soap Creek." Benton County was officially referring to it as "Tampico" in 1854.

Life In The First Oregon Settlements

The first year in the new country was a very hard one for most pioneers. Most of the emigration into the southern end of the Willamette Valley arrived in the late fall with little more than themselves and the clothes on their backs.

David D. Davis arrived in the southern Willamette Valley on November 4, 1847. The *Oregon Spectator* reported their arrival:

> *"I have the pleasure to announce to you the safe arrival by the southern route of a fourth company of immigrants of 20 or more wagons. This party left St. Joseph on the 22d June (May) being in the rearward of so large an immigration fared but badly until they took the S. route.-Finding on it an abundance of feed, their teams rapidly recuperated and upon arrival here were in fine condition. From the best information I can get they have made the most saving trip that has ever yet been made from Fort Hall, having lost but four animals on the road (which were stolen by Indians). - The party kept no guard, and it is remarkable they lost no more; a woman was wounded in the arm by an arrow. So terrible had the Kanyon been described to them that they were expecting daily to arrive at it until they came into the settlement and declared there is no Kanyon on the road. They brought with them 80 sheep."*

The Benjamin Davis family is another example of the hard times. They had only seventy-five cents when they reached their settlement a few miles north of Skinners. They sold their cow for some corn. Later they sold their oxen to buy other commodities. Before the first winter was over, they met others that were even needier. They shared their supplies with them and finished the season on a diet of boiled wheat.

The rugged life brought out the best in most people. Sharing was a very important part of their lives. Cooperation and helping neighbors was a "must." Barn raisings and house raisings were common-place and were a social event. Early pioneers got their pleasure in socializing with and helping neighbors.

There was little cash around at that time. The barter method of buying and selling was often used. The merchant became the person relied upon to evaluate his customers trading stock in addition to evaluating the commodities he had for sale and other commodities offered in exchange.

One good thing about the barter system was that it lessened the cases of armed robbery. Actually however, there were few criminals to be found in these pioneer settlements. Jails were not prevalent. The Soap Creek settlement had one but mainly to take care of the minor offenders or rowdies who disturbed the peace of the community.

Another development of this rugged pioneer life was that it encouraged individual resourcefulness. There just were no rewards for those who would not work. Ambition, strength of character, honesty, and dependability were things that men would strive for and expected to find in others. Men were measured by these admirable qualities. There was plenty of work that had to be done.

The Davis Family And Measles Arrive in Soap Creek

The first year in the Soap Creek settlement was little different for The Davis family than for most other settlers. An outbreak of measles took Hannah's life on June 15, 1848. That was only one month after the Davises arrived In Soap Creek on May 15th.

Contrary to popular belief, the measles virus was not carried to Oregon, or California, by emigrants along the Oregon Trail in either 1846 or 1847. Although measles was rampant in the United States in 1846 & 1847, it was not carried westward by emigrants using the Oregon Trail. Many diaries were written about the trail. They even mention sickness and death from many of the diseases common to that time. However none of the diaries mention "measles" as one of those diseases. Indians were already dying in Oregon Country before the 1847 emigrants arrived.

Indians Introduce Measles In Oregon

Robert Boyd reported in the *Oregon Historical Quarterly*, Volume 95 Number 1, that the measles virus was introduced into the northwest by Indians at Fort Nez Perce during the last of July 1847. A war party of two hundred Walla-Walla and Kye-use Indians headed by Chief Peo-Peo-mox-mox, Chief of the Walla-Walla Indian Tribe brought the measles to the northwest. The war party had been out for eighteen months to northern California. The foray was a total disaster with many of the young men dying of measles. When news of the disaster reached Fort Nez Pierce, the Indians sent messengers in all directions to carry the story. The messengers probably carried the measles virus with them to their home communities. (RB)

The epidemic spread and after only two weeks large numbers of Indians were coming down with the disease. News, rumors, misinformation, and lies, spread throughout the area leading to the infamous "Whitman Massacre" of November 29, 1947. One particular vindictive rumor that Dr. Whitman was poisoning Indians he was treating, was probably spread by a disenfranchised Hudson's Bay Company trapper. (RB)

The spread of the virus by Indians was supplemented when emigrants from the United States began catching it from the Indians at Whitman Mission and carrying it down the Columbia. (RB)

Indians suffered most of the losses because their manner of treating measles was counterproductive. It seems that the natives induced a fever by using sweat lodges when fever was not already present. They treated the fervor with cold water baths. The sweating and cold water treatment was associated with the increased mortality among the Cayuse, upper Chinook, Cowlitz, and Calapooya Indians. (RB)

Persons with measles running a fever

from measles should be kept warm. One reaction of fast succession of fever with cold is a chill. People running a fever from measles were known to die after drinking a cool glass of water.

A March 16, 1848, letter by James Douglas, a Hudson's Bay Company Factor, said the measles had gone so far south as to cause inferior return of furs from the lower Umpqua River. (RB)

David and Hannah Davis arrived at Soap Creek with their family on May 15, 1848, according to government records. The measles virus has an incubation period of fourteen days, so she was exposed to the disease a few days after they arrived and started building their new home alongside the trail on the bluff overlooking Soap Creek. She died on June 15, 1848, as shown on her headstone near the south entrance to the west side of New English Cemetery south of Monmouth, Oregon.

But Life Must Go On

David Davis was a resourceful man and had good judgment, or good fortune if you prefer. He arrived at the settlement with some livestock and equipment. He had been a blacksmith, a farmer and livestock raiser. He was a good manager and, with his leadership, the wagon train had reached the settlement with a flock of sheep.

The published 1853 inventory of personal and real property for the Soap Creek Precinct showed that the Davises had thirty-five head of cattle, sixty sheep, twenty hogs, five horses, a clock and a watch. Improvements on the land were valued at twelve hundred dollars. The combined value of real and personal property was more than thirty five hundred dollars, a sizable sum for that time. (EE/DRD) A sale of about 20 acres of the land in 1994 shows that David D. Davis' Donation Land Claim land alone was worth almost $1,280,000 in 1994.

Life in the early settlement was one with a homespun economy. The sixty sheep at the Davis place must have produced many fine garments to keep the people warm and protected. Carding tools and spinning wheels were found in most of the early homes. In some early communities there was a law that required every household to have a trained person to do the spinning. It was essential since most of the basic needs of the early settlers were provided for in the form of raw materials and hand labor turned them into usable commodities.

Fireplaces were used to heat the main rooms of a house while a special fireplace with a built-in baking oven was sometimes used in the kitchen. However, cast iron stoves were becoming popular. Kitchen fireplaces were surrounded by a variety of special wrought iron tools to help the cook with roasting, toasting, boiling and frying. Other handmade wooden tools to help the cook with her work were found around the kitchen.

Thomas Davis was a carpenter and it was probably during these early years that he became the skilled artist that he was in carving. He carved the fiddles that he played at dances throughout the southern Willamette Valley. Alice Delcina Sims Davis gave me the parts to an uncompleted violin that Thomas Davis had carved just before his death. The parts mysteriously disappeared in the late 1940's. Thomas Davis handed down his skill to his son, Charles Elmer Davis. A grandson, Clarence Thomas Davis, was proud of his ability to carve detailed sailing ships (in or out of bottles). Clarence and his brother James carved cooking tools.

Meshach Davis was a wagon-maker skilled at turning out wooden parts for wagons and furniture. He was skilled at forging wagon parts, a skill that provided him with the ability to make iron cooking gadgets.

Early pioneers had large families. There could be two dozen people around a table when it was spread for some special dinner such as Christmas. The housewife of that time was as comfortable in her home as her modern counterpart is in the midst of all her convenient appliances - probably more comfortable.

There was always a lot of work to be done

in the pioneer home. There was cooking, spinning, weaving, sewing, mending, darning, sweeping, cleaning, washing and caring for her family. And that was just the inside work. She had the chores of looking after the chickens, milking a family cow, and tending the vegetable garden. With all of this, the housewife and mother could have the help of her children if they were well trained and set to the task.

The sight of one of these early pioneer kitchens might turn away a modern housewife with all of her gadgets. However, we should remember that the women of that time managed pretty well. They could do great things with their equipment. Mothers became the grandmothers whose houses the children of later generations wanted to go to for any reason or no reason other than it was Grandmother's House.

David D. Davis Marries Sarah Bowman

After Hannah's death in 1848, David D. Davis married Sarah Bowman in 1852. Several of Sarah's children moved into the Davis household. David had four unmarried children living at home. The Davis household increased to eight or more and had outgrown the first house that he had built hastily back in 1848. There were several farm buildings at that location. He farmed his three hundred twenty acre farm that extended a mile to the east along the Scott-Applegate Trail.

Probably more important to his decision to move, it became apparent that his first house would not be on the main road. Preliminary plans for County Road # 3 called for the road to pass through Soap Creek Valley in a straight line. It would pass three fourths of a mile north of the Davis home. People would have to go out of their way to patronize his store or mill.

Regardless of the reason, David D. Davis chose to move into town, but finding that there were no towns, he started his own. Joseph Hunter told Dr. Blake: *"In (1853), D. D. Davis bought the land and built the first residence in the town site of Tampico. This residence was used as a store and hotel * * * *."*

James Anderson O'Neil, one of Oregon's earliest politicians and experienced in setting up grist mills, established a store in the vacated Davis residence. Joseph Hunter told Dr. Blake that he purchased some books from James O'Neil at this store in the old Davis home on Soap Creek in 1853.

Wagon Ruts

The Applegate Trail went up the hill seven hundred fifty feet after crossing Soap Creek. It turned due north for over half a mile along the west boundary line of David D. Davis Donation Land Claim. The vegetation line along the west boundary of the claim is in the old Applegate Wagon Road. It appears that the GLO Surveyor used that trail as the west boundary of David D. Davis' Donation Land Claim. Traces of the old wagon road are obscured only by a thick growth of young fir trees. Before the white man started settling in this country in 1846, the Indians kept most of the trees off the land by constantly burning the hills and prairies. Although this section of the Scott-Applegate Trail was only used from 1846 through 1853, the wagon road was significant in the history of the Oregon settlers and should be preserved. (BZ.)

There is no accurate record of the number of emigrants or emigrant wagons entering the Willamette Valley from the south. There were only about one hundred fifty wagons of record that entered the Scott-Applegate Trail at the fork in the road in 1846 and 1847. They were headed for the southern Willamette Valley. Many of the one hundred fifty wagons broke apart and were abandoned along the trail. Some emigrants stopped to settle farther south in the Willamette Valley. There were probably some who came through that were not recorded. Many more settlers who passed through, or settled in, the Soap Creek Valley, came over the northern route of the Oregon Trail.

It is not realistic to assume that all of

the traces were made by emigrants from the Southern Route. The first wagons to cross Soap Creek probably came to Oregon by the northern route. Eugene Skinner, J. C. Avery, Levi Scott, Thomas Reed, and Hiram Lewis brought wagons into Benton County from the northern Willamette Valley before the 1846 emigrants arrived via the Southern Route.

The crossing and traces located in sections 24 & 25 of T10S, R5W Wm. between Soap Creek and the hill should be preserved as part of the history of Oregon. The first commercial business in the area was established along the old wagon road by James Anderson O'Neil, one of the first settlers in Oregon. It was used by the emigrants and by pioneers, and was the first north-south commercial wagon road in pre-territorial Oregon Country. It was probably used as an alternate crossing by earlier trappers and drovers. The Scott-Applegate Trail served as seed for many later north-south roads including the present day interstate (also international) freeway system on the Pacific Coast.

David D. Davis' Donation Land Claim

David D. Davis and his family settled in Soap Creek Valley on May 15, 1848, on six hundred forty acres of land. The exact configuration of the squatter's claim is unknown, however it must have included the land within his Donation Land Claim. David D. Davis filed application # 40 on three hundred twenty acres under the Donation Land Claim Act of 1850 on June 30, 1850. The land was located in sections 23 and 24, Township 10 South, Range 5 West of the Willamette Meridian in Soap Creek Valley where the Scott-Applegate Trail crossed Soap Creek. He received his patent, #4515 to three hundred twenty and one tenth (320.1) acres of land from President Ulysses S. Grant on October 4, 1875, twenty-five years later and fifteen years after his death. (BLM)

David D. Davis' Big Disappointment

This is an oversimplification of what happened. There is no doubt that David D. Davis was planning to receive a full section, six hundred forty acres of land, from the United States government. Previous land grant acts gave a full section of land to men meeting other requirements of the specific act.

David D. Davis had planned his overland journey to Oregon on the assumption that he would receive a full section. That was the general assumption. James Neall wrote:

> *"The prevailing expectations of the Oregon settlers was that Congress would pass an act of Donation to each settler a section of 640 acres of land, and it was this expectation, when I found myself landed here with all my business arrangements served, to secure this land before returning."*

James Neall got homesick and returned to the United *States "over what was known as the Applegate Cutoff"* in the spring of 1848. James Neall was a single man expecting to return to Oregon to claim his section of 640 acres of land. He traveled south through Soap Creek Valley on the Applegate Cutoff. David D. Davis built his first house on Soap Creek, only a few feet from the Applegate Trail. They both had the same expectation-receiving a section of land. (JN)

David D. Davis received more than one devastating blow on June 15, 1848, when his beloved wife died. At that time he could not see into the future and realize that the United States was about to penalize him because of his wife's death. He continued his expectation of receiving a section of land up until the 1850 Donation Land Act finally passed.

David D. Davis, Meshach Davis, George W. Roberts, William Beatty, and William J. Crouch were the only landowners in Tampico before 1860.

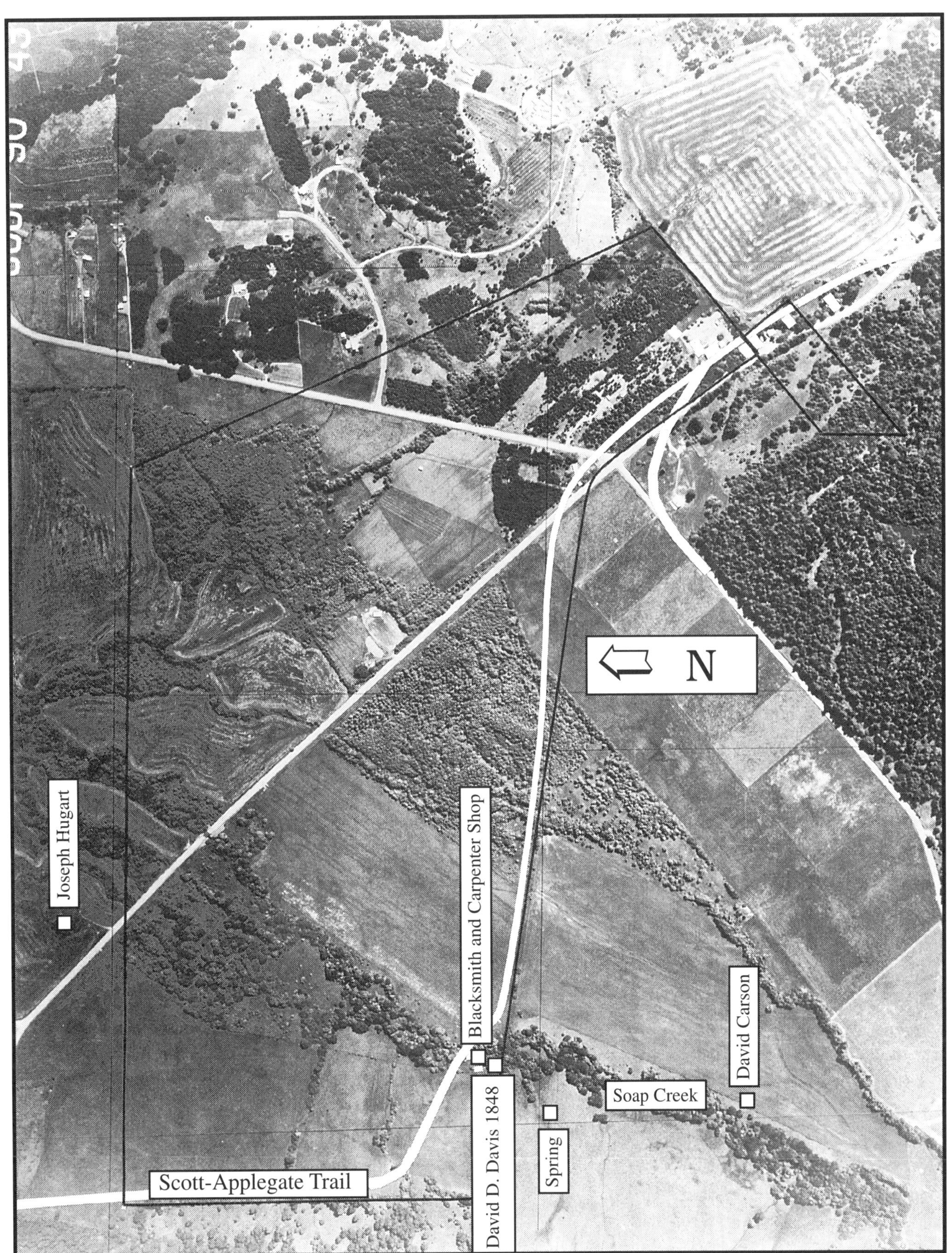
N
Joseph Hugart
Blacksmith and Carpenter Shop
David Carson
Soap Creek
David D. Davis 1848
Spring
Scott-Applegate Trail

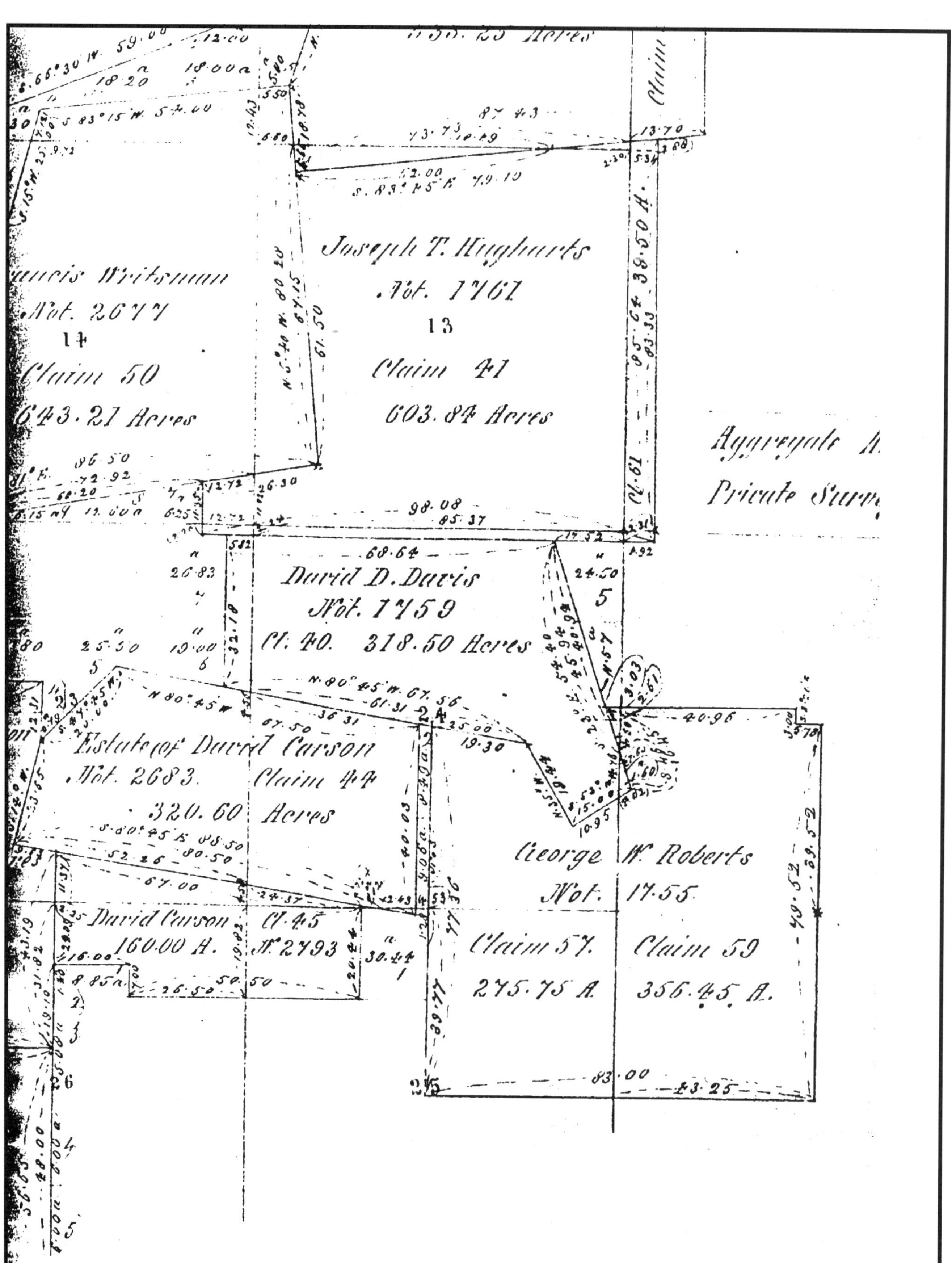

Joseph T. Hughurts
Not. 1761
13
Claim 41
603.84 Acres
Not. 2677
14
Claim 50
643.21 Acres
David D. Davis
Not. 1759
Cl. 40. 318.50 Acres
Estate of David Carson
Not. 2683.
Claim 44
320.60 Acres
David Carson
160.00 A.
Cl. 45
No. 2793
George W. Roberts
Not. 1755
Claim 57.
275.75 A.
Claim 59
356.45 A.

Donation Land Claim Bearing Tree and Marker

The southwest corner of David D. Davis' claim was the base point in describing other property in the area. David D. Davis claimed only one quarter of the land circled around the corner. George W. Roberts claimed the other three quarters.

Although David D. Davis came into the Soap Creek Valley the second year, he was the third person to file a claim in his area. John Wiles filed Donation Land Claim # 2 and Green Berry Smith filed Donation Land Claim # 5. Both were a mile or more north of David D. Davis' Donation Land Claim # 40. Jacob Modie filed claim #46. George Roberts filed claims #'s 57 & 59, and David Carson filed claims #'s 44 & 45 next to the Davis claim.

David D. Davis must have done some scurrying around to make his application fit into the legal requirements of the Act. The land that he settled on in 1847 or 1848 contained six hundred forty acres. The land described in Notification 1759 allows only three hundred twenty acres. Documentation shows that he refined his claim in 1850 after Hannah's three hundred twenty acres had been stripped from his claim. Perusal of other claims files show that settlement dates in 1850 were normal. However, Monroe Hodges' Donation Notification Claim file contains a statement sworn to by David D. Davis that he knew Hodges' after the thirtieth day of May 1848. The same document shows that Davis had established his residence on his claim in the valley on May 15, 1848. The 1850 Donation Claims Act only reduced the boundaries of his claim.

Granting Donation Land Claims

A Surveyor from the Government Land Office arrived in Soap creek to administer the Applications for Donation Land Claims. The Surveyor was charged with Administering the Act as it applied to each of the settlers making applications. He was also faced with the reality that land had not only been claimed, but land had also been sold or exchanged for many years.

The Surveyor used the procedure that was used in most of the early land grants known as "Grand-Fathering In." The Surveyor looked at the land that the claimant possessed at the time of the survey. He surveyed the land and applied the technicalities of the Act. David D. Davis' claim was cut down from one section of land to one-half section of land sometime between 1847 and 1853, either before or after he filed the application.

Negotiating may have taken place to allow him keep both residences and limit the amount of land to three hundred twenty acres. The two residences were over a mile apart.

The Surveyor made the final survey and laid out the corners, boundaries, and wrote the legal meets and bounds description of the land to be allowed under the claim.

Donation Land Act of 1850 Had Loopholes A Slave In Soap Creek Valley

The Oregon Donation Land Act of 1850

was intended to provided free land to white adult emigrants to the new territory. An unusual feature of the Act is that it allowed a man's wife to claim the same amount of land as was in her husband's claim. Before long, the legal age of marriage for women in the Oregon Territory was twelve.

David Carson claimed land next to David D. Davis. He also claimed land for a common law wife, Letitia. Letitia had been David Carson's slave in Kentucky and he brought her to the Oregon Country as his common law wife when he emigrated in 1847. Upon David Carson's death in 1853, Letitia sued the executor of her husband's estate for the money from the sale of David Carson's claim applicable to their relationship.

It was illegal to own slaves in Oregon. Common Law Marriages have never been recognized since James Anderson O'Neil sold his copies of the Iowa Statutes to the provincial government 1843. Oregon patterned its statutes after Iowa law. The question of whether David Carson had found a "loophole" in the act had to be decided in court.

CHAPTER 12

Old Tampico

The Town Stood When the West Was New and Men Were Men

From Arthur King's Tampico Epitaph

This chapter is dedicated to Edwin Erwin Davis, co-author with David Ronald Davis, of "Our Davis Pioneer Ancestors." Erwin contributed the funds for this Benton County marker. He is the only living grandchild of Thomas W. Davis, son of David D. Davis.

It is hard to imagine that an entire town was once located in this quiet valley. It has been said that despite its short existence tales of rowdiness and general lawlessness have survived to this day.

However, reading available samples of these tales fails to show that early Oregon pioneers were any different than their descendants are a hundred and fifty years later. Preachers are still telling stories about other preachers. Country people still fight country people. City people have replaced their fists with guns, but still fight other city people.

Town of Tampico Memorial Marker

Horses still race down the stretch. People can still lose their shirts, cows, and farms gambling. It is still considered entertainment.

Colorful tales of fist fights, gambling, stagecoach robberies, murder, horse racing, tent revivals, drunken sprees, and hangings persisted in the stories of former residents and neighbors until the land was finally purchased by the US Army during World War II.

The area was not completely lawless. Most of the residents were honest and hard working citizens who supported healthy and productive families. Many held prominent positions in local government, taught school, or otherwise figured positively in the affairs of their community. Perhaps it was the nostalgia of these people, passing away hours in the comfort of one another's company that most encouraged and nourished the tales of long-ago Tampico Town.

Folks from the surrounding area were attracted to this town on weekends and on special occasions. The crowd could reach a thousand or more. The Tampico Race Track was one attraction that drew sizable crowds. Scores of gamblers would come to Tampico to bet on the horses during racing seasons. They would remain for weeks. Tampico helped Corvallis build its reputation for street races. This encouraged development of a lower subculture within the community.

There were men who lost everything and ended up bankrupt because temptation to bet was great and opportunity was readily available. Even in a frontier settlement, without much cash, this was possible because the gamblers would accept personal property as well as cash.

Saturdays were big days for Tampico. The men would gather for shooting matches. Men could meet to settle their differences with fist fights. Most would fight for the entertainment.

Hills And Valleys Burned

It is hard to realize that this tranquil little valley with all of its fir trees was barren of most timber and undergrowth in the mid 1800's. Many oak and aspen trees survived devastating fires. Some oak trees can live through the fires after they are seven or eight years old. The Indians followed the practice of burning the grass and underbrush each year to herd the game birds and animals into places where they could be killed more easily. When the first emigrants arrived in the southern Willamette Valley, they found it charred from the previous summer's grass fires. It was not easy for the emigrants and settlers to find feed for their animals the first winter.

A few of the settlers such as William Beatty and David D. Davis went to the hills to dig up fir trees to plant around their property. Some of the trees planted by Beatty are still standing on the west side of Tampico Road just south of Soap Creek Road. Some trees

Water-color painted by William Ball under the direction of historian John Horner in 1925. John Horner prepared notes from personal reminiscences of Soap Creek/Tampico. William Ball had access to the original town site and painted from the notes under the personal suprvision of John Horner.

OSU Horner Museum

planted by David D. Davis across Tampico Road mark the entrance to the Davis compound.

A large double fir tree and a large oak more than three feet in diameter still stand close to where the Tampico School House once stood on the hill overlooking the town.

First Soap Creek, Then Tampico

A "town" is any significant collection of dwellings and other buildings larger than a village, but not incorporated. David D. Davis was the first to build in Tampico in 1853. The town probably existed until the late 1860's.

The town commonly known as "Soap Creek," later as "Tampico," evolved in the Soap Creek Settlement after 1847. Emigrants began settling in the Soap Creek area late in 1846. Most of the emigrants became farmers. Goods and services were available only in the northern part of the Willamette Valley. A few emigrants established small businesses to meet the people's need for goods and services. A business and residential community began to develop along the Scott-Applegate Trail just south of Soap Creek.

Oregon's First Mail Route

The United States government began its support of the settlers. The August 6, 1850, issue of *Oregon Spectator* printed the following advertisement for mail service in the southern Willamette and Umpqua Valleys.

> *"5028 From Oregon City at 6 a.m. twice a month on the 5th and 19th by Linn City, Yamhill Falls (Lafayette,) Salem, O'Neal's or Nesmith's mills, J. C. Avery's or Marysville, Eugene F. Skinner's (Eugene,) Elijah Bristow's to Levi Scott's in Umpqua Valley 200 miles and back between 6 am on the 12th and 26th at 8 p.m. on the 17th and 31st of each month."*

Using present day geography the route started at Oregon City and went through Linn City, the Tualatin Valley, over Bald Peak to Lafayette, Salem, Ellendale west of Dallas, crossed Soap Creek near the old D. D. Davis residence, Tampico, Corvallis, Eugene, Elijah Bristow's east of the Willamette River and north of Cresswell, to Levi Scott's place in Scott's Valley east of Yoncolla.

Pack animals were used to carry the first mail and supplies through the southern Willamette and Umpqua Valleys.

The United States government established a Post Office at Soap Creek on November 4, 1854, and appointed David D. Davis as "Soap Creek's" first and only Postmaster. The Soap Creek Post Office existed from November 4, 1854, until December 3, 1857, when the name was changed to Tampico and William J. Crouch was appointed Postmaster.

David D. Davis was a successful entrepreneur. He established a way station, general store, farm and a hotel. He sold the store and way station to William J. Crouch in 1857. The Post Office was part of the sale and Crouch was appointed Postmaster of "Tampico" on December 3, 1857. William J. Crouch served as Tampico's first and only Postmaster until November 4, 1860,

The Soap Creek and Tampico Post Offices were placed in "Geographic Names Information System" file in 1993. Soap Creek Post Office was in the first David D. Davis residence, the Tampico Post Office in the second David D. Davis residence. Bob Zybach was instrumental in filling in the blanks. He documented his case from his own research and information developed in this chapter and the previous chapter of this book.

The "Tampico" name originated soon after the David D. Davis family moved there in 1853. However, the first known recorded use of the name was when William J. Crouch was appointed Postmaster in 1857. Dr. Blake credits David D. Davis for giving the settlement the name "Tampico." Frank McDonald, a contemporary writer, merely said it was "a skamp from Arkansaw." John B. Horner wrote

Roberts Boarding House *Arcade Saloon* *Crouch's Store* *Davis Home and Hotel*

Tampico Town Site

Buildings were lined up along near where these buildings now stand.

Only a few oak trees grew here in the 1850s. The Indians kept the vegetation burned over. A surveyor tied the first Davis House almost a mile west to two tie points established in this field. It was a clear shot. The Applegate Trail ran along the base of the hill in back of the buildings on the right, between the buildings right of center, and below the buildings on the left of the photograph.

in the 2/20/1926 issue of the *Gazette-Times:* "D. D. Davis, who gave Tampico its name, conducted a variety store * * * *."

"Tampico" was a city and port of Mexico. It is in Tamaulipas State on the north bank of the Panuco River about seven miles from the Gulf of Mexico. It is two hundred ten miles north of Mexico City. "Tampico" was occupied by American forces in 1846 during the Mexican War.

J. B. Horner wrote that Tampico was among the early Willamette Valley towns that had disappeared. Tampico was one of the principal stage stations west of the Willamette River for many years. The lively little town was on the State Road from Portland to Jacksonville via Lafayette, Dallas, Corvallis, Eugene, Roseburg, Canyonville, and Grants Pass. *Oregon Historical Quarterly* (Vol. 55, 1954) says that "Tampico was rip Snortin' in 1853, but faded fast."

Buildings Of Tampico Introduction

Tampico Town has been the subject of many stories. All of the stories seem to fit any neighborhood to this day. The only exception is that Tampico had a race track not found in an average neighborhood, then or now. Preachers are still telling stories about preachers. Kids and teachers are still telling tales out of school. Fist fights are still prevalent in rural areas. Fists have been replaced with ouzies in urban and suburban neighborhoods — but that's progress.

During the 1920's and 1930's Dr. N. E. Blake and John Horner speculated about the locations of the buildings in Soap Creek and Tampico Town. Most of their stories had some validity, but some were clouded by interpretation when a literal meaning was available.

Frank McDonald's song was the only contemporary writing found through extensive research on the Soap Creek - Tampico Town era. His only aim in wording the song seems to be to paint Tampico as he perceived it to be, in a humorous light and following his own interests. After allowing him literary license, there is no reason to believe that his writing is not accurate. He presses the entertainment and the gaudy sides of Tampico.

McDonald gives the only known portrayal of the layout of Tampico. He tells of the two residences of David D. Davis being on one of the two streets in Tampico and Tampico businesses being on the other.

Frank McDonald taught school in the Tampico School House on the hill overlooking Tampico and the David D. Davis residences. He had an exalted view of the entire Town of Tampico and everything that went on there.

TAMPICO

By Frank McDonald (1858)

Oregon is a pleasant place
for dancing, fun and foli-o,
But you may search it o're and o're,
You'll find no place like Tampico

Chorus:
Hurrah, hurrah for Tampico.
Three Cheers for our town Tampico.
Corvallis never can take the shine
to it we never will resign.
2
You will wonder where it took its name
It happened about two years ago,
A rambling scamp from Arkansaw
for mischief called it Tampico.
3
And now the name still sticks to the place,
Perhaps it will long continue so,
perchance some degenerate race
will drop the name of Tampico.
4
Our town is not extensive now,
being but two houses in a row
and opposite on the other street,
is the city-dell of Tampico.
5
And lots of goods are there for sale,
silks, pantaloons and calico
and then just twice a week the mail
Deposits freight at Tampico.
6
Saturday night the boys all meet
And all the bands are sure to go,
To make amendments for the week
With a social Spree at Tampico
7
Egg-nog first circulates around,
Then comes the fiddle and the bow
Off goes the coats to the merry sounds,
and a hoe-down starts in Tampico.
8
Now they shake the heal and toe,
And nimbly they go two and fro,
all care's resting until the morn
And shout hurrah for Tampico.
9
They care not for priest, pope, or king
But with them in the realms below,
They part resolving to meet again
Next Saturday night in Tampico.
10
But singing school is now the rage,
There all the boys are sure to go,
From north to south and all around
The neighborhood to Tampico.
11
To school each Saturday night they go,
And sweetly they sing Sol-me-do
The natives they are astonished soon
With harmony in Tampico.
12
But the time I do remember well
It happened just before last winter's snow,
There was scarce a day but you'd hear tell
Of fuss or fight in Tampico.
13
And one man swore he saw a whale

And all believed it to be so,
Then all the small craft took in sale
And scampered in to Tampico.
14
About that time there was to be,
In our neighborhood and down below,
A many a dance and social time
Around our dear old Tampico.
15
But now alas each dreary night
With heavy grief treads to and fros
Still waiting till the sign is right
For another dance in Tampico.

Benton County Records contained helpful information about events after 1854 or 1855 when Benton County began keeping records. Very little hard information was available before 1854 except Donation Land Claim Records.

Joseph Hunter, Old-timer Interviewed by Dr. N. E. Blake

Joseph Hunter was a young man clerking in his fathers store in Tampico in 1858. Dr. N. E. Blake interviewed him in his home in Ashland on January 24, 1926 and recorded his impressions of what the old timer told him.

Almost seventy years had gone by since Joseph Hunter worked in the store owned by William J. Crouch and Ira Hunter. Tampico Town had disappeared many years before and it is doubtful that Hunter had been in the area in a long time.

John Horner said that "tintype" portraits were the fad in Tampico. Joseph Hunter, a young swain of eighteen years with a dyed mustache, a broad brimmed hat, and Sunday coat, had his picture taken. The Daguerreotype was still clear in 1926. Sixty-eight years later *"Joseph C. Hunter was photographed again, this time in a group of four generations of which he was the patriarch, a fine ripe old gentleman beloved by his posterity."* (NEB)

Horner, Professor of History and head of the department at Oregon Agricultural College, gave several dissertations on the town of Tampico. Most of the information is within the time spanned by the existence of the Soap Creek community without identifying the town's beginning or its ending. Joseph Hunter was the kid next door, only a little younger than Thomas Davis.

David D. Davis First Settler At Tampico Town Site

The David D. Davis family had lived in their first hastily built home on the west side of Soap Creek since 1848. David D. Davis required a large house because he had a large family. He operated a way station, a store, a hotel, and a post office from the home before he built other buildings to house the increased activity. The Professor Horner that grew up in Soap Creek Valley told Dr. Blake that the Davis residence was on Soap Creek near a spring. Traces of the family orchard remain on a short bluff where the residence once stood overlooking Soap Creek.

David D. Davis built another permanent home in 1853. It was a mile due east of the first home and was the first building in the Town of Tampico. It also was in the pass

Tampico Street As They Look Now
Davis Street — Left.
This secluded street leads to the Davis Compound.
Tampico Road — Right.
The City-del of Tampico

where the Scott-Applegate Trail passed from the Willamette Valley into the Soap Creek Valley.

David D. Davis built his second home near the southeastern corner of his Donation Land Claim. Frank McDonald wrote that there "*were two houses in a row.*" They were set back from the Territorial Road more than most of the businesses. (FM)

The GLO Surveyor (on July 10, 1854) noted David D. Davis' second residence was north fifteen degrees east of the southwest corner of his donation land claim and south sixty five degrees west of the southeast corner. Donald Mario Alcatraz, Jr., a mathematics teacher and sixth generation descendant of David D. and Hannah Davis, says that it was two hundred fifty-two and one-half feet from the southeast boundary of the claim and one hundred sixty one and seven tenths feet from Tampico Road. It was twenty feet from the Scott-Applegate Trail marked on GLO maps as "The Road to Marysville". (BLM)

The house was very close to the eastward bend in the present driveway. The Scott-Applegate Trail was between the house and the foot of the hill.

The second house described by Frank McDonald in 1859 may have been built between 1854 and 1859 where a residence stands in 1996. The configuration and condition of the fruit trees at the site show they are the survivors of the Davis family orchard.

A pasture ran from the compound to the back of the Donation Land Claim. (BLM)

Frank McDonald, in the "Tampico" song, says in verse 4: "*Our town is not extensive now, being but two houses in a row and opposite on the other street, is the city-dell of Tampico.*"

The present lay of the land in Tampico supports the Frank McDonald verse. A driveway or street branches off Tampico Road about five hundred feet south of Soap Creek Road.

The private street or driveway runs along the base of a hill from Tampico Road to where David D. Davis built his second residence. There is a spring on the southeast edge of the David D. Davis Land Claim near where the home once stood. There is a spring on the George W. Roberts Donation Land Claim about forty feet from the Davis spring. Both Springs have been improved with brick liners and cement caps. The first spring probably supplied the Davises with water. The second spring is located to the rear of where Crouch's store was and probably supplied his store and residence.

David D. Davis probably had several buildings in the area but the only things of interest shown on July 10, 1854, GLO Survey Notes were the Davis house, a pasture behind the Davis house, a yard, and the Scott-Applegate Trail passing through the yard.

Exploding Boats

David D. Davis made regular trips on riverboats to lower Willamette River markets to buy goods for his new store in Tampico. He was on one of these buying trips when he barely escaped death in the most tragic disaster in Willamette River steamboat history. The disaster occurred at dockside in Canemah, above Oregon City. At 6:30 a.m. April 8, 1854, the "*Gazelle*" was tied up for a fifteen minute stop at the Canemah Docks. In preparation for rapid departure, the engineer crowded on a heavy head of steam without opening the safety valves. About sixty people were aboard when at 6:40 a.m. both boilers went up with a deafening explosion. Twenty people were killed outright. Another thirty were injured. Four more died later. The pilot of the "*Willamet*" lying alongside was killed by flying debris. The "*Gazelle*" sank where she was tied. The *Oregon Spectator* listed David Davis among the injured. (Vol. 22, #7, page 1, 4/14/1854.)

Some blamed the steamship company for poor equipment, but the tragedy was charged to the engineer, who had tied down the safety valve so that no steam could escape. A coroner's jury found the explosion "resulted from the gross and culpable negligence of First Engineer, Moses Tonie, in knowingly carrying more steam than was safe and neglecting to keep sufficient water in the boilers."

The "Gazelle," was a side-wheeler built by Page, Bacon & Company for the Willamette Falls Canal, Milling and Transportation Company of Linn City. She made her trial run on March 18, 1854. She went into immediate regular service. The wreck of the "*Gazelle*" was sold, moved below the falls, and restored as the "*Senorita.*"

The "*Gazelle*" was not the first riverboat mishap on the upper Willamette River. The "*Sholewater*" suffered the first boiler explosion in Oregon. A flue blew injuring several persons and damaging the boat. The boat was rebuilt and renamed the "*Fenix,*" for the fabled bird hatched from the ashes of disaster. However bad fortunes continued to plague the boat and she was renamed two more times.

The "*Canemah*" was below Champoeg when she blew a boiler flue in the summer of 1853. One passenger, Marion Holcroft, was killed and two or three others were scalded. The boat was restored and placed in active service.

(See also the *Oregon Statesman,* Corvallis Run, 4/24/1854, Page 2, Column 4. Davis is shown as #13.)

An aside: Chester Oliver Davis probably knew of this great grandfather's narrow scrape with death when, as a fourteen year old boy in 1907, he began working on riverboats. Although Chester told great stories about his seagoing days, he did not seem very impressed with riverboats. He did mention that the riverboats wandered around in farmer's fields in streams not much wider than the boats themselves. Sometimes they could not turn the boat around and had to back out of harbors on the Yamhill River. He was impressed when he saw pigs climbing trees out over the water as the riverboat passed under them.

Back To Tampico

Most of the Town of Tampico was on the George W. Roberts Donation Land Claim on August 23, 1859. The buildings were said to be cheaply constructed. The Territorial Road (now known as Tampico Road) ran from northwest to southeast through the Roberts property.

Tampico Road, the town's main street, was up the hill west of the Davis houses showing Joseph Hunter was right when he penned "And opposite on the other street, is the city-del of Tampico."

The Oregon and California Stage Company established stage lines running north and south. It had way stations about eight or ten miles apart all of the way from Portland to San Francisco. Stations were fully equipped with a complete change of eight or ten horses. There were extra horses to be used in case of sickness or disability of any of the regular string of horses. The stages carried the United States mail and express as well as passengers.

Overnight facilities were provided at the way stations. David D. Davis, and other way station operators, boarded the hostler and the drivers who stopped there in consideration for passengers who were brought to the hotel every day for dinner. Some passengers stayed overnight.

The Davis residence was used as a way station, store, post office, hotel, and livery stable. He operated the store for several years. David D. Davis was appointed Postmaster of Soap Creek December 4, 1854. David D. Davis had built a store house on the corner of his Donation Land Claim next to the Roberts claim in 1856 or 1857. (BLM)

Tampico began to expand in 1857 when David D. Davis sold the way station, store and post office to Ira Hunter and W. J. Crouch on December 3, 1857. Real estate is not mentioned in the transaction so it is assumed that W. J. Crouch or Ira Hunter built a new building on land Crouch purchased from George W. Roberts on December 1, 1857. It was next door, only six and one-half feet away from the Davis Store House.

However, "Crouch's Store" could have remained in the Davis store building. This conclusion is supported by Crouch's sale of the property in 1859, fourteen months before Crouch vacated the postal appointment and the Post Office was closed.

Left, from the top: Trees at the entrance from Tampico Road to Davis Compound. Davis home site was in and off lower right corner of photo. View northeast across the yard from the Davis home site. Reverse view from far end of above photo.
Right, from the bottom: View across yard to Davis home site near shrub at center. Exit from Davis yard. Exit from

Beatty and Roberts may have been taking in boarders in 1857 because Beatty bought land from Roberts on December 1, 1856. (BCR Book B, Page 385: Book C, Page 440.)

David D. Davis kept the residence and continued to operate the hotel and livery stable. Some say that David D. Davis operated a variety store in his store house. Saturday night dances were held in the Davis residence. (Did Tampico have a Casino?) People would come and board for weeks and even months to bet on the horses, play poker at high stakes gaming tables, and have a good time. Most of this ended in 1859 when the law closed David D. Davis' gaming table down thus discouraging other operators.

David D. Davis and his two oldest sons, Meshach (Mac) and Thomas (Tom) were accomplished musicians on the mandolin, banjo, and fiddle. Each of them could play most other instruments. Meshach preferred to play the mandolin. Tom was in demand on the fiddle. Their father liked to play almost any musical instrument. They moved from instrument to instrument with ease as required by the music. They made their own instruments. Each of them played at Saturday night dances where-ever he was, until his death.

Thomas W. Davis was carving a fiddle from dogwood just before his death in 1890. The unfinished fiddle was handed at his death in 1890 — through his son, Charles Elmer, to this writer.

First Boarding House In Tampico

James Anderson O'Neil and William Beatty ran the first boarding house and livery stable in Tampico. There was a corral around the livery stable. Bronco buster Dave English roped and rode wild horses as long as they could buck for one dollar.

William Beatty built a new boarding house on the west side of the road, about six hundred feet south of the Soap Creek Road junction. The boarding house was almost directly across from the entrance into the David D. Davis compound. Dr. Blake said that William

Beatty Fir Trees Planted in 1858

Beatty planted fir trees along the road on the east side and the north side of his boarding house. David Blake helped Beatty plant the trees. Some of the trees are still there, off Tampico Road four to six hundred feet south of the Soap Creek Road junction.

William Beatty's boarding house was west of the row of trees along Tampico Road. It was south of the row of trees that runs ninety degrees to Tampico Road. There is a depression in the hillside at the spot at or near where the Beatty's boarding house once stood. The depression is probably the remains of the "fruit house" or "cellar."

Pioneers grew their own food and had to provide for its storage. Before the advent of ice boxes, refrigerators, and freezers, this meant building their own cold storage "fruit houses" or "cellars."

A fruit house was dug into the side of a hill. A small "log cabin" was built into the hillside. It could be built with either logs, or large split logs with logs on top. Dirt was piled high on the sides and on top to keep it as cool as possible and to keep it from freezing in winter. A shake roof was built to keep the dirt as dry as possible. Apples, pears, potatoes, onions, and other vegetables would keep for many months when stored in a fruit house. Canned goods would keep better than in a warm house. Meat could be stored for only a very short time.

A cellar was the same as a fruit house, except it was under a house. Rural houses were built on mud sills and posts so it was easy to add a cellar. Today's city dwelling activists are forcing this pioneer heritage into extinction in their effort to protect rural people from themselves. Building codes are stringent and increase costs. It is no longer practicable to build a fruit cellar except in remote places.

Site of Robert's Boarding House, Saloon, and Store.

Roberts' Boarding House, Saloon, and Store

At the other end of Tampico, Wash Roberts operated a boarding house at the top of the hill at the south end of Tampico. It was a half mile south of Soap Creek Road at the top of the hill.

Government Land Office surveyor's field notes place the Roberts' house south thirty degrees east of the southeast corner of David D. Davis Donation Land Claim, and south twenty-five degrees west of the northeast corner of the land claim. (BLM) Several large foundation rocks were recently removed from the Roberts' boarding house site during reconstruction of the spring. They were between the spring and some old poplar trees that remain on the property. Roberts' boarding house was near Tampico Road at the top of the hill.

Joseph Hunter lived in the Roberts' boarding house. John Horner says Roberts also had a saloon. Roberts and Crouch were merchants selling satin and silk to pioneers that spun their own thread to weave into cloth.

Bill Bowers built the Arcade Saloon in

A Survivor, Bill Bower's Arcade Saloon, circa 1900

1858. Bowers was the owner and the bartender. Dr. Blake says there was a livery stable north of the saloon.

Bill Bowers' Saloon was on a sloping shelf below Tampico Road between Roberts' boarding house and Crouch's Store.

Crouch & Co. Store

The Crouch & Co. Store owned by W. J. Crouch and Ira Hunter was north of the livery stable. The business was renamed "Crouch and Company" when it was purchased from David D. Davis in December 1857.

Benton County Records (Book C, Page 440) and Dr. Blake's records show that Crouch had property next to David D. Davis' Store House. William J. Crouch purchased the land from Wash Roberts. The William J. Crouch property was four hundred forty feet wide along both sides of Tampico Road southeast of the Davis property. Crouch subdivided the land as the "Tampico Town Plot" subdivision in October 1857.

Water was available from a spring near the rear of the store building, about thirty feet from David D. Davis' Donation Land Claim.

Frank McDonald referred to Roberts' store and Crouch's store when he wrote *"And lots of goods are there for sale, silks, pantaloons and calico and then just twice a week the mail deposits freight at Tampico."* Crouch and Company did not do a very good business under Crouch's guiding hand.

Tampico Town Plot Aborted

William J. Crouch recorded a subdivision of land titled "Plot of the Town of Tampico" that some writers have used to signal the change in name from Soap Creek to Tampico. Crouch filed the plot in Benton County, Oregon on October 27, 1857. Crouch acquired the land from George W. Roberts on December 1, 1857, for one hundred forty dollars.

The subdivided land was carved out of the George W. Roberts' Donation Land Claim that was adjacent to the southeastern boundary of the David D. Davis Donation Land Claim. The plot contained slightly more than ten acres of land on both sides of the Portland and Umpqua Valley Road.

Meshach R. Davis purchased the identically described land (same meets, same bounds, same words) from William J. Crouch for four hundred dollars on September 9, 1859. Crouch had improved the land during the twenty-two months he owned it.

Green B. Smith purchased the identically described land from Meshach R. Davis for four hundred dollars on January 22, 1860.

The project was aborted when Green Berry Smith recorded his cancellation and annulment of the plot on January 23, 1860.

The Tampico Town Plot was never a serious factor in life of Tampico. Crouch owned the land and he and his store were its sole occupants with the possible exception of Bower's Saloon. However, it appears that the Bowers Saloon was built south of the Town Plot. There is no evidence that anything was different because the plot was aborted and canceled in 1860. No subdivided lots were sold from the subdivision. The two sales of the subdivided land were described by meets and bounds identical to the original acquisition. No reference was made to a subdivision. The subdivision was not consummated-and the project was aborted.

Mrs. Eunice Brown Flickinger told an interviewer for Benton County Historical Records Survey in 1938 that "Tampico was considered a tough town but I was so young I never knew much about it. There was a saloon there and a store. Billy Picketts kept the store." Mrs. Flickinger's age is not given but most of her education was obtained in the Tampico School.

Meshach Davis probably operated the store for the short time. There is no information explaining why Meshach Davis owned the property and operated the store for such a short time. However, the three Davis boys, Meshach, Thomas, and William may have been yanks in a rebel community.

Plot of the Town of Tampico,
Benton County. O.

State of Oregon
Benton County } S.S.

On this 23rd day of January 1860 before the undersigned recorder of Benton Co. personally came Green B Smith, the present proprietor of the within named Town of Tampico; and acknowledges and declares, that he is the owner of the entire town of Tampico, and that the record thereof is hereby cancelled and annulled: to the extent that said town aforesaid may be no longer considered a town—

Green B. Smith

Acknowledged and declared before me the undersigned recorder as aforesaid the date above written

Thomas B. Ordeneal
Recorder of Benton County

4th St. · 3rd St. · 2nd St. · 1st St. · Back St. · A St. · B St. · C St. · Road · N

Notes of the Survey of the Town of Tampico.
Course of the Streets

First Street, or the Territorial Road	South	37°	East,	60 feet wide
Second Street	"	"	"	50 " "
Third	"	"	"	" " "
Fourth	"	"	"	" " "
Back	"	"	"	20 " "
A	"	53°	West	25 " "
B	"	"	"	40½ " "
C	"	"	"	25 " "

Eight Blocks—of Eight Lots each—Lots numbered 1 and 8 4 and 5 in Blocks numbered 1,2,3,4,5,6,7 and 8 are 25 feet by 100 feet.
Lots numbered 1,2,3,6,7,8 in Blocks numbered 2,3,6 and 7 are 50 feet by 100 feet.
Lots numbered 2,3,4,5,6,7, in Blocks numbered 1,4,5 and 8 are 50 feet by 100 feet long

Magnetic var from 16° to 20° 15' East.

Surveyed for William J. Crouch
October 27th A.D. 1857.

Recorded Nov. 10th 1857
J. H. B. Ordeneal
Recorder.

B. W. Wilson
By G. H. Wilson

Aborted Tampico Town Plot

There is a story going around that Green Berry Smith, a settler in Soap Creek Valley, bought the subdivision from Crouch and aborted the subdivision the same day to put Crouch out of business. The story is not supported by the facts. Green Berry Smith bought the subdivision from Meshach Davis, not Crouch. But then, the Davises were the more likely target.

Meshach Davis bought the subdivision from Crouch for four hundred dollars. Meshach was David D. Davis' oldest son. David D. Davis was fined one thousand dollars for operating a poker table a couple of months after Meshach sold the store. David died August 31, 1860, several months later. The brothers Davis sold out in 1864.

1858 Tampico School House

David Blake and Mr. Shrum built the Tampico School House in 1858. The school district purchased the property from William Beatty on January 24, 1859. The school building overlooked Tampico from a small piece of property directly across Territorial Road from the Davis Store House.

The purchase of the school house property was recorded in Benton County Records Book E, Page 213. The property was small, about fifty by one hundred thirty-two feet. The school was on a shelf of land on the hillside three hundred twenty-one feet up the hill from Tampico Road. It sat directly across Tampico Road and up the hill from the Davis store house. The school house was said to be about eighteen feet by twenty-four feet.

A sign of the times survives

The School District gave William Beatty one hundred dollars for the sixty-five hundred square foot parcel. There is a large double fir tree near the lower end of the property. A large oak over three and a half feet in diameter stands nearby. There was a spring on the hill in back of the property that has been improved recently.

The Tampico building was not the first schoolhouse in the Soap Creek Settlement. There are at least two references to the Soap Creek School being the first school in Benton County. David Fagan says the first school in the Soap Creek Settlement was built in 1847. This is not hard to understand. David Carson, Thomas Read, D. D. Stroud, Robert W. Russell, The Carters, J. S. Halter, Green Berry Smith and others arrived in Soap Creek with their families late in 1846. David D. Davis and others arrived in Soap Creek in late 1847 or early 1848.

John E. Smith said the first schoolhouse in the Soap Creek Settlement started in a log schoolhouse in 1849 or earlier. Dr. Blake says that Joseph Hunter purchased a spelling book and an arithmetic book from James O'Neil who had a store in the home of David D. Davis in 1853.

The first evidence of the use of the name "Tampico" was when William Crouch was appointed Postmaster of Tampico in December 3, 1857, ten years after the school opened. Earlier schools carried the Soap Creek School name.

The school served the educational needs of the community. It also served as a meeting place for community and social functions. Religious services were held there on Sunday and it is said that as many as forty saddle horses and several ox teams would be tied nearby. People attended the Baptist services from far and near.

Elisha Vineyard was the first teacher at the new Tampico school. He was later the first Benton County School Superintendent. Frank McDonald was known as the clever

Irishman that taught his own treatise on mathematics. McDonald died in a fire on his claim in the mountains. Some say he was murdered but no one was brought to trial.

T. J. Stites, John Greek Springer, Ed. V. Price, Sam Berry, and a man named Noschker taught at Tampico at various times.

Eunice (Brown) Flickinger, daughter of G. W. Brown and Mary Ann Todd Brown, lived on Soap Creek near the Polk County line. She went to the school, probably during the middle to late 1860's. Her teachers were Sam Berry, Mr. Price, and Mr. Noschker. The store was still there at that time and was operated by Billy Picketts.

Another Tampico School House was built in 1923 and survived until 1942. Hugh Govier, a former student at the school, says that it was built at the junction of Soap Creek Road with Tampico Road. It was on one of the two concrete foundations under the David D. Davis memorial monument. The play shed was in the middle of where Soap Creek Road has been extended toward Coffin Butte.

Blacksmith And Carpentry Shops

Tampico had a blacksmith shop that was first owned and operated by William Griffin and later by Jacob Modie. Modie was a Justice of The Peace, a farmer and a very good friend of David D. Davis. He shod horses and made wrought iron hardware. Jacob Modie's Donation Land Claim # 46 was a mile or so southwest of David D. Davis'.

Dr. Blake said that the blacksmith and woodworking shop was on the west side of Soap Creek and north of the first Davis cabin. It was close enough to Soap Creek to harness the creek for power to operate the lathe to make wagon spokes and furniture parts.

Meshach (Mac) Davis, oldest son of David and Hannah Davis, ran the carpenter's shop in the back of the blacksmith shop. Meshach operated the water-powered lathe and turned wagon parts and made furniture. He worked with the blacksmith to make wagons for the community. He was also the town carpenter. Thomas Davis also knew how to work with wood and probably worked with Meshach.

Tampico Race Track

Joseph Hunter told Dr. Blake that the Tampico Race Track "was north of town in the road running down toward the John Wiles place and was six hundred yards long. It was kept scraped and in good condition, and many exciting races were held. In one race Joseph Hunter won a cow, calf and mule from his opponent, (Jesse Brown) which left the latter almost bankrupt."

During the 1860's, each race track was unique, there was no standard length, and no standard shape. There were some straight tracks as short as four hundred forty yards long. One-heat races over shorter distances on oval tracks finally became the rule.

Joseph Hunter's eyewitness reminiscence contains the only known clues about the Tampico Racetrack. John Horner seems to

Tampico Race Track

have picked up on these clues and enlarged on them.

John Horner said that Ben Bold, owned by James Griffin, and Jack of Clubs, owned by Jehial Kendall, trained and established their speed on this track. Silver Tail was trained on the track and later sold for one thousand dollars to George Coggins of LaGrande.

Local tradition places the race track on the David D. Davis Donation Land Claim. There is an open field about a half mile north of Tampico, south of Tampico Road, and east of Soap Creek. It can only be seen from that part of Tampico Road, and from the air. The open field could adapt to an oval track about six hundred yards long. By running the front straightway twice, at the start and at the finish of a race, it could run one mile races. It would be a full blown race track by today's standards.

However, Joseph Hunter told Dr. Blake that the race track was in the road north of Town. Bob Zybach, Oregon State University, Oregon Research Forests, believes that the race track was a straight track, not an oval one, and that it was in Tampico Road in the flat stretch of Soap Creek Valley north of Tampico.

Bob Zybach's site and straight track interpretation of evidence appears to have a more logical explanation and location. His site is a literal interpretation of Dr. Blake's note on the Joseph Hunter interview, literally "it was in the road north of town". Hunter also brags that it "was 600 yards long," and 600 yard races were held. The Tampico Race Track was a long track, not an oval one. Hunter would have bragged about the longer race that could be held on an oval track.

There is no record of what type or how many races were held over any length of time, except for John Horner's embellishments. He lists the names of three horses that infer thoroughbred racing. However, some variation of sprint or street racing appears likely. The first known record of thoroughbred horses started in 1865. The list of thoroughbred horses does not contain any of the three Horner names.

Joseph Hunter said the track was scraped and in good condition. County Road #3 was surveyed, and probably built, through smooth the level prairie in Soap Creek Valley. The survey shows a straight stretch of road north from the center of Tampico over a mile and a quarter long. There is a two-thousand-foot section between the foot of the hill and Soap Creek that would provide space for a six hundred yard track.

An aerial photo clearly shows that the straight section remains in Tampico Road north of town.

Nearby Corvallis had a reputation for street races about this time. Tampico's six-hundred-yard horse races held in the road adds credibility to Corvallis' reputation for street racing. Or was its Tampico's close proximity to Corvallis that gave Corvallis its reputation. Either way, Corvallis' early day reputation for street races adds credibility to Tampico's having races in the road. It must have given the Corvallis do-gooders that closed David D. Davis' poker table down something else to do.

Tampico Jail

The Tampico jail was so well built that it was the last building to go. It finally burned in a forest fire. C. A. Williams, J. G. Myers, and Jacob Modie and others served as Justices of the Peace at different times. The jail location is unknown. Some say it is under the David D. Davis commemorative stone at the junction of Tampico Road and Soap Creek Road. It appears that the cement foundation at that location was there before the second Tampico School was built in 1923.

There is evidence that there were several other buildings in Tampico between Soap Creek Road and Wash Roberts Boarding house. However, history left no clue to their identity.

A Serious Side Of Tampico

Tampico had a more serious side. All was

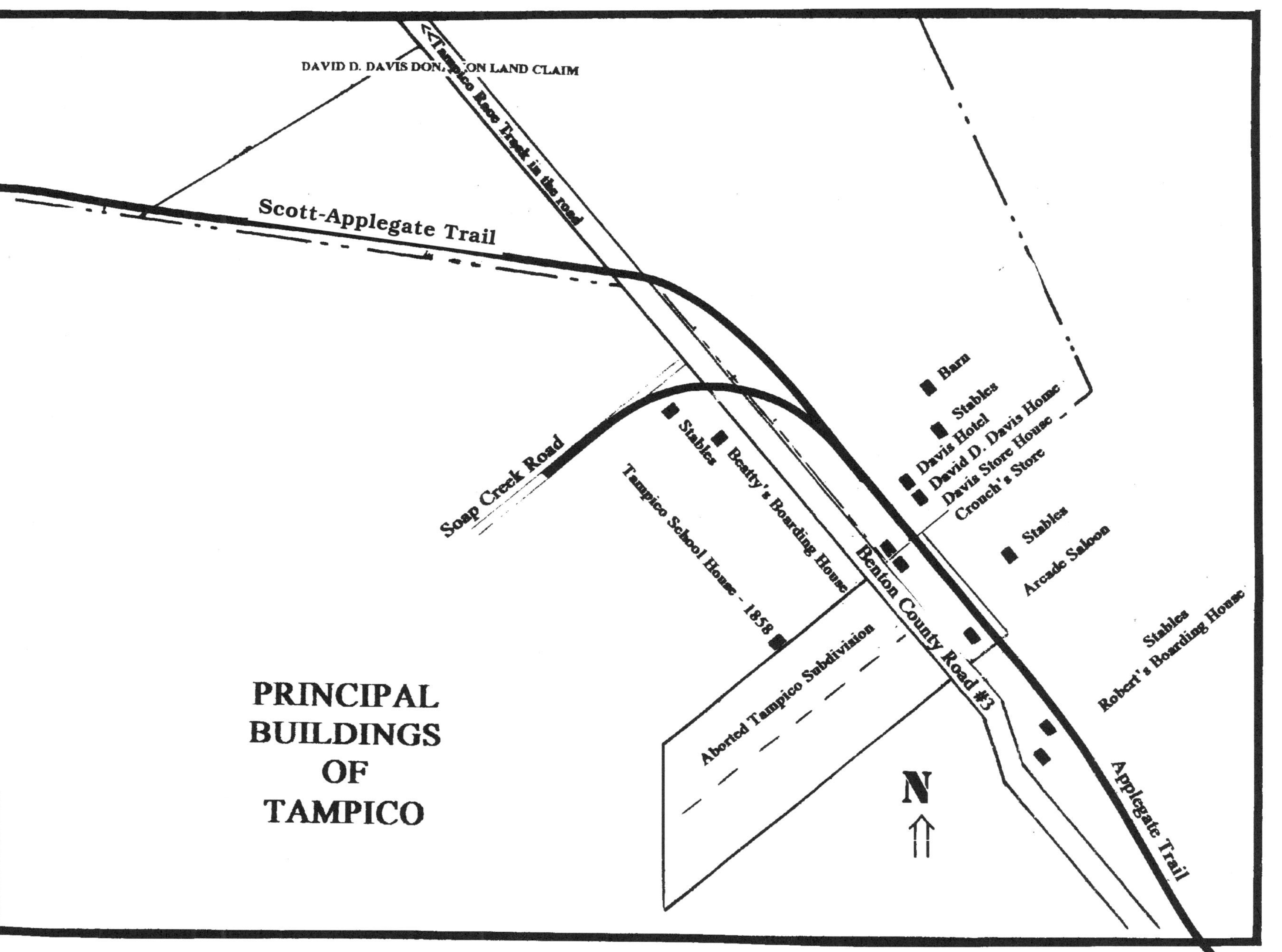
PRINCIPAL
BUILDINGS
OF
TAMPICO
N
DAVID D. DAVIS DONA ON LAND CLAIM
<<Ta ico Race Track in the road
Scott-Applegate Trail
Soap Creek Road
Stables
Beatty's Boarding House
Tampico School House - 1858
Aborted Tampico Subdivision
Benton County Road #3
Barn
Stables
Davis Hotel
David D. Davis Home
Davis Store House
Crouch's Store
Stables
Arcade Saloon
Stables
Robert's Boarding House
Applegate Trail

not just fun and frolic. The school house became the meeting place for many social functions. Jacob Modie, a farmer and owner of the blacksmith shop, was a very good friend to David D. Davis. He encouraged gatherings in the school and conducted debates and taught singing. He later became Benton County Assessor.

The children played in the school yard. They played games such as youngsters do today. The boys played marbles, horse shoes, a game called One Old Cat, and a variation of a game becoming known as baseball. The girls enjoyed jump rope, ante-over, blackman, and a game called Catching The Dutchman.

Religious Side Of Tampico

Religious services were conducted for the town and community at the school. People came riding or driving in from near and far to attend the services. As many as forty saddle horses and several yokes of oxen were tied nearby. Tampico never had a regular church structure or organization although the Baptists tried hard to establish a church. Services were informal. Great evangelist preachers like Elder Joab Powell and Doctor Reuben Hill (minister and physician) conducted protracted meetings from time to time. When the word got around that such meetings were scheduled, folks came in such numbers that the town became filled to overflowing. The good townsfolk took the overflow crowd into their houses and barns for overnight lodging.

Elder Joab Powell, The Pony Preacher

Professor J. B. Horner, historian of Oregon Agricultural College (now Oregon State University) gave a good account of pioneer conditions that prevailed in Tampico when Joab Powell came to preach. His report was made in the June 19, 1922, issue of the *Gazette-Times.*

Horner wrote that Tampico was among the early Willamette Valley towns that had disappeared. Tampico was one of the principal stage stations west of the Willamette River for many years. The lively little town was on the state road from Portland to Jacksonville via Lafayette, Dallas, Corvallis, Eugene, Canyonville, Roseburg, and Grants Pass.

B. Horner wrote:

> *"Tampico was, therefore, the community center for this portion of the country. Baptists who were strong in that area, regularly held their conventions there. The Rev. Joab Powell and his friend Dr. Hill, were principal speakers at these conventions and they drew crowds from all parts of the Willamette Valley. The meetings developed into revivals at which many prominent people were converted, among which was James H. Slater, a young clerk in Corvallis, but later U. S. Senator from Oregon.*
>
> *"Hotel accommodations being meager, the visiting members were distributed throughout the neighborhood. Among the neighborhood was Mr. John Wiles, a thrifty farmer who lived a mile away. He owned twenty-six hundred acres of land enclosed by a nine rail double-stake-and-rider worm fence, which was hog tight, mule high and bull strong. His was one of the largest and most hospitable homes in the vicinity, and many guests were received by Mr. and Mrs. Wiles.*
>
> *"One night after the service forty or more of the visitors were apportioned to the Wiles home. The bedrooms were filled, the floors were covered with beds, and some of the men went to the barn for the night's lodging, among whom were Mr. Wiles and the Rev. Mr. Powell. They shared the same blankets. Toward morning the air became quite cool and the Rev. Mr. Powell complained that he could not sleep. Mr. Wiles whispered to him to remain quiet for a few minutes. In a short time the loud snoring in the hay loft indicated that all were asleep again and Mr. Wiles*

quietly and slowly withdrew the coverlids from two young men snoring near them and spread the blankets over himself and the minister. Mr. Powell said nothing but his massive form of 300 pounds shook the hay, indicating that he was giggling. When Mr. Wiles asked him what was the matter he said, 'Last night I preached on the text, 'He that provideth not for his household hath denied the faith and is worse than an infidel,' and now you have gone one better for you have provided for the preacher also'.

"There being no more sleep in store for the plain, old-fashoned preacher and his resourceful friend that morning, the pair withdrew from the nasal chorus which by that time had developed considerable rhythm and dynamics yet lacking in the other charms of modern sheet music."

Soap Creek Post Office
David D. Davis, Postmaster

In a few short years this part of the Soap Creek Settlement near where South Road crosses Soap Creek grew and took on the shape of a town. Soap Creek was geographically excellent for economic growth and development. The businesses were joined by a Post Office on November 4, 1854. David D. Davis became the first and only Postmaster of Soap Creek.

William J. Crouch purchased the new store and way station from D. D. Davis. Crouch was appointed first and only Postmaster of Tampico on December 3, 1857. Tampico was between the Scott-Applegate Trail and the new Territorial Road about a mile east of Soap Creek. The Tampico Post office was closed November 4, 1860.

Pack animals carried the first mail through Soap Creek. After roads were improved, a stage coach followed the route bringing people, goods, and mail to the Soap Creek area. However, pack animals still carried the mail and supplies for several years during rainy winter months when muddy roads were impassable to stage coaches. Thomas Morgan was one of the proudest men as he drove his six horses, handling the lines and sounding the bugle to announce to the community the arrival of the stage.

New United States Geological Survey documents show the Soap Creek Post Office at the site of David D. Davis' first home and will soon show the first Tampico Post Office on the southeastern corner of his Donation Land Claim.

Green Berry Smith
The Town Money Lender

Tampico never had a bank so the lending and borrowing could only be done by individuals using a personal note. A store-

Green Berry Smith

OSU Research Forrest

keeper or business man might carry credit on his books when he could afford it. Some individuals might loan out money, if they had any, to certain friends whom they could trust. Many of these notes receivable were still around when the lender's estate papers were filed.

There was one man in Tampico who took his lending very seriously. He was Green Berry Smith. He often loaned money at a going rate of 12% interest. Of course, he cautioned all borrowers not to take money that they could not return on payday. He seldom refused a borrower.

Green Berry Smith became the most powerful and influential landowner in the Soap Creek neighborhood. He was often involved in litigation with his neighbors. In time Mr. Smith had a sizable amount of real estate. He had over 9,000 acres in the Soap Creek and Tampico areas. He also had another strip a mile wide and eight miles long located south of Corvallis.

Benton County

Benton County was officially created from Polk County by the Provisional Government of Oregon Country on December 23, 1847. That was less than two months after David D. Davis arrived in the Willamette Valley. Benton County ran from two and one-half miles north of Soap Creek to the California Border, and from the Willamette River and the Cascades to the Pacific Ocean. That includes all of the Oregon Country southwest of Soap Creek.

The Territorial government carved parts or all of Lane, Douglas, Jackson, Josephine, Curry and Coos Counties out of Benton County in 1851. Benton County still extended from the Willamette River to the Pacific Ocean, but its northern and southern boundaries were established where they are today. Lincoln County was formed in 1893 and Benton County took on its present form with six hundred seventy-nine square miles of land area.

James Anderson O'Neil was elected Justice for Yamhill District in 1843 and Judge of Polk County in 1845 when Districts were redistricted into Counties. Justices and Judges governed their respective Districts, and Counties. O'Neil was Justice over the Benton County area when it was within Yamhill District, then Judge when it was within Polk County. (*Directory of Oregon History*, edited by Howard McKinley Corning.) The *Oregon Historical Quarterly*, Vol. 60, 1959 p-255 says O'Neil was appointed "magistrate" in Yamhill District at the July 5, 1843, meeting.

Benton County is one of seven in the United States named honoring Senator Thomas Hart Benton of Missouri, a long-time advocate for the Oregon Country.

The area was originally inhabited by several small bands of Kalapua Indians. Many of the Kalapua Indians died of the same diseases that took the lives of six persons from the Davis household; Jane, Rebecca, Rachel, David, Hannah and Sarah (Bowman) Davis.

James Anderson O'Neil (O'Neal)

Tampico had its celebrity. James Anderson O'Neil, or O'Neal, is sometimes confused with James O'Neill (with two "l's"), an early Portland Mayor and Indian Agent. Ralph Friedman wrote:

> *"The facts about James Anderson O'Neil are dramatic enough without making him a Mayor or an Indian Agent. About him swirled the currents and fogs of early white settlement in the Oregon country. Directly or peripherally he was associated with much of the history making that led to Americanization of the territory."*

James Anderson O'Neil was born in Georgia on January 26, in 1800. He arrived in Oregon with the second expedition of Nathaniel Wyeth in 1834. He was thirty-four at the time. O'Neil worked with Wyeth in building Fort Hall on the westward journey. Nat Wyeth returned home to brood over his failure to set up a fur gathering empire. O'Neil and some others stayed in the Willamette Valley.

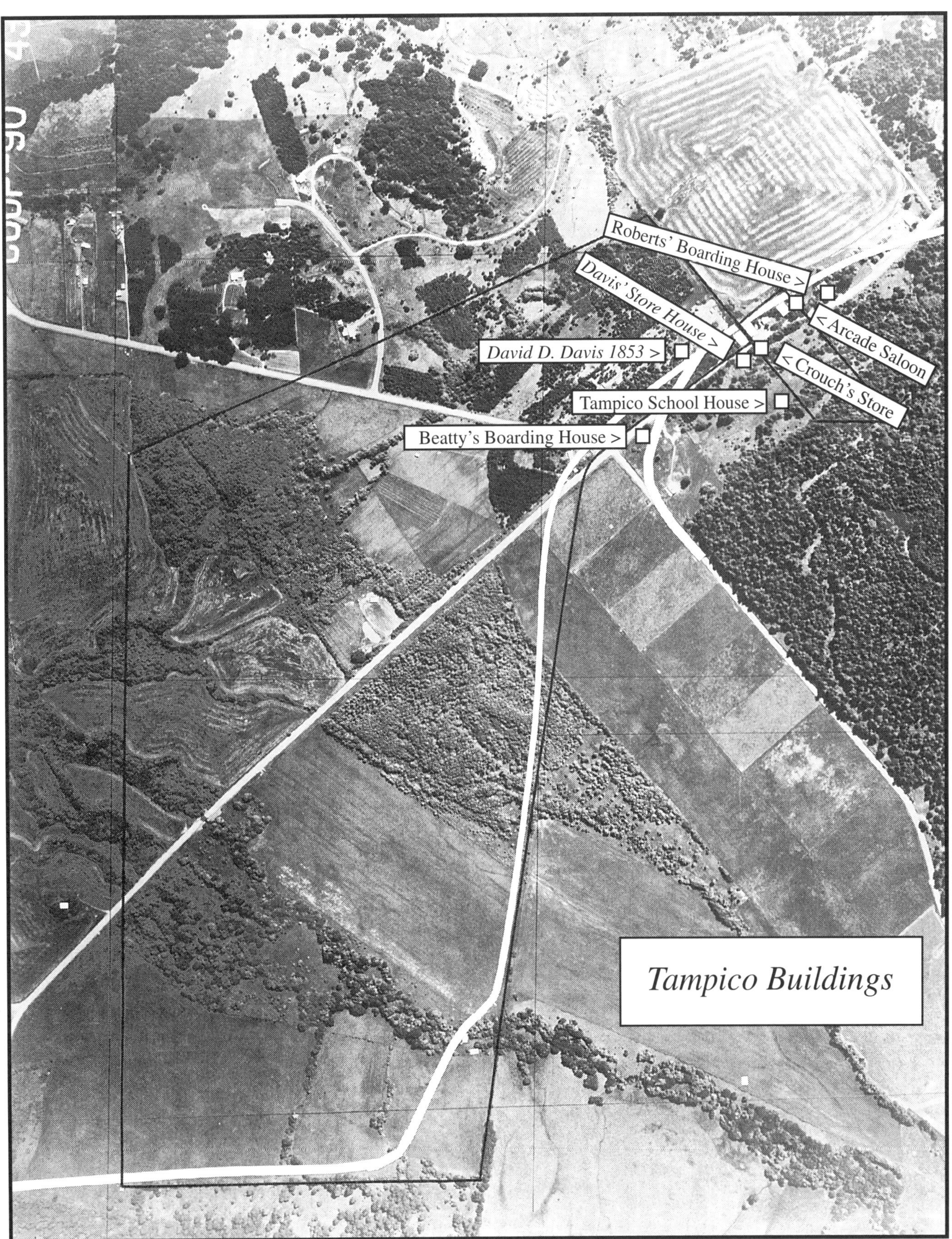
Roberts' Boarding House >
Davis' Store House >
David D. Davis 1853 >
< Arcade Saloon
< Crouch's Store
Tampico School House >
Beatty's Boarding House >
Tampico Buildings

A year after he arrived in Oregon, O'Neil took up land on the west bank of the Willamette, at what became Wheatland. He was along side Jason Lee in his temperance effort and contributed to Lee's efforts to abolish Ewing Young's enterprise in manufacturing ardent spirits.

James A. O'Neil was one of the eleven members of the Willamette Cattle Company that went to the San Francisco Bay area in 1837 when the tyrant John McLoughlin refused to sell beef cattle. This was a major concern for the American settlers. They reached Oregon in mid-October 1837 with Spanish cattle after this nations first long cattle drive.

O'Neil found something missing in his life. He began attending revival meetings at the Methodist Mission where the preaching of Reverend David Leslie deeply moved him. One day in December 1840 he stepped forward to become a convert. He became so dedicated that he was made a missionary aide.

James O'Neil signed everything he could get his hands on that might speed the day when the British could be gotten rid of. He particularly liked the bill of particulars against Dr. John McLoughlin, written March 23, 1843, accusing him of being a despot, a swindler, and a crooked landlord. He presided over the "Wolf Meetings." (AH) The second meeting that set up bounties for predatory animals. The real purpose of this meeting was to appoint a committee of twelve to consider the propriety of taking measures for the civil and military protection of this colony.

O'Neil was on the appointed committee of twelve. The committee of twelve did their work and called the next meeting for May 2, 1843, the meeting at which Oregon was born. O'Neil was appointed to Oregon's First Legislature, a group of nine. He had the "Statutes of Iowa," which he sold to the government, along with "Guide to Judges," and "Jefferson's Manual" for $10.50. These became the first library books purchased by the provisional government.

James Anderson O'Neil's Wheatland Ferry

The Wheatland Ferry, the only ferryboat operated by the State of Oregon over one hundred fifty years later, still crosses the Willamette River a few miles north of Salem.

James Anderson O'Neil and A. Beers employed Lindsay Applegate to help build a ferry boat during the winter of 1843-1844. Lindsay Applegate and his brother, Charles Applgate, had arrived with the 1943 immigration and were wintering at the old abandoned Methodist mission across and slightly upriver from O'Neil's place. Jesse A.Applegate, Lindsay's son, related that "He first caulked the openings between the planks in the bottom of the boat, and then poured in hot pitch. It was a large boat. He used a bushel or two of literature he found in the old house. Tracts and other pamphlets that had been left there by one of the missionaries were forced into the cracks with a chisel and hammer."

James Anderson O'Neil sold the rights to his land claim on the west bank of the Willamette River about seventeen miles above Campoeg to Daniel Matheny in the spring of 1844. The boat was included in the transaction. Matheny started operating the Wheatland Ferry. (HMC p.95.)

James A. O'Neil completed the first grist mill on Ellendale Creek near LaCreole Creek west of Dallas in Polk County early in 1845. He opened a store and a small community developed. He sold the mill to James W. Nesmith and Henry Owen in 1849. He held on to the store and was appointed postmaster of "O'Neal's Mills" on January 8, 1850. He sold the store to Nesmith. James W. Nesmith was appointed Postmaster of "Nesmith" on August 21, 1850.

Buena Vista

Reason B. Hall platted the town of Liberty early in the 1850's. In the early years of Oregon, names of budding municipalities were readily changed. Recalling the Mexican War Battle Of Buena Vista in which some of his relatives had fought, Hall renamed his town Buena Vista. Buena Vista means *beautiful view* in Spanish. (HMC p.139)

James Anderson O'Neil established a mercantile business in Buena Vista in the early 1850's.

James A. O'Neil erected a woolen mill soon after selling his gristmill to Nesmith. The woolen mill shut down in 1857 after changing hands several times. (AH)

James O'Neil settled down on a farm near Lewisville in Polk County a few years after he sold O'Neil Mills to Nesmith. While at O'Neil's Mills, O'Neil became acquainted with William J. and Sarah Bowman. The Bowmans moved to a Donation Land Claim in the Lukiamute River Valley about the same time O'Neil moved there. (AH)

Over the next several years James O'Neil had several business holdings. He was living at the ferry landing in Buena vista in 1851 where he built the first commercial business, a warehouse. He was managing a store in the old Davis residence in Tampico in 1853. O'Neil operated a Boarding house in Tampico with William Beatty. (AH)

William Bowman died during this time and James O'Neil took over managing the farm for his widow, Sarah Bowman. Like the blacksmith, Jacob Modie, James O'Neil "had several irons in the fire" at one time. (AH)

James A. O'Neil had his last fling at glory and power while he was at Tampico. The Territorial Legislature of 1853-1854 appointed him as one of the commissioners to build the Oregon-California railroad. The undertaking was never completed.

In 1855 he married Talitha C. Bowman, David D. Davis' stepdaughter, the daughter of Sarah (Bowman) Davis. Sarah was David's second wife. James O'Neil was appointed guardian of David and Sarah Davis' two daughters after David and Sarah's deaths. He was also appointed guardian of William Davis, David's youngest son by his first wife, Hannah.

James O'Neil withdrew from the store and boarding house in Tampico and settled down on the Bowman farm near Lewisville in Polk County soon after being married. James O'Neil became well known in the Tampico settlement while he operated the store in the first Davis residence. He was also known for his connection with the Beatty Boarding House, store and livery stable.

EPITAPH

By Arthur King

Old Tampico the town stood when
The West was new and men were men;
In olden days a lovely town
which Father Time hath leveled down.

But now the old-time stage coach wheel
With squeaking brake against the steel
No longer echoes far and wide
Along the rugged mountain side.

Old time has worn the buildings down,
Yet history of the famous town
tells how it looked, so I am told.
When men were men in days of old.

[Arthur King was the grandson of Solomon King of King's Valley.
From a clipping once owned by Mrs. Josephine Wells, Corvallis, Oregon]

CHAPTER 13

Sad Days in Tampico

Disease spread through early Oregon settlements like wildfire. Diseases caused so much fear in the early pioneers that the fear carried down through the succeeding generations.

Thomas W. Davis' fear was such a fear. It was passed down to Charles Elmer Davis, Thomas' son, and Alice Delcina Sims Davis, his daughter in law. Charles Elmer and Alice passed it down to their son Chester Oliver Davis. Chester was afraid that his mother would give tuberculosis to his grandchildren and thought that his mother gave the disease to his wife, Isaphene M. Aydelotte Davis. She was in a Tuberculosis Sanitarium from 1937 to 1940.

Alice Delcina Sims Davis' fear came from Thomas W. Davis, and knowing that half

Headstones in New English Cemetery, Monmouth, Oregon
David D.Davis, Hannah Donahoe Davis, Rachel Davis, Rebecca Davis

of her husband's family members died of consumption and measles in the early settlements in the southern Willamette Valley.

There was a lot of confusion about tuberculosis, commonly known as consumption in earlier days and TB later. Most of the confusion was due to people's attitude toward TB as a subject not to be discussed during the first hundred years of Oregon history. It was feared. It was a killer. It was The White Plague.

Alice Davis advised that people should move to the Redmond-Prineville area, or Arizona, for better health and to cure or avoid tuberculosis in particular. She conveyed the impression that Thomas Davis had moved from the valley to Prineville, Oregon, either to avoid getting the disease or, more probably, as a cure. Thomas Davis knew Monroe Hodges, founder of Prineville, when Hodges was on his Donation Land Claim in Soap Creek Valley.

Charles Elmer Davis' only visit to the Soap Creek - Tampico area was with his son, James Albert Davis, in 1931. He wanted to see where his grandfather and grandmother first settled in the southern valley. Alice Delcina Davis explained that he had not been able to bring himself to visit there because he was saddened that many of his relatives had died in the settlements of the southern valley. Other settlers in the area had been hard(er) hit in a series of epidemics, including measles and consumption. She said that his grandmother, Hannah Davis, had died in a measles epidemic. He was particularly disturbed that his grandmother and several of the children had died in the southern valley. The Davis family and the settlement was almost "wiped out."

Hannah Davis Dies At Soap Creek

Hannah Donahoe Davis, David D. Davis' beloved wife was the first of the Davises to die at Soap Creek on June 15, 1848 during a measles epidemic. The headstone of Hannah Davis shows that David D. Davis "wrote it in stone" that his beloved wife Hannah died on June 15, 1848.

There are some people who say she could have died on the trail, however, these rumors are without foundation.

Lester Hulin, in writing his day-by-day journal about the trip, does not mention the death of Hannah Davis although he does mention the death of the Kimball's child early in the trip. Lester Hulin would have mentioned the death of his friend's wife, Hannah Donahoe Davis.

David and Hannah Davis arrived in Oregon at Skinner's cabin on November 4, 1847. They arrived at Soap Creek with their family on May 15, 1848, according to government records. The measles virus has an incubation period of fourteen days, so she was exposed to it a few days after they arrived and started building their new home alongside the trail on the bluff overlooking Soap Creek. She died on June 15, 1848, as shown on her headstone in New English Cemetery south of Monmouth, Oregon.

David D. Davis and the eight children were saddened by the death of his beloved wife and their mother. David D. Davis' responsibilities to his family increased by the absence of their mother. There were three teenage girls and two boys to help with some of his added tasks.

Three Davis Children Die

Jane Davis, the oldest daughter was born in 1832 in Dearborn County, Indiana. She married John F. Winters on August 6, 1849, at Soap Creek and left the Davis household. Their first daughter, Samantha Jane, was born in 1850. A second daughter, Sarepta Ellen, was born in 1852. Jane died late the following year on December 3, 1853, at the age of twenty-one. Jane's early death may be the reason some thought Hannah Ann was the oldest child. (EE/DRD)

Rebecca Davis, the third daughter of David and Hannah, was born in Dearborn County, Indiana in 1835. She died in 1851 at the age of sixteen. (EE/DRD)

Rachel Davis, the youngest daughter of David and Hannah, was born in Iowa in

1844. She died in 1854 about the age of ten. (EE/DRD)

David D. Davis had lost his wife and three daughters in less than six years. The three girls may have died of typhoid fever although they may have died of tuberculosis or measles.

David D. Davis Marries Sarah Bowman

David D. Davis married a second time. He married Sarah Bowman, the widow of William Bowman, in 1852.

William and Sarah Bowman had emigrated from Indiana, Illinois, and Missouri. They had six children; Artimesa, Talitha, Nancy, William, Sarah and Elisha.

Artimesa had moved to Lewis County, Washington. Talitha married James A. O'Neil in 1855. O'Neil was a respected business man in Tampico and a good friend and associate of David D. Davis.

William and Sarah were the only children remaining at home. They moved into the Davis household with their mother. David & Sarah had two children before 1860. Hannah was born May 20, 1854. Mary Jane Davis was born in November 1857.

David D. Davis Dies At Tampico

The *Oregon Weekly Union* for the week of September 14, 1860 reported David D. Davis' passing on August 31, 1860. He died of consumption at the age of 54.

David D. Davis had prepared and executed his will on August 20, 1860 in anticipation of his death. It was filed for probate on September 5, 1860.

David D. Davis' will provided the best interpretation of how his real estate, including the remainder of his donation land claim, was to be divided

David D. Davis' Last Will And Testament

"In the name of God, Amen-

"I David D. Davis of the Town of Tampico in the County of Benton in the State of Oregon being of sound mind and memory but in feeble health do therefore make ordain publish and declare this to be my last Will and Testament.

"That is to say, First after all my lawful debts are paid and discharged that the residue of my estate and personal I give bequeath and dispose of as follows: To my beloved wife Sarah A. Davis Ninety Eight Acres of land to be taken from the South end of my farm and East of the public highway, with all the improvements and appurtenances situated thereon during the term of her natural life and after her death to be divided equally between my two little daughters Hannah and Mary Jane. To my sons Meshach R. Davis, Thomas W. Davis and William D. Davis all the remainder of my real estate equally between them reserving the portion falling to William D. Davis for the use and benefit of my wife and two little daughters Hannah and Mary Jane until such time as the said William D. Davis shall arrive at legal age. To my daughter Ann Hendricks one brown American mare about ten years old now in the hands of her husband. To my daughter Elizabeth Baxter a certain sorrel mare known by the name of Lizzie also one milch cow. To my son-in-law John Winters for the use of my two grand daughters, the children of his deceased wife Jane equally the amount which the said John Winters is due me which amount is about sixty dollars. To my daughter Hannah one half breed mare and colt in the care of Caswell Hendricks. I give bequeath and devise all the rest residue and remainder of my personal estate to my beloved wife for use of herself and my children Hannah and Mary Jane and after her death if there should be any remaining to be divided equally between said Hannah and Mary Jane. In Witness Where of I have here unto

subscribed my name and affix my seal this twentieth day of August in the year of our Lord, One Thousand Eight Hundred Sixty."
"SIGNED David D. Davis"

The will was witnessed by Zebulon Sheets, John Wiles, and Jacob Modie and filed with Benton County Clerk, E. S. Prham.

Actual documents distributing the estate were not found. However, recorded sales of the land by the heirs reflect the distribution. Benton County Deed Records show that Meshach R. Davis, Thomas W. Davis, and William Davis, as individuals, sold inherited land from the David D. Davis Donation Land Claim to John Wiles during February 1864. In the division of the land in the Donation Land Claim, divided interests in the land on the east side of Tampico Road went to Meshach R. Davis and Sarah Davis. Thomas W. and William Davis received divided interest in the land on the west side of the road.

The aerial map of section clearly shows the division on the east side of Tampico Road with a straight line change in vegetation. About ninety-eight acres on the south side of the division line went to David D. Davis' wife Sarah Davis in life estate. Meshach R. Davis sold sixty-one acres "off the northeast part" of the Donation Land Claim. This loosely describes the rest of the land on the east side of Tampico Road. Meshach later sold the remainder of his interest of ten undescribed acres.

Thomas Davis sold seventy-four acres being all of the claim west of Soap Creek and west of Tampico Road. William D. Davis sold seventy acres off the north part of the Donation Land Claim. By the process of elimination (being the remainder of the claim) this loosely describes the rest of the land on the west side of Tampico Road.

David D. Davis sold eight acres off the Donation Land Claim to William Beatty before the former's death. All the three hundred twenty acres in the Donation Land Claim are accounted for.

Benton County Deed Records show that Meshach R. Davis and Thomas W. Davis sold several acres of land that had been acquired by David D. Davis outside the Donation Land Claim.

Sarah (Bowman) Davis' Death

Sarah (Bowman) Davis died in 1861, the year after David D. Davis' death. Talitha O'Neil assumed responsibility for raising her two half sisters, Hannah and Mary Jane Davis. Her spouse, James O'Neil was appointed to be their guardian in accordance with the wishes expressed by David D. Davis in his Last Will and Testament.

Hanna and Mary Jane Davis property went into trust for them. They ultimately received and disposed of the property. Thomas Davis married Missouri Hall in 1867 and moved from the area in 1868. He advised James O'Neil, guardian of Hannah and Mary Jane Davis, Thomas' half-sisters:

> *"I write you a few lines to let you know that we are well at present whoping you are enjoying the same. I have the crop taken care of. Your part is in the granary. It contains one hundred and thirty bushels of oats and thirty-five of wheat. And about three tun of hey. I am going away and cannot see to it any longer. I fastened the doors up good and fast. Mack Davis is going to move there in a short time and he can tend to things then. So no more at present. But remain Your obedient servent."*
> SIGNED Thos. D. Davis

James Anderson O'Neil (O'Neal))

James Anderson O'Neil (O'Neal) was appointed guardian of Hannah and Mary Jane Davis upon the death of their mother, Sarah (Bowman) Davis.

He was fifty-five in 1855 when he married Talitha C. Bowman, one of David D. Davis' six step children. Talitha was the daughter of William Bowman deceased and

Sarah Bowman Davis. O'Neil became the guardian of Hannah and Mary Jane Davis under the provisions of David D. Davis' will. O'Neil was also appointed guardian for William Davis, David and Hannah's youngest son.

James and Talitha O'Neil probably lived on the estate of Sarah Bowman Davis near Lewisville in Polk County being managed by James O'Neil. Ralph Friedman says James and Talitha O'Neil settled down on the farm. He must have come from a hardy folk, for a Portland newspaper dated May 5, 1917, said of him: "He died in Polk County at 74. None of the other members of his generation of this family died so young." (RF)

James Anderson O'Neil died in Polk County in September 1874 at the age of seventy-four. He was buried on the farm. When his farm fell into other hands, his body was removed to a private burial ground as Hart Cemetery. Hart Cemetery is on a hilltop forest clearing southwest of Falls City junction on Oregon 223.

David, Hannah, Rachel, And Rebecca Davis Moved To Monmouth Now May They Rest In Peace

Edward Erwin Davis and David Ronald Davis found the headstones of David, Hannah, Rachel and Rebecca at the southeast corner of the west section of the New English Cemetery. The cemetery is on old highway 99W a mile or so south of Monmouth, Oregon. The headstones are less than fifty feet off the old highway that divides the cemetery. They are between the south road and the southern edge of the cemetery.

They were moved from a cemetery near Tampico to New English Cemetery when Camp Adair was established in 1943. David D. Davis' headstone was missing until 1991. The Benton County Historical Museum found the headstone. David Ronald Davis retrieved the headstone and returned it to its rightful place in 1991.

David D. Davis, Hannah Davis, Rachel, and Rebecca Davis' travels in death have

Soap Creek Valley in late 1980s viewed from Lewisburg Saddle

Photo by Bob Zybach

been almost as great in death as they were in life. May we now work to "Let them rest in peace."

Conclusion Of Soap Creek Saga On A Personal Note

David D. Davis did not record any fond memories of his adventures in Soap Creek. These were not the "good old days." His years in Soap Creek appear quite miserable.

David D. Davis' Soap Creek saga started with the death of his beloved wife, Hannah, soon after he arrived there. It ended in his own death, that was soon followed by the death of his second wife, Sarah. Three of David and Hannah Davis' children also died at Soap Creek.

These factors controlled the life of Thomas Davis, son of David and Hannah, so much that the sadness was instilled in the life of Charles Elmer Davis, his son living with him - my grandfather. My grandfather and my own father never talked about the "good old days" had by their pioneer ancestors.

Charles Elmer Davis visited the Soap Creek area only once, in 1930 or 1931 when he was about sixty years old. On that occasion my grandmother, Alice Delcina Sims Davis, said that he had never visited the place where his family had first settled in Oregon. She said that many of his family had died in the early days in settlements in the southern Willamette Valley and that grandfather was so saddened that he could not get enough courage to visit the place even though we were not very far away. He wanted to visit the place, where his family had first settled, shortly before he died in 1942.

My father, Chester Oliver Davis, never visited Soap Creek. The Charles Elmer's branch of Davis family tradition said that the Davises lost everything but a few personal items and maybe some loose stock emigrating to Oregon — Then many lost their lives.

Thus the saga of David D. Davis is complete: An emigrant-pioneer through life, birth-to-death, shore-to-shore, and coast-to-coast from the Atlantic-to-the-Pacific.

1807-Pennsylvania-to-Oregon-1860

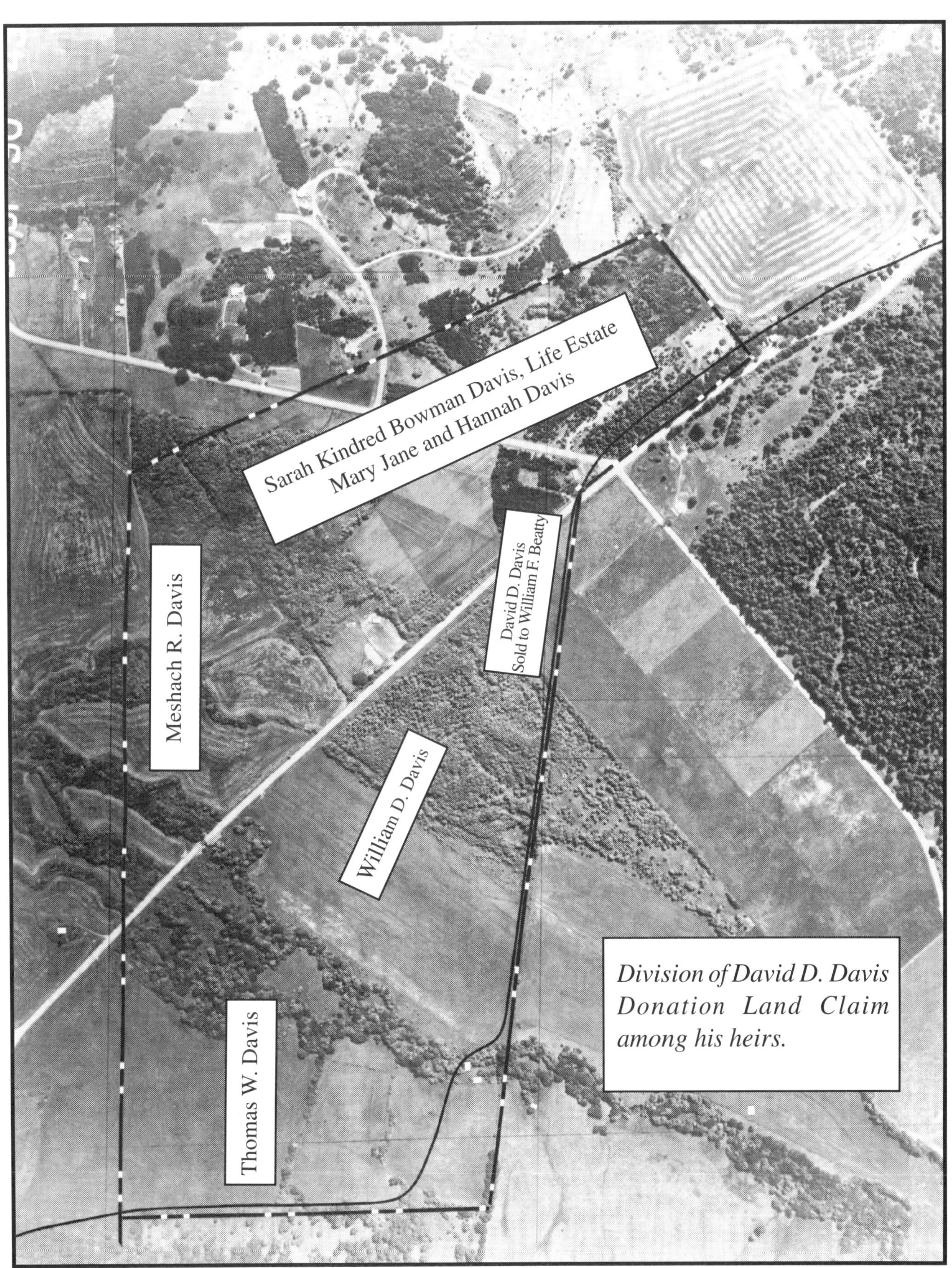

Division of David D. Davis Donation Land Claim among his heirs.

OREGON TRAIL 1846 – 1847

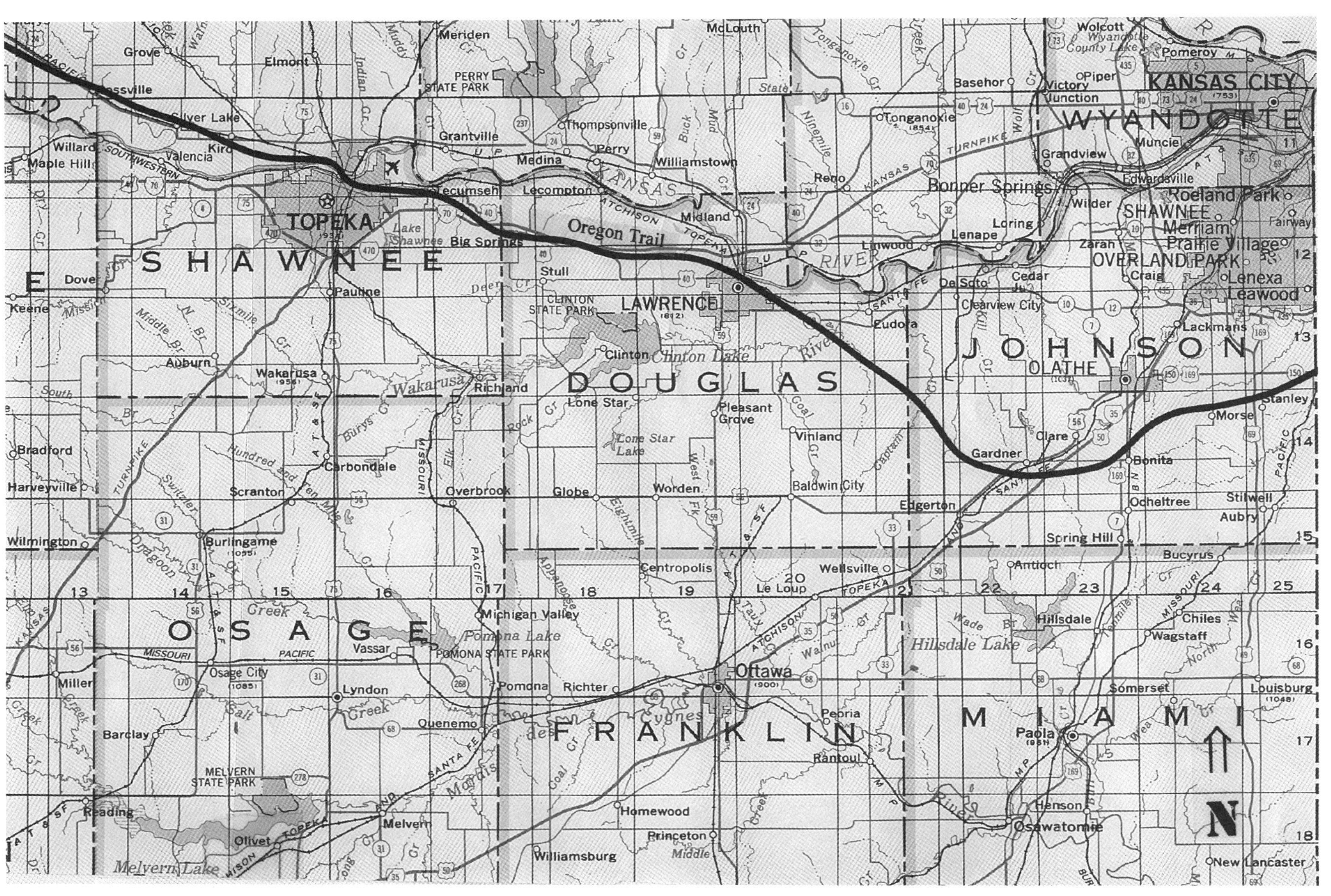

SOUTHERN ROUTE TO OREGON

MAP 3

OREGON TRAIL 1846 – 1847

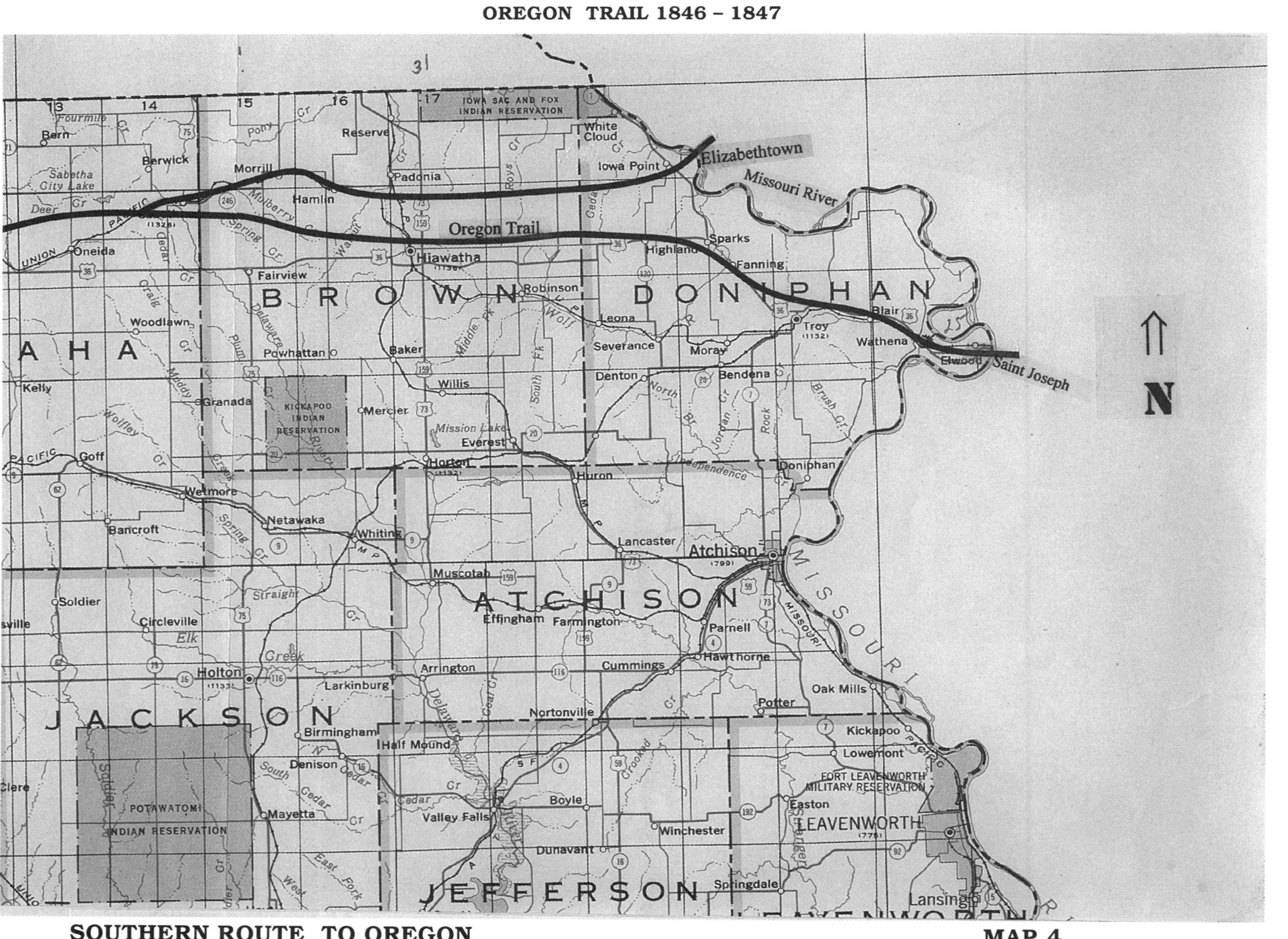

SOUTHERN ROUTE TO OREGON

MAP 4

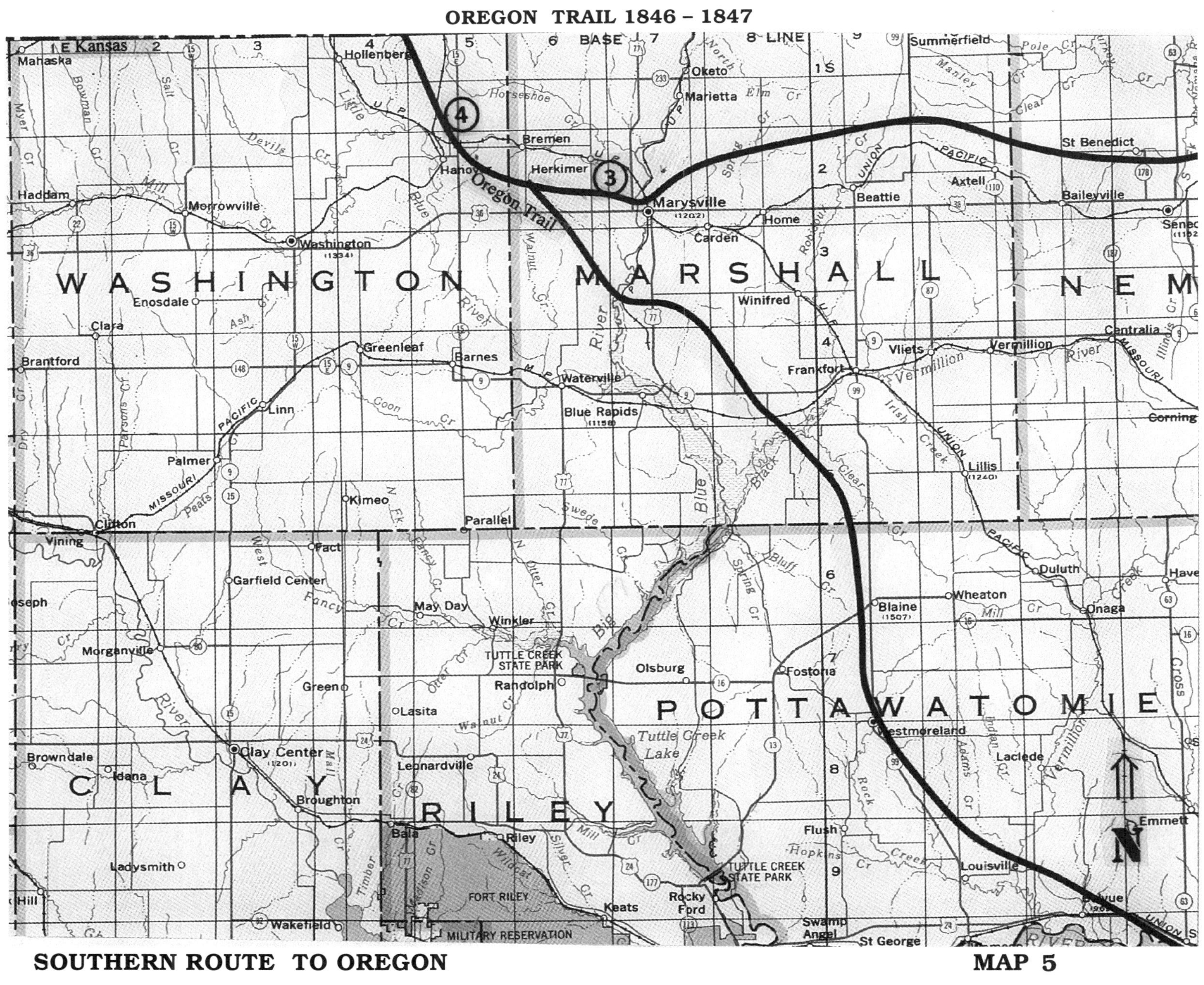

OREGON TRAIL 1846 – 1847
WASHINGTON
MARSHALL
CLAY
RILEY
POTTAWATOMIE
Oregon Trail
Marysville
Washington
Clay Center
Tuttle Creek Lake
FORT RILEY
MILITARY RESERVATION
SOUTHERN ROUTE TO OREGON
MAP 5

OREGON TRAIL 1846 – 1847

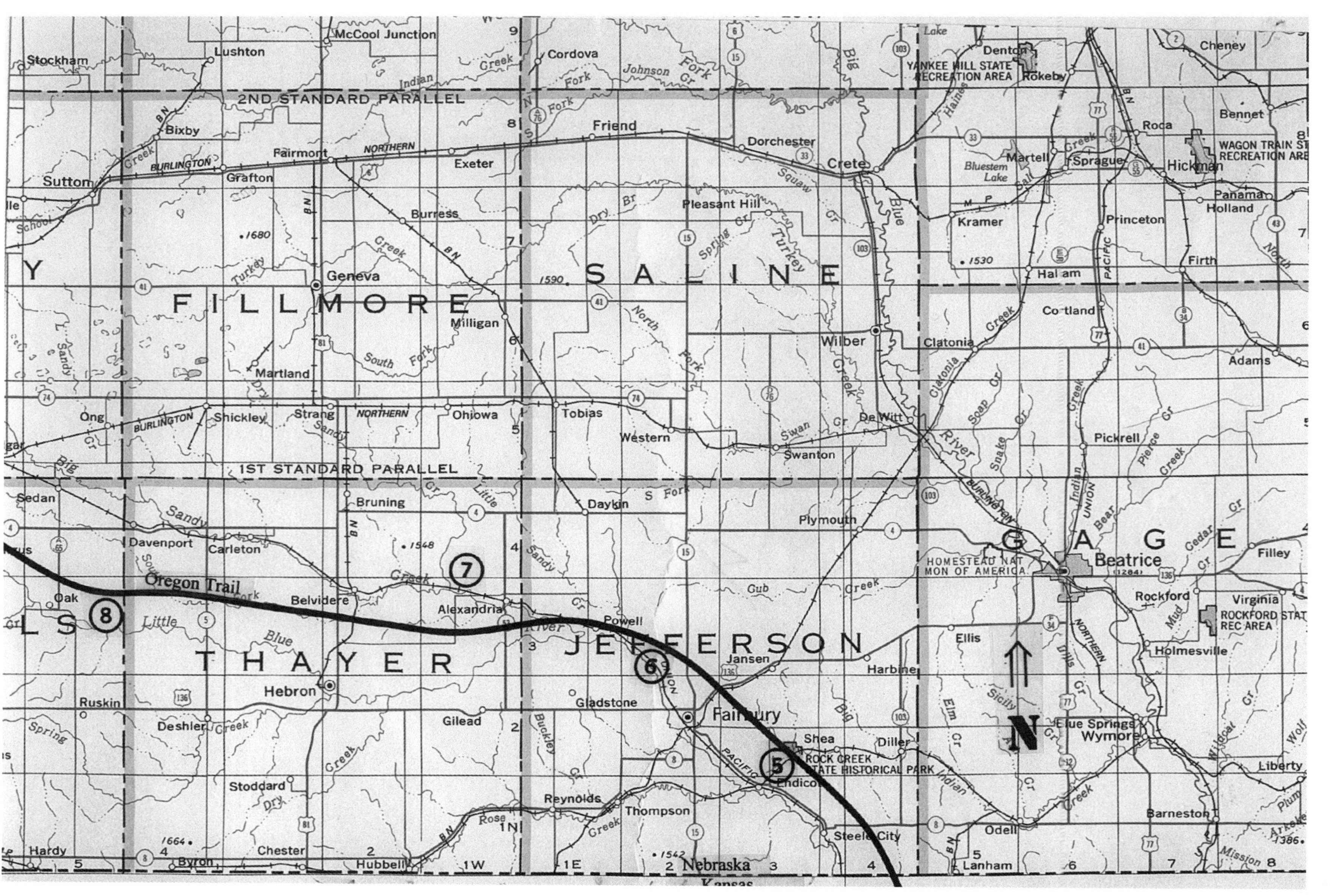

SOUTHERN ROUTE TO OREGON

MAP 6

OREGON TRAIL 1846 – 1847

SOUTHERN ROUTE TO OREGON

MAP 7

OREGON TRAIL 1846 – 1847

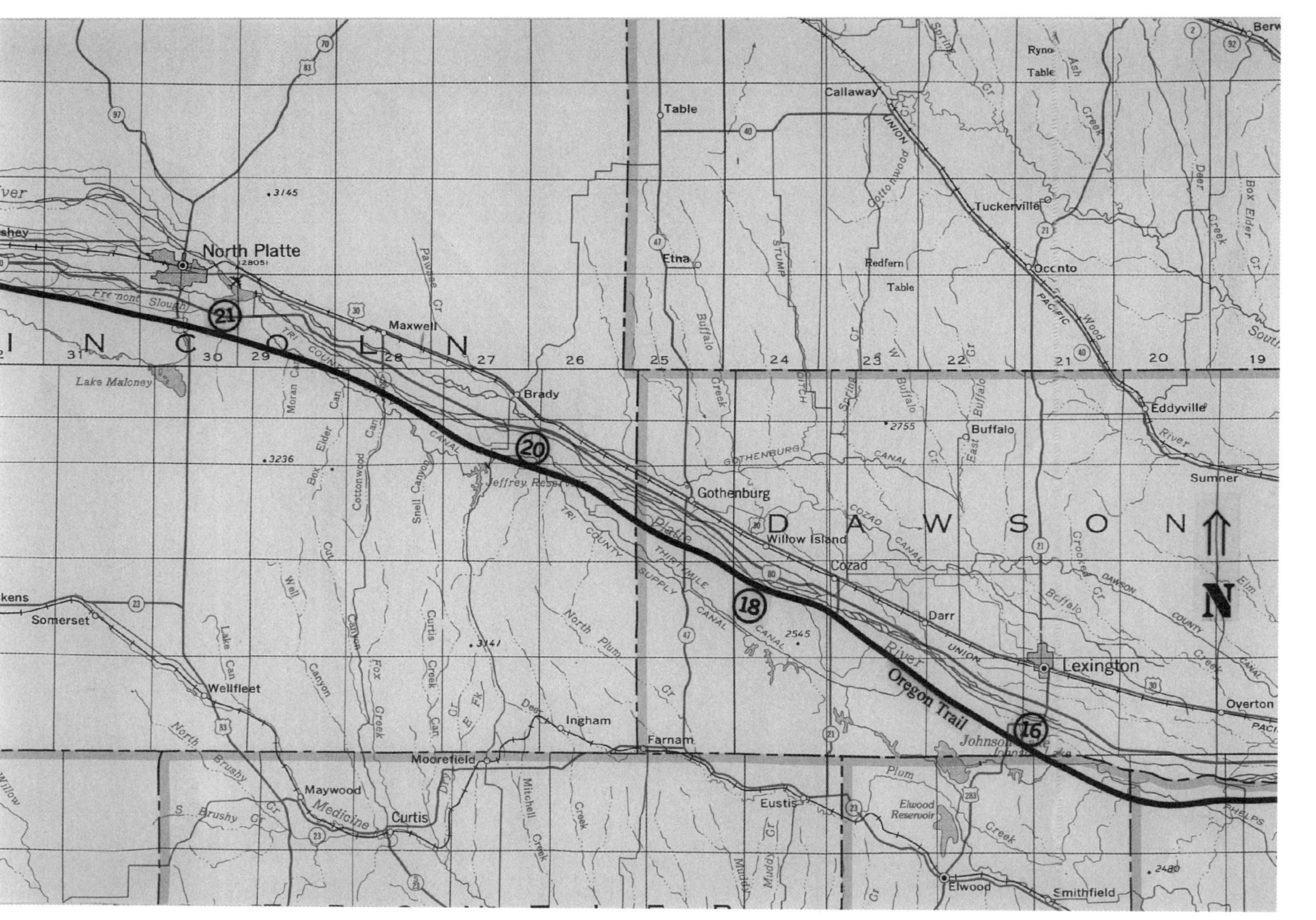

SOUTHERN ROUTE TO OREGON

MAP 8

OREGON TRAIL 1846 – 1847

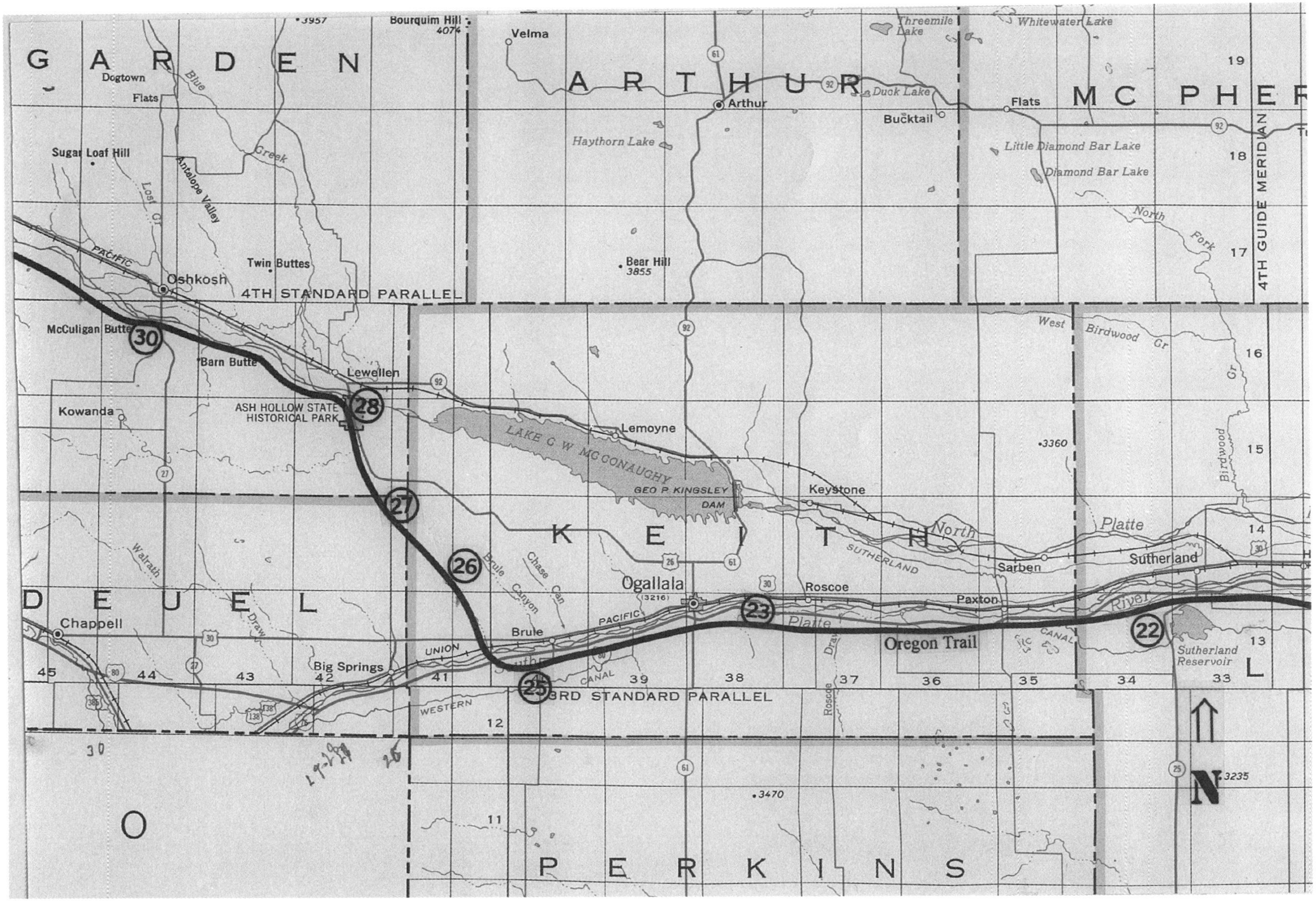

SOUTHERN ROUTE TO OREGON

MAP 9

OREGON TRAIL 1846 – 1847

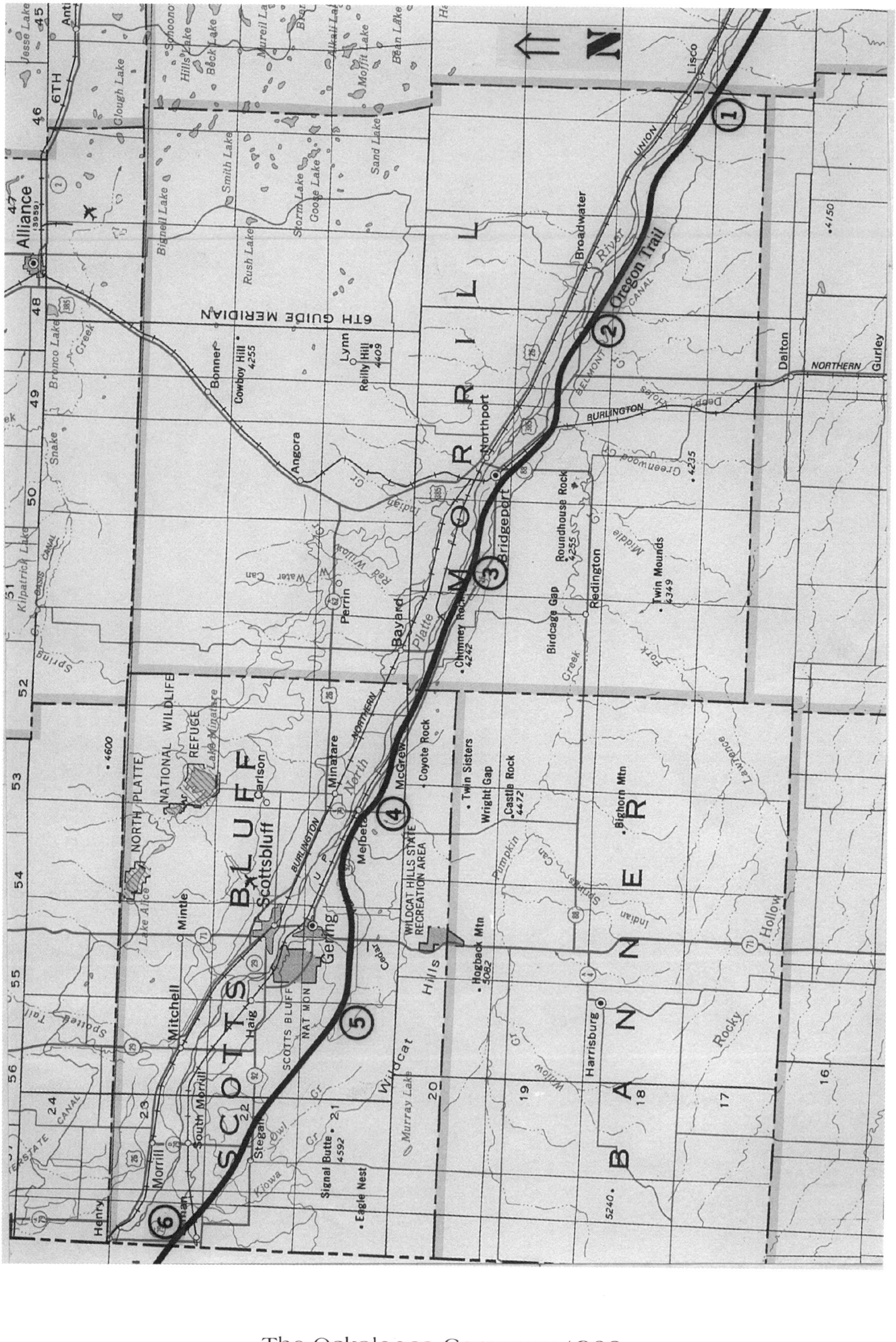

MAP 10

SOUTHERN ROUTE TO OREGON

OREGON TRAIL 1846 – 1847

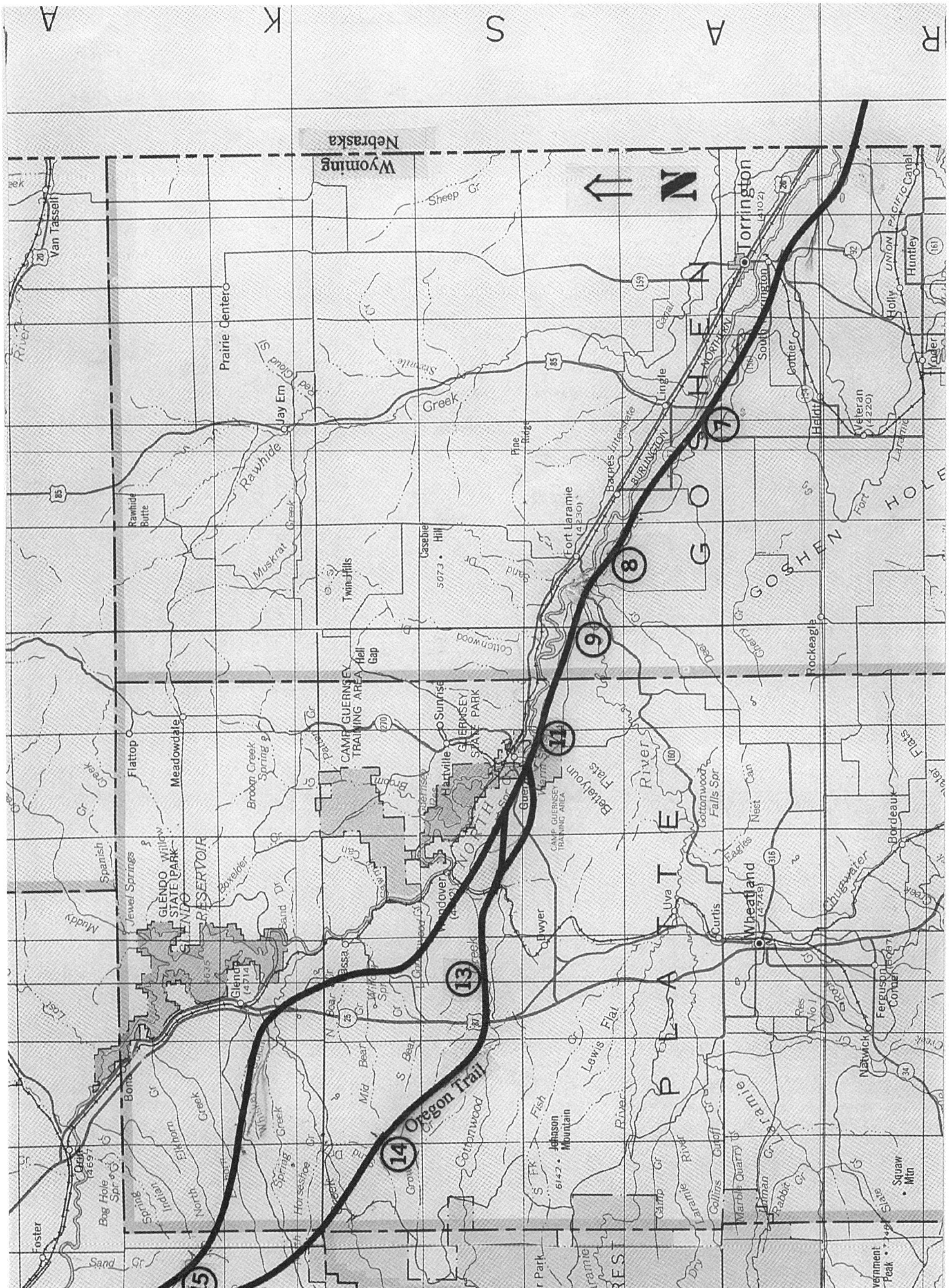

SOUTHERN ROUTE TO OREGON

MAP 11

OREGON TRAIL 1846 – 1847

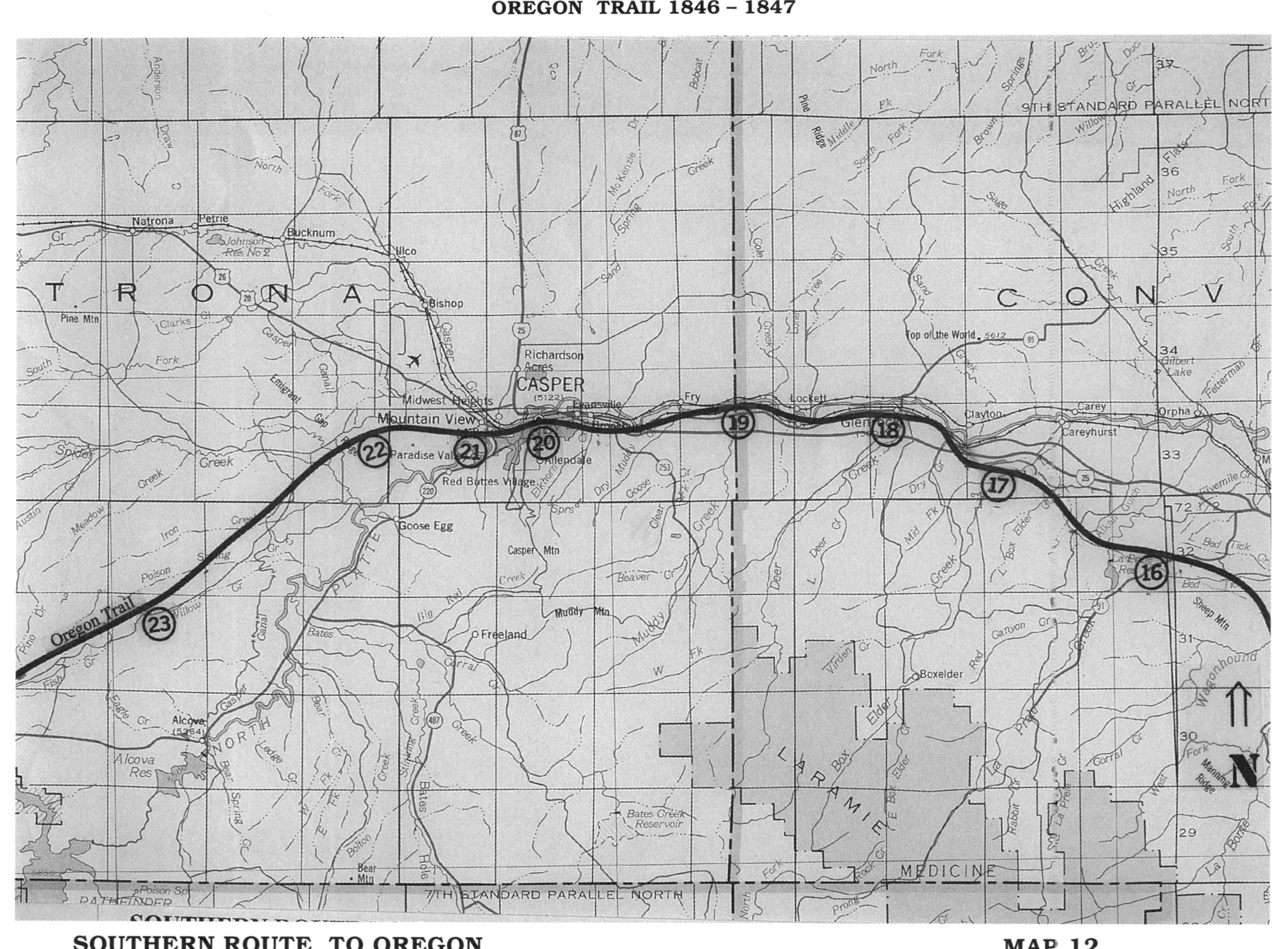

SOUTHERN ROUTE TO OREGON

MAP 12

OREGON TRAIL 1846 – 1847

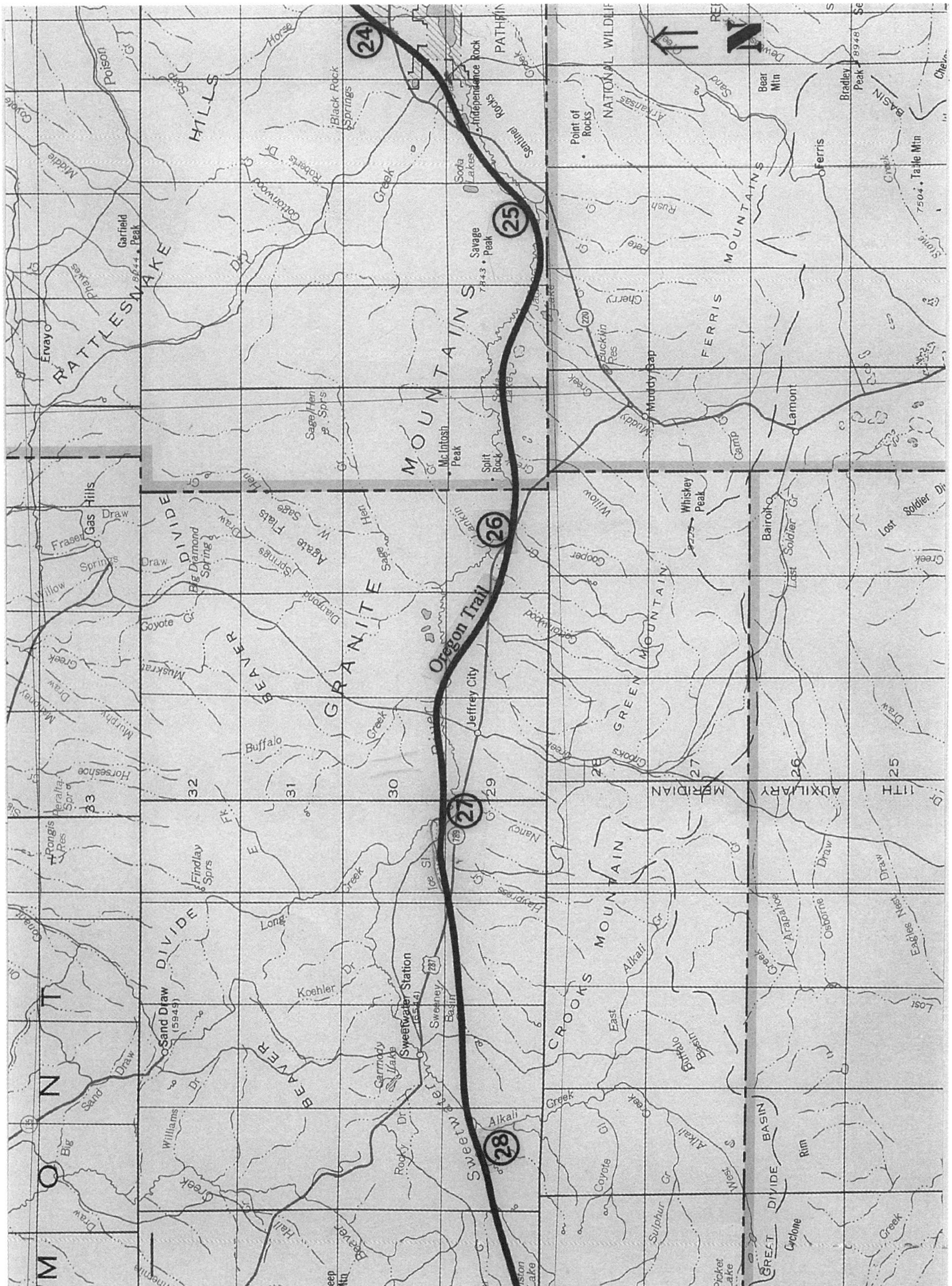

SOUTHERN ROUTE TO OREGON

MAP 13

OREGON TRAIL 1846 – 1847

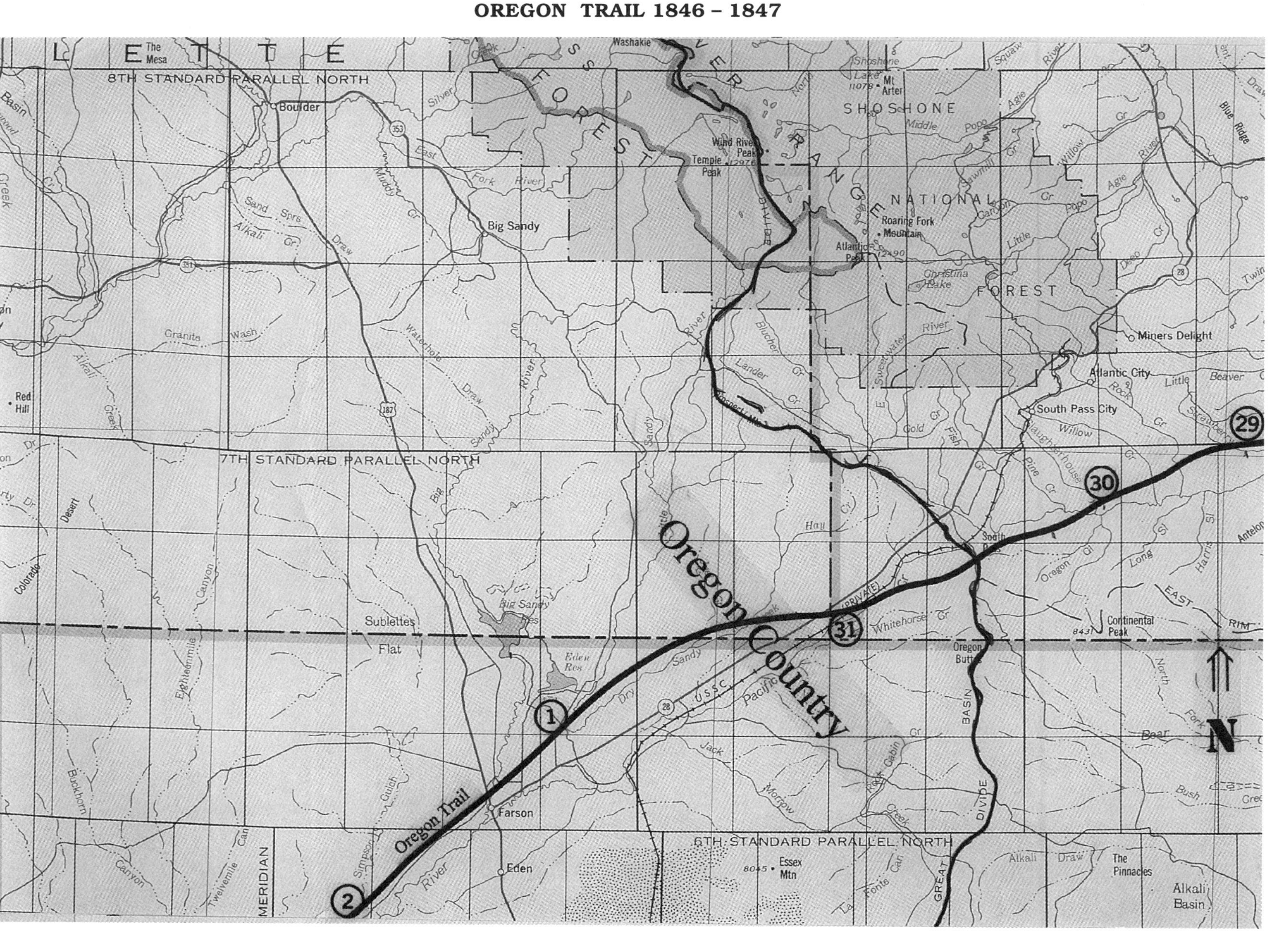

SOUTHERN ROUTE TO OREGON

MAP 14

OREGON TRAIL 1846 – 1847

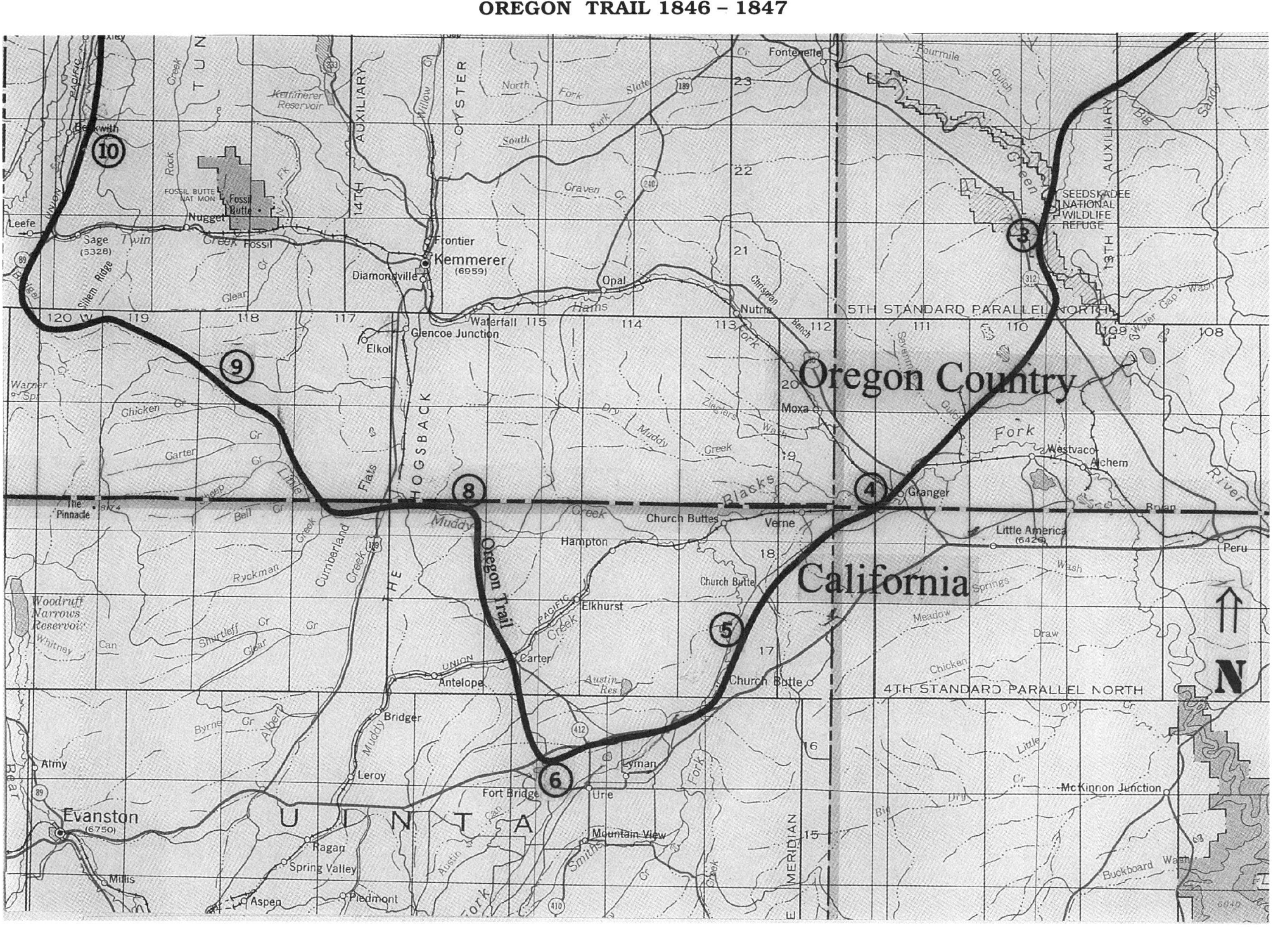

SOUTHERN ROUTE TO OREGON

MAP 15

OREGON TRAIL 1846 – 1847

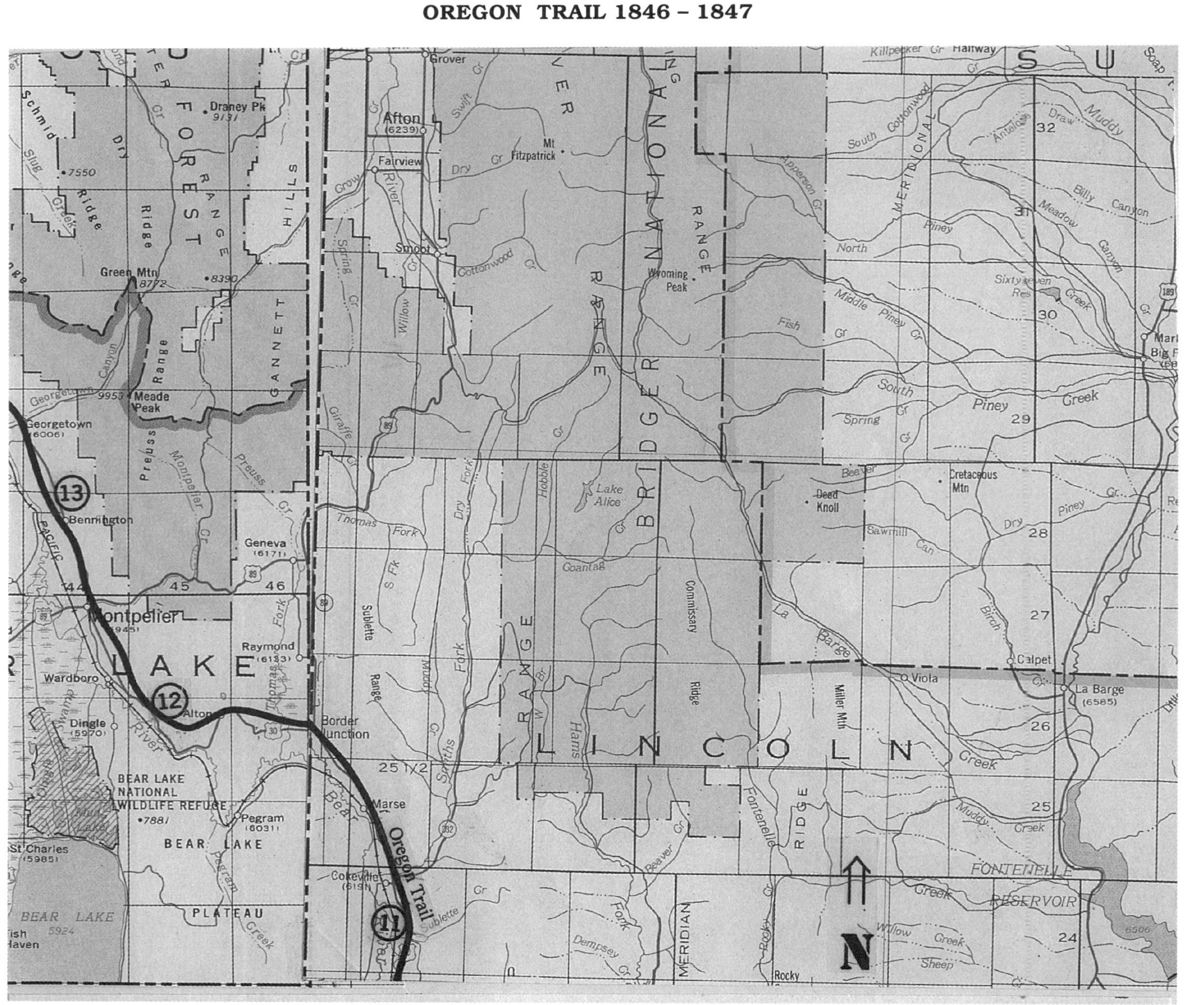

SOUTHERN ROUTE TO OREGON

MAP 16

OREGON TRAIL 1846 – 1847

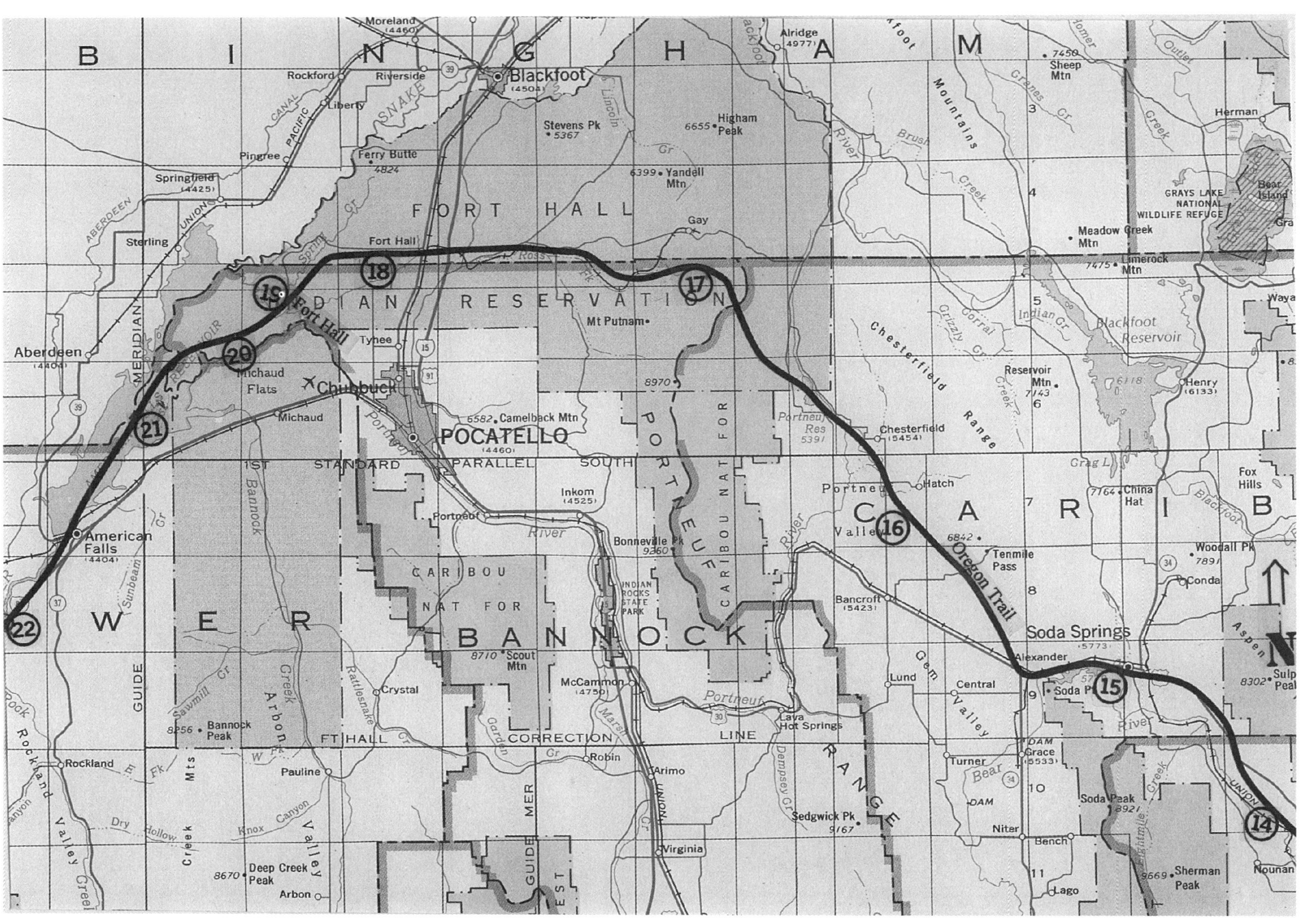

SOUTHERN ROUTE TO OREGON

MAP 17

OREGON TRAIL 1846 – 1847

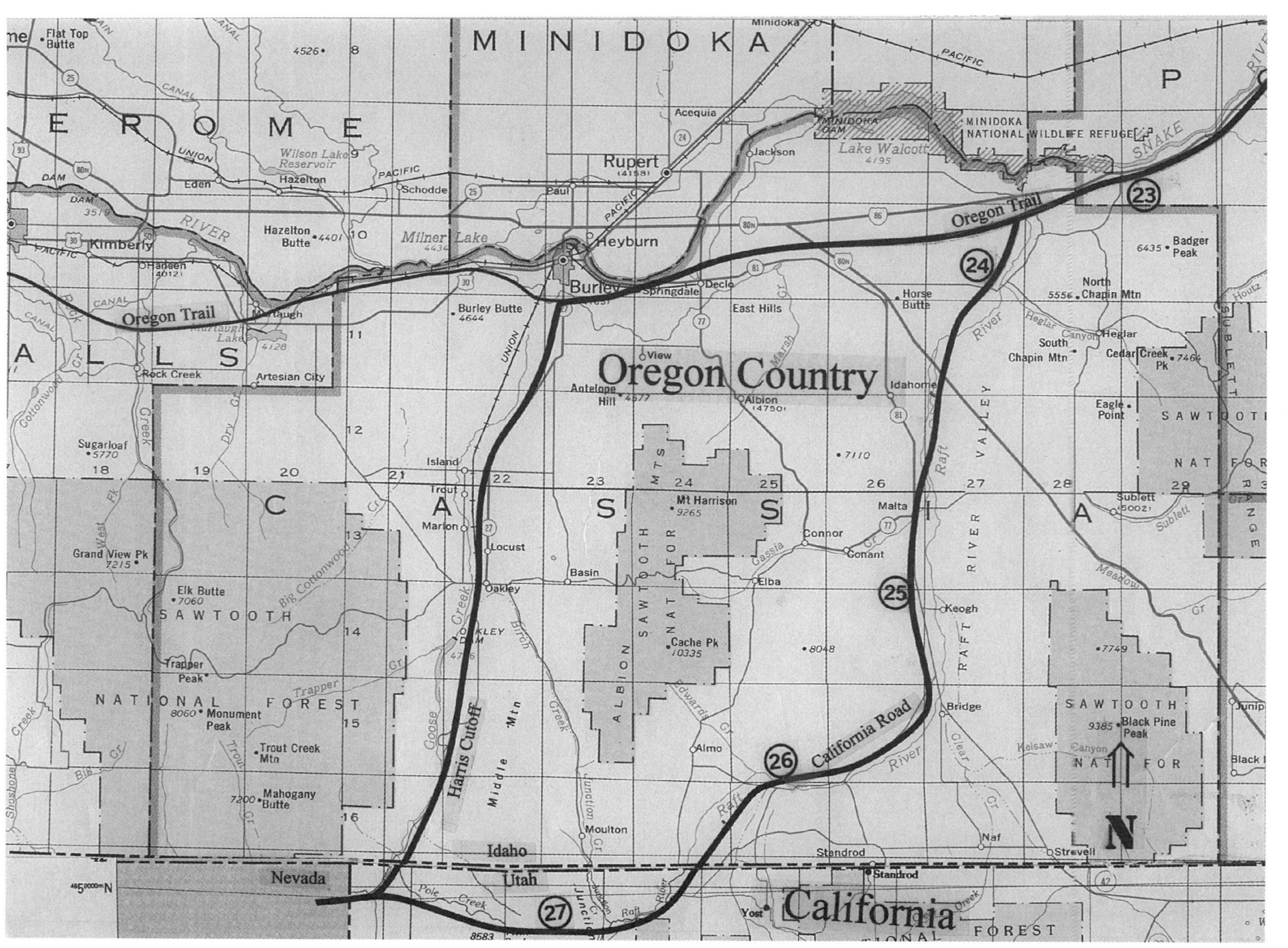

SOUTHERN ROUTE TO OREGON

MAP 18

OREGON TRAIL 1846 – 1847

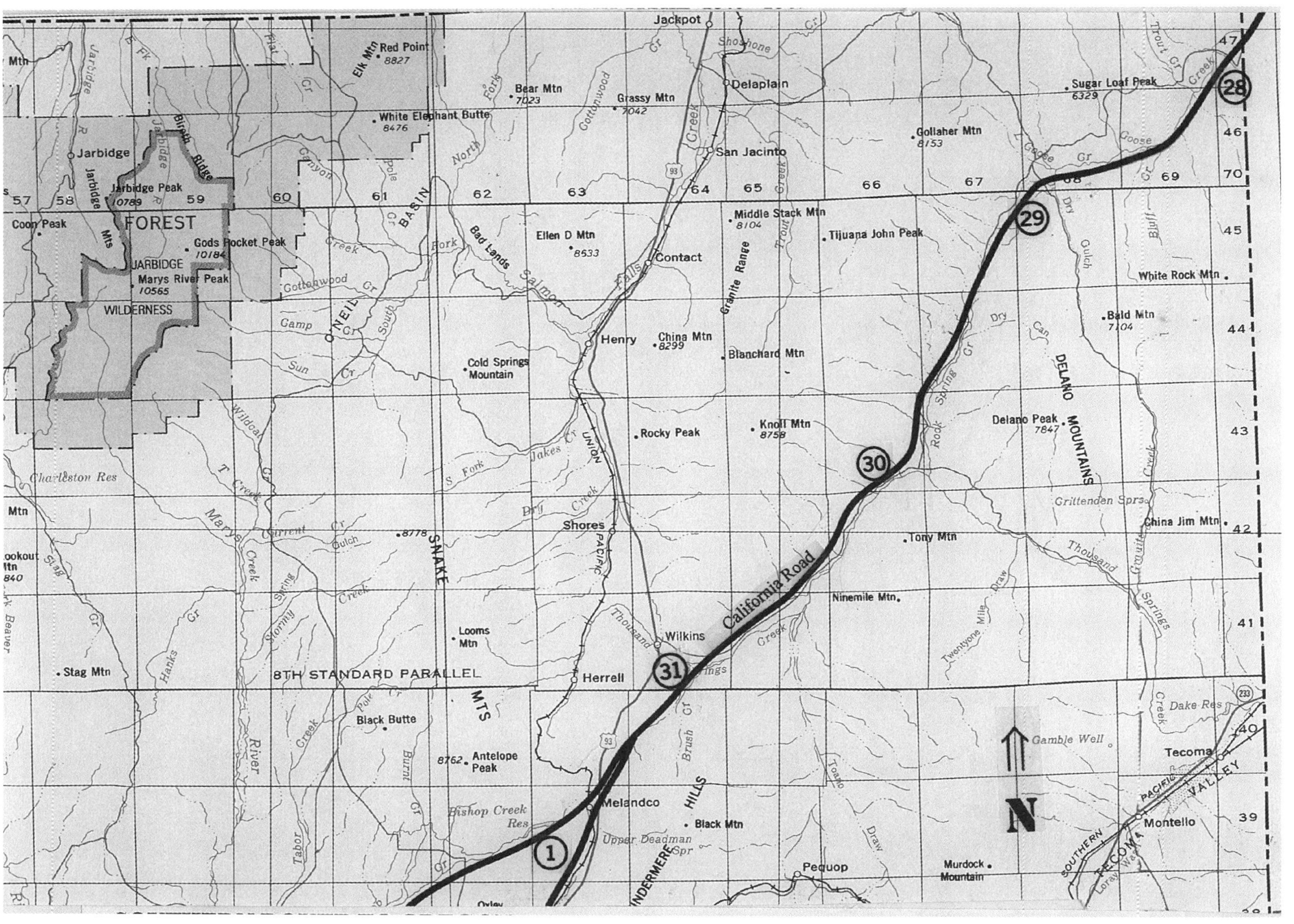

SOUTHERN ROUTE TO OREGON

MAP 19

OREGON TRAIL 1846 – 1847

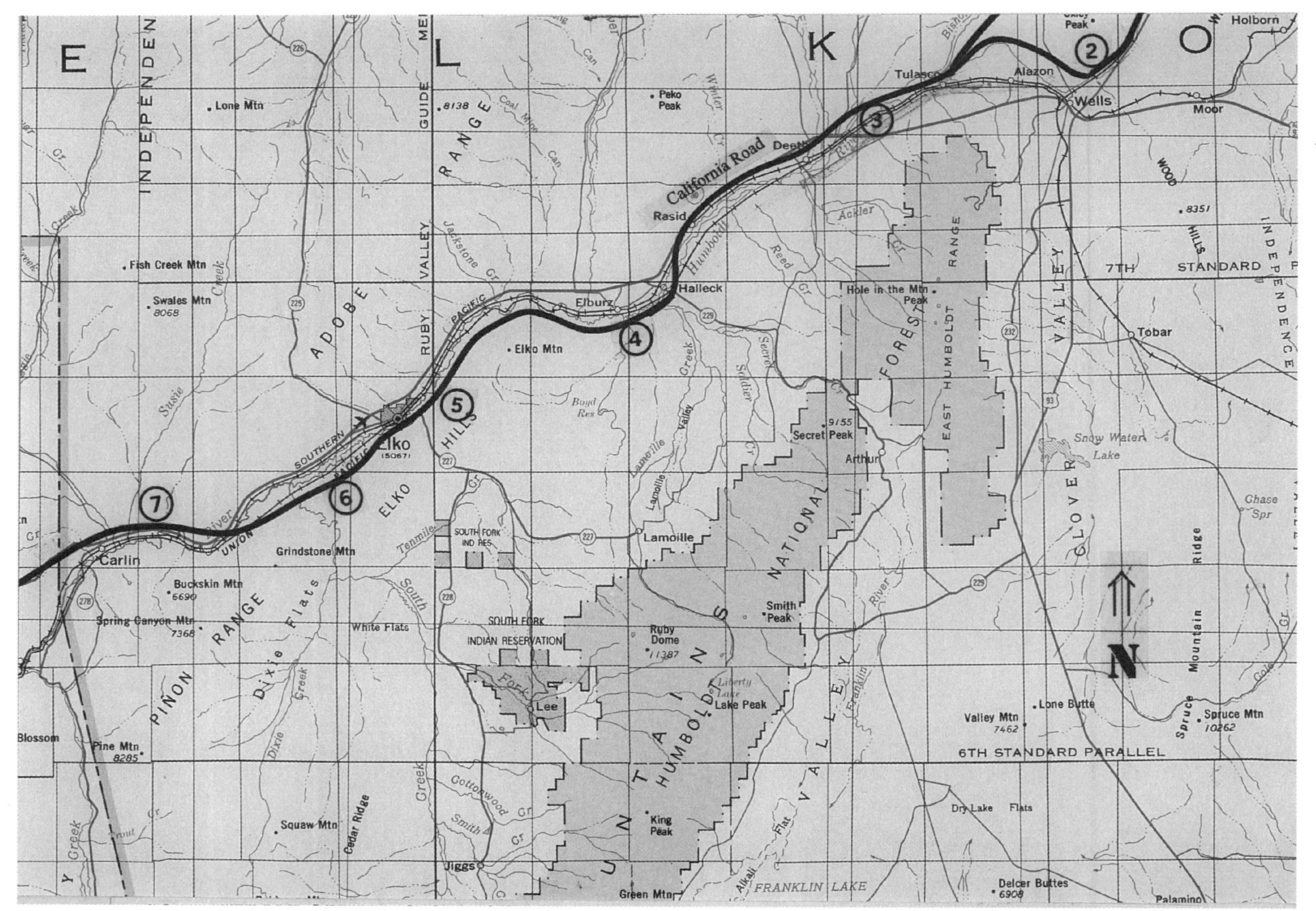

SOUTHERN ROUTE TO OREGON

MAP 20

OREGON TRAIL 1846 – 1847

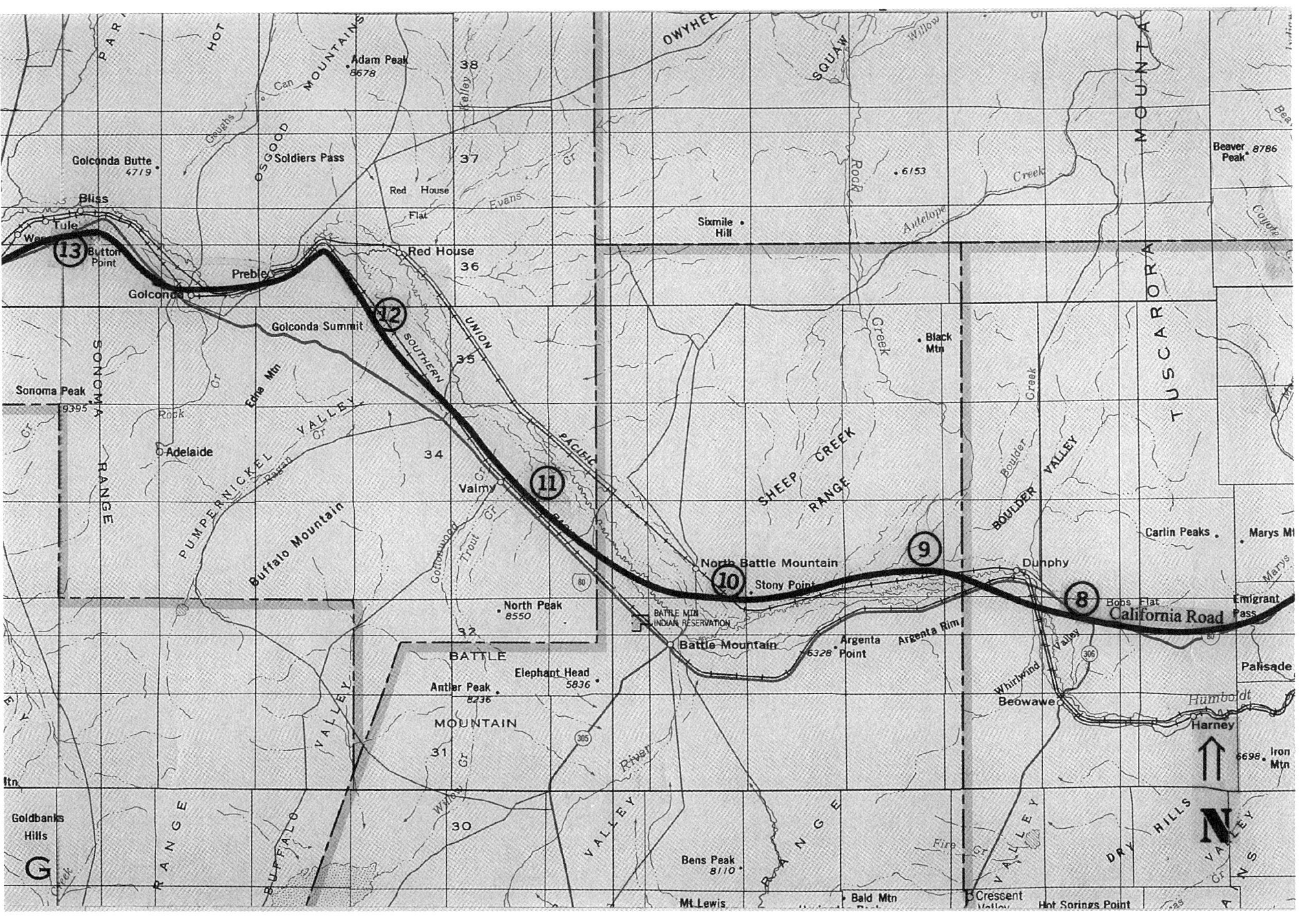

SOUTHERN ROUTE TO OREGON

MAP 21

OREGON TRAIL 1846 – 1847

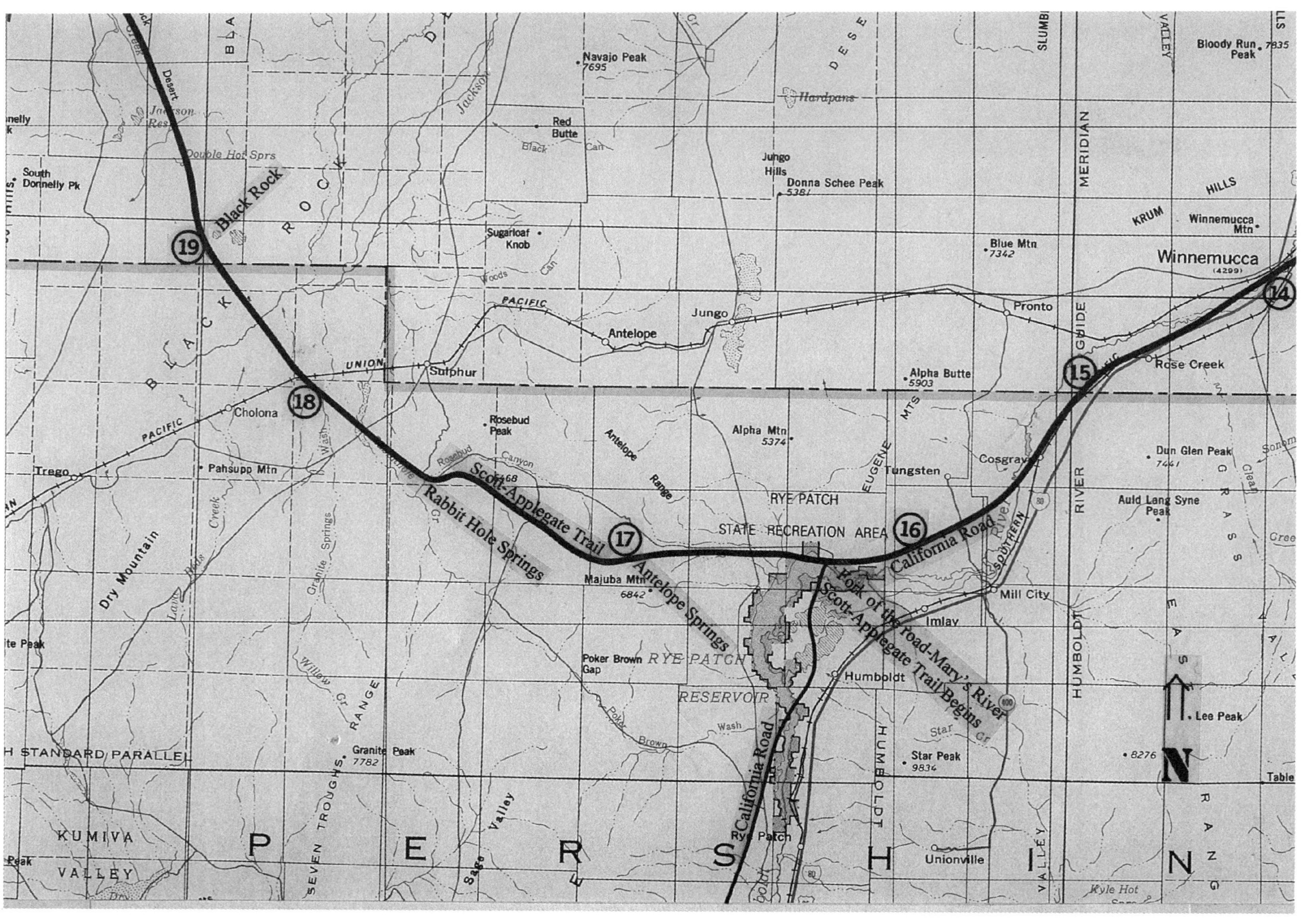

SOUTHERN ROUTE TO OREGON

MAP 22

OREGON TRAIL 1846 – 1847

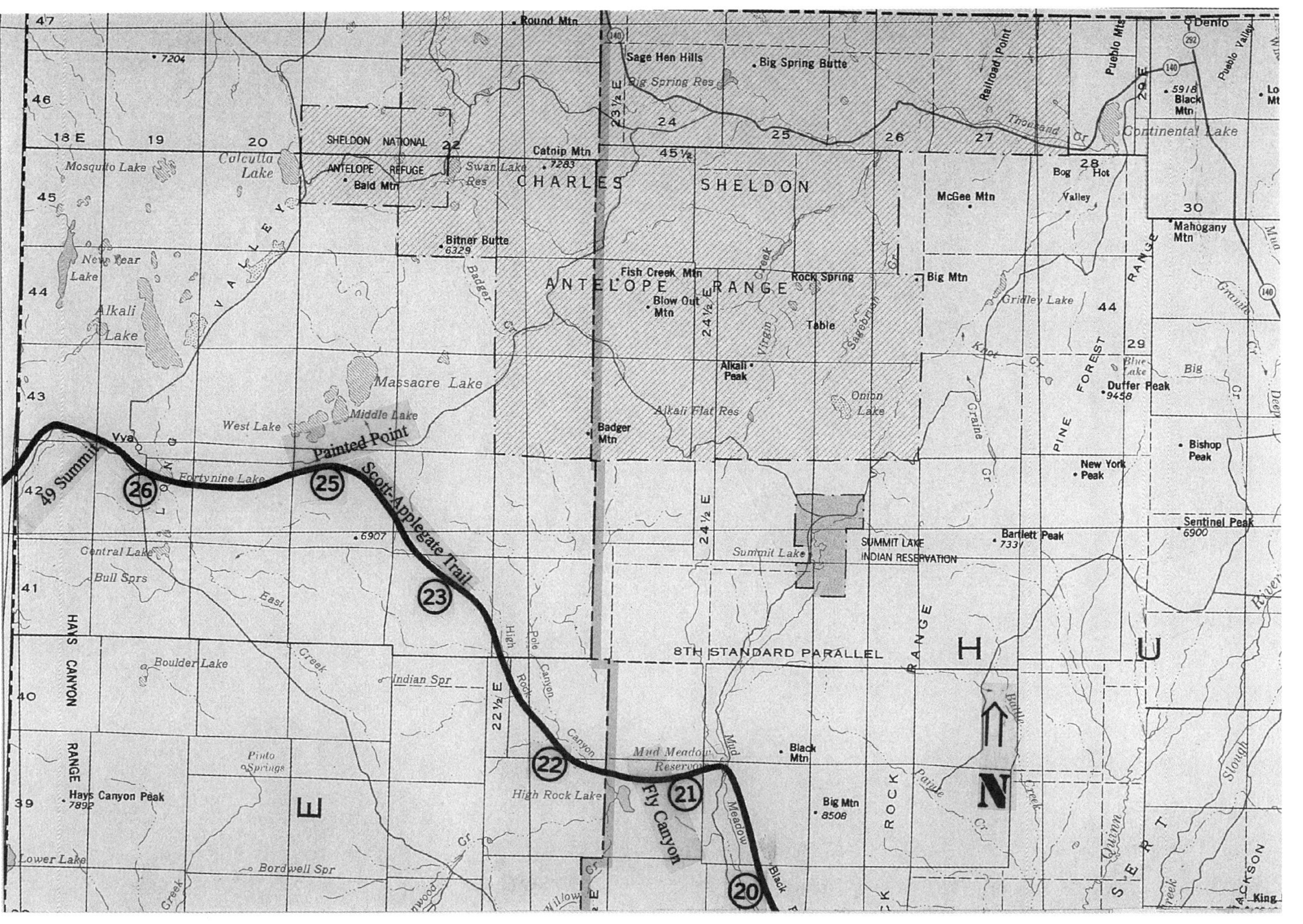

SOUTHERN ROUTE TO OREGON

MAP 23

OREGON TRAIL 1846 – 1847

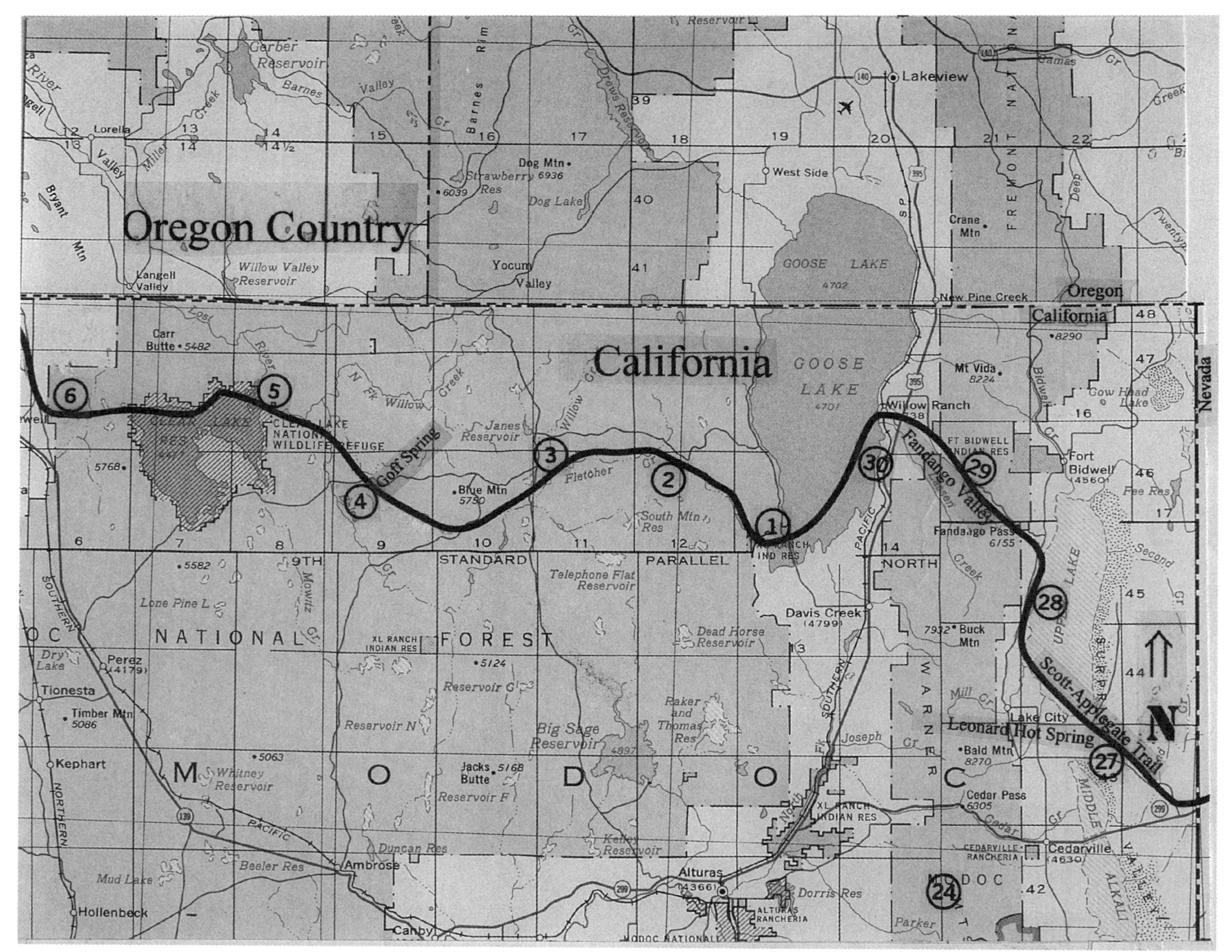

SOUTHERN ROUTE TO OREGON

MAP 24

OREGON TRAIL 1846 – 1847

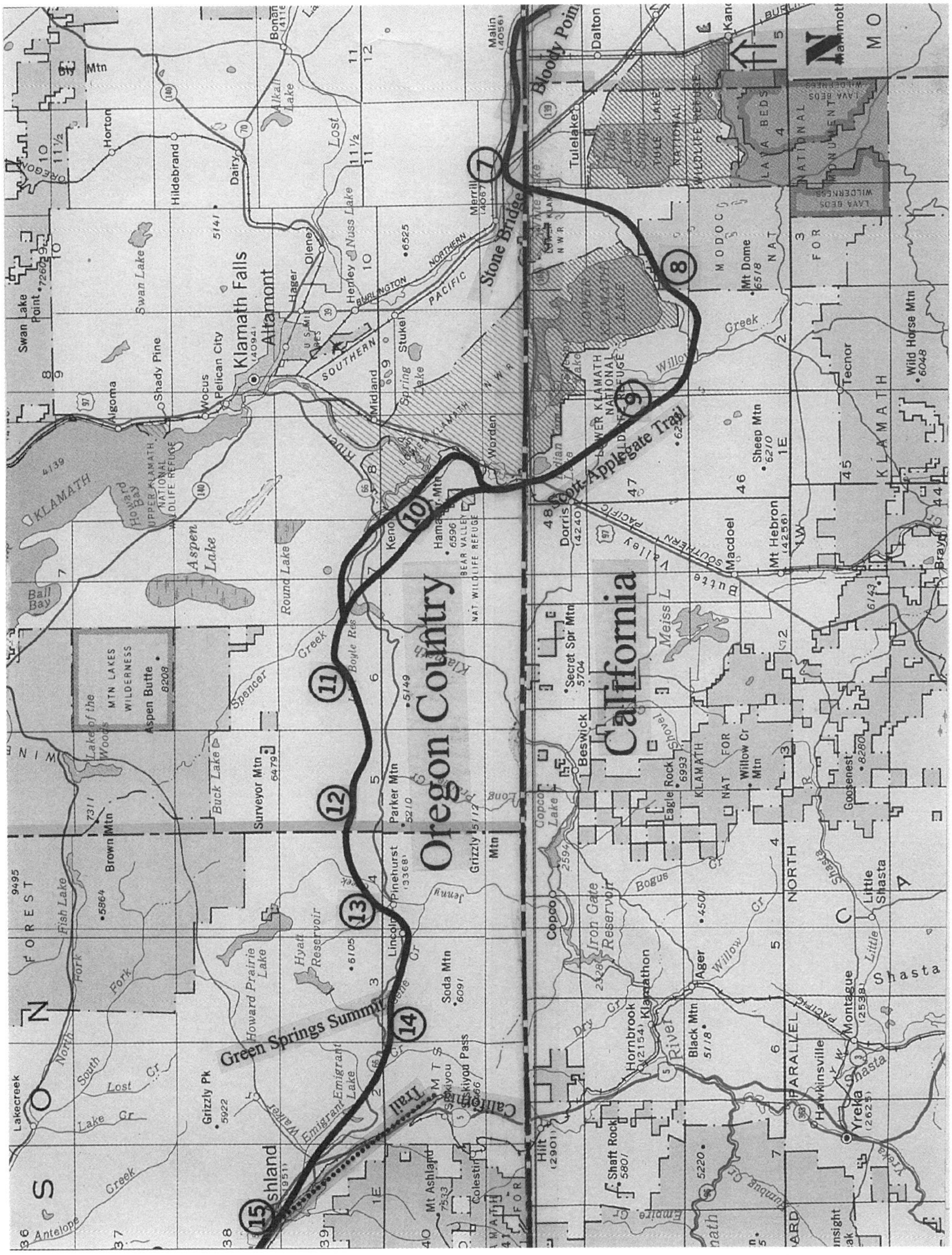

SOUTHERN ROUTE TO OREGON

MAP 25

OREGON TRAIL 1846 – 1847

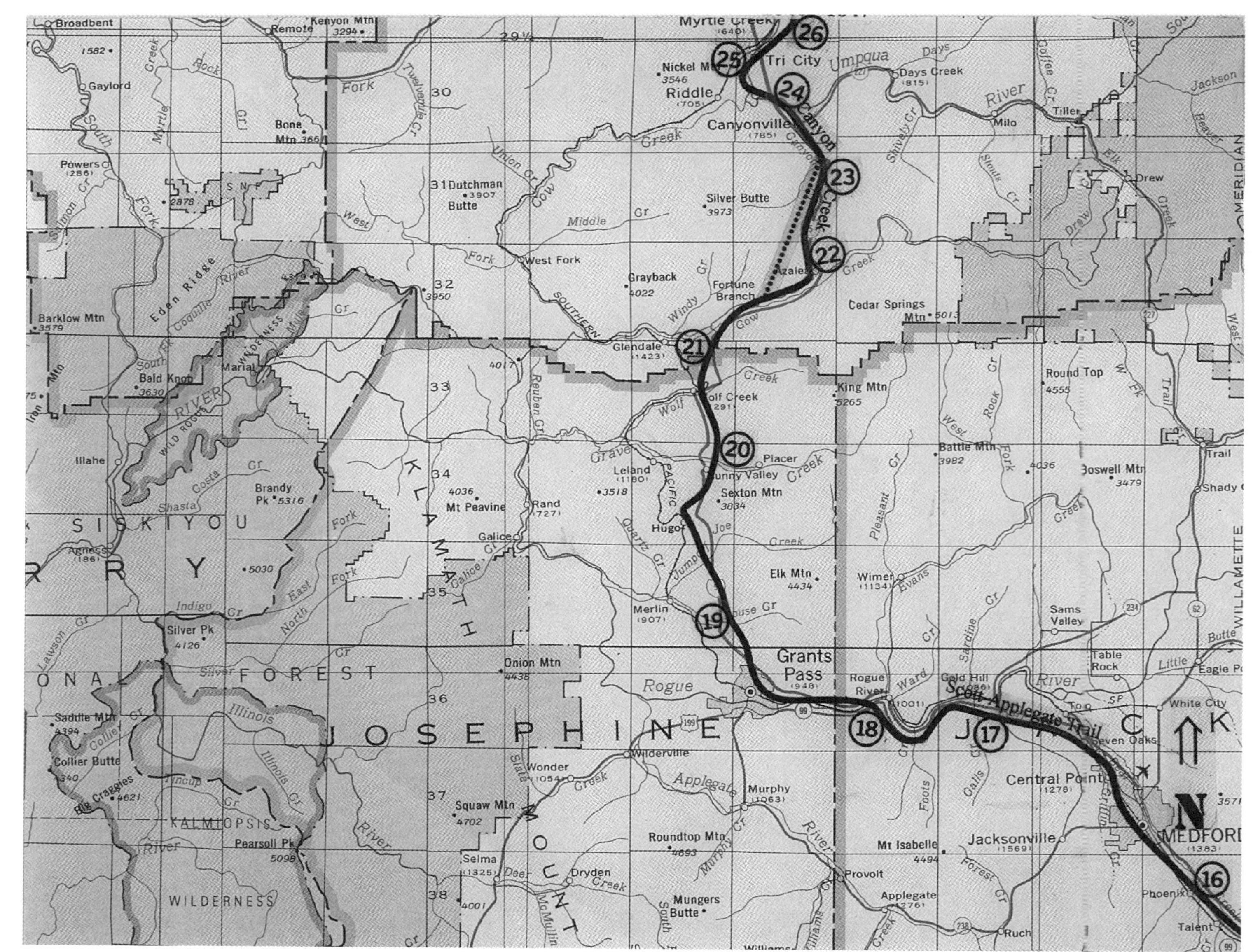

SOUTHERN ROUTE TO OREGON

MAP 26

OREGON TRAIL 1846 – 1847

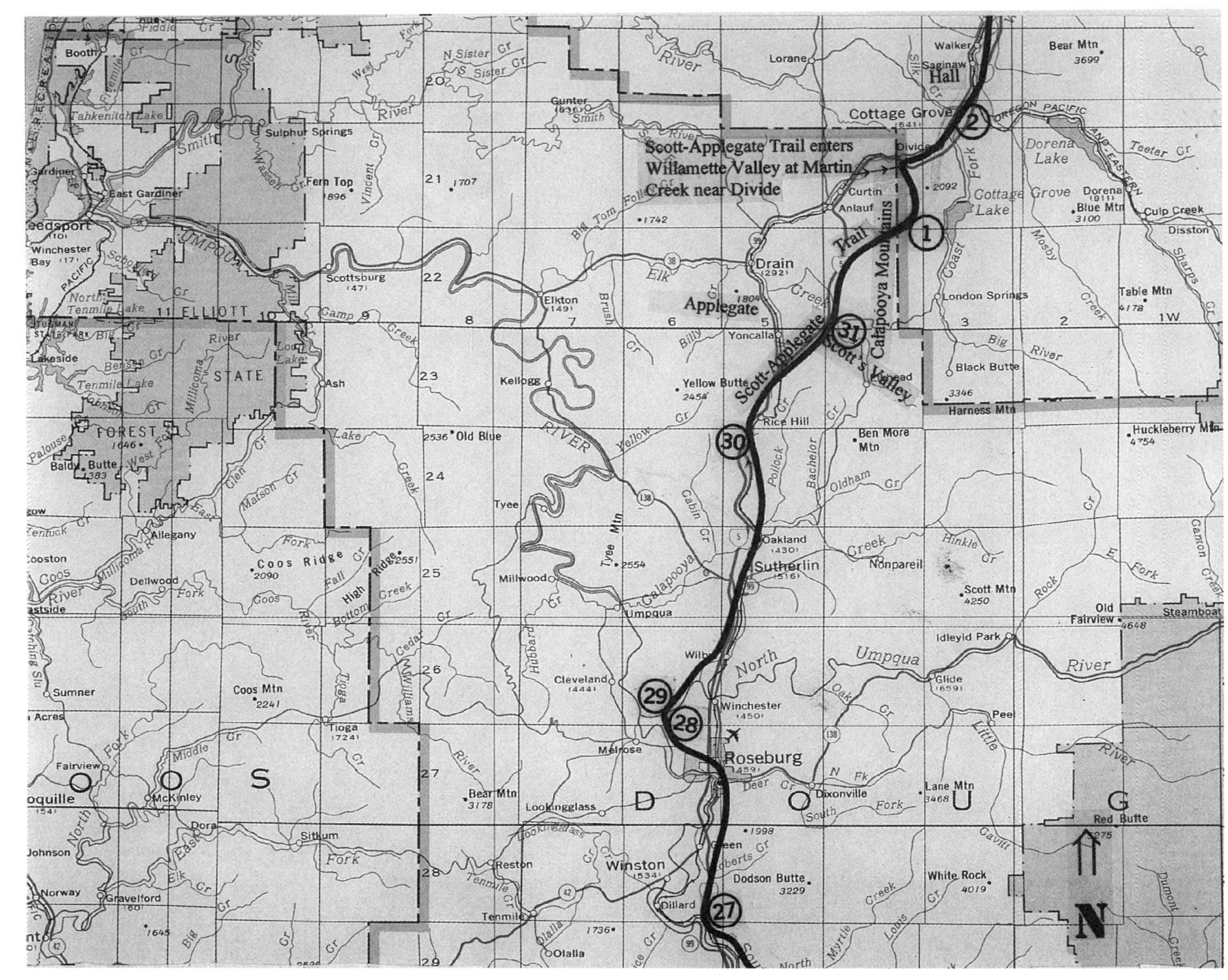

SOUTHERN ROUTE TO OREGON

MAP 27

OREGON TRAIL 1846 – 1847

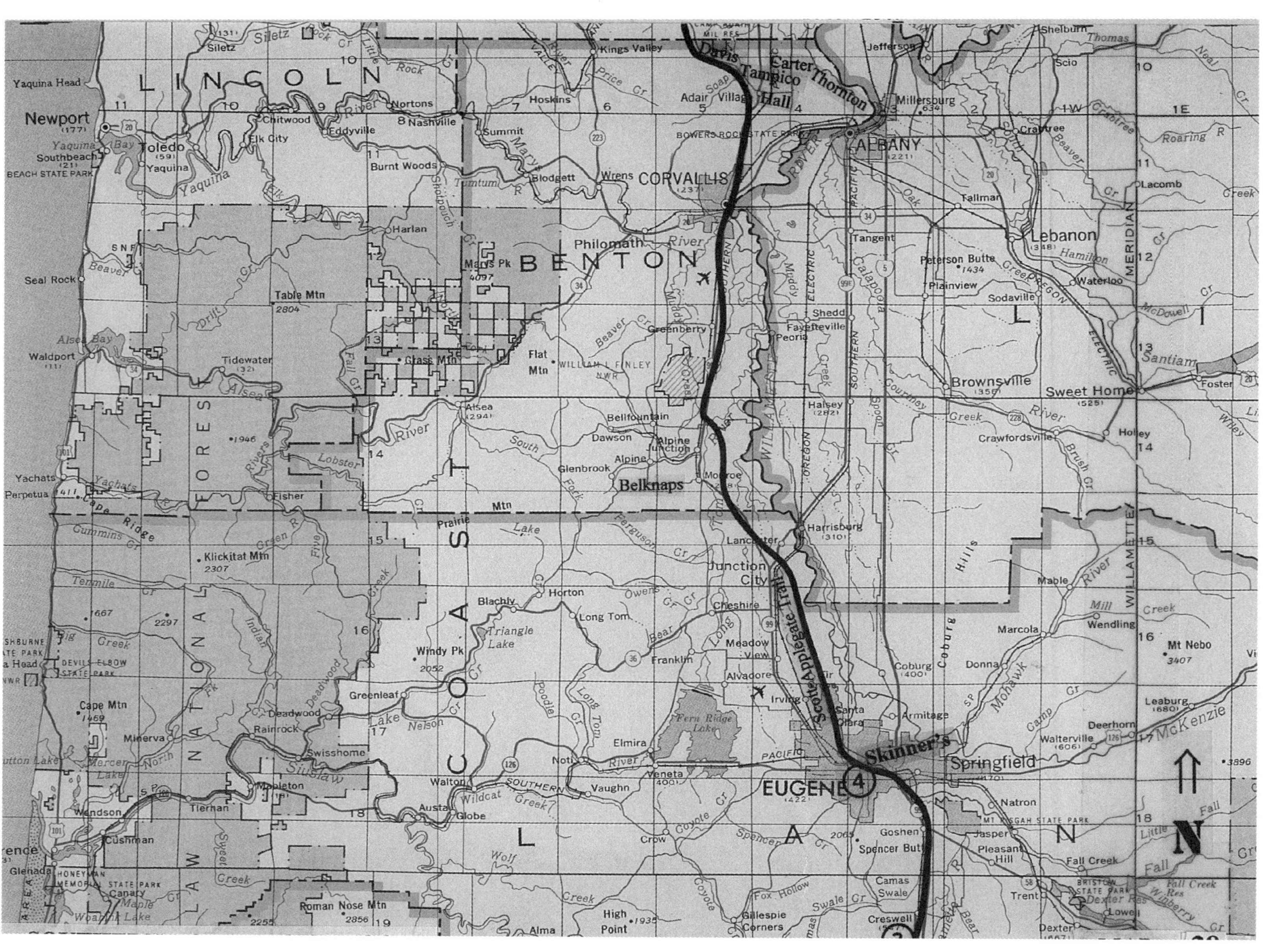

SOUTHERN ROUTE TO OREGON

MAP 28

OREGON TRAIL 1846 – 1847

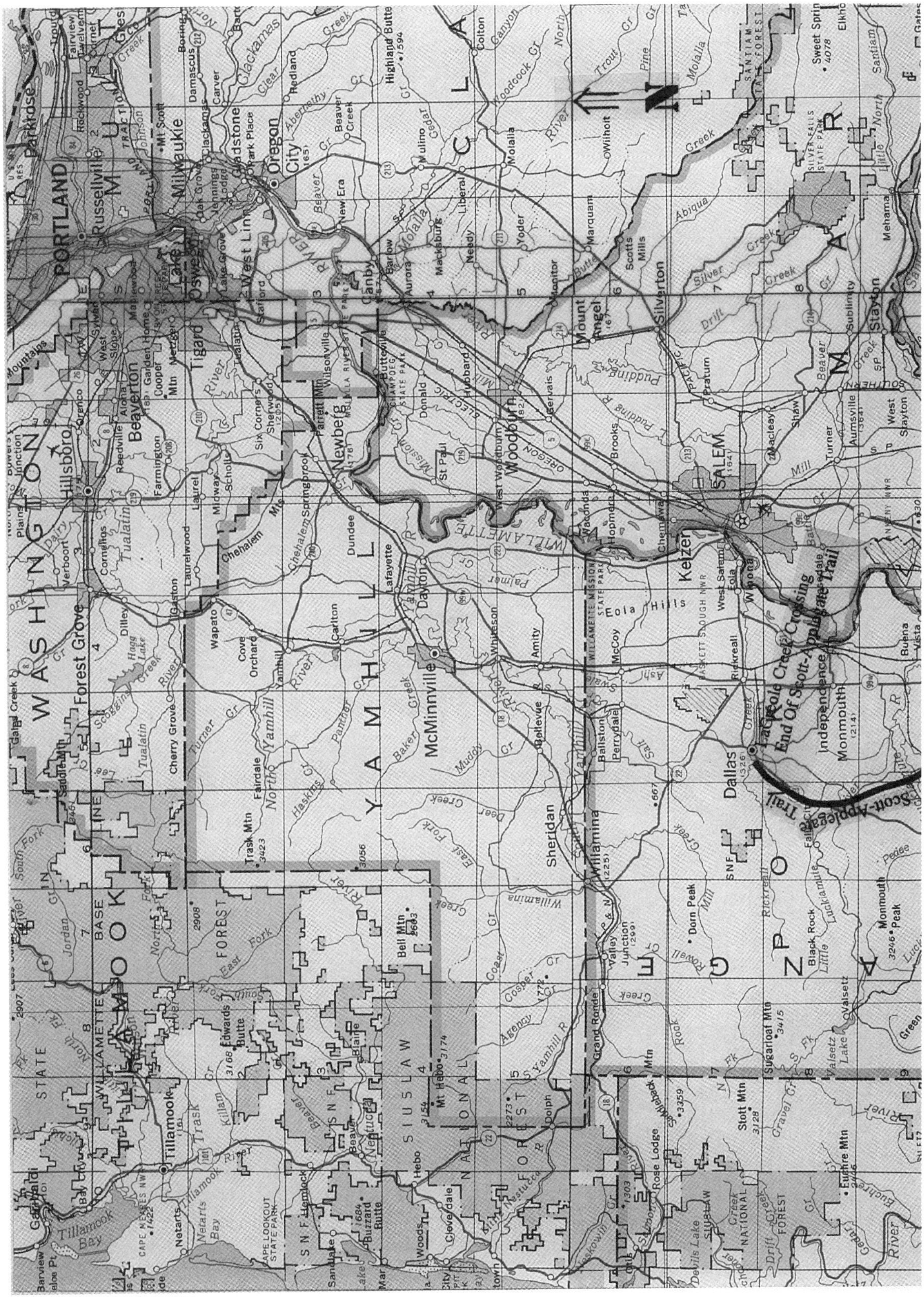

SOUTHERN ROUTE TO OREGON

MAP 29

APPENDIX

Roll of Honor

The Oskaloosa Company

(Information is not complete.)

Families

Belknap, Oren (son of Jonas), **and**
Nancy Starr
and four children (BCM)

Belknap, Ransom Amos(son of Jesse) **and**
Mahala Starr (Daughter Of Jeramiah)
Lucinda Jane
Sara M.(BCM)

Blach (Bloch) & Family (LH)(JNH)(HHH)
Brishinel, Daniel and Eunice Oliver (PWC)
Cline, George Family*#
Joseph, Lewis, Jane Emily
Peter
Cooper Family# (PWC)
Davis, David D. *
Hannah Donahoe
Jane
(Hannah) Ann
Rebecca
Meshach
Thomas
Elizabeth
Rachel
William. (EE&DRD)
Fullison Family#. (PWC)
Gilbert, Lorenzo Dow (son of Phiness)
Hannah Belknap (daughter of Jesse)
Philander
George (HHH)
Jane
Riley
Phineas (BCM)
Hill Family* (PWC)
Peak, Abe Family# (PWC)
Mr. Kimble & Family* (PWC)(JNH)(LH)(HHH)
McKee Family*#. (PWC)(LH)
Read, Reason Family*#,
Mary Margaret
Adeline
Joseph
Samson
Read, David (PWC)
Stanton Family* (PWC)
Starr, Samuel Fletcher (son of Moses)
Tolitha Cumi Belknap (dau. of Jesse)
Elizabeth Jane
Leander James (BCM)
Watts Family (BCM)

Single Men

Blair, Prior (HHH)
Cane Gustave * (PWC)
Chapin, James (HHH)
Crawford, Peter W. *# (PWC)
Coryell, Lewis (HHH);
Davis William (HHH)
Denis (JNH);
Harty, James N. (JNH);
Hills, Cornelius Joel
Hughes, E. (JNH);
Hulin, Lester (LH)(HHH)
Judson* (PWC)
Manbeing, Jerry * (PWC)
McKean (LH)
Molten, Bill *(PWC)

Mulligan, Charnel (HHH)
Nobel, Henry (HHH)
Ross (LH)
Lewis Savage* (PWC)
Simpsons*# (PWC)
Stearns, Isaac (HHH)
Towner (LH)
Wheeler*# (PWC)
Wheeler, Jason (HHH)

Note:

* Probably from Indiana, part of George Cline Party.

Withdrew from Oskaloosa Company to go with McKee as Captain.

Known Scott-Applegate Trail Emigrants are in bold type.

(LH) Source: Lane CHS Typescript of Lester Hulin's original handwritten journal.

(JNH) Source: Reproduction of James N. Harty's of original letter home.

(PWC) Source: Peter W. Crawfords reminiscences written to Bancroft1862-1878.

(HHH) Source: Hallie Hills Huntington as told by her grandfather, Cornelius Joel Hills. Some information confirmed by his son, her father.

BIBLIOGRAPHY

Bibliography — And More

(With Key to Text)

Beckham, Stephen Dow. *"Report to Applegate Trail Coalition."* Applegate Trail: Impressions and Experiences of Emigrants and other Travelers. A county by county compilation that results in fragmentation of documents. Plastic bound soft cover, 300 pages. Self-published.
(SDB)

Benton County Museum, Philomath, Oregon. Miscellaneous papers file including: Horner story 2/20/1926;
Flickinger story 7/25/1938; Frank McDonald-1858 song & Jacob Modie story; Tampico Historical Research Form 576; *Gazette-Times* Horner story 6/19/1922; Historical Research Form 779-Tampico; Crouch's Town Plot 10/27/1857;
Belknap family genealogy.
(BCM)

Benton County Recorder, Corvallis, Oregon, Record of Deeds, books: C-440, E-212, E-212, F-521, F-530, and others.
(BCR)

Benton County Surveyor, Corvallis, Oregon: Crouch's Town Plot 10/27/1857; GLO Area sketch 6/14/1882; GLO first survey map of D. D. Davis DLC; Typed copies of GLO Surveyor filed notes on subdivisions; Arial Sectional Map.
(BCS)

Boyd, Robert. *"The Pacific Northwest Measles Epidemic of 1847-1848."* Paper in Oregon HistoricalQuarterly 1994 spring issue Vol. 95, Number 1.
(RB)

Brenneman, Roderick. Information about the site of Roberts' Boarding house and history of Tampico obtained over forty years. Some of the pictures show his property. Private conversations.

Bureau of Land Management, successor to the General Land Office. GLO Maps and Surveyor's Field Notes, DLC's 40, 44, 45, 57, 59, & 60.1300 NE 44th Avenue, Portland, Oregon.
(BLM)

Card, Douglas. *"River Road Ruts."* Newsletter of the Lane County Applegate Trail Committee, 1272 Jackson, Eugene, Oregon. Vol. 2, No.3, July 1995. Private Conversations.
(DC)

Carter, Tolbert. Letters to Corvallis Newspaper re. *"Pioneer Days."* Transactions Of The thirty-fourth Annual Reunion Of The Oregon Pioneer Association, June 14, 1906.
(TC)

Collins, James Layton, Co-author Levi Scott. James Layton Collins collaborated with Levi Scott by rewriting from Scott's notes, with Scott's assistance. James Layton Collins' original handwritten manuscript was approved by Levi Scott. Dean Collins received the handwritten manuscript upon his father, James Layton Collins', death. An "exact presentation of the manuscript's material in final form" was reviewed at the Douglas County Historical Society and Museum. The manuscript is Copyrighted

by Dean Collins. Margaret Ballard now holds the Copyright. James Layton Collins was a boy of thirteen years who did a man's work driving a team of oxen pulling a wagon over the Scott-Applegate Trail in 1846. He is as capable witness in his own right as any other. He witnessed the events as they took place and Scott was a lifelong friend until Scott's death.
(LS)

Corning, Howard McKinley, forward by Philip H. Parish. *"Willamette Landings"* Second Edition 1973. A history of river boats, boating, and landings on the Willamette River. Oregon Historical Society book.
(HMC)

Crawford, Medoreum. *"Journal Of Medoreum Crawford."* Paperback by Ye Galleon Press, Fairfield, Washington.
(MC)

Crawford, Peter W. *"Narrative of Overland Journey To Oregon."* Peter W. Crawford was a bull-whacker with the Oskaloosa Company for a short time as it traveled in northeastern Kansas. The company divided while still in northeastern Kansas and Crawford went with a new company under Captain McKee. He identified Davis as the Captain of the Company. He includes several tall tales of his overland journey that are retold in this book. This is probably the first use of Peter W. Crawford's work. It is a recollections manuscript that was directed to Bancroft. Apparently it took sixteen years, from 1862 to 1878, to write. A photo-copy of the original hand-written manuscript written for Bancroft contains 345 pages. It seems unlikely that tales in this volume attributed to Peter W. Crawford have been published before. Bancroft Library, University of California -UCB.
(PWC)

Davidson, T. L. *"By The Southern Route Into Oregon." "T. L. Davidson's narrative. At the pioneers Camp meeting Salem, Oregon, Friday, June 14th, 1878. "* Nine hand-written pages plus cover page. Left Burlington, Iowa, as a thirteen year old boy with about 45 wagons. Met Levi Scott at Fort Hall and about 25 wagons and 50 or 60 people chose to go "on what was called the Southern Route at that time." Another documentation of "the Southern Route" name for the trail – source: may be Levi Scott. Recollections manuscript reproduction, Bancroft Library, UCB.
(TLD)

Davis, Edward Erwin & David Ronald. *"Our Davis Pioneer Ancestors."* A genealogical/geographical/historical study of the David D. and Hannah Davis family. Source of vital statistics of the Davis Family members and more. Bound book published by authors, Cornelius/Lincoln City, Oregon. 75 plus pages.
(EE/DRD)

Dunning, Michael. Guide assistance through and around the Tampico area of the David D. Davis Tampico Home Site with the approval of John and Patricia Dunning. Without Mike's help there would be no pictures of David D. Davis' Tampico home site.

Ralph Friedman. *"This Side Of Oregon."* A group of stories about Oregon people, places and things. Information about James Anderson O'Neil. Soft cover book published by The Caxton Printers, Ltd., Caldwell, Idaho. 304 pages plus index.
(RF)

Franzwa, Gregory M. *"The Oregon Trail Revisited, Fourth Edition."* Current soft cover trail guide. Over 450 pages. Patrice Press, Inc., 1701 South Eighth St., St. Louis, Missouri.
— *"Maps Of The Oregon Trail."* Complete set of Oregon Trail Maps – Independence to The Dalles and the Barlow road to Oregon City. Used extensively for pointing to the trail of The Oskaloosa Company from the Kansas-Nebraska state line to Raft River.
(GMF)

Gaston, John. *"The Centennial History*

of Oregon" about "Mrs. Catharine S. Davis." Pg.433-35.
(JG)

Garrison, Abraham Henry. "*Reminiscence, Over the Oregon Trail in 1846.*" Oregon-California Trails Association, Overland Journal Vol. 11, No. 2, Summer, 1993. Copy of original manuscript OHS #874. Reminiscence of fourteen year old boy. It was written in 1903, forty seven years after the journey.
(AHG)

Hammond Inc. Licensed use of map in Funk & Wagnalls New Encyclopedia (MCMLXXIX) retitled Westward Growth of the United States.

Helfrich, Devere & Helen. "*Applegate Trail (I)*", #9-1971;
— "*Applegate Trail II,*" #14-1976. Sanctioned by Klamath County Historical Society. A detailed historical documentation of travel on the "Applegate Trail." Study material used in developing the Scott-Applegate history. Used extensively as a source of present day names along the Applegate Trail. Recommended reading. Devere and/or Helen Helfrich photographed the Applegate Trail. Soft cover books, published by and under the name of "Klamath Echoes", Klamath Falls, Oregon.
(D/HH)

Holmes, Kenneth L. "*Ewing Young, Master Trapper.*" Hard cover published by Binfords & Mort, Portland.
(KLH)

Holt, Arlie. Miscellaneous research papers providing the genealogical data for the James Anderson O'Neil and the William Bowman families and Mary Jane and Hannah Davis
(AH)

Holt, Thomas. "*Holt's Journal.*" A public statement of Thomas Holt's rescue mission to bring beleaguered emigrants out of the Umpqua Mountains and South Umpqua Valley in December 1846 and January 1847. A no nonsense journal including costs, numbers, dates and places. Published in the Oregon Spectator March 18, 1847, Vol. 2 No. 3.
(T H)

Hulin, Lester. "*1847 Diary Of Applegate Trail To Oregon.*" "Day Book," bound reproduction of typescript by Lane County Pioneer-Historical Society, Eugene, Oregon (1959) 30 pages. Gilbert Hulin owns the original and keeps it in a safe deposit box. A no nonsense logbook, with days, dates, distances and notes. Lester Hulin is responsible for the day-by-day progress of the story from St. Joseph, Missouri on May 22nd, 1847 to Eugene, Oregon on November 3rd, 1847. Without Lester Hulin — the Overland Journey to Oregon of would be fiction. His contribution makes it history because they were traveling together. Lester Hulin daily notes are quoted (script type) in their entirety on a daily basis, footnotes are not necessary.
(LH)

Huntington, Hallie Hills. "*Cornelius Hills Crosses The Plains.*" 11 page article in "Lane County Historical Society" publication, 2161 Madison St., Eugene, Oregon (1962.) Hallie Hills Huntington was a granddaughter of Cornelius Hills.
(HHH)

Hussar, Linda. "*Fandango Pass — Dance or Massacre.*" 15 page article in "The Journal Of The Modod County Historical Society, No 13 — 1991," "Warner Mountains Issue." 600 South Main Street, Altars, California.
(MCHS)

Mattes, Merrill J. "*Platte River Road Narratives.*" Hard bound book. A descriptivc bibliography of travel over the Great Oregon Trail. University of Illinois Press, Urbana and Chicago. ORHS Ref. 016.9178/ M435p.

"OTA Revolution." Overland Journal Vol.13, No. 4. Winter 1995-1996
(MJM)

McDonnell, Marlene. *"When School Bells Rang."* Paperback. History of schools of Benton County, Oregon. Published by Mac Publications, Rte 1, Box 125, Philomath, Oregon 97370
(MM)

Meares, Lt. John. *"The Memorial of Lt. John Meares of The Royal Navy: Dated 30th April, 1790, and presented To The House Of Commons, May 13, 1790, Containing Every Particular Respecting The Capture Of The Vessels in Nootka Sound."* 5th printing by Ye Galleon Press, Fairfield, Washington 1985.
(JM)

Morgan, Dale (Editor). *"Overland in 1846".* A compilation of contemporary narratives by emigrants traveling to Oregon and California. Paperback Bison Books, University of Nebraska Press, Lincoln & London in 2 volumes.
(DM)

Morgan, Dale L. *"Jedediah Smith and the Opening of the West."* Source of documentation of the internal information on Hudson's Bay Company. Soft cover published by University Of Nebraska Press, Lincoln.
(DLM)

Mulkey, Erbee. *"To Fandango Valley With Love."* History and lore of Fandango Valley. Self published.
(EM)

National Archives. Donation Certificate #4518, Oregon City. David D. Davis Donation Land Claim file: Certificate No. 4518 and Notification No. 1707 and related documents.
(NA)

Neall, James. *"A Down-Easter in the Far West."* Edited by Martin Schmitt and K. Keith Richard. Publication No. 5 of the Oregon Book Society, Limited Edition. OHS 979.404, N3481d.
(JN)

Nesmith, James Willis (With Biographical Sketch by Harriet K. M'Arthur.) *"Two Addresses: The Occasional Address, and Annual Address, by Hon. J. W. Nesmith.* Ye Galleon Press,
Fairfield, Washington, 1978.
(JWN)

Ochico Review. Newspaper. August 30, 1890 - Vol. 6, No 12. Prineville, Oregon.
(OR)

Oregon State Highway Department, Historical Files. Right of Way, County Road Documents. Exhibit A., File 49218, Territorial Highway, #200, Benton, Lane & Douglas Counties, May 27, 1976.
(OSH)

Oregon Spectator. Newspaper. November 25, 1847 - Vol. II, No.22. Oregon City, Oregon
(OS)

Parker, Martha Berry. *"Washington and Oregon, A Map History of the Oregon Country."* Page 28 shows a division of established forts in Oregon Country. Undocumented. Ye Galleon Press, Fairfield, Washington.
(MBP)

Peltier, Jerome. *"Black Harris."* A 162 page history of America's Rocky Mountain fur trade with biographical sketches of Moses (Black) Harris, mountain man, explorer, guide on the trails to Oregon. A hard bound book published by Ye Galleon Press, Fairfield, Washington
(JP)

Preston, Ralph N. *"Early Oregon Atlas",* Binford & Mort Publishing, Portland, Oregon, publisher. Softbound book with reproductions of historical maps and photos.
(RNP)

Pringle, Virgil K. *"Overland in 1846."* Morgan, Dale editor. See Dale Morgan. A journal of one man's overland journey to Oregon over the Southern Route. He drove the second wagon into the Willamette Valley. Pringle's diary was used extensively in the chapters on the California road and the Scott-Applegate Trail. His works supports Lester Hulin's Oregon Trail route through the Black Hills west of Guernsey.
(VP)

Rand McNally & Company. Funk & Wagnalls New Encyclopedia (MCMLXXIX), Vols. 4, 10, 18, 24,
(FW)

Ross, Alexander, first Astorian to sign on. *"Adventures of the First Settlers on the Oregon or Columbia River 1810-1813."* History of the building, operating, and British capturing the first American colony on the Columbia River. University of Nebraska Press, Lincoln and London.
(AR)

Russell, I. C. *Forth Annual Report of the United States Geological Survey in 1884.*
(ICR)

Scott, Levi. *"From Independence to Independence.* "T. L. Davidson identifies Levi Scott as piloting the Albert Davidson company of the 1847 emigration. See James Layton Collins.
(LS)

Slacum, William A. *"Memorial of William A Slacum."* An official United States Government document. Slacum's report to President Jackson through Secretary of State, John Forsythe. Extensive use of this report on British activities in jointly controlled territory, and on activities of American Citizens in the Columbia River region. Ye Galleon Press, Fairfield, Washington.
(Most passages footnoted "Slacum". (WAS)

Thornton, Jesse Quinn. *"Oregon And California in 1848."* Arno Press, A New York Times Company. OHRS 917.92, T 3950 1973.
(JQT)

Tompkins, Jim. *"Politically on Their Own,"* Oregon History Magazine, Vol. 37, No.2. Oregon Historical Society, 1200 SW Park Ave., Portland, Oregon 97205.
(JT)

Townley, John M. *"The Trail West."* Hard bound book (1847 portion). Detailed source book of contemporary writers traveling the Oregon Trail showing, author, library of record, publisher, dates, short summary of narrative and opinions of Townley.
(JMT)

Townsend, John Kirk. *"Oregon; Or A Short History Of A Long Journey."* Narrative of a journey across the Rocky Mountains, to the Columbia River in 1834 with Nathaniel Wyeth. Hard bound book reprinted by Ye Galleon Press, Fairfield, Washington 1970.
(JKT)

U.S. Geological Survey, Denver, Colorado. *"Topographical Pull Sheet - Maps by States."* Scale 1:500,000. The base document is the most accurate available.

VanZandt, Franklin K. *"Geological Survey Professional Paper 909, Boundaries of the United States and the Several States."* 1974.
(FKVZ)

Webber, Bert. *"Diary of Welborn Beeson in 1853."* 80 pages soft cover published by Webb Research Group, Grant's Pass, Oregon. Diary of Welborn Beeson with comments and introduction by Bert Webber.
BW)

Wells, Harry L. *"History of Siskiyou County, California."* (1881) The body count shown by Wells for the Bloody Point Massacre is disputed. The counts used here are for two

separate and distinct counts shown by Wells. It is assumed, but not known, that the count includes some, or all of six packers, three guides, and one runner from the first wagon train. There is no indication of casualties on the two wagon trains other than the runner. When more information comes to light, it should be evaluated together with how it can now be known after one hundred forty-four years when it was not known in 1881.
(HLW)

Winterbotham, Jerry, 753 Templeton St., Brownsville, Oregon 97327. *"Umpqua, The Lost County of Oregon."* Soft cover history of Umpqua County, Oregon.
(JW)

Wyeth, Nathaniel Jarvis. *"Journal of Nathan Jarvis Wyeth."* Hard cover, Ye Galleon Press, Fairfield, Washington.
(NJW)

Zybach, Bob. *"Historic Soap Creek Valley."* Bob Zybach was historian of the Oregon State University Research Forrest including the Soap Creek and Tampico areas. He is an authority in that area and also supplied loads of unwritten information. 32 page Auto Tour Manual of/by the Oregon State University Research Forest, Corvallis, Oregon.
(BZ)

INDEX

Names, Places, Etc.

C

G

H

I

J

K

L

M

N

O

P

Q

R

S

T